Self-Help

Concepts and
Applications

Self-Help

Concepts and Applications

Edited by

Alfred H. Katz, DSW
Hannah L. Hedrick, PhD
Daryl Holtz Isenberg, PhD
Leslie M. Thompson, PhD
Therese Goodrich
Dr. Austin H. Kutscher

The Charles Press, Publishers
Philadelphia

The Charles Press, Publishers
Post Office Box 15715
Philadelphia, PA 19103

Library of Congress Cataloging-in-Publication Data

Self-help: concepts and applications/edited by Alfred H. Katz
 [et al.].
 p.   cm.
 Includes bibliographical references.
 ISBN 0-914783-56-4
 1. Self-care, Health. 2. Self-help groups—United States.
 I. Katz, Alfred H. (Alfred Hyman), 1916-
 RA776.S4536   1991
 362.1'0425—dc20   91-28890
                                                         CIP

Printed in the United States of America

ISBN 0-914783-56-4

Editors

Alfred H. Katz, DSW
Emeritus Professor of Public Health and Social Welfare,
UCLA School of Public Health, Los Angeles, California

Hannah L. Hedrick, PhD
Director, Department of Information Analysis
and Publications, Medical Education Group,
American Medical Association, Chicago, Illinois

Daryl Holtz Isenberg, PhD
Director, Illinois Self-Help Center,
Evanston, Illinois

Leslie M. Thompson, PhD
Provost for Graduate Studies and Research,
Texas Woman's University, Denton, Texas

Therese Goodrich
Executive Director, The Compassionate Friends,
Oak Brook, Illinois

Dr. Austin H. Kutscher
President, American Institute of Life-Threatening
Illness and Loss; Department of Psychiatry, College
of Physicians and Surgeons, Columbia University,
New York, New York

Contributors

Michael K. Bartalos, MD
Director, Institute for Genetic Medicine;
Department of Pediatrics, College of
Physicians and Surgeons, Columbia University,
New York, New York

Harold H. Benjamin, PhD
President, The Wellness Community–National,
Santa Monica, California

Rev. Lewis R. Bigler, MDiv, MA
Chaplain, Roswell Park Cancer Institute;
Pastoral Counselor and Family Therapist,
The Pastoral Counseling Group,
Buffalo, New York

Leonard D. Borman, PhD
Former Executive Director, The Self-Help Center,
Evanston, Illinois

Vicki Bruce, BA, RN
Northern Illinois Chapter,
National Multiple Sclerosis Society,
Chicago, Illinois

David F. Cella, PhD
Director, Division of Psychosocial Oncology,
The Rush Cancer Center, Rush-Presbyterian
St. Luke's Medical Center,
Chicago, Illinois

Patricia A. Clickener
Self-Help for Hard-of-Hearing People,
Chicago, Illinois

Sr. Alice L. Cullinan, PhD
Clinical Psychologist, Newburgh Counseling
Service, Newburgh, New York

Robert E. Emerick, PhD
Associate Professor of Sociology,
San Diego State University,
San Diego, California

Carol J. Farran, DNSc
Assistant Professor of Nursing,
Rush University College of Nursing,
Chicago, Illinois

Rev. Perry T. Fuller, MDiv, DMin
Marriage and Family Therapist, Addictions
Counselor, The Pastoral Counseling Group,
Buffalo, New York

Allen I. Goldberg, MD, MM
Medical Director, Respiratory Care,
Children's Memorial Hospital, Chicago, Illinois

David Haber, PhD
Associate Professor, School of Allied
Health Sciences, University of Texas,
Galveston, Texas

Elaine K. Harris, MA
President, Sjögren's Syndrome Foundation,
Port Washington, New York

Hannah L. Hedrick, PhD
Director, Department of Information Analysis
and Publications, Medical Education Group,
American Medical Association, Chicago, Illinois

Ann Hughes
Coordinator, SKIP of Illinois (North Suburbs),
Gurnee, Illinois

Steve Hughes
Coordinator, SKIP of Illinois (North Suburbs),
Gurnee, Illinois

Daryl Holtz Isenberg, PhD
Director, Illinois Self-Help Center,
Evanston, Illinois

Alfred H. Katz, DSW
Emeritus Professor of Public Health and Social Welfare,
UCLA School of Public Health, Los Angeles, California

Jeffrey M. Kauffman, PhD
Director, Center for the Care of Community Institutions,
Bala Cynwyd, Pennsylvania

Dennis Klass, PhD
Department of Religion, Webster University,
St. Louis, Missouri

C. Everett Koop, MD, ScD
Surgeon General of the U.S. Public Health Service,
1981–1989

Kathryn D. Kramer, PhD
Psychologist and Research Scientist,
Psychosocial Research Division, University of
North Carolina, Chapel Hill, North Carolina

Cecelia Kwa, MB, BS, MPH
Research Assistant, UCLA School of Public Health,
Los Angeles, California

Edward J. Madara, MS
Director, American Self-Help Clearinghouse,
St. Clares–Riverside Medical Center,
Denville, New Jersey

Carl A. Maida, PhD
Assistant Research Anthropologist, UCLA School
of Public Health, Los Angeles, California

Carlos J.M. Martini, MD
Vice President, Medical Education Group,
American Medical Association, Chicago, Illinois

Chris McDonald
Indiana Regional Coordinator,
The Compassionate Friends, Valparaiso, Indiana

Maureen A. Milligan, PhD
Instructor, University of Texas School of
Allied Health Sciences, Galveston, Texas

Geraldine Monbrod-Framburg
Alzheimer's Disease Center, Rush University,
Chicago, Illinois

Fitzhugh Mullan, MD
Director, Bureau of Health Professions,
U.S. Public Health Service,
Rockville, Maryland

Kermit B. Nash, PhD
Professor of Social Work, University of North Carolina,
Chapel Hill, North Carolina

Virginia B. Newbern, PhD, RN
Professor and Director, Continuing Education Program,
University of Southern Mississippi School of Nursing,
Hattiesburg, Mississippi

William G. Pheifer, MS, RN
College of Health Sciences, Old Dominion University,
Norfolk, Virginia

Kathleen A. Pistone, PhD
Bereavement Counselor, Widows and Widowers,
Yonkers, New York

Sharon Romness, PhD
Northern Illinois Chapter
National Multiple Sclerosis Society,
Chicago, Illinois

Cynthia Russell, DNSc
Alzheimer's Disease Center, Rush University
Chicago, Illinois

Joanne G. Schwartzberg, MD
Medical Director, Home Health Service of Chicago,
North; Consultant, Department of Geriatric Health,
American Medical Association, Chicago, Illinois

Howard K. Shapiro, PhD
Founder and Director of Scientific Program,
National Foundation for Peroneal Muscular Atrophy,
Philadelphia, Pennsylvania

Phyllis R. Silverman, PhD
Co-Director of Child Bereavement Study,
Harvard Medical School; Department of
Psychiatry, Massachusetts General Hospital,
Boston, Massachusetts

Catherine Smith-Wilson, MA
Assistant Director, Illinois Self-Help Center,
Winnetka, Illinois

Gayle Strauss, EdD
Computer Consultant, UCLA School of Public Health,
Los Angeles, California

Leslie M. Thompson, PhD
Provost for Graduate Studies and Research,
Texas Woman's University, Denton, Texas

David S. Tulsky, PhD
Assistant Professor, The California School
of Professional Psychology, Los Angeles Campus,
Alhambra, California

Contents

Self-Help Applications

Foreword

C. Everett Koop, MD

In 1987, as I was preparing for the Surgeon General's Workshop on Self-Help and Public Health, several of my colleagues in the health field asked me if I felt it was wise to invest the power and prestige of the Office of the Surgeon General in the self-help movement. I responded with an emphatic "Yes!" My years as a medical practitioner, as well as my own first-hand experience, had taught me how important self-help groups are in assisting their members in dealing with problems, stress, hardship and pain. As a pediatric surgeon in the 1940s, I observed that one of the most important ways I could help struggling families was by introducing them to one another. The benefits of mutual peer support were also experienced by our medical staff as we came together to deal with our own grief and stress in reference to dying children. Today, the benefits of mutual aid are experienced by millions of people who turn to others with a similar problem to attempt to deal with their isolation, powerlessness, alienation, and the awful feeling that nobody understands.

So my participation in the self-help movement neither began nor ended with that 1987 workshop. Beyond my personal participation, I had included self-help groups as an integral part of nearly all of the Surgeon General's workshops convened during my decade in that office. At that time, I was primarily concerned with how the Public Health Service and other federal agencies could acknowledge more fully the benefits of self-help in health care delivery, especially in dealing with those conditions that are not clear-cut diseases and for which there are no highly specific treatments. The anguished parents of a mentally or physically impaired child, the sorrowful child who grows up in an alcoholic home, the person grieving over the loss of a spouse, a person disfigured in an auto accident or a fire, the infertile couple may not fit into traditional disease categories—but they all do need help. Frequently, the best place for them to get it is by joining with others to provide emotional support and to share information about common concerns.

The reluctance of my colleagues to accept this type of help as part of health care indicated that in 1987, the educational systems and practices of medical and other health professionals had not caught up with the self-help movement. So I asked the participants at the workshop to formulate recommendations on developing partnerships between self-help groups and the health care delivery system to improve the health and well-being of the public. I also asked for suggestions on how to educate the public and the health professions on the use and benefits of self-help groups, on how to use organized research to expand the current knowledge of how self-help groups work, their benefits and their limitations, and on how to start and support self-help groups as part of a health care delivery system.

Some of the outcomes of those recommendations are reported in the first chapter of this book, which itself addresses the recommendation to sponsor an informational campaign aimed at the general public, human service professionals, and self-helpers. I suggested a book by a commercial publisher, and as far as I know, this is the first book in this country to combine self-help concepts and applications.

As the following chapters indicate, much progress has been made. Professional associations in the human services are increasingly recognizing self-help as an important element in the range of helping methods. Health and human service providers are learning that they can indeed provide a superior service when they help their patients and clients find appropriate peer support. This book provides an invaluable tool in our efforts to develop the partnerships and networks through which we can affect public policy, and brings us closer to the day when self-help groups will be universally accepted as an important element in the range of helping methods.

A final and very important note. When I first learned of plans for this book, I encouraged the editors to stress in the opening chapter that the future of health care in these troubled times requires cooperation between organized medicine and self-help groups to achieve the best care for the lowest cost. That was the message I delivered as Surgeon General in my dealings with professional associations, government agencies and the private sector, and that is the message I will continue to deliver through my talks, writings and media presentations.

Introduction

Self-Help/Mutual Aid Groups in Strategies for Health

Leonard D. Borman, PhD

Self-help/mutual aid groups have already been recognized for the enormous benefits they provide to members, their families and to society. These groups make low-cost or no-cost resources available to vast segments of the population coping with developmental disabilities, chronic conditions and other afflictions. In addition to strengthening the voluntary component of society, they provide new resources to be used by professionals and agencies. But little attention has been directed to the issues, findings and implications of such groups as they relate to prevention activities, and even less to their existing and potential contributions to holistic health. I believe that self-help/mutual aid groups are developing new strategies for lowering the incidence of disease and other disorders. These strategies, many of which emphasize the development of positive mental attitudes, are applicable in primary, secondary and tertiary settings.

Research has made it clear that individuals who have the support of such groups are better off emotionally than those who face problems alone. George Albee, former president of the American Psychological Association (APA), suggests that the talents and knowledge of mental health professionals can best be used in encouraging self-help/mutual aid groups, in developing more and larger groups, in monitoring their progress and in providing consultation when it is requested.

The APA recognizes six interventions: crisis intervention; stress management by behavioral methods; individual therapy; group therapy; family therapy and psychopharmacology. Self-help/mutual aid groups provide a seventh intervention—support mechanisms for the other six, whose characteristics are of crucial importance for professionals and agencies, especially for those concerned with a holistic approach.

CHARACTERISTICS OF SELF-HELP GROUPS

Shift in Human Service Paradigms

The critical way in which self-help/mutual aid groups contribute to the paradigm shift in human services lies in their limited dependence on professionals and professional services, in spite of the fact that many have been launched by professionals. These groups focus on *peer support and education*. While they consider the latest scientific findings, as well as invite professionals to their meetings, they rely heavily on *experiential learning* rather than on formal training. This move to knowledge based on experience is a major shift.

The human service paradigm shift also includes an emphasis on using a *network approach* to an identified population, for which information, support and other help are provided. Unlike most professional services, self-help groups are not preoccupied with one-on-one, case-by-case relationships. They do not presume to provide treatment. It is not the professional *treaters* who play an important role in such groups, but the *treated* themselves, and often family members and friends.

The involvement of family members and friends is critical, and this too is a major shift in conventional human service delivery. Moreover, there is a heavy focus on the emotional, social and spiritual dimensions of the affliction, rather than solely on the physical or technical. Thus the self-help/mutual aid group approach is holistic, an approach that is used rarely by professionals, many of whom address only their specialty areas.

Another important shift is that there is no dependence on fees for service; moreover, few self-help groups seek public grants. Their survival depends on donations, on the sale of their literature, and on voluntary support and commitment from their participants and friends.

Proactive Adaptive Capacity

Although the general class of social organization to which self-help groups belong is ancient and is found in all societies, those that are formed around common afflictions represent a new arrangement in responding to modern-day dangers and threats. It matters little whether the threat comes from some modern technology, from heart surgery or from hemodialysis, or whether it is a threat based on a reaction to stress, or whether it is due to an addiction, to violent behavior or to trauma.

Reaching out and linking individuals to appropriate groups is the common concern of all self-help organizations. Voluntary activity that extends in a radiating fashion is essential to the development, maintenance and expansion of groups, and to the recruitment of participants. Many of the groups do not have adequate resources, and they need a great deal of assistance and encouragement from others who have the connections to patient populations that could benefit from what the groups offer. The media also play an important role by linking individuals through local newspaper stories, through columns such as Ann Landers, and through TV programs such as Phil Donahue.

The groups themselves do as much as they can to take a proactive stance. They are prepared to make free presentations about what they do to hospitals, clinics and service organizations. Also related to the proactive approach are the helping mechanisms provided by the groups that emerge primarily from natural situations and experiences in everyday life rather than from formalized therapy, training or rehabilitation programs. The helper therapy principle is the one that reaches out and helps others in pain. This approach is far different from the professional agency intake procedure that waits for an individual to be motivated to walk into a clinic before help is provided.

Focus on Total Population

Self-help groups are similar to specialized professionals in that they each focus on a specific population, but they differ in that the groups can reach vast segments of society. They may be found in dispersed communities, with chapters and networks wherever there is interest. Because of the radiation effect of such groups and their activities, they have unlimited potential for focusing on prevention, a potential that is still largely a hidden, untapped resource.

Delivery System Articulation

Self-help groups represent a service that can be and has been initiated, developed and articulated with existing professional delivery systems. The pattern of founding groups in collaboration with professionals appears to be continuing, but the potential of additional types of articulation has hardly been tapped.

When considering types of potential articulation, it is important to remember that a key role of self-help groups lies in the momentum and direction they take with guidance from professionals. We must avoid confusion with *self-care* programs, which are largely dependent on professionals. While professional management, skills and resources are not essential for self-help groups, there is a role they can play. Social instruments, such as professionally developed self-help clearinghouses, can be enormously stimulating to self-help groups. With ongoing advice and assistance, centers and clearinghouses are able to put out directories, have a telephone service, conduct workshops, develop training courses, conduct research and publish findings.

Increasing Knowledge Base

The increasing knowledge base about self-help groups is a developing resource that needs to find its way into the human service arena. Students across the human service professions need to articulate their particular disciplines and theory with the work of these groups. We need to expand the knowledge about group process, about the emergence of particular groups, about the pathways by which individuals find their way into groups, about the outcome of group participation, and about the roles of professionals and agencies.

DEVELOPMENTS IN THE SELF-HELP MOVEMENT

Research in Burgeoning Growth

Significant research has been devoted to examining and explaining the reasons underlying the burgeoning growth and development in self-help activities, groups and centers. The studies show that self-help groups are increasing so rapidly that it is almost impossible to keep track of them. Within individual groups the growth is similarly impressive. Alcoholics Anonymous has more than doubled the number of its chapters in the past ten years, embracing more than 40,000 groups in 100 countries. Groups involved with epilepsy, parents who have lost their children and families of individuals with Alzheimer's disease show similar growth patterns.

Another indication of the impressive growth of this movement is found in the increasing number of self-help centers and clearinghouses. Since I founded the first such center in the country at Northwestern University in 1974, we have witnessed the opening of more than 30 centers across the U.S. and Canada. Typical activities include compiling information and publishing directories, providing referrals by telephone and conducting training sessions. These centers and clearinghouses are providing important new roles for professionals, an involvement that will continue in coming years.

At least four major factors have contributed to the growth in self-help activities, groups and centers:

1. *Changes in family and neighborhood roles.* The extended family units that once supported their members trying to cope with these conditions have been so eroded that they no longer have the resources to provide adequate assistance. Added to family instability and the increasing number of single-parent households is an increasingly high mobility rate. It is easy to see why self-help groups have become quasi-extended families.
2. *Populist movements.* People are asserting their right to participate in decisions that affect them. We have seen the increasing strength of

women, blacks, youth and persons with disabling conditions as they struggle to participate in activities that are meaningful to their goals and aspirations.

3. *Lethal life styles.* Occupational and living hazards, including depression and addiction, have been offered as still another impetus to the growth of self-help and mutual aid. Practicing professionals and students have joined those from many other walks of life in turning to support groups to meet their personal needs, a role quite different from the supportive and referral roles to which they also contribute.

4. *Limited professional services.* It is difficult to develop professional techniques to respond to all the problems emanating from a traumatic life experience. There is no easily "evoked expertise" to support parents who lose their children or to prepare a child who will be teased about hair loss caused by cancer treatment. Leaders in the self-help movement need to take the initiative in working with professionals to explore appropriate expanded roles.

Nature of Helping Mechanisms

We have accumulated extensive findings to assist us in understanding why self-help/mutual aid groups are so effective and in identifying desirable helping mechanisms. The factors discussed below are particularly representative of the new strategies that we have indicated and are also helpful in providing the bases for new approaches.

INSTANT IDENTITY

If you look at any of these groups, you will see that their members share some common experience. Before they found "their" group, they may have felt unique and alone in their suffering. These relationships are established through a process used by many groups. In a meeting of Compassionate Friends, sessions begin with everyone identifying themselves and describing how they lost their child. Members are able to identify those who can most closely relate to their own situation. They especially want to talk to someone who lost a child in the same way. This focusing on something similar is a vital mechanism in self-help groups.

HELPER THERAPY PRINCIPLE

What Frank Riessman called the "helper therapy principle" has been described by Irving Yalom as altruism. Both applications are based on the simple notion that if you help someone else, they might not benefit, but you usually do. Caring and compassionate response to the needs of a fellow group member, even at great personal inconvenience, is typical.

NETWORKS

John Naisbitt in *Megatrends* and Marilyn Ferguson in *The Aquarian Conspiracy* emphasize the importance of networking, with specific references to self-help groups, reinforcing a concept held by such groups from the beginning, that networks are essential for connecting individual people within a group. Attendance at meetings is important, but the network is the heart of the quasi-extended family. When comparing group therapy to the encounter movement and to self-help groups, we have found that some of the most important help goes on not in the group therapy or encounter session, but in intrapersonal networking. People call each other at 10:00 or 11:00 at night; they read a newsletter with tips on diet and exercise; they read a story about people who have survived heart surgery or who are dealing with child abuse or breast cancer. In studies on widows throughout the U.S. and Canada, Mort Lieberman and I found that one of the widows' most powerful mechanisms was being connected to the network that allowed them to call another person who had been through the experience. The network is particularly valuable in our mobile society.

TEACHINGS AND BELIEFS

Another extremely powerful mechanism is the development of teachings and beliefs, of an ideology, around the condition that allow people to cope. Paul Antze describes this ideology as a "fixed community of beliefs." This teaching or value system, focused on a particular condition, malady or affliction, is so powerful that it allows you to continue to face each day. Norman Cousins' writings on the importance of positive emotions, Irving Yalom's work on psychotherapy, and Herbert Benson's studies of the relaxation and response provided by belief systems are promoting recognition that this kind of ideology is almost critical in empowering people to deal with ongoing concerns.

Unlike group therapy, which is basically under the control of a professional leader and which may last a few weeks or months, these belief systems have an enduring quality. They do not rely on the leadership of an individual professional, but on the developing ideologies, teachings and writings of the groups. A little culture is developed that persists through time; members can plug into these teachings, which provide a very powerful mechanism for coping.

GATHERING INFORMATION

Groups provide a major service by becoming centers for both scientific and experiential information. Each group develops knowledge about the important literature and shares it with group members. In response to a request from a group for assistance, professionals can help in collecting information, designing a questionnaire and getting money for research. But the groups themselves manage to pull together impressive literature collections. At the first national conference of SHARE, a group formed for women who have had miscarriages or stillbirths, I was amazed to see that they had probably the best collection of materials on this problem of any source in the world.

GRASSROOTS LEADERSHIP

Most of the founders of self-help groups in the U.S. have been persons, or relatives of persons, who have the conditions they are concerned about. Jolly K co-founded Parents Anonymous, the child-abuse group, with Leonard Leiber. Orville Kelly founded Make Today Count, for people with cancer. Marjorie Guthrie founded the Group to Combat Huntington's Disease, which killed her husband, Woody. This grassroots leadership role demonstrates the importance of peer involvement. The professional may assist members in learning what to do and how to do it, but the members themselves must eventually take the important roles.

LOVE: THE UNDERLYING MECHANISM

All of these mechanisms—the instant identity, the helper therapy principle, the network, the belief system, the collected information, the initiative taken by group members themselves—are based on a central underlying mechanism: love. Members of these groups share a selfless caring that is quite different from the impersonality that frequently occurs in our bureaucratic systems. In 1950, Sorokin described the effects of caring and compassionate love:

> Love is literally a life-giving force. . . . Altruistic people have on the average a far greater duration of life than egotistic persons. Love annuls loneliness and is the best antidote to suicidal and morbid tendencies. Love . . . beautifies anything that it touches. Love is goodness itself. Love is freedom at its loftiest. Love is fearless and is the best remedy for any fear. Love is the most creative power, an accessible and effective means to real peace of mind and supreme happiness. It is the best therapy against hate, insanity, misery, death and destruction. Finally, it is the only means of transcending the narrow limits of Lilliputian egos and of making our true self co-existent with the richest manifold infinity (*Altruistic Love*, pp. v-vi).

The Role of Professionals

The self-help/mutual aid movement has not been an entirely grassroots indigenous effort; it has been encouraged by professionals who have played important roles during the past several decades, beginning with the work of psychiatrist Henry Tiebout and physician William Silkworth in their early encouragement of AA. Tiebout recognized that AA provided spiritual assistance that he simply could not offer. Recovery Inc., the large mental health group, was founded by psychiatrist Abraham Low more than 40 years ago because he was concerned with the problems of stigma and the difficulties of the families and relatives of the mentally ill. Low's books and tapes are still used, and there are now about a thousand Recovery groups meeting throughout the U.S.

The involvement of Leonard Leiber in co-founding Parents Anonymous is equally significant. When Jolly K came to him in the early 1970s and expressed concern about herself and others who beat their children, he advised Jolly to put an ad in the paper that said, "Parents, do you lose your cool with your kids? If so, call Jolly. . . . " They began to get calls from parents who wanted help in overcoming their outbursts of rage. The two worked closely in establishing Parents Anonymous, and there are now more than 1500 chapters throughout the U.S., Canada and Europe. Professionals have played and will continue to play very important roles in all phases of self-help group establishment and growth.

In "Special Roles of Mental Health Professionals in Self-Help Group Development" (*Prevention in Human Services*, 1983, pp. 69-70), Lauriann Chutis outlines a number of useful roles that can be undertaken by mental health professionals in providing mutually satisfying service to self-help/ mutual aid groups:

1. *Community Organizer*: "setting goals, handling publicity and achieving legitimacy in the community"
2. *Technical Assistant*: "in the development of press releases, brochures, newsletters, public service announcements and techniques for acquiring speaking engagements with local and civic groups"
3. *Source of Legitimacy*: "providing the group with the stamp of approval"
4. *Liaison to the Professional Community*: "for the purpose of support, referrals and back-up"
5. *Group Co-Leader*: "participating in the actual meeting of the self-help group, providing leadership, support and resource information"
6. *Mental Health Consultant*: "offering information about resources, group process, leadership and helping skills that are outside the scope of the self-help group"

In "Expanded Roles in Holistic Prevention for Allied Health Professionals" (*Journal of Allied Health*, November 1985), Hannah L. Hedrick points out that allied health professionals can also assume significant roles with self-help groups. Hedrick emphasizes the holistic prevention roles in a section on "Developing Self-Help Group Partnerships for Holistic Prevention." She also mentions the opportunities for allied health professionals to get involved in activities such as self-help fairs and workshops through which lay people and professionals can learn more about self-help principles and about how to form groups.

Professionals as Recipients of Self-Help

It is crucial to recognize that many professionals do not function in groups as professionals, but rather as peers, as people who cooperate with others and who try to broaden the boundary lines of what needs to be done to encourage the cooperation of the groups themselves in reaching out and helping others. They also recognize the usefulness of self-help groups when they themselves have problems. A group of lawyers in Chicago, concerned about the high incidence of alcoholism among judges and attorneys, has come together to provide peer support. Teachers in the Chicago school system have asked about self-help to deal with burnout. The American Psychological Association has established a program for psychologists faced with problems related to burnout and stress. And so many other examples could be cited.

Implications of Growth

To date, more than 30 self-help/mutual aid centers or clearinghouses have been established in the U.S., and they are constantly increasing their services. Canada is developing clearinghouses in its major cities, as are countries in Europe. The World Health Organization has recognized the value of establishing an information and coordination center in Belgium. Self-help has been described in Washington circles as a "new social instrument," a new kind of institution that provides a new kind of assistance. During the summer of 1985, Illinois passed House Bill 26, providing for the establishment of a statewide self-help clearinghouse. There are now three other statewide clearinghouses in the country—in New York, New Jersey and California.

More directories are being developed so that people will know how to connect with a group. Many of our clearinghouses distribute such directories. A growing number of workshops are now being conducted, with increasing collaboration between professionals and the community, as they come together to share information on their various respective roles and to define new levels of cooperation and partnership.

WORKING TOGETHER

Working together, we are providing some very important sources of help for vast segments of our population. We are extending the pathways by which individuals find their way into self-help groups. We will continue to expand the knowledge about group processes that work with these populations. We will continue to expand the contributions that may be made by professionals and agencies. And working together, we will increase awareness of the new strategies for holistic health that can be developed through partnerships between professionals and self-help groups.

Self-Help
Concepts

1

Self-Help Groups: Empowerment Through Policy and Partnerships

Hannah L. Hedrick, PhD, Daryl Holtz Isenberg, PhD, and Carlos J.M. Martini, MD

Autonomous grassroots self-help groups, which operate without professional control and without a great deal of professional involvement, came of age during the 1980s. Publications as varied as *American Medical News, Good Housekeeping,* the *Journal of the American Medical Association, New Woman, The New York Times, People, Psychology Today, Vogue* and *The Wall Street Journal* featured articles on self-help groups. Phil Donahue, Ann Landers, Oprah Winfrey, and other media figures referred with increasing frequency to the benefits provided by peer support groups in dealing with a multitude of problems. Oprah asserted on June 21, 1990, in connection with a program on addictions to self-help groups, that her show would not exist without such groups. Numerous health and human service providers, health care facilities and employee assistance programs included referral to self-help groups among their services.

The media dramatization and documentation introduced in the 1980s served as a powerful catalyst for increased acceptance of self-help groups. Jacobs and Goodman reported in 1989 that almost all of the national and local docudramas on the "disease of the week," depicting people affected by AIDS, Alzheimer's disease, cancer, child abuse, domestic violence and mental illness involved "a successful self-help group as part of the plot" and that "actual self-help groups are frequently promoted at the end." The authors conjectured that "no other format for delivering mental health service enjoys the media attention currently focused on the self-help groups," as "hundreds of millions have watched these unintentional advertisements" (pp. 538-539).

3

Dramatization specifically intended to connect self-help groups with healthy behavior included numerous references to self-help groups delivered through Health and Science Network (HSN) programs for a variety of conditions. A new 1991 program, "Support Services for Children with Cancer," was featured in the May 1991 issue of *HSN Program Guide*. "Children with Cancer" concluded with a "hopeful message" section that focused on the necessity of providing help by "introducing the sick child and the child's family to others who have had similar experiences." The HSN footage included a group of teenage cancer patients "discussing the problems they face in trying to lead normal lives." In the program, Emy Hyans, a pediatric social worker, described these group meetings as one of the best tools she has seen for helping patients deal with the many emotional problems their condition causes. The February 1991 *Good Housekeeping* contained Lisa Belasco's "Groups to Help Women Through Hard Times" as a complement to its 50-page special section on women's health.

This attention in popular and educational media moves us closer to the day when, in the words of former Surgeon General C. Everett Koop, "the self-help way will be accorded the respect it deserves as one of many established helping methods." In 1990, Dr. Koop urged "professional associations in the human services to recognize self-help as an important element in the range of helping methods," while praising "vanguard teaching professionals [who] have introduced the study of self-help into professional training schools . . . [and] professional researchers and writers who genuinely understand self-help." Dr. Koop also emphasized the "important economic reasons why self-helpers and professionals should coordinate their efforts to help people: Professionals who understand self-help can properly refer people to self-help groups, and self-helpers who understand when professional guidance is needed can suggest it to their group members . . . A partnership between professional traditional care and the self-help movement can provide a superior service" (Romeder 1990, pp. xi-xii).

The following material focuses on policy and partnership activities related to the growth of autonomous grassroots self-help groups for persons affected by life-threatening conditions. The qualifier "autonomous" indicates that this chapter deals primarily with groups run for and by members, with service providers participating in various roles at the request of the group. Support groups organized and conducted by professionals no doubt provide a great deal of mutual support.* In general, however, independently

---

*While for policy purposes it may be desirable or even necessary to differentiate between autonomous grassroots self-help groups led by group members and support groups organized and led by health and human services providers, care must be taken to avoid creating "us" and "them" categories. The numerous properties of various types of self-help organizations demonstrated in Thomas J. Powell's *Self-Help Organizations and Professional Practice* (1987) point to the difficulties in developing a definition that does not exclude or offend some type of group. The "Working Definition of Self Help" (*National Self-Help Network News,* 1990) contains the caveat that among the many independently operating self-help groups that meet around the world, not all fit neatly into the parameters and principles in the working definition.

operating groups emphasizing personal mutual aid and equality enhance the empowerment experienced by members. In "Mutual Help Organizations: Interpretations in the Literature" (1970), Marie Killilea includes constructive action toward shared goals as a primary characteristic of self-help groups (Robinson 1981). This shared goal usually deals with ways of coping with the condition; while self-help groups may devote their activities to social change as well as to personal mutual aid, those that concentrate entirely on social activism or advocacy would not be included in most definitions of self-help groups (Romeder 1990, p. 33).

Members of autonomous self-help groups are empowered not only because they *learn* by doing, but also because they are *changed* by doing. David Robinson (1981), coordinator of the World Health Organization's 1980 study on self-help groups concerned with health problems, contends that the "doing something" that changes people is collective self-help: the self-help group provides "practical solutions to specific difficulties and gives members an opportunity to build . . . a new set of relationships—for some, even a new way of life." Members of independently operating self-help groups also tend to assume responsibility for dealing with their common problem; while outside resources may be used, "self-reliance and self-determination at the basic group level are required to solve the problem." (pp. 186-187).

In addition to the empowerment provided by this peer action orientation, autonomous grassroots groups usually exhibit several of the following characteristics and benefits:

- *A Common Problem.* The common problem enables members to immediately identify with one another; when group members share similar feelings about their common problem, they may experience what Canada's Jean-Marie Romeder (1990) calls *resonance.*
- *Mutual Aid/Helper Therapy.* The term "helper therapy principle" was coined by Frank Riessman (1965) to describe the phenomenon of self-help group members learning that as they give help, they receive help. An explosion of new research by psychologists, epidemiologists and neuroscientists has revealed that "the benefits of helping other people flow back to the helper" (Growald and Luks 1988, p. 51). Through involvement in a self-help group, "the problem they saw only as a liability (such as epilepsy or depression) becomes an asset because the experience enables them to empathize with and guide others" (Thiers 1987, p. 16).
- *Network for Support.* Members provide a network of emotional and social support through regular meetings, telephone calls, newsletters, friendly visits, special gatherings and computers.
- *Shared Information.* Through the group process and written material, members capture and perpetuate wisdoms or teachings for successful coping.

- *Low Cost.* Expenses are shared through collections at meetings, minimal membership dues or fund-raising projects.
- *Unconditional Love.* Self-help members are usually encouraged to share their deepest feelings in an environment characterized by "unconditional love," a term used to indicate a nonjudgmental, caring attitude. Self-help pioneer Leonard Borman stressed that unconditional love is the underlying mechanism of self-help groups.
- *The "Prosumer" Concept.* Members of self-help groups frequently acquire a special ability to help, based on their development as "prosumers," a word coined by Alvin Toffler to reflect the fact that the ability of self-helper consumers of the health care system to exchange knowledge and experiences empowers them to provide services related to their condition. In an application of the helper therapy principle, this mutual exchange empowers group members to assist one another in ways that differ from the help given by a professional or a member of the general population.
- *Equality.* Although equality is not mentioned in many of the familiar definitions of self-help groups, the authors agree with Jean-Marie Romeder (1990) that equality is a common attribute of self-help groups: "Two people who have experienced similar crises tend to treat each other as equals, whatever their differences. The spirit and practice of equality are reinforced or intensified by mutual aid and the resonance that accompanies it" (p. 31).

The following examination of the increasing acceptance of autonomous grassroots self-help groups during the 1980s focuses on four major topics:

1. Issues and strategies involved in developing national policies supportive of self-help.
2. Contributions of self-help clearinghouses (including a case history of the Illinois Self-Help Center).
3. Selected national meetings and publications focusing on self-help and professional partnerships and on the intervention and health protection role of self-help groups.
4. The formation and activities of the National Council on Self-Help and Public Health.

DEVELOPING POLICIES SUPPORTIVE OF SELF-HELP

The topic of developing policies supportive of self-help has traditionally aroused strong concern, even alarm, in the self-help community. Self-helpers fear that formal policies would limit or deform the growth and freedom of their burgeoning yet fragile movement. Is it possible to develop a definition of policy that would nurture self-help groups for vulnerable populations, which may not be well-informed about or have ready access to information about self-help groups and which may not understand the ways in which self-help groups could meet those needs? As the authors use the term "policy"—the formulation of proposals intended to construct a path leading to an ultimate goal (in this case, the goal of increased empowerment through self-help groups)—the answer is yes.

With this definition in mind, the authors have identified four situations that make it desirable to form partnerships to develop and promote policies supportive of self-help groups:

1. While self-help groups will probably continue to flourish among middle-class populations, even without supportive policies, vulnerable groups impacted by severe, limiting conditions (including those with chronic conditions, older Americans and members of underserved multicultural populations) may not gain adequate access to self-help groups.
2. The growth of the self-help movement, while glorious, has not been particularly efficient. Appropriate policies could reduce the overlap, duplication and misuse of resources.
3. Although self-help happens locally, national policies are required to ensure that self-help groups are included in discussions about and proposals for a reorganized U.S. health care system.
4. Formal policies at the national level would complement and support the various individual partnerships and alliances. Public and private sector organizations can encourage integration of self-help groups into the health care system from the top down while self-help groups are encouraging integration from the bottom up.

The ability to address these policy issues requires "mainstreaming" information on the efficacy of self-help groups, improving communication between self-helpers and health care providers, gaining recognition of the contributions of self-help groups to public health, disseminating information about the current and potential ability of groups to support behavior change and increasing the support of influential organizations.

Efficacy Studies

Given the amount of information that exists about efficacy studies, it is somewhat surprising that many policymakers appear to be ignorant of the degree to which the health benefits of such groups have been studied. David Robinson (1981) concluded that "self-help groups . . . have the potential for making a significant contribution to raising the overall health standards of the community. They may be a model for an important element in a much-needed new approach to health and health care" (p. 190). Katz (1986) pointed out in the middle of the decade that "Two groups of scientific stud-ies of health and well-being have in the past few years demonstrated that fellowship, connectedness and identity support are . . . indispensable to well-being and to the maintenance of physical and mental health" (p. 6). Katz cited leading social epidemiologist John Cassel's recommendations that embody the use of self-help approaches and recent research from neuro-physiology regarding the use of patient groups in life-threatening condi-tions.

In the fall of 1987, Kurtz and Powell assured professionals that self-help groups are effective at least part of the time, citing reviews of a still immature but growing body of research. Since that time, resources about effectiveness research have increased, with such valuable additions as Louis Medvene's "Selected Highlights of Research of Effectiveness of Self-Help Groups" (updated since it was initially prepared in conjunction with the 1987 Sur-geon General's Workshop on Self-Help and Public Health), Arpad Barath's 1990 study on *Self-Help and Its Support Systems in Europe, 1979-1989: A Critical Review,* and Linda Farris Kurtz's "The Self-Help Movement: Review of the Past Decade of Research" (1990). Barath's study emphasized results of effectiveness research among cancer groups in Britain, parents of British children with disabilities, and hypertensives in Croatia for their strong evi-dence on the effectiveness of self-help groups. The international bibliogra-phy in Barath's book reflects the growing empirical evidence on the effectiveness of self-help groups to the well-being of their members.

The work of Katz and Maida generally confirmed literature reports of social-psychological issues and coping strategies in life-threatening illnesses. The group data showed possibly significant differences in the effects of vary-ing styles of group functioning and group composition, which, if validated, could have important implications for health professionals' knowledge and practice regarding the use of patient groups in life-threatening conditions. In "Evaluating Self-Help Groups" (1990), Francine Lavoie, Canadian pioneer in research on self-help groups, reported findings that self-help groups make a unique contribution "to the well-being of their members by offering them services that are likely to help them resolve their difficulties to some degree" (p. 91).

Information on these efficacy studies needs to be more widespread if health and human service providers, government agencies and potential funding sources are to be supportive of policies supporting self-help groups. As Martini and his colleagues pointed out in *Participation in Health* (1983), multidisciplinary research is still needed on precisely how consumer partici-pation affects health care. In 1990, Romeder echoed the continuing need for studies to define more clearly which activities of self-help groups provided effective help and why they are effective. Lavoie (1990) also concluded that knowledge of the advantages and limitations of self-help groups is vital to avoid "planning social policies or interventions on the basis of false prem-ises" (p. 75).

The Center for Self-Help Research and Knowledge, established in 1989 through a five-year grant from the National Institute of Mental Health, conducts research on coordination of self-help and professional service providers, development of more effective self-help group programs, how to enable persons with mental illness to use mainstream self-help groups, and how to create interaction between the public mental health system and consumer-run, self-help–based programs. The Center invites leaders and researchers across the country to develop joint proposals, share data, support small pilot projects, provide technical assistance and disseminate knowledge.

In spite of this significant body of completed and in-process research, there is a great need for more research, especially on strategies for delineating and maintaining quality assurance in groups (i.e., how to avoid dangerous activities). Additional significant assessment of efficacy and quality assurance would be most helpful as we attempt to incorporate self-help objectives and mechanisms into the rapidly changing health care delivery systems. Special effort should be made to incorporate self-help efficacy studies into epidemiological research, particularly in relationship to changing behavioral risk factors.

Improved Communication: A Prerequisite

Convincing efficacy studies that can support policy development depend heavily on cooperation between self-helpers and service providers. Although progress was made during the 1980s, inadequate communication continues to be identified as an impediment to partnerships between professionals and individuals dealing with life-threatening conditions and their sequelae. In spite of significant attention at meetings and in publications, a survey conducted for the 1987 Surgeon General's Workshop revealed that self-helpers responded vehemently and at length about the relationship between self-help groups and the traditional health care system. Although some respondents reported that communication was "improving," many continued to view the relationship as "very hostile," with "lots of mutual distrust" (*Executive Summary,* 1987, p. 3). As Miriam Stewart pointed out in her excellent review of "Professional Interface with Mutual-Aid Self-Help Groups" (1990), 12 studies have examined professional relationships with self-help groups; "the overriding concern was professional lack of information on self-help groups" (p. 1154).

The Surgeon General continued to draw attention to the importance of consumer/provider communication in his closing remarks to the March 13-15, 1989, conference on "Growing Up and Getting Medical Care: Youth with Special Health Care Needs." Reporting that "self-help groups tend to be somewhat hostile toward organized medicine, and doctors particularly appear to be suspicious of the more informal support groups," Dr. Koop called for engineering a partnership between self-help groups and doctors in order to dissipate the present hostility and suspicion; "the result would be an outstanding combination of supportive and preventive care with diagnostic and therapeutic management" (p. 45).

The importance of making "every effort . . . to support and nourish the development of a genuine partnership between health, social services, and self-help communities" was again emphasized by Dr. Koop in his foreword to *The Self-Help Way: Mutual Aid and Health* (Romeder 1990, p. xi). In the same publication, Francine Lavoie identified the importance of further study of "the relationship between self-help groups and human services professionals," because "self-help groups complement existing traditional resources" (p. 91).

One suspicion of health and human service providers is that the primary purpose of self-help groups is to seek alternatives to traditional treatment. Yet a report of research studies conducted by Mort Lieberman (1988) indicated that "most people who participate in self-help groups also avail themselves of a variety of professional and social support services." In fact, "Participants in self-help groups were found to use both professional and social support more often than a group of nonparticipants matched by level of distress" (p. 166). In "Patient Self-Help Groups for the Families of Children with Cancer" (1988), Grace Monaco provided evidence that self-help groups do not encourage negative attitudes toward doctors and treatment.

Nonetheless, as reported in the April 14, 1989 issue of *American Medical News,* some members of the medical and health professions continued to express skepticism "about the intent of these lay-led organizations" and feared "that any information disseminated among participants would be anti-medical and even injurious" (Hinz, p. 10). Exactly two years after the workshop on self-help and public health, the September 21, 1989 issue of *Chicago Medicine* reported that "physicians seem suspect of the movement" (French, p. 10).

Recognizing the Self-Help Group Role in Public Health

The activities of the National Council on Self-Help and Public Health appear to be reducing this suspicion. The most stunning result of improved communication is the inclusion of three objectives supporting self-help groups and clearinghouses in Healthy People 2000. This type of recognition legitimizes the longstanding acceptance of some experts of the contributions of such groups to public health, while skeptics await more extensive definitive research documenting effectivenss.

At the beginning of the decade, David Robinson (1981) published a number of articles on the topic of self-help groups in primary health care. Based on his research, Robinson concluded that meeting with others helps self-help group members to solve some common health problems. McEwen, Martini and Elkins (1983) placed the contributions of self-help groups in the context of empowering individuals to function on their own behalf in maintaining and promoting health, in preventing disease, in detecting and treating illness, in restoring health, or in adapting to continuing disability. In the middle of the decade, Daniel J. Anderson observed in *Living with a Chronic Illness* (1986) that groups of parents concerned either about preventing drug use or eliminating drug abuse among their children "could well become an important community-based prevention program" (p. 22) and that participation in self-help groups "can lead to the primary prevention of any number of other disabling psychological and physical conditions" (p. 30).

One of the most supportive correlations between self-help groups and intervention in mental and emotional disabilities appeared in *The Prevention of Mental-Emotional Disabilities* (1986), which reported that "Studies of such groups have shown improvement for members on various measures of mental health" (p. 14). The publication referred to the research indicating that "People coming together in self-help networks to share their problems . . . offset some of the identified risks" (p. 2). Mutual support groups are identified as having immediate potential for reducing mental-emotional disabilities and are included as one of the four components of prevention. Alzheimer's support groups and widower mutual help groups are given special credit for their potential or demonstrated effectiveness in reducing mental-emotional disabilities.

Another blueprint for action vis-à-vis the contributions of self-help groups to public health appeared in the report of *The Health Policy Agenda for the American People* (1987). The report emanated from a five-year collaborative effort involving representatives of 172 health, health-related, business, government and consumer groups; the project was coordinated and largely financed by the American Medical Association. In conjunction with reducing disease and injury and on promoting healthy behaviors, the 271-page report encourages dissemination of information about self-help groups and regional coordination of self-help efforts: "Self-help groups should make their presence known in a community through coalitions to develop and distribute directories of their services. The establishment of self-help clearinghouses should be considered by self-help groups and their supporters as a means of integrating these efforts at the state level" (p. 83).

The extent to which self-help groups are accepted as part of the continuum of care in the mental health field is reflected in the extensive references to self-help appearing in Jack and Joanne Nottingham's *The Professional and Family Caregiver—Dilemmas, Rewards, and New Directions* (1990). This collection of papers from the conference of inaugurating the Rosalynn Carter Institute for Human Development includes support groups as part of caregiving in a holistic context and encourages caregivers not only to refer clients groups but also to benefit from groups themselves. In "The Professional and the Family Caregiver: Medical/Psychiatric Issues," Harold McPheeters strongly recommended that family and professional caregivers seek and use self-help groups; . . . "they can often provide the practical guidance and support that [the caregiver] and the client need in a way that no professional can" (p. 48). Richard Edwards, former president of the National Association of Social Workers, included caregiver support groups among the variety of social services specifically targeted to handle the objective and subjective burdens on caregivers.

State public health agencies have also demonstrated increased responsiveness to integrating self-help activities into policies and programs. The April 1990 statewide conference on the future of public health in California, sponsored by the California Coalition for the Future of Public Health, featured two specific sessions related to self-help groups: Thomasina Borkman and Ernest Kurtz presented "Powerlessness vs. Control: The Twelve-Step Model of Self-Help Recovery from Alcohol and Drug Problems," and Amye Leong (then chair of the National Council on Self-Help and Public Health) presented "Self-Help Groups and Public Health Agencies: A Partnership for Wellness." The "Policy Papers" prepared as California's response to the Institute of Medicine's report, *The Future of Public Health* (1990), described self-help groups as providing a maximum impact at a minimum cost. Although given credit for working "directly with those individuals in most urgent need who have decided to make a change in the unhealthy patterns of their lives," self-help groups were perceived as being "generally invisible to the policy process" (Hafey, Hildebrand and Spain, p. 3).

During 1990, the National Council on Self-Help and Public Health approached public health organizations in other states about the possibility of including self-help groups in projects related to the future of public health. As an alternate Council member, Linda Randolph, Director of the Office of Public Health of the New York State Department of Health, created a strong link with her office and with other public health entities in New York. Hannah Hedrick, Council chair, communicated with coordinators of the Colorado Action for Healthy People project about strategies for including self-help groups as contributors to public health and for developing some kind of clearinghouse to serve the area. The executive director of the Illinois Public Health Association, Jeffrey Todd, offered to put information about self-help groups in *Viewpoint,* the IPHA newsletter, and in the Early Childhood Disability Clearinghouse. The effects of these contacts were apparent in the increased attention given to self-help groups at the fall 1990 meeting of the American Public Health Association, with presentations by Thomasina Borkman, Leslie Borck Jameson and Mary Huber.

Support for the public health contributions of self-help groups has been consistently provided by Tom Ferguson, director of the Center for Self-Care Studies and founder of *Medical Self-Care,* a quarterly magazine that focuses on information and resources related to self-care/self-help issues. Ferguson provides effective empowerment tools through the Center, his writings, and radio and TV appearances; his work has been cited by John Naisbitt in *Megatrends* as representing "the essence of the shift from institutional help to self-help." In "Sharing the Uncertainty" (1987), Ferguson attributed a major role to the self-help movement in "conquering disease through knowledge" and cited self-help groups and clearinghouses as making "one of the biggest contributions to self-care knowledge" (p. 132).

Former Surgeon General C. Everett Koop has referred frequently to the role of self-help groups in accepting "the burden of disease prevention and of health promotion in the United States" (*Growing Up and Getting Medical Care,* 1989, p. 45). The ability of self-help groups to bear this burden is widely recognized in Canada (*Achieving Health for All,* 1986), where the Health Promotion Contributions Program of Health and Welfare Canada "offers financial support to groups serving four specific populations: children and youth, women, the elderly, and the disabled" (Wollert 1987, p. 2).

A Strong Argument: Groups Help Support Behavior Change

Self-helpers report with enthusiasm the many ways in which groups support healthy behaviors. Individuals with a life-limiting condition and also their families who attend self-help group meetings frequently learn techniques for everything from reducing stress to developing healthy eating habits, yet people outside a specific self-help group are not generally aware of the extent to which self-help groups collect and share information that is primarily protective or preventive.

Self-help groups for persons affected by strokes are among those with a long history of prevention activities, both for their members and for people who have not been affected by stroke. *Stroke Connection,* published by the Courage Stroke Network, is written by and for families and professionals to foster communication and sharing of information, interests and experiences. Stroke survivors are encouraged to assume responsibility for their own health. Gary Goldberg's articles on "Preventing the Risk of Another Stroke" (1988) and "Reducing Your Risk of Stroke" (1990) exemplify how a self-help publication related to a life-threatening condition can be used to promote health and prevent disease and injury.

Testimony and research involving the risk-reduction role of self-help groups related to domestic violence are also relatively easy to locate because of the comparatively long history of groups such as Parents Anonymous. Groups are reported to be effective in educating their members and the public about the necessity of changing behavior to prevent or alleviate the condition and are frequently mentioned as complements to the practice of counselors and others.

At the turn of the decade, Anne H. Cohn, executive director of the National Committee for Prevention of Child Abuse, strongly supported the value of groups related to abuse in "The Prevention of Child Abuse: What Do We Know about What Works?" (1981) and in "The Treatment of Child Abuse" (1979). Clients who participated in a Parents Anonymous self-help group "were much more likely to have reduced propensity for future abuse by the end of treatment than [other] clients (53% versus 38%)" (p. 201). C.H. Kempe and R.E. Helfer's *The Battered Child* (1980) contained two references to self-help groups for families involved in child abuse and neglect. Helen Alexander's "Long-Term Treatment" included the statement that Parents Anonymous had "been particularly effective in working with abusive families" (p. 290). The ways in which good relationships between health and human service providers and self-help groups contribute to the effectiveness of the intervention role of such groups were summarized in Hamilton's chapter on minorities in Katz and Bender's *Helping One Another: Self-Help in a Changing World* (1988).

Even groups for such recently-discovered conditions as HIV infection are recognized for their public health contributions and their ability to support behavior change. Roger Ricklef's "Bleak Prognosis" article in the *Wall Street Journal* (February 11, 1988) clearly connected the role of self-help groups for persons with AIDS in promoting healthful behavioral change: "Often support-group members help steer one another away from self-destructive behavior" (p. 17). The health care professionals quoted in "AIDS Care" (September 23/30, 1989) found "the self-help work of groups like Alcoholics Anonymous and Narcotics Anonymous to be beneficial in their approach to health care" (p. 43). Groups specifically for individuals impacted by HIV infection were cited for encouraging empowerment by allowing peers to discuss anxiety, fear, stigmatization, rejection and death, as well as practical issues such as filling out Medicare forms and talking to health care professionals.

Similar emphasis was given to the health protection roles of groups for people impacted by HIV infection and AIDS at an international workshop on AIDS: "The Contribution of Self-Help Groups to Prevention and Care," organized for December 6-8, 1989, by the International Information Centre on Self-Help and Health on behalf of the World Health Organization's Regional Office for Europe. The report boldly declared that "collective self-help has a major role to play in every aspect of health and that its particular contribution in the field of HIV/AIDS needs to be properly understood." Attendees explored the contributions of such groups to "government-sponsored preventive measures, public campaigns and health education activities." The enormous benefits of participating in a group are succinctly and convincingly described, including the fact that "as a result of participation in a group, many members feel 'empowered' for the first time" (p. 6). The report also acknowledged the important contributions of such groups in promoting an improved climate for HIV and AIDS prevention. The recommendations to the WHO Regional Office for Europe point out the need for help for those groups that "are ready to undertake a greater role in health promotion" (p. 9). Recommendations to member states included one in support of self-help clearinghouses and one to build a greater awareness of self-help groups in the education provided to all professionals working with people with HIV and AIDS.

As weighty a publication as *Population Reports* (September 1989) similarly praised the tremendous empowerment provided by self-help groups for persons impacted by HIV infection. Peer groups were cited as imperative to the success of approaches to educating against AIDS, and were specifically mentioned as providing the "knowledge, emotions, and skills [that] reinforce healthful changes." The information, services and support provided by these groups was presented as being able to "persuade people to change their behavior and to maintain new behavior." Empowerment was emphasized in the conclusion that "people at high risk and people infected with HIV can contribute to the solution of the AIDS problem" (p. 27).

CASE HISTORY: TEST POSITIVE AWARE NETWORK

Test Positive Aware Network (TPA), a Chicago-based "non-therapeutic support fellowship and information network for people affected by HIV," exemplifies the willingness of many groups to undertake a conscious role in health protection and early intervention, both for its members and for the public. TPA provides its members with an amazing number of tools to improve their health and the quality of their lives. The carefully arranged books, pamphlets and handouts in the resource room include articles from *JAMA* and the *New England Journal of Medicine,* the latest information from the FDA, and books on visualization, meditation and affirmation. Meeting topics embrace mainstream medical therapies, experimental drug studies, complementary or holistic therapies, nutrition, stress management and "safer sex." Service providers make presentations, but members are always provided with an opportunity to share information about and techniques for changing behaviors to improve their health and the quality of their lives. Stress reduction and exercise classes are conducted several times a week and are frequently built into the context of the twice-weekly fellowship meetings, each of which draws from 50 to 120 attendees. Health education and promotion concepts are frequently included in additional meetings for subgroups, such as heterosexual couples, beginning and advanced HIV groups and a Hispanic-speaking group.

Acceptance by the provider community helped TPA receive funding to develop a one-day training module, including a videotape, for organizing peer-directed support, adding to its phenomenal growth. Celebrating its fifth birthday in July 1991, TPA had provided orientation to more than 2500 people, and nearly 3000 more had asked to be placed on the mailing list for its newsletter, *Positively Aware.* Typical contents included a well-researched feature article, health education and risk reduction information, AIDS information articles, a summary of news stories from the previous 30 days, a report of clinical trials and medical therapies, international AIDS news and a list of resources. Thousands of additional copies of the newsletter were distributed each month to physicians' offices, hospitals and locations frequented by persons at risk for HIV infection.

Increasing Support in Organizational Policies

Throughout the 1980s, mental health and social work organizations increasingly manifested their agreement with the contention of McEwen, Martini and Elkins (1983) that members of self-help groups "can make a valuable contribution in undergraduate and postgraduate education of doctors, nurses, social workers, and related health professionals" (p. 197). C. Everett Koop placed professionals who introduced the study of self-help into professional training schools among the "vanguard." After a decade of increasing attention to self-help groups, two influential national professional organizations in the United States, the American Medical Association (AMA) and the American Hospital Association (AHA), were in a position to move into that vanguard.

At the 1988 Symposium on the Impact of Life-Threatening Conditions, Carlos J.M. Martini, vice president for the AMA Medical Education Group, summarized the many self-help group activities coordinated or supported by AMA staff. At the national level, these activities included self-help programs and open meetings at a number of AMA meetings (including the National Leadership Conference and the National Conference for Impaired Professionals), the initial meeting with Surgeon General Koop that culminated in the Surgeon General's Workshop on Self-Help and Public Health, cosponsoring and cochairing the Symposium on the Impact of Life-Threatening Conditions, a number of publications promoting the involvement of health and human service providers in self-help groups, and leadership on the *National Council on Self-Help and Public Health.* In spring of 1991, the AMA health office organized the Association's first on-site self-help groups for individuals impacted by the Persian Gulf conflict.

By early 1990, AMA policies included references to self-help groups for a variety of conditions, including physicians and their families affected by malpractice suits and groups for persons impacted by HIV infection. *HIV Infection and Disease* (1989) contained several positive references to self-help groups, self-help groups were included in the AMA psychosocial guidelines, and the proposed *National Directory of Self-Help Groups for AIDS* was cited as a current AMA project in preventive medicine and public health. The 1989 AMA *Encyclopedia of Medicine* included "Self-Help Organizations" as one of six major sections. The AMA journal and newspaper have featured dozens of major articles on and references to self-help groups. The AMA Employee Assistance Program, instituted in 1989, provided information about and referrals to self-help groups, with guidance from the Illinois Self-Help Center's directory. The May 1991 issue of *Connections,* an AMA newsletter for state and specialty medical societies, contained two references to self-help groups in its front-page article on "Resource Guides Help Americans Cope with War."

Self-help groups were equally promoted in the summer 1991 *Target 2000: A Newsletter of the AMA's Healthier Youth by the Year 2000 Project,* which reported on self-help groups as "a relatively new resource for adolescents." The helper therapy principle is reflected in "Self-Help Programs Let a Youth's Problem Be Part of the Solution":

> The health problems facing many of today's adolescents are compounded by the minimal resources available to deal with these issues, as well as by a youth's tendency to talk about problems more readily with peers than adults. One solution can be found in the mutual aid/self-help movement, in which peers help one another and themselves in dealing with a common problem. Mutual aid/self-help programs are not meant to replace professional services, but they can supplement them, as well as prevent the need for them (p. 1).

The increased involvement of the American Hospital Association was due in large part to AHA staff member Barbara Giloth, who had a history of support for the self-help movement. Believing that self-help groups could help people cope with chronic disease and other stressful health events, Ms. Giloth presented "Hospital Involvement with Self-Help Support Groups" at the meeting of the November 1981 American Public Health Association. Throughout 1986, she provided the Illinois Self-Help Center with guidance for projects with the Illinois Hospital Association, and in 1987 she completed a collaborative project with the Center—the 270-page *Directory of National Self-Help/Mutual Aid Resources*. Giloth also played a major role in the Surgeon General's Workshop on Self-Help and Public Health (securing funding for a research project and promoting the workshop to 2500 subscribers of the AHA newsletter, *Promoting Health*) and in the development of the National Council on Self-Help and Public Health.

Giloth incorporated self-help into numerous AHA patient education and health promotion activities, such as a live teleconference broadcast via satellite through the American Rehabilitation Educational Network on May 19, 1987. During the same year, her AHA unit developed a self-help group communications kit, *Sharing Caring,* which was sent to all AHA member hospitals. A study conducted by the AHA Center for Health Promotion found that "more than half of all hospitals currently participate in or offer self-help programs for patients, their families, hospital staff members, and the community." The kit included guidelines, a resource list, a list of state and local clearinghouses, samples of media pieces, and five case studies describing different examples of hospital/self-help relationships.

SELF-HELP CLEARINGHOUSE CONTRIBUTIONS

Organizations formed to provide support to self-help groups and to put consumers in touch with such groups have had limited success in developing favorable policy. Identified as "centers" or "clearinghouses," these organizations are frequently started by self-help group advocates, sometimes a "lone pioneer," wanting to make groups available to more people in need. Prior to 1974, there was only one clearinghouse in the United States established solely to assist self-help groups in these areas. The findings of President Carter's Commission on Mental Health, published in 1978, recommended the establishment of clearinghouses in every federal region to gather and retain information on self-help groups, to develop local directories, and to conduct workshops and programs for group representatives and professionals.

A decade later, Dr. Koop repeatedly emphasized the importance of clearinghouses in developing referral and recruitment systems, assisting in starting and maintaining groups, forming networks and coalitions, developing advocacy programs, and developing audiovisual and print guides for use by individuals interested in starting and maintaining groups. By 1989, nine statewide clearinghouses were developed and 46 local clearinghouses provided services in an additional 15 states, covering geographic areas that included 53 percent of the U.S. population ("Year 2000 National Health Objectives: Comments from the NCSHPH," 1989).

Borck Jameson and Aronowitz's "The Role of the Self-Help Clearinghouse" (1982) and Wollert's "Human Services and the Self-Help Clearinghouse Concept" (1987) present the history of the development of clearinghouses, the services they provide and the issues that need to be addressed when starting or running a clearinghouse. In 1990, Arpad Barath cited as model "pioneer clearinghouses" (1) a 1975 nationwide support network founded in Germany by researchers, policymakers and self-helpers, which became the German National Clearinghouse (NAKOS) in 1984; (2) Trefpunt Zelfhulp, the Flemish Clearinghouse in Leuven, which grew out of a government-initiated research project in 1979-80; (3) the Nottingham Self-Help Groups Project (NSHGP), established in Britain as a result of innovative participant-action research in self-help; and (4) the New Jersey Self-Help Clearinghouse (1981), identified as the first statewide system in the U.S. to support self-help groups.

In *Self-Help and Its Support Systems in Europe* (presented in part at the Jordana CRONICAT '89, "Volunteers in Self-Help for the Chronically Ill," in Manresa, Spain), Barath (1990) identified clearinghouses or centers as providing the primary organized support systems for self-help groups. Barath called for "thoughtful critical evaluation of major constraints to the development of self-help support systems . . . based on sound research methodologies and unbiased professional guidance" (p. 2). In 1990, Edward Madara outlined similar contributions in "Maximizing the Potential for Community Self-Help Through Clearinghouse Approaches." While focusing on the roles of self-help groups in mental health and prevention, Madara described examples of clearinghouse strategies and accomplishments and advocated for the "development of an integrated and multidisciplinary self-help clearinghouse approach to increasing the awareness, utilization, and development of mutual aid self-help groups in the community" (p. 109). Like Wollert, he pointed out that "many more groups and new support networks could be developed in other states and on a national basis if encouragement and support were available" (p. 134).

In the United States, two clearinghouses have been specifically organized to function at the national level. The National Self-Help Clearinghouse, founded in 1976, encourages and conducts training activities, provides speakers for professional, lay and public policy audiences, sponsors a Women's Self-Help Center, and publishes manuals, training materials and *The Self-Help Reporter* newsletter. Founder Frank Riessman solicits and shares information throughout the world, keeps a sensitive finger on the pulse of the self-help movement, and alerts self-helpers and self-help advocates to potential dangers.

The New Jersey Self-Help Clearinghouse (1981) and the American Self-Help Clearinghouse (1990), both founded by Edward Madara at St. Clares–Riverside Medical Center, maintain information on clearinghouses, publish the national *Self-Help Sourcebook,* and distribute the mutual aid/self-help network computer software and database for the use of other clearinghouses in the United States and Canada. The *Sourcebook* contains information on more than 600 national and model self-help groups, on self-help clearinghouses, on national 800 numbers, and on ideas and resources for starting a group. Madara, known internationally for his support for clearinghouses and for his active promotion of "electronic self-help," is responsible for dozens of articles in publications ranging from the *Cleveland Plain Dealer* to *The Futurist.* In "The Computerized Self-Help Clearinghouse: Using 'High Tech' to Promote 'High Touch' Support Networks," Madara, Kalafat and Miller (1988) described "the nation's first statewide, computerized Self-Help Clearinghouse . . . which adapts . . . approaches from the computer and telecommunications field to referral, consultation, networking and epidemiological research efforts with self-help groups" (p. 39).

Communication among U.S. clearinghouses was facilitated by the New Jersey Self-Help Clearinghouse, which was instrumental in founding the National Network of Mutual Help Centers (NNMHC) in 1985. The two purposes of the NNMHC, identified as "the professional organization for the more than 80 self-help clearinghouses located throughout the country," are to coordinate interclearinghouse communication and to provide assistance to organizations that are opening new clearinghouses (*National Self Help Network News,* 1990, pp. 2-3). The specific goals are to promote and support mutual help by increasing the awareness, utilization and development of self-help groups and to share resources, facilitate interclearinghouse communication and promote other activities that enhance clearinghouse operation.

The national and regional clearinghouses established solely to assist self-help groups provide varying kinds of support and may differ in structure and purpose, but most include the empowerment of grassroots autonomous self-help groups as a major part of their mission. As Madara has stated, "promoting the birth of self-help organizations and networks" is considered by many to be "the primary value of a self-help clearinghouse." Autonomous groups organized and run by volunteers have little or no time, money or energy to devote to activities beyond meeting the needs of group members. They may not be aware of existing organizational materials and may not have the skills or resources to reach out to others in need. Such groups turn to clearinghouses to provide technical support, conduct research, provide professional education and increase public awareness, as well as to provide information about and referral to their group, assist in developing group leadership (a sensitive topic), identify new members and guide the group in obtaining local resources.

Each U.S. self-help clearinghouse has its own character of goverance, support and focus. Some operate from a store-front office and serve a local area, while others serve a network of centers. Some receive most of their support from a single source, such as the state, a university or a health care institution, while others scramble for funds through benefits, grants, donations, sale of materials and special projects. Some have a professional staff, others combine professionals and volunteers, and others are run totally by self-helpers. Staff time can vary from a total of ten hours per week to the full-time services of ten or more staff members. That all of the U.S. clearinghouses operate within the constraints of a combined budget of less than 5 million dollars and fewer than 100 full-time staff positions ("Year 2000 National Health Objectives: Comments from the NCSHPH," 1989) attests to the incredible cost-effectiveness of these heavily volunteer operations.

In addition to the generic clearinghouses serving self-help groups in specific regions are the clearinghouses that serve self-help groups related to a single condition. The International Polio Network (IPN), founded by the Gazette International Networking Institute's Gini Laurie, has greatly facilitated the growth of groups for people affected by the late effects of poliomyelitis. Motivated by the loss of three siblings to polio, Laurie was a pioneer in "finding expert personal experience among those whose lives were on the line" (*Rehabilitation Gazette,* 1990, p.11). A 1987 National Health Interview Survey uncovered 1.6 million polio survivors in the United States alone (*Polio Network of Illinois,* 1990); the *1990 Post-Polio Directory* includes 300 groups serving these survivors, their family members, and their formal and informal caregivers in all 50 states. The directory also lists health professionals, clinics and international resources. IPN's newsletter, *Polio Network News,* promotes networking among and carries information to thousands of polio survivors, support group members, physicians and other health professionals, and resource centers. IPN is strongly networked with the general self-help community, and the newsletter is as informative as any published by a generic clearinghouse.

Organizations serving a number of related conditions, such as the Alliance for Genetics Support Groups and the National Organization for Rare Disorders, also function as clearinghouses. The Alliance, with 112 organizational members, focuses on peer support and on self-helper and professional relationships through its publications and at conferences. The March 1990 National Conference on Peer Support Training resulted in a helpful resource guide and abstracts.

For information outside the United States, the International Centre on Self-Help and Health, in Leuven, Belgium, is an invaluable resource; publications include a summary of the most important papers on World Health Organization involvement in self-help and health, reports on self-help and mutual aid in health, and information on health leadership development for self-help and mutual aid clearinghouses. The International Information Centre also publishes the *International Newsletter,* and cosponsors, with the University of Zagreb, the annual Interuniversity Postgraduate Program on Self-Help and Mutual Aid, which brings together representatives and researchers from all parts of the world.

At their best, clearinghouses provide advocacy and protection for fragile autonomous groups, enable groups to develop and achieve their goals, and enhance communication with the various communities of interest. They assist without subverting the self-help group's capability for empowerment. Clearinghouses that are sensitive to the fragility of groups organized and run by their members can help to maintain the autonomy and grassroots nature of such groups. The clearinghouse role is welcomed by self-help groups as long as staff and volunteers support the self-help ethos. But groups may express concern or even alarm about possible subversion of the self-help ethos when clearinghouses encourage public/private sector partnerships and relationships between self-help groups and service providers. Some groups are also uncomfortable with being promoted as complementary to other health services. In addition, clearinghouses are in danger of being perceived as competing with self-help groups for limited funds or of being perceived as placing more importance on their own survival than on providing support to groups.

Lack of Support for Clearinghouses

A 1987 survey conducted by Wollert substantiated that the most serious obstacle plaguing clearinghouses was the low level of available funding. Based on the responses from the sites surveyed, Wollert attributed this lack of funding to the fact that "policy makers have not yet fully appreciated the contributions that clearinghouses offer in the fields of health and human services" (p. 6). Barath's study (1990) indicates the success of clearinghouses in legitimizing, encouraging and mobilizing nonprofessional health responses; facilitating local and national planning in primary health care; and providing the material and impetus for public debates on the role of self-help in primary health care. But as he reminds us, we do not yet have a system for developing clearinghouses at the local, national and international level, in accordance with the principles and guidelines set forth at the January 1986 meeting of self-help experts initiated by WHO. As the report of the workshop states, fewer than a third of European member states were supporting self-help to any significant extent. Only the Federal Republic of Germany, Belgium and the United Kingdom reported a significant amount of resources, activity and results.

This lack of support may be partly due to the fact that information about clearinghouses and their activities is fragmented and difficult to come by. Several newsletters are distributed fairly widely, including *Self-Help Horizons* (National Council on Self-Help and Public Health, in conjunction with the National Project for Self-Help Groups), the *Self-Helper* (California Self-Help Center), the *Reporter* (National Self-Help Clearinghouse), *Initiative: The Self-Help Newsletter* (Canadian Council on Social Development), *International Newsletter* (International Centre on Self-Help and Health, Leuven, Belgium), *Mutual Aid and Self-Help* (National Self-Help Support Center, London), the *Barnraiser* (Illinois Self-Help Center), *Helping Ourselves* (Michigan Self-Help Clearinghouse), *Polio Network News* (International Polio Network), the regular news sheet of the Alliance for Genetic Support Groups and the *National Self-Help Network News* (National Network of Mutual Help Centers).

In spite of their vulnerability to the vagaries of support, clearinghouses received considerable recognition during the 1980s; by 1989, publications as varied as the National Health Information Center's *Healthfinder* and *Newsweek* included clearinghouses in their supportive pieces on self-help groups. The *Healthfinder* on "Family Care" referred readers to the National Self-Help Clearinghouse (New York), the Self-Help Center (Illinois) and the Self-Help Clearinghouse (New Jersey). The *Whole Earth Review* (Winter 1987) informed its readers that "Self-Help Clearinghouses help callers locate a support group for their specific health problem, or can assist in the formation of a group when none is available" (Cosgrove, p. 132). The list provided in the February 5, 1990 *Newsweek* article entitled "Unite and Conquer" included the New York, Illinois, California, Massachusetts and Minnesota clearinghouses.

The Illinois Self-Help Center

Like many other clearinghouses, the Illinois Self-Help Center, established in 1974, responds to the needs of groups and individuals, including those affected by life-threatening conditions. The spectrum includes (1) linking individuals with groups or assisting individuals in starting a group; (2) providing services to help new and existing groups resolve specific problems (i.e., leadership skills, continuity, public awareness and acceptance, fundraising strategies, and organization and structure); (3) acting as a conduit to the public on the benefits of self-help groups to people with a life-threatening condition and to their formal and informal caregivers; and (4) educating professionals, institutions and corporations about the roles, benefits and cost-effectiveness of self-help groups. In addition, the Self-Help Center has made a special effort to provide information about specific groups meeting the needs of people served by hospitals, corporations, employee assistance programs and social service agencies. The Center took an early lead in initiating and developing partnerships supportive of the self-help movement. Three Center activities merit expanded discussion due to their influence on local or national policy development.

RESOURCE / REFERRAL CENTER

The resource center function of clearinghouses is a vital service to the groups and to the community. Groups that have not developed a mechanism to reach out to potential members depend on the clearinghouse to provide a first contact with individuals in need of a group. The Illinois Self-Help Center's database maintains information on more than 3500 meetings of self-help groups throughout the state, on the national headquarters of 400 self-help organizations and on 100 national helplines. The Center's toll-free statewide telephone line provides information about self-help groups to professionals and consumers. The Directory of Self-Help and Mutual Aid Groups in Illinois, prepared bi-annually, lists more than 2400 groups in the metropolitan Chicago area and Illinois, representing more than 350 areas of concerns. More than 2500 copies of each edition of the *Directory* are distributed or sold, primarily to professionals or institutions.

PUBLIC AWARENESS

The Illinois Self-Help Center has a long history of initiating and participating in activities at local and national levels to increase public awareness and self-help group outreach. While serving on the President's Commission on Mental Health in 1978, Leonard Borman identified self-help groups as valuable community resources and pointed out the need to maintain lists of such groups and encourage their growth. Since then, the Center has fostered placement of hundreds of self-help articles and announcements of Center events, including Dr. Koop's public service announcements, in newspapers, newsletters, magazines and journals, and on television and radio stations. It is a distribution center for the *Report of the Surgeon General's Workshop on Self-Help and Public Health*. To encourage use of self-help groups by employee assistance programs, it has developed a video emphasizing services for corporations.

BUILDING PUBLIC / PRIVATE SECTOR PARTNERSHIPS

The Illinois Self-Help Center has from its inception demonstrated an unusual initiative in emphasizing partnerships and alliances. In the early 1970s, founder Leonard Borman established collaborative projects with the University of Chicago and Northwestern University and established national self-help networks. In 1974, he hosted a national Self-Help Exploratory Workshop, funded by the W. Clement and Jessie V. Stone Foundation and attended by 70 pioneering self-help leaders and professionals. As director, Daryl Isenberg has expanded working relationships with professional, voluntary and educational organizations, such as the American Association of Retired Persons, the American Medical Association, the Foundation of Thanatology, the Governor's Office for Voluntary Action, Blue Cross/Blue Shield, the National Easter Seal Society, the Illinois Hospital Association and the University of Illinois at Chicago School of Public Health.

The Center has made a special effort to take self-help to underserved populations. Housed within the Bethel New Life Church, the Urban Self-Help Project was formed with a variety of local groups to serve people dependent on drugs, single parents, teen mothers, persons with epilepsy, persons seeking to quit smoking and abused women. The Center has responded to other types of needs by coordinating a phone response system for people affected by physical and sexual abuse. The Center also focused partnership activities on projects involving older Americans, caregivers and mental health consumers. Through Project SLICD (Statewide Library Information for Caregivers of Disabled), the Center and the Illinois State Library provide information about support groups through a federally funded network linking more than 600 public libraries with five regional information centers. The Center has also initiated cooperative programs with a number of Illinois state agencies, including the Department of Aging, the Department of Mental Health, the Department of Children and Family Services, the Department of Public Health, DASA Prevention and the Institute for Developmental Disabilities.

Many of the partnership-building activities initiated by the Illinois Self-Help Center have had a national impact. In 1985, the unique combination of self-helpers and supporters of self-help from Illinois approached Surgeon General C. Everett Koop about conducting a national meeting to focus on the public health contributions of self-help groups. Dr. Koop, who had featured self-help groups at many of his workshops, offered his advice and support. Securing seed money from the W. Clement and Jesse V. Stone Foundation, the Illinois Self-Help Center was eventually awarded a Maternal and Child Health Bureau grant to administer the landmark Surgeon General's Workshop on Self-Help and Public Health. Representatives from other clearinghouses were included in the early planning meetings and later on the steering committee. Prior to and during the planning for the 1987 Surgeon General's Workshop, the Center sponsored quarterly regional symposia involving self-help groups, professional associations, corporations, insurers and others in outreach activities, networking and disseminating information. The Center was even more centrally involved in instigating, planning and conducting the April 1989 national symposium on the Impact of Life-

Threatening Conditions: Self-Help Groups and Health Care Providers in Partnership.

NATIONAL MEETINGS AND PUBLICATIONS

Policymakers and health care providers would have a greater understanding of the contributions of self-help groups to public health if they were aware of the multitude of national meetings and publications presenting the outcomes of self-help group membership. The representative examples described below were selected on the basis of the authors' involvement in initiating, planning, conducting or participating in the meetings and initiatives and on their familiarity with the national publications. Selection was also determined by the impact of the meeting or publication on developing policy supportive of the self-help movement. No attempt is made to report on the annual meetings of dozens of national self-help organizations, many of which focused on the relationships between self-helpers and health and human service providers.

National Meetings

SURGEON GENERAL KOOP'S WORKSHOPS

Throughout the 1980s, strong, direct recognition of the contributions of self-help groups to the health care delivery system was provided by the Office of the Surgeon General of the Public Health Service. During the second half of the decade, Dr. C. Everett Koop conducted a Surgeon General's Workshop on Self-Help and Public Health, guided health and human service agencies on incorporating self-help in their policies and funding proposals, established the National Council on Self-Help and Public Health, filmed public service announcements on the benefits of self-help groups, and established a connection between self-help groups and the National Museum of Health and Medicine. Deputy Surgeon General Faye G. Abdellah was heavily involved in these and other activities that did much to legitimize self-help groups in the eyes of federal agencies and of health and human service providers. Dr. Abdellah personally participated in the planning meetings for the 1987 workshop, attended all the meetings of the National Council on Self-Help and Public Health, and guided the Council in its ongoing communication with public health and other national agencies.

The effects of the Surgeon General's endorsement and active leadership cannot be overestimated. Dr. Koop's declaration that he wanted increased access to self-help groups to be the most important legacy of his tenure as Surgeon General culminated a professional lifetime of support for the self-help group concept of people coming together to help one another. In fact, the first Surgeon General's workshop (December 1982), which focused on children with disabilities and their families, included a presentation by Sick Kids Need Involved Parents (now Sick Kids Need Involved People). The April 1987 Surgeon General's Workshop on Children with HIV Infection and Their Families included a presentation on "A Mother's Viewpoint," in which the presenting mother lamented the fact that stigma limited access to peer support groups.

It was the landmark invitational Surgeon General's Workshop on Self-Help and Public Health, conducted in September 1987, that drew national attention to the major contributions self-help groups were making to public health, initiated specific activities, and charted some future directions. Many of the hundreds of tasks and strategies suggested by workshop participants related to ongoing goals and activities of the self-help movement. Building national and regional public/private sector partnerships emerged as a top priority. Workshop participants also recommended increased efforts to communicate with the public and with health and human service providers about the value of self-help groups, about the intervention and health promotion roles of self-help groups, and about the importance of conducting organized research to expand current knowledge of how self-help groups work. The blueprint for activities in the 1990s included a White House Conference on Self-Help, a National Self-Help Week and an International Year of Self-Help.

The 1987 workshop itself gathered together various strands of support and began to weave them into a recognizable pattern. Included in that pattern were other activities reflecting the Surgeon General's advocacy for self-help. The September 1988 Surgeon General's Conference on Building Community-Based Service Systems for Children with Special Health Care Needs recognized the importance of community-based peer support groups. At the March 1989 Surgeon General's Conference on Growing Up and Getting Medical Care: Youth with Special Health Care Needs, Dr. Koop requested the Bureau of Maternal and Child Health to work closely with the Alliance of Genetic Support Groups and other self-help group consortia to develop teaching resources for young patients and their families.

In addition, the 1987 workshop stimulated studies, such as Louis Medvene's "Selected Highlights of Research on Effectiveness of Self-Help Groups" and Richard Wollert's *Survey of Self-Help Clearinghouses in North America* (1988). The references to the workshop in publications as varied as *Social Policy* (Fall 1987) and *Foundation News* (July/August 1988) attest to the ongoing stimulus provided by national meetings. That workshop also served as the major springboard for Dr. Koop's suggestions that the National Museum of Health and Medicine create a bridge between the medical profession and the self-help movement.

GENETIC SUPPORT GROUPS: VOLUNTEERS AND PROFESSIONALS AS PARTNERS

The June 1985 symposium, Genetic Support Groups: Volunteers and Professionals as Partners, examined how a "professional-voluntary" partnership could "promote maximum health care and social and psychological functioning for genetically affected individuals and their families." Major tracks were devoted to self-help groups as an emerging social resource. The concept of networking to communicate with health professionals and the public about the value of self-help groups and to impact on policies related to genetic disorders permeated these tracks. Leonard Borman, Frank Riessman, Hannah Hedrick and other self-help leaders were on the planning committee of the program. Subsequent to the meeting, the Mid-Atlantic Regional Human Genetics Network (MARHGN) and the National Organization for Rare Disorders (NORD) brought together groups related to a number of disorders to strengthen communication with health professionals and the public. The symposium also created a new coalition of voluntary organizations and professionals, the Alliance of Genetics Support Groups, which has some clearinghouse functions. The Alliance sponsored the 1990 National Conference on Peer Support Training, which brought consumers and professionals together to "strengthen critical working relationships." With support from a Maternal and Child Health project, the Alliance publishes an information sheet that promotes policies supportive of genetic services and of the role of self-help groups in those services.

SYMPOSIUM ON THE IMPACT OF LIFE-THREATENING CONDITIONS

The first national self-help group event stimulated by the 1987 Workshop on Self-Help and Public Health was the 1989 Symposium on the Impact of Life-Threatening Conditions: Self-Help Groups and Health Care Providers in Partnership. Exemplifying the Illinois Self-Help Center's initiatives in using public awareness and outreach to promote alliance-building, the Symposium was co-sponsored by the New York-based Foundation of Thanatology. Dr. Austin H. Kutscher, Foundation president, and Hannah Hedrick, representing both the AMA and the Center, chaired the event. Support was provided by the American Medical Association, the Administration on Aging, the University of Illinois at Chicago School of Public Health, the American Association of Retired Persons, and the National Council on Self-Help and Public Health. Outcomes of the Symposium included a set of publications, increased attention to self-help groups on the part of many of the participating organizations and a number of partnership activities.

The first multidisciplinary national meeting devoted exclusively to improving relationships between self-helpers and health and human service providers, the Symposium was attended by nearly 300 people from across the country and Canada, including representatives from 75 different self-help groups. More than 50 organizations actively participated in planning and promoting the meeting. Two self-help organizations—The Compassionate Friends and Test Positive Aware Network—had representatives on the steering committee. The Alliance of Genetic Support Groups, Alzheimer's Disease and Related Disorders, Care for Life (children dependent on technology), Courage Stroke Network, The Healing Community, Let's Face It (facial disfigurement), Moving to Overcome Violence (domestic violence), the National Mental Health Consumers Association, SHHH (Self-Help for Hard-of-Hearing People), the American Hospital Association, Sears Roebuck, the Illinois Governor's Office for Volunteer Action, Baylor University, Georgia Southern College and Texas Woman's University were among the organizations and institutions providing leadership to the working committees and participating in the symposium.

Participants advocated a mutual vision: a health care system in which self-help groups are recognized as complements to clinical practice. In addition to lay self-helpers, Symposium speakers included nationally renowned professionals and researchers from throughout the U.S. and Canada, many of whom had also experienced life-threatening conditions. The meeting was organized around seven major tracks: serious and chronic illness (including numerous sections on cancer and AIDS), disabilities, mental health problems, bereavement, older Americans and caregivers, adolescent health, and policy, research and evaluation. Each track contained multiple breakout sessions, with bereavement presentations included in most of the tracks. During two-hour roundtable discussion, lay leaders from more than 21 self-help groups interacted with participants, surrounded by a panorama of self-help group displays and videos.

As indicated by audience response, by requests for copies of abstracts, biographic sketches and lists of participants, and by comprehensive articles in the *Journal of the American Medical Association* (May 5, 1989), *American Medical News* (April 14, 1989), *Chicago Medicine* (September 21, 1989), the *Illinois Self-Help Center Barnraiser* (Summer 1989) and various self-help group and clearinghouse newsletters, the keynote and policy presentations at the Symposium struck responsive chords in the self-help and provider communities. The overarching focus was provided by Al Katz's *Partners in Wellness* and by his keynote address on the same topic. Dr. Katz acknowledged the role of the Symposium in "understanding and facilitating the relationship between professional providers and agencies and the tremendous social resource represented by self-help groups and their members."

Symposium keynoter Fitzhugh Mullan was also widely quoted in the *JAMA* and *AMN* pieces. Dr. Mullan's paper described his transformation "from a provider to a recipient of medical service" who consequently sought the company of others going through a similar experience with cancer. He and his wife joined an informal group of cancer patients, led by a physician. Interested in formalizing the "veterans helping rookies" mutual aid process, Dr. Mullan went on to found the National Coalition for Cancer Survivorship. Encouraged by the "enlightened humanism" achieved by the end of the 80s, he predicted a new "social contract" that "will include people who have already had the condition or who are coping with the condition as part of the basic prescription on how we care for people with an illness or with a condition." Appointed director of the Bureau of Health Professions in 1990, Dr. Mullan was positioned to continue to promote improved communication between health care professionals and self-helpers and to facilitate partnership projects to increase access to self-help groups.

Symposium presentations embodied this new social contract. Partnership models included the cooperative track on Older Americans and Their Caregivers, developed by the Illinois Self-Help Center. The track included more than 25 presentations by organizations such as Alzheimer's Family Care Hospice, the Chicago Department on Aging and Disability, the Creighton Center for Healthy Aging, North Shore Senior Center, the Healing Community and Home Health Service of Chicago. Sessions were devoted to improving collaboration with geriatric health professionals, removing barriers to participation, increasing participation of religious congregations and the work sector, preparing hospital staff and discharge personnel to use self-help groups and using self-help groups to promote healthy behaviors. The American Association of Retired Persons reported on its landmark study of medication and bereavement, with strong endorsement for self-help groups.

The Symposium theme was strongly reflected in Joanne G. Schwartzberg's presentations on "Increasing the Participation of Older Persons and Family Caregivers in Self-Help Groups" and on "Physicians, Patients and Self-Help Groups". As the medical director for Home Health Service of Chicago–North, as director of the AMA Department of Geriatric Health and as a self-help group participant, Dr. Schwartzberg's research and personal experiences have made her a strong advocate for using self-help groups to empower older persons to assume control over their life decisions; peer-to-peer meetings were presented as a mechanism for retaining "patient control." Dr. Schwartzberg predicted that "referral to self-help groups would become part of the comprehensive long-term treatment plan for patients, just as it now is often part of the home health agency's discharge plan."

"Unity in diversity" emerged as the theme of the mental health track, which pulled together the diverse ways in which self-help manifests in the mental health area. The diversity was exemplified in the presentations on GROW, Recovery Inc., Adult Children of Alcoholics, the Manic Depressive and Depressive Association of Chicago and the Mental Health Consumers of Alaska. Family support groups were covered in the presentation from the Alliance of the Mentally Ill of Greater Chicago. As pointed out by presenter Robert Emerick, who reported on a study of 104 ex-mental patient self-help groups, the mental health self-help movement is composed of many different types of groups, from politically conservative groups promoting "alternative therapy" to radical anti-psychiatry groups that promote "social change" activities. Although some health care providers fear that the latter dominate, Emerick's study revealed that most of the groups are moderate in their group affiliation, group structure and political philosophy. By and large the presentations presented evidence that peer-led self-help groups have value as an adjunct to psychiatric or other forms of treatment. This evidence was consistent with the March 1989 conclusions of Jacobs and Goodman in "Psychology and Self-Help Groups: Predictions on a Partnership."

BUILDING SELF-HELP INTO MEETINGS OF PROFESSIONAL ORGANIZATIONS

In order to reach human service providers unlikely to attend special meetings such as those described above, self-helpers and self-help advocates have participated in the meetings of voluntary and professional organizations. Communicating with health and human service providers about the benefits of participating in self-help groups was a frequent topic. Groups such as the American Cancer Society, the Association for the Care of Children's Health, the Foundation of Thanatology, the March of Dimes Foundation and the National Easter Seal Society continued their practice of encouraging sessions on self-help at the national and local levels. Self-help groups were also promoted at meetings such as the biennial post-polio symposia sponsored by the Gazette International Networking Institute.

Groups related to a specific disorder also integrated self-help groups into the programs of their national meetings. For example, the March 1990 National Conference on Phobias and Related Anxiety Disorders, sponsored by the Phobia Society of America, contained workshops on "Adapting the 12-Step Recovery Approach for Panic Disorder" and "How to Develop a Non-Profit Corporation for Self-Help Support Groups." Throughout the 1980s, self-help topics appeared on the programs of a number of meetings conducted by the American Association for Respiratory Care Foundation, the American Hospital Association, the American Medical Association, the American Medical Association Auxiliary, the American Society of Allied Health Professions and the American Society of Radiologic Technologists Educational Foundation.

The AMA sponsored two programs on self-help at National Leadership Conferences. During the seminar on Self-Help Groups for AIDS Patients, Families, and Professionals at the February 1988 Leadership Conference, physicians and self-helpers spoke about the difficulties and benefits of developing self-help groups around a life-threatening, stigmatizing condition. Sessions on and meeting of "anonymous" groups are a regular feature at the annual conference on impaired professionals. State meetings of various professional groups reflected the involvement of allied health professionals in groups helping people to cope with conditions treated by the profession. In 1990, in the area of radiologic technology alone, one national and two regional meetings featured keynote addresses on the roles of health professionals in self-help groups and the contributions of group participation to personal and professional empowerment. In October 1990, the American Society of Radiologic Technologists Educational Foundation awarded continuing education credits to a seminar on the positive impact of self-help groups on cancer survivors and on the roles of radiologic technologists in directing patients to self-help group resources.

Representatives from all over the world also heard the May 31, 1990 presentation by the Dominican Republic's Ambassador to the United Nations, Julia Tavares de Alvarez, at the conference on "Aging in the Americas: Challenges for the 90s." The ambassador envisioned a self-help/mutual aid program through a proposed Senior Peace Corps: "Given the limited resources available, self-help and mutual aid should be of paramount importance in Third World medical care of the aged."

National Publications

Unfortunately, many of the presentations described above are not published, thereby diminishing their potential impact on improving communication or forming supportive policy. Fortunately, increased coverage in national publications has stimulated communication between the two groups. As early as 1981, David Robinson, who conducted extensive studies of self-help groups concerned with health problems, was able to report that "There is hardly any wide-circulation magazine or professional journal that has not carried an article on . . . the activities of some particular self-help group." Two 1976 books presenting information about national publications were praised by Robinson for their pioneering efforts to assemble "some of the scattered information on specific groups in developed countries in order to determine what self-help groups do": Katz and Bender's *The Strength in Us: Self-Help Groups in the Modern World* and Caplan and Killilea's *Support Systems and Mutual Help: Multidisciplinary Explorations*. Another 1976 professional publication–the *Journal of Applied Behavioral Science*— devoted a special issue to self-help groups, with good bibliographical information in Katz and Bender's "Self-Help Groups in Western Society: History and Prospects." These and other sources of bibliographies about national publications, right up to Katz and Bender's *Helping One Another—Self Help Groups in a Changing World* (1988), are easily retrieved through traditional literature search techniques.

PUBLICATIONS FOR PROFESSIONALS PROMOTE SELF-HELP

Articles supporting self-help groups appear frequently in publications serving mental health professionals and social workers and usually encourage improved communication with self-help groups. As early as 1965, the *Encyclopedia of Social Work* contained Katz's entry on "Self-Help Groups." In the *Psychiatric Therapies* (1984) section on "Self-Help Groups," the authors concluded that "self-help groups are a useful addition to contemporary psychotherapy." Mort Lieberman's "Self-help Groups and Psychiatry" appeared in 1986 in the *American Psychiatric Association Annual Review* (5:744-760), and the National Association of Social Workers published Powell's *Self-*

help Organizations and Professional Practice in 1987 and *Working with Self-Help* in 1990. *Social Work with Groups* (Fall 1987) published Powell and Kurtz's "Three Approaches to Understanding Self-Help Groups," which encouraged professionals "to augment their understanding of how groups work in order to help clients make effective use of them."

In the *Journal of Counseling and Development,* Riordan and Beggs (1987) commented on the positive shift in attitudes: "Recent literature now reflects not only a receding ambivalence but a strong trend toward symbiotic cohabitation. . . . The emphasis is now on ways in which these groups can be used selectively as an adjunct to the therapeutic process or as an entire component in the mental health care delivery system." In spite of the fact that "self-help groups have proven their success and have been of help to thousands of people," the authors label existing research as "primitive" and point out the "pressing need for research regarding the effectiveness of self-help groups as an adjunct to health care systems" (pp. 427-428). Other core publications encouraged counseling and human development professionals to participate in the mutual referral system that can result from service-provider participation in self-help groups. In "Self-Help Movement Gains Strength, Offers Hope" (Thiers 1987) emphasized how the professional and self-help systems work together. Counselors refer clients to groups, and "when group members perceive that someone needs more help than a weekly support meeting, they will refer that member to a counselor" (p. 16).

Dan Hurley's "Getting Help from Helping Others" in the January 1988 *Psychology Today* reported on the proliferation of groups, clearinghouses and attention during the past 15 years, aided by "the increasing number of referrals by psychologists, physicians and social agencies," while admitting that there is "tension between academics and self-helpers" (p. 67). The creation of more than 40 clearinghouses, the formation of the International Network for Mutual Help Centers (1985) and the 1987 Surgeon General's Workshop were cited as evidence that self-help groups were an important social phenomenon. As indicated by its title, Jacob and Goodman's "Psychology and Self-Help Groups: Predictions on a Partnership (*American Psychologist,* March 1989) reported on the "increased legitimacy of self-help groups," predicting that they "will assume a central role in the nation's mental health delivery system over the next two decades," with massive increases in the use of the self-help group format to deliver mental health services. Also predicted were "a place in public policy, acceptance into graduate curricula . . . and collaborative relationships with a variety of professional disciplines" (p. 536). Support in the mental health field culminated in the special issue on self-help groups in the *American Journal of Community Psychology* in 1991.

Articles in publications for professionals less frequently associated with self-help groups also began to appear in the mid 1980s. The professional journal for physician assistants, *Physician Assistant,* promoted self-help groups and clearinghouses in February 1987 by including the concept in "Community Resources: An Overlooked Tool." Authors Bulman and Rosenbaum offered strong support for the "self-help groups . . . available to address almost every conceivable medical, emotional, and social problem" (p. 55). Four articles aimed at educating allied health professionals were published between November 1985 and May 1988 in the *Journal of Allied Health*. The third (May 1987) summarized roles of allied health professionals in self-help groups, as presented at the April symposium on Allied Health Sciences and Life-Threatening Illness sponsored by the Foundation of Thanatology.

INFORMATION TO PHYSICIANS INCREASES

Publications for physicians reflected a noticeable increase in information about self-help groups in general and groups for physicians in particular during the 1980s. Manber's December 10, 1984 cover story in *Medical World News* called patient support groups "a burgeoning natural resource for physicians, patients, and their families." With more than half a dozen full pages of text, three pages of lists of self-help groups and clearinghouses, and several pages of photographs, it remains one of the most supportive and comprehensive reports in the professional medical press.

Although much shorter, Kathleen Gaioni's "Rx: Self-Help" (July/August 1988) contains a remarkably eloquent testimonial for professional use of self-help groups. The physician author reported that she "prescribes" self-help groups for her patients as often as she prescribes "erythromycin or non-steroidals or calcium channel blockers," counting herself among those physicians for whom it is not enough "simply to diagnose and medicate," or even "to educate and comfort." Especially for patients "coping with exceedingly stressful medical problems," she prescribes "informal, member-run groups . . . composed of people who share a common problem, illness, or handicap." In addition to quoting Dr. Koop and the outcomes of the 1987 Workshop on Self-Help and Public Health, Gaioni describes the empowerment provided by self-help groups in terms that could be quoted in a self-help group handbook:

> Groups provide vast experiential knowledge and practical coping skills, not only for patients but often for the 'hidden patients,' their spouses and their families.
> These non-profit groups have an immense normalizing effect on members. . . . Such groups seem to go past the pathology to recognize and nurture members' strengths and competence.
> Self-help groups provide patients with the rare opportunity to learn from positive role models—those who have been there.
> [Members] often experience an increased sense of needed self-worth and self-esteem as they begin to see how their experience with adversity enables them to help others in the mutual aid group.

Many work to educate the general public . . . [on] prevention of the disorder.

All [groups] seem strikingly able to equip and empower patients to cope with handicaps, pain, disfigurement, disease and death.

In addition to these eminently quotable quotes, Gaioni included a brief directory of self-help groups related to ten specialty practices, including pediatricians, ophthalmologists, dermatologists, neurologists, oncologists, otolaryngologists, urologists, orthopedists, gynecologists and psychiatrists, as well as information on clearinghouses and other sources for locating groups. The *New Physician* is circulated primarily to members, residents and educators.

Hundreds of thousands of practicing physicians have been receiving a fairly regular dose of self-help group information in dozens of articles, editorials and letters to the editor with positive references to self-help groups for life-compromising conditions in *American Medical News* (AMN) and the *Journal of the American Medical Association* alone. Some feature articles, such as the ones on Compassionate Friends (a bereavement group), Mothers of AIDS Patients (MAP), support groups for physicians dealing with AIDS, and "Doctors in AA" covered several pages and were illustrated with photographs.

Relationships with professionals were explored in "Support Group Helps Mothers Share Grief"; several pages of the January 22/29, 1988, issue of *American Medical News* reported on the peer support operations of Mothers of AIDS Patients. The profound changes resulting from the helper therapy principle are reflected in comments such as, "When you make a commitment to helping, your life goes a different way" (Staver, p. 29). While articles containing words related to self-help in the title, such as Staver's, are retrievable from the *AMN* Index, titles without identifiable key words in the title are lost to the literature. For example, Ann-Christine d'Adesky's " 'New Eclecticism' Approach to AIDS" (September 23/20, 1988), which addresses integrating community health care into clinical care at three New York hospitals, incorporates perceptive and knowledgeable references to self-help groups addressing the spectrum of concerns related to AIDS care. This article, like many others in *AMN* and *JAMA,* also contains positive references to twelve-step, "anonymous" groups: "As more needle-sharing IV drug users and women recently have contracted AIDS, Stuy-Poly has found the self-help work of groups like Alcoholics Anonymous and Narcotics Anonymous to be beneficial in their approach to health care" (p. 43). Comments typically indicate an assumption that autonomous self-help groups are considered as part of the standard of care.

Gregory French's September 1989 feature article in *Chicago Medicine* on "Self-Help Groups: More than a Band-Aid Treatment?" reflects some of the self-helper/service provider polemics reported during the Symposium on the Impact of Life-Threatening Conditions, as indicated by its cover illustration of a patient being pulled in different directions. But the author concluded the piece with a quotation reflecting Dr. Koop's belief that the self-help movement "ought to be regarded as a valuable partner of the formal health-care system," a system in which "professionals serve as a resource to the groups, and the self-helpers also serve as a resource to the professional" (pp. 10-13). Physicians have even been informed about electronic access to self-help group meetings in articles written for specialty publications, such as "Networking via Computer" (*Computer News for Physicians,* May 1986) and "The Social Engineering Agency" (*The Psychiatric Times,* May 1987). The former includes references to sobriety-saving on-line AA meetings and to the New Jersey Self-Help Clearinghouse; the latter indicates that self-help groups have literally saved the lives of people with a stigmatizing condition.

TURNING THE TIDE: GROUPS FOR PHYSICIANS

Physicians who have personally experienced the benefits derived from membership in a self-help group are generally strong advocates for using groups to complement medical interventions. In "The Injured Self, Addiction, and Our Call to Medicine: Understanding and Managing Addicted Physicians" (July 12, 1985), E.J. Khantzian, himself a physician, called for both the peer assistance provided by impaired physician committees and the "invaluable" help provided by Alcoholics Anonymous and Narcotics Anonymous. AA and NA are described as being "as effective for physicians as they are for those from other walks of life . . . . AA is one of the most ingenious, dynamic psychological approaches for helping people with life's problems. For many, it goes beyond providing support and becomes the basis for significant and permanent psychological growth and change."

International Doctors in AA (IDAA) is suggested as a means to "help physician alcoholics and addicts overcome their shame and fear of exposure and accept the benefits of AA, NA, and other treatment alternatives" (p. 251). Hinz's "Physicians Can't Shut Eyes to Drug, Alcohol Abuse, MD, Former Addict, Says" (July 3/10, 1987) is equally supportive of the role of self-help groups for physicians, contending that the "big answer" to helping recovering substance abusers, including physicians and students, is "to go to AA meetings and hear the stories" (p. 52). Another form of addiction physicians address in groups is the addiction to work or activity. According to *Medical World News* (March 10, 1986), groups began to form around this condition in 1985, when groups began, independently of each other, in Westchester, New York, and in Houston. Group members feel "without a doubt" that the group has "made a difference in their lives" (p. 113).

Just as self-help groups may help professionals with a special problem or condition, they may also help physicians and their families deal with the challenges created by the practice of medicine. In "A Place to Go to Talk about the Pain" (August 12, 1988), Samples concluded that self-help groups "may contribute to a process of change in the medical family itself, by strengthening mutual support . . . [and by] equipping physicians to better handle stress in a time of critical change" (p. 47). Samples draws examples from self-help groups dealing with malpractice suits, job crises, family difficulties and professional stress, but all come to the self-help group "to reduce their sense of isolation" (p. 41). After resolving the original condition, members may stay to resolve other issues, such as workaholism engendered by "the dysfunctional family system of medicine" (p. 44). The article differentiates between mandatory "authoritarian" groups and voluntary "leaderless" groups. In the latter model, a different person volunteers each time to start the meeting, after which individuals speak as they are ready, bounded by the simple rules of confidentiality and no advice giving. "Starting a Physician Support Group," a 13-minute videotape produced by Health Sciences Consortium in Chapel Hill, North Carolina, emphasized that these groups are oriented toward sharing unconditional support.

One of the most supportive pieces published in *AMN* was "Doctors in AA" (January 12, 1990). While acknowledging that "AA still provokes ambivalence within the medical profession" and that "the profession as a whole continues to be ignorant of AA or to regard it with suspicion," physician author C. Thomas Anderson presented AA in an almost entirely favorable light: "Physicians who do join AA report tremendous benefits to themselves as individuals and as practitioners. Indeed, the benefits for physicians may be greater than those for the overall chemically dependent population. . . . Physicians in AA speak . . . of dramatic transformations that take place in their lives as a result of membership" (p. 46). They even contend that "AA makes them better practitioners" and that AA is "a model for treatment of chronic disease" (p. 47).

Although some physicians may reject AA because its effectiveness cannot be explained in scientific terms or tested in controlled studies, the American Society of Addiction Medicine (ASAM) adopted a resolution in 1979 identifying AA as a resource: "Whereas self-help groups, particularly Alcoholics Anonymous, have been a tremendous help in recovery to many thousands of alcoholics, their friends, and families, therefore be it resolved that the American Medical Society on Alcoholism and other Drug Dependencies (now ASAM) encourages all physicians . . . to develop relationships of maximal cooperation with self-help groups such as Alcoholics Anonymous" (p. 48).

Anderson's is not the only article advocating self-help groups for physicians dealing with specific condition. A number of articles about AIDS in *American Medical News* have pointed out the need for groups for providers dealing with AIDS patients and their families. At least one article, Sari Staver's "AIDS MDs Cope with Frustrations in Support Group" (June 5, 1987), was devoted entirely to this topic, strongly encouraging physician involvement: "The support is important because insensitive colleagues often make these physicians feel like 'second-class' citizens. . . . There is a stigma about being labeled an AIDS doctor. . . . I think the group helps give us the strength to get through the day" (p. 34).

A single author, Flora Johnson Skelly, published five major articles with extensive references to self-help in 1990-91 alone. "Permission Granted" (May 25, 1990) discussed John-Henry Pfifferling's advocacy for physician use of support groups to deal with stress and other problems. "Going It Together" (September 21, 1990) focused entirely on the use of support groups to deal with stress among residents. "Scenes from a Marriage" (September 21, 1990) described the Menninger Clinic's use of a support group structure as part of its annual week-long program on physician marriages. A three-part series on how physicians respond to mistakes they make culminated in "Escape to Reality" (December 14, 1990), which strongly advocated use of support groups for dealing with stress and figuring out what to do in the event of a mistake. In June 1991, Skelly's piece on psychosocial support for people with cancer, "Cancer and the Mind," placed self-help groups in the context of that form of support. While acknowledging that "historically, physicians have tended to be somewhat wary of peer support, particularly when it is not professionally led," Skelly reported that "studies indicate that peer support, as ordinarily conducted, does not encourage negative attitudes toward physicians or treatment, or divert patients from conventional care." Skelly quoted the lament by Dr. David Spiegel, one of the country's leading researchers on the effects of psychosocial interventions on cancer, that "It's a shame such inexpensive, helpful techniques are not more available."

In his introduction to *The Self-Help Way* (1990), Dr. Koop acknowledged the "serious work still to be done to get professional associations in the human services to recognize self-help as an important element in the range of helping methods. Many professionals still believe that . . . transformation, change, and healing are the prerogative of an elite who possess knowledge and techniques bestowed by specialized training institutions" (p. xi). It is no wonder, then, that health and human service providers continue to deprive themselves of the empowerment provided by self-help group membership. As J.H. Pfifferling pointed out in "Permission Granted" (May 25, 1990), these professionals are frequently taught "to repress their emotions, deny their physical needs, and demand perfection from themselves and others." Pfifferling advised that "the best advice on how to deal with a problem typically comes from other people who are dealing or have dealt with the same problem" (p. 39).

NATIONAL COUNCIL ON SELF-HELP AND PUBLIC HEALTH

The improved communication between self-helpers and service providers stimulated by national meetings and publications was enhanced by a number of special initiatives in the 1980s. Shortly after the 1987 Surgeon General's Workshop on Self-Help and Public Health, the office of Surgeon General C. Everett Koop facilitated establishment of a 501c9 entity, the National Council on Self-Help and Public Health. The Council was established to be a focus of national representation for self-help and to advise the Surgeon General's office in implementing workshop recommendations. At its first meeting in June 1988, the Council developed a statement of purpose, drafted by-laws and formed committees to develop implementation plans.

The Council placed a priority on encouraging active partnerships among self-help groups, health and human service providers, government agencies and other components of the public, private and voluntary sectors. These partnerships are being used to increase roles for and the use of self-help groups in maintaining and promoting health. Specific Council projects included consultation in the development and distribution of the Surgeon General's public service announcements supporting self-help groups. In keeping with the Surgeon General's Workshop, the Council is particularly interested in increasing networking with minority groups and underserved populations and with demonstrating sensitivity to definitions of self-help groups formulated by minorities.

The Council secured funding from the Maternal and Child Health Bureau to establish the National Project for Self-Help Groups. With a major emphasis on integrating self-help into health training and services, the National Project disseminates information about federal grants, maintains a network of researchers in self-help and publishes *Self-Help Horizons*. In early 1991, this newsletter was being distributed to 1100 organizations and individuals.

In its early years, the Council was also involved in the expansion of the self-help group component of DIRLINE (the Directory of Information Resources on Line), available at the National Library of Medicine (NLM) 24 hours a day, seven days a week. The system can be accessed from a variety of terminals connected to the NLM's computer facility or from the TELENET nationwide communications network. During mid-1988, the Council informed the self-help community about the ability of this computerized database to respond to public inquiries about health, biomedical and special interest organizations. The American Self-Help Clearinghouse, national groups and regional clearinghouses provide information to DIRLINE; information about local groups continues to be coordinated through the local and national self-help clearinghouses.

During 1990-91, the Council initiated or accomplished a number of specific outcomes related to the three major goals of the National Project for Self-Help Groups. In connection with increasing public and professional awareness of the concept, uses and benefits of self-help groups, the Council and the Project published and distributed *Self-Help Horizons,* developed relationships with a number of databases that are including or will include self-help group information, presented exhibits or provided materials for a number of national and state meetings (including the Healthy People 2000 Conference), initiated a project to compile concept papers for publication in professional journals, met and established relationships with more than a dozen national agencies and organizations, and arranged for an ongoing exhibit on self-help groups at the National Museum of Health and Medicine.

The key collaborative strategies include plans for presentations at conferences. Strong working relationships have been established with health professional and key self-help groups and with publishers interested in presenting the outcomes of these relationships in books, journals and newsletters.

Council members participated in numerous projects designed to advise public health agencies on ways to incorporate self-help approaches into their projects, including communications and meetings with staff from the Office of Disease Prevention and Health Promotion, which resulted in specific references to the value of self-help groups and clearinghouses in *Healthy People 2000*. Information, materials and other technical assistance have been supplied in response to requests from the Public Health Service agencies with which relationships were established in 1989, as well as from agencies with which relationships were established in 1990. The Council continues to facilitate the implementation of the recommendations from the Surgeon General's Workshop on Self-Help and Public Health through *Self-Help Horizons,* through book chapters and articles, through encouraging distribution of the Report of the workshop, and through numerous contacts with potential funders.

Cooperative Projects with Federal Agencies

Throughout 1989 and 1990, much of the attention of the Council was directed toward establishing relationships with federal agencies. The communication initiated in late 1987 and early 1988 by Dr. Koop continued at the June 1, 1989, Council meeting attended by representatives from ten agencies: Alcohol, Drug Abuse, and Mental Health Administration (ADAMHA); Bureau of Health Professions (BHPr); Centers for Disease Control (CDC); Food and Drug Administration (FDA); Health Resources and Services Administration (HRSA); Indian Health Services (IHS); Maternal and Child Health Bureau (MCHB); National Institutes of Health (NIH); Office of Disease Prevention and Health Promotion (ODPHP); and the President's Council on Physical Fitness and Sports (PCPFS). The representatives who made presentations were generally knowledgeable about self-help groups in the context supported by the Council; several reported extensively on activities and initiatives in keeping with the Council mission and objectives. Representatives from these and additional federal and national organizations attended the October 1990 Council meeting.

ALCOHOL, DRUG ABUSE, AND MENTAL HEALTH ADMINISTRATION

During the June 1989 meeting, an agenda was established for mutual activities with the Alcohol, Drug Abuse, and Mental Health Administration (ADAMHA), which had already attempted to interject self-help concepts into technical activities for state agencies, including state mental health and substance abuse programs. FDA administrator Frederick K. Goodwin indicated that the new ADAMHA focus on drug abuse treatment improvement would address "treatment and aftercare services in which self-help will play a large role," and that ADAMHA would integrate references to and information about self-help groups in publications and activities. In 1990, the guidance previously provided by Heddy Hibbard, who played a key role in the Surgeon General's Workshop and the Council, was continued by the new ADAMHA liaison, Anna Marsh. ADAMHA and the Council established the mutual goals of broadening the constituency for self-help, of building coalitions and of working with all institutes to encourage a self-help approach.

ADAMHA, with extensive capabilities for providing technical assistance on self-help groups to the states, expressed particular interest in being involved in programs involving researchers. The Council was invited to provide input into various technical assistance activities that would bring the people involved in self-help research in contact with people evaluating treatment programs. At the October 1989 ADAMHA-sponsored national conference on "Treatment of Adolescents with Alcohol, Drug Abuse, and Mental Health Problems," Thomasina Borkman, representing the National Project for Self-Help Groups, participated in a panel on "An Overview of Self-Help and Adolescents." Margaret Duthie of the New Jersey Self-Help Clearinghouse focused on self-help groups available to teens with mental and emotional problems.

Staff members of ADAMHA's National Institute of Mental Health, also in attendance at the October 1990 meeting, reported the NIMH history of providing support and funding for consumer-run services and businesses. They emphasized the importance of receiving information about self-help groups and clearinghouses in order to determine additional ways in which ADAMHA and NIMH can stimulate the development of self-help groups.

BUREAU OF HEALTH PROFESSIONS

The relationship of the Council with the Bureau of Health Professions (BHPr), established at the 1989 meeting by representative Howard Kelley, took a giant step forward when Fitzhugh Mullan was appointed director of the BHPr in 1990. In 1989, Kelley had expressed the interest of the BHPr (which is part of Health Resources Services Administration) in exploring how to incorporate self-help group concepts into educational programs for health professionals; he perceived that such materials would be useful not only for health care professionals, but also for public health personnel, policy analysts and environmental health personnel, including epidemiologists.

Dr. Mullan had addressed the Council in June 1989, prior to his BHPr appointment, about the Symposium on the Impact of Life-Threatening Conditions: Self-Help Groups and Health Care Providers in Partnership, at which he had delivered a keynote presentation on "Self-Help Groups and Public Health: Rewriting the Social Contract in Health." At that early meeting, Dr.

Mullan indicated that the Council could be useful in redefining the doctor/ patient relationship as one in which "people who have already had the condition or who are coping with the condition" will be included "as part of the basic prescription on how we care for people with an illness or condition." Dr. Mullan's experiences with self-help groups include assistance in organizing and maintaining the National Coalition for Cancer Survivorship, which was five years old in 1990.

At the October 1990 meeting, Dr. Mullan requested information from the Council about training and education related to self-help groups in schools for the health professions and offered the assistance of the BHPr in circulating information about curricular innovations. He advised the Council, self-help groups and self-help advocates to become articulate in public policy; if they wish to hasten this participatory system, they must identify what exists and what needs to be developed and then help the self-help movement find these "alternative" ways to impact curricula and the professional life style.

HEALTH RESOURCES AND SERVICES ADMINISTRATION

Interaction with the Health Resources and Services Administration (HRSA) has been frequent and constant since the June 1989 meeting, when the Council was introduced to liaison Florence Fiori. Dr. Fiori has actively supported the Council by encouraging interaction with the National Health Council (NHC), making a presentation to Grantmakers in Health, and communicating with various state and local health officials. She keeps HRSA officials, including administrator Robert Harmon, informed about self-help group issues and encourages HRSA to function as an outlet for self-help resources, including those developed by the Council.

With her guidance, the Council developed plans to establish relationships with various HRSA divisions and to communicate with the leadership of the associations that represent state and local health officials. During the October 1990 meeting, Dr. Fiori shared helpful suggestions with the Council and offered to send the list of self-help clearinghouses compiled by the American Self-Help Clearinghouse to the 600 community health centers across the country. At the February 1991 meeting, preliminary plans were developed to conduct in-service training for federal agency staffs and to provide assistance in integrating self-help in agency activities.

INDIAN HEALTH SERVICE

The Indian Health Service (IHS), established in 1955 primarily to assist Native Americans in accessing the health care system, was very supportive of developing cooperative activities with the Council, in keeping with increased interest in self-help groups in IHS health care initiatives. Offers were made to assist in identifying resources to support self-help and to develop strategies for involving Native Americans in self-help groups promoting healthy behaviors. LeMyra DeBruyn, primary author of *A Community Approach to Suicide and Violence,* published by the Special Initiatives Team of the IHS Mental Health Programs Branch, communicated with the Council about the possibility of including self-help groups as part of a community-based program to reduce violent behavior.

At the October 1990 Council meeting, IHS representatives Yvonne Jackson, George McCoy and Nikki Solomon expressed interest in the role of self-help clearinghouses in providing information about and referral to existing self-help groups. They commented on the great need for health education that will result in actual behavior change and on the IHS belief that self-help groups are particularly beneficial in assisting Native Americans in learning to manage their own health problems. Groups are needed in the areas of smoking, substance abuse, stress, family violence and chronic illness (especially diabetes). The 1400 Community Health Representatives, paraprofessionals who are indigenous to reservations and who provide health care there, could be invaluable in incorporating self-help in these activities. The IHS representatives pointed out that Council members or local clearinghouse representatives could train these natural helpers in strategies to promote self-help group development and participation.

MATERNAL AND CHILD HEALTH BUREAU

The Maternal and Child Health Bureau (MCHB), one of four bureaus in HRSA, has a remarkable history of support for self-help groups and for improving relationships between self-helpers and health and human service providers. Funds through MCHB have supported parts of many major workshops, meetings and initiatives containing self-help components. Resources and bibliographies have long included self-help groups as sources of information and peer support. During the 1980s, MCHB provided funding and sometimes staff support for the Surgeon General's Workshop on Handicapped Children and their Families (1982), Genetics Support Groups: Volunteers and Professionals as Partners (1986), the Surgeon General's Workshop on Self-Help and Public Health (1987), the Alliance of Genetic Support Groups, the formation of the National Council on Self-Help and Public Health, and the National Project for Self-Help Groups.

With guidance from MCHB Project Officers Heddy Hibbard, Donna English and Diana Denboba, the National Project for Self-Help Groups focused on MCHB issues relating to youth empowerment and parent self-help groups. Technical assistance was provided in cooperation with MCHB grant recipients, such as the National Center for Youth with Disabilities and the Adolescent Employment Readiness Center at Children's Hospital in Washington, DC. The three project officers assisted the National Project in developing working relationships with the Association of Maternal and Child Health Programs and the network of MCHB state officials. Working relationships were also developed with the National Center for Family-Centered Care of the Association for the Care of Children's Health and with the Federation for Children with Special Needs.

OFFICE OF DISEASE PREVENTION AND HEALTH PROMOTION

M. Michael McGinnis, Deputy Assistant Secretary for Health and Director of the Office of Disease Prevention and Health Promotion, attended the June 1989 Council meeting and expressed strong support for self-help. Dr. McGinnis acknowledged that "self-help groups are an integral element in producing the motivation" that results in healthy changes in behavior. Throughout 1989, ODPHP liaison Angela Mickalide, who had been involved in the 1987 workshop, worked with the Council to spread information about self-help through the National Information Center, to develop a statement about the risk reduction of self-help groups for the year 2000 and to build support for self-help groups into the dissemination activities of the *Guide to Clinical Preventive Services,* released in May 1989.

In 1990, self-help supporter Linda Harris, who had participated in the Symposium on the Impact of Life-Threatening Conditions, was assigned as the ODPHP liaison with the Council and continued the strong support provided by her predecessor for including self-help in the national health objectives for the year 2000. As a member of the Year 2000 National Health Objectives Consortium, the Council participated fully in all planning activities, was listed as a sponsor of the September 1990 Healthy People 2000 Conference, and developed an exhibit with a graphic display and a video for the conference, including a 30-minute video provided by Edward Madara and the American Self-Help Clearinghouse.

The Council submitted 41 pages of comments on the draft document that later became *Healthy People 2000.* Seven of the eleven categories for which testimony was developed were directly related to life-threatening conditions: mental and behavioral disorders, alcohol and other drugs, maternal and infant health, violent and abuse behavior, HIV infection, other chronic disorders and cancer. Comments related to the vitality and independence of older people also focused on preventing life-threatening conditions. The commentary requested a "flagship" objective calling for a 20 percent increase in the number of people who know about and are able to access relevant self-help groups. The commentary also emphasized the current and potential contributions of autonomous grassroots self-help groups to facilitate healthy changes in behavior that both reduce morbidity and disability and improve the quality of life.

Healthy People 2000 included three objectives with specific recommendations related to self-help groups: one related to chronic and disabling conditions, one to mental health and one to self-help clearinghouses. The first called for an "increase to at least 40 percent the proportion of people with chronic and disabling conditions who receive formal patient education including information about community and self-help group resources as an integral part of the management of their condition." The second called for an "increase to at least 20 percent the proportion of people aged 18 and older who seek help in coping with personal and emotional problems." The third objective called for "establishing mutual help clearinghouses in at least 25 states."

OFFICE OF MINORITY HEALTH

The relationship between the Council and the Office of Minority Health (OMH) was initiated at the October 1990 meeting, during which representative Georgia Buggs reported that the agency was indirectly supporting self-help vis-à-vis community projects established in 1975 as an outcome of the Black and Minority Task Force Report. Ms. Buggs offered to "tease out" information about self-help activities going on in OMH-funded projects and to request various programs to target resources and efforts to minority populations. For example, self-help groups could be among the community groups that will be used to assist in developing health-risk education programs through grants for up to $50,000 per year for community-based organizations, $75,000 per year for national organizations.

Ms. Buggs also reported that OMH would be open to suggestions to include a self-help segment in conferences and workshops. She also advised the Council, self-help clearinghouses and self-help groups to encourage the OMH Resource Center, which conducts a speakers bureau, to include self-help in resources related to the six problem areas it is currently addressing, including infant mortality, chemical dependency and homicide/suicide. The Council will use the Task Force Report as the basis for providing guidance about including self-help concepts and models in OMH workshops and activities, while the OMH will distribute the list of U.S. self-help clearinghouses to their grantees and consider the role of the OMH Resource Center as a possible avenue for disseminating information about the Council and about the contributions of self-help groups. Subsequently, the OMH awarded a grant of $20,000 to the California Self-Help Center to convene a conference on self-help groups for young men of color in April 1991.

Cooperative Projects with National Organizations

While the primary focus of the Council was on establishing relationships with federal agencies, Council members also pursued cooperative projects with a number of other national organizations.

NATIONAL MUSEUM OF HEALTH AND MEDICINE

The National Museum of Health and Medicine (NMHM) has enormous potential for educating all sectors about self-help groups related to the various conditions exhibited at the Museum. Dr. Koop created awareness of this potential when, as chair of the NMHM board, he announced during a museum planning forum that the museum should act as a bridge between the medical profession and the self-help movement. Council members communicated with NMHM staff throughout development of the national health objectives for the year 2000, and museum director Marc Micozzi and Orla O'Reilly attended the October 1990 Council meeting. As a result, arrangements were made for ongoing communication about developing a self-help group and Council exhibit at the museum and as part of portable traveling exhibits. Resource materials demonstrating the location of self-help clearinghouses and information about national self-help models would also be made available.

HEALTHY PEOPLE 2000 COOPERATIVE AGREEMENTS

Following Michael McGinnis's recommendation, Council member Barbara Giloth contacted the nine organizations receiving cooperative agreements to implement the recommendations related to the national health objectives for the year 2000 and asked them to consider current and potential roles for self-help groups. From information provided by Council chair Hannah Hedrick, the Summer 1991 issue of *Target 2000: A Newsletter of the AMA's Healthier Youth by the Year 2000 Project,* featured an item on self-help groups and peer-helper programs with references to the American Self-Help Clearinghouse. On November 28, 1990, Marilyn Johnson, Director of the Community Health Coalition Project of the National Medical Association, invited the Council to make a brief presentation at one of the pilot sites for the NMA cooperative project. Although unable to participate in this event, the Council developed a plan for ongoing communication with the NMA and other cooperative agreement recipients interested in incorporating self-help group activities in their projects.

NATIONAL SAFE KIDS CAMPAIGN

When Angela Mickalide moved from the ODPHP to the National SAFE KIDS Campaign, she encouraged the Council to communicate with this organization about potential roles for self-help groups. SAFE KIDS, which has received funding for five years to focus on unintentional injury and risk prevention, serves 90 grassroots coalitions around the country. The office focuses on education, environment, enactment/enforcement and evaluation of specific interventions. The focus in 1989 was on bicycles; in 1990, on burns. The office recognizes the potential contributions of self-help groups in that many of the individuals most committed to prevention are those who were themselves involved in injuries. At the October 1990 Council meeting, Dr. Mickalide agreed to guide the Council in determining cooperative or complementary activities.

Joan Parks, Senior Health Education Administrator at Metropolitan Life
Insurance Company and Managing Editor of the Health and Safety Education
Division, was responsive to suggestions from Council member Hannah
Hedrick to incorporate references to self-help groups in *Your Guide to
Healthy Living*. Distributed in April 1990, the pamphlet contains several
"door openers" for self-help groups. The first page talks about the value of
"a support group or 'buddy' system" to help people change eating habits,
exercise regularly or stop smoking. At least half of the resources are agencies
that would have information about self-help groups. Alcoholics Anonymous
has a separate listing, and there is a reference to local directories of "Self-
Help/Mutual Aid Groups."

Ms. Parks has also encouraged Metropolitan Life to consider additional
ways in which self-help groups and resources could be appropriately presented in educational materials. The October 1988 *Health Action* pamphlet
contained a strong recommendation for The Compassionate Friends;
"When a Child Dies: Thoughts for Parents" contained a parent's declaration
that "only other bereaved parents can fully understand the overwhelming
emotions that follow the death of a child."

In written and spoken communication with Council chair Hannah Hedrick,
Miriam Jacobson, Director of the Prevention Leadership Forum (a cooperative initiative of the Washington Business Group on Health and the ODPHP),
expressed interest in examining the roles of self-help groups in conjunction
with the Forum's goals of improving the quality and quantity of worksite
health promotion. Self-help groups were perceived as among the "new players" being considered to enrich the field of worksite health promotion and
as being a means for developing projects aimed at underserved populations.
Rick Birkel, who was instrumental in getting references to self-help groups
included in the mental health section of the national health objectives for the
year 2000 when he served as director of the Office of Prevention at the
National Mental Health Association, manages the National Worksite Health
Promotion Resource Center, which welcomes information on self-help
groups.

Sharing Information About Self-Help Resources

In addition to cooperating with federal agencies and other organizations, the
Council seeks to locate and disseminate information supportive of service
provider referrals to and membership in self-help groups. The Council
encourages expansion of the retrieval assistance available through clearing-

houses, which can be contacted for practical guides for starting and maintaining groups, including the roles of professionals wishing to be supportive of such groups.

AMERICAN SELF-HELP CLEARINGHOUSE

The best single source of information about individual clearinghouses is the American Self-Help Clearinghouse, which publishes *The Self-Help Sourcebook: Finding and Forming Mutual Aid Self-Help Groups.* The American Self-Help Clearinghouse has been particularly helpful to the Council, with its functions of maintaining information on clearinghouses and distributing the mutual aid/self-help network computer software and database for the use of other clearinghouses in the U.S. and Canada. Clearinghouse director Ed Madara is a consummate networker, committed to providing assistance in forming groups where they are most needed.

NATIONAL HEALTH INFORMATION CENTER

The ODPHP National Health Information Center (ONHIC), a federally sponsored information and referral service of the Office of Disease Prevention and Health Promotion, has collected a description of the Council and its services, a copy of materials the Council distributes, topics of inquiries the Council is able to answer, as well as a contact person. This information is used to assist in responses to requests for health information from health professionals and the general public and in channeling inquiries to appropriate organizations. ONHIC maintains a library with files on some 800 health topics; produces directories, resources guides and bibliographies (*Healthfinders, Health Information Resources in the Federal Government, Locating Funds for Health Promotion Projects,* and *Staying Healthy: A Bibliography of Health Promotion Materials);* and maintains an on-line directory of more than 1000 health-related organizations (accessible to the public through DIRLINE, part of the National Library of Medicine's MEDLARS system).

RESEARCH NETWORK

The Council also encourages researchers, clearinghouses and self-help groups to explore the roles of professionals and to examine issues of concerns to professionals, such as quality control, potential harm and competition. The Council is committed to making information available about major activities related to self-help and public health, such as the *Report of the Surgeon General's Workshop on Self-Help and Public Health,* which lose much of their potential impact because they do not reach a large audience. One of the original goals of the Council, establishing collaborative research needs, was addressed by two activities being coordinated by the National Project office: a self-help research network (with 104 members in mid-1990) and a November 1990 meeting of self-help social science researchers and youth/parent self-help groups to identify research needs.

ACCESSING THE CANADIAN NETWORK

The Council's relationship with the self-help movement in Canada was actually initiated during the 1987 Surgeon General's Workshop on Self-Help and Public Health; the conference packet contained a copy of a 1986 publication, "Achieving Health for All," which recognized the importance of self-help and mutual aid groups in achieving Canadian public health goals. Hector Balthazar and Jean-Marie Romeder, nationally recognized self-help activists and publishers, participated in the 1989 Symposium on the Impact of Life-Threatening Conditions. At the October 1990 Council meeting, Balthazar reported on the growth of the self-help movement in Canada, from no clearinghouses in 1980 to seven in 1990. Unlike the United States, where clearinghouses have developed locally, the Canadian Department of Health and Welfare established three different models of clearinghouses and is comparing the outcomes to see which model works best.

MOVING FORWARD

Autonomous self-help groups worked hard during the 1980s to increase policies supportive of self-help, establish clearinghouses, participate in national meetings and promote self-help through national publications. The National Council on Self-Help and Public Health worked hard to establish cooperative relationships with federal agencies and other organizations. To build on this momentum, we must continue our efforts to support clearinghouses and centers, stimulate and disseminate information about effectiveness research, expand existing networks and cooperative activities, and develop national and international objectives.

Including self-help in national and international meetings is one of the most effective mechanisms for getting the word out. Individual initiative can ensure that self-help is a part of a meeting, as evidenced by Thomas Powell's presentation at the December 5, 1990 meeting of state-level departments of mental health sponsored by the National Association of State Mental Health Program Directors and by Thomasina Borkman's presentation on collaboration at the 1991 National Conference on Drug Abuse Research and Practice. Meetings in 1992 include an international self-help conference in Ottawa in September.

Our greatest challenge in developing policies supportive of increasing access to autonomous, grassroots self-help groups may be to develop mechanisms to evaluate the efficacy of varying self-help groups models and to develop strategies for delineating and maintaining quality assurance in ways that are acceptable to autonomous groups. Evaluation tools, such as the Client Satisfaction Questionnaire, are currently being used to measure member satisfaction with self-help groups (Kurtz 1990), but researchers admit that "continued evaluation of process and outcome, using both quantitative and qualitative methods, is needed" (Kurtz, p. 111).

A number of such evaluations were getting underway in mid-1991, frequently in connection with the growing attention to the positive impact of "psychosocial support" in general. In "Psychosocial Factors in Maternal Phenylketonuria: Prevention of Unplanned Pregnancies," published in the March 1991 issue of the *American Journal of Public Health,* the authors announced their plan to include "intensive examination" of social support, defined "more precisely in terms of the nature of support networks, [and] the importance of peers versus family, the role of perceived as opposed to actual support provided" (p. 303). It is especially heartening that the authors recognize the importance of support networks in prevention, i.e., the effectiveness of peer support in family planning: "It appears that social support for birth control and positive attitudes about contraception each have a very significant influence on the reported contraceptive behavior of young women with PKU" (p. 303).

Empowerment

Policies and partnerships designed to promote self-help groups for persons impacted by life-compromising conditions will benefit the growth of the autonomous self-help group movement to the extent that they recognize the importance of empowerment. Only when there is genuine collaboration among professionals and self-help group members, viewed as resources rather than as clients, can empowerment be achieved. Can we develop a tool to measure this empowerment, this expansion of palpable energy created when a number of people gather to help one another? Do reports of greater life satisfaction, higher scores on self-esteem measures, and decreased depression (Rappaport 1985) convey this benefit? Barath (1990) cites medical sociologist Alf Trojan's study showing that more than 80 to 90 percent of 232 members from 65 disease-related groups demonstrated increased social activation, improved sense of well-being and "self-competence," better understanding of the disease and more rational use of medical services and medication, but can we measure the process that transforms people with life-threatening conditions from passive patients to empowered givers?

It is this process that is referenced time and time again, not only in self-help publications, but also in the popular publications cited elsewhere in this chapter. During the first half of 1990 alone, multiple-page articles appeared in mainstream publications as diverse as *Newsweek* (February 5), *The New Yorker* (April 23), and *New Woman* (June). The articles all refer to the empowerment that comes from peers helping one another and thereby helping themselves. In the "Notes and Comment" section of *The New Yorker's* editorial feature, "The Talk of the Town," the editorial "we" describes "the miracle of human connectedness" in a meeting of Compassionate Friends. In "this giving and taking," strangers could be so "receptive to each other's truths" that they could "begin to heal. . . . The energy of equality flowed without hindrance. . . . We all experienced a growing sense of excitement and privilege at living in our own time." What tool could measure this "growing sense of excitement and privilege," or the "unconditional love" and "helping others" cited by Victoria Secunda (1990) as the "transforming" elements in group meetings?

A Pressing Need

All is not well in the self-help world. Clearinghouses that serve self-help groups, one of the major partners, are being closed or are cutting back at a time when they are most needed. Three of the four clearinghouses represented on the planning committee for the 1987 Surgeon General's Workshop are closed or operating with only volunteer staff; the Minnesota Self-Help Network closed in 1989, the New York City Clearinghouse closed in 1990, and the Self-Help Center in Illinois is trying to handle referral calls and put out a directory with an all-volunteer staff. The New York State Clearinghouse closed in early 1991, and those in Massachusetts, Connecticut and Michigan are facing major funding cutbacks and possible closure.

Foundations are not impervious to the need for contributions to self-help groups. In the July/August 1988 issue of *Foundation News,* Roger Williams' supportive article, "The Wave of Self-Help," reported that "Mutual support groups are a lifesaver for the growing number of people who want help—and are willing to give it, too." The "increasing number of referrals made to self-help groups by physicians and other professionals" is cited as "the best measure of success" and as an indication of a reduction in professional criticism. In the article, which was motivated by Dr. Koop's support of self-help and the 1987 workshop, Williams reported that self-help groups are "funded by at least two dozen foundations."

In mid-1991, however, neither foundations nor public agencies were rushing to support clearinghouses. Perhaps publications such as this one, which tell the self-help story, will convince public and private funding sources that they can get a tremendous bang for the dollars they give to support the clearinghouses that nurture self-help groups. As Raymond Fowler, Chief Executive Officer of the American Psychological Association, pointed out in 1990, "The most important change now taking place in mental health care has to do not with the mental health professionals—it has to do with people helping themselves and helping each other. . . . There is, within the community, a healing power if we have the will to help mobilize it" (Nottingham, 1990, p. 62).

Clearinghouses and the groups they serve will continue to work together to find a way to mobilize that healing power. For as Dr. Koop stated in June 1990, "the future of health care in these troubled times requires cooperation between organized medicine and self-help groups to achieve the best care for the lowest cost."

REFERENCES

Achieving Health for All: A Framework for Health Promotion. Ottawa: Canadian Ministry of National Health and Welfare, 1986.

AIDS education—a beginning. *Population Reports* Series L(8), September 1989.

Alexander, H. Long-Term Treatment. In C.H. Kempe and R.E. Helfer, eds., *The Battered Child.* Chicago: University of Chicago Press, 1980.

Anderson, C.T. Doctors in AA. *AMN,* January 12, 1990, pp. 33, 46-48.

Anderson, D.J. *Living with a Chronic Illness.* Center City, MN: Hazeldon Foundation, 1986.

Barath, A. *Self-Help and Its Support Systems in Europe, 1979-1989: A Critical Review.* (Copies available from Department of Health Psychology, Medical School of Zagreb, Zagreb, Yugoslavia.)

The Barnraiser, Summer 1989. Chicago: Illinois Self-Help Center.

Belasco, L. The better way. *Good Housekeeping,* February 1991, p. 245.

Bernstein, A.D., ed. *Self-Help Groups for People Dealing with AIDS: You Are Not Alone.* Denville, NJ: Self-Help Clearinghouse, St. Clares–Riverside Medical Center, 1988.

Borck, L., and E. Aronowitz. The Role of the Self-Help Clearinghouse. In L.D. Borman, L. Borck, R. Hess, and F. Pasquale, eds., *Helping People to Help Themselves: Self-Help and Prevention.* New York: Haworth Press, 1982.

Borkman, T.J. Self-Help Mutual Aid Groups: A Different Helping Paradigm? Unpublished manuscript prepared for the Surgeon General's Workshop on Self-Help and Public Health, 1987.

————. Self-Help Groups at the Turning Point: Emerging Egalitarian Alliances with the Formal Health Care System? Presentation at the annual meeting of the Association for Voluntary Action Scholars, Seattle, September 27, 1989. (Published in *Am. J. Community Psychology,* May 1990.)

————. Experiential, Professional, and Lay Frames of Reference. In Thomas Powell, ed., *Working with Self-Help.* Silver Spring, MD: National Association of Social Workers, 1990.

Borman, L.D., L. Borck, R. Hess, and F. Pasquale, eds. Help yourself—& others too. *The Rotarian* 143(1):12-15, 1983.

————. Self-Help/Mutual Aid Groups: Strategies for Prevention. In *Directory of Self-Help/Mutual Aid Groups.* Evanston, IL: The Self-Help Center, 1988.

————. *Helping People to Help Themselves: Self-Help and Prevention.* New York: Haworth Press, 1982.

Breo, D.L. Panel's chairman urges radical change in U.S. war on AIDS. *AMN,* June 17, 1988, pp. 1, 58.

————. Coping with the AIDS crisis. *AMN,* July 31, 1987, pp. 3, 27-28.

Bulman, J.A., and J. Rosenbaum. Community resources: an overlooked tool. *Physician Assistant* 11(2):51, 55-56, 1987.

Carroll, C.A. The Function of Protective Services in Child Abuse and Neglect. In C.H. Kempe and R.E. Helfer, eds., *The Battered Child.* Chicago: University of Chicago Press, 1980.

Check, W.A. 'Public health problem' of violence receives epidemiologic attention. *JAMA* 254(7):881-892, 1985.

Cohn, A.H. The Prevention of Child Abuse: What Do We Know about What Works? In J.E. Leavitt, ed., *Child Abuse and Neglect: Research and Innovation.* The Hague: Martinus Nijhoff, 1983.

_____. The Treatment of Child Abuse: What Do We Know about What Works? In J.E. Leavitt, ed., *Child Abuse and Neglect: Research and Innovation.* The Hague: Martinus Nijhoff, 1983.

d'Adesky, A.C. 'New Eclecticism' approach to AIDS. *AMN,* September 23/30, 1988, pp. 3, 43-46.

De Alvarez, J. Third Age Development in the Third World: Empowerment and the Rights of the Elderly. Statement at the conference on "Aging in the Americas: Challenges for the 90s," May 31, 1990. (Available from Edward J. Madara, St. Clares–Riverside Medical Center, Denville, NJ.)

DeBruyn, L.M., K. Hymbaugh, and N. Valdez. *A Community Approach to Suicide and Violence.* Albuquerque: Indian Health Service Mental Programs Branch, 1988.

Directory of National Self-Help/Mutual Aid Resources. Chicago: American Hospital Association, 1988.

Directory of Self-Help/Mutual Aid Groups. Evanston, IL: The Self-Help Center, 1988.

Edwards, R.L. Professional and Family Caregivers: A Social Work Perspective. In J. Nottingham and J. Nottingham, eds., *The Professional and Family Caregiver— Dilemmas, Rewards and New Directions.* Americus, GA: Georgia Southwestern College, 1990.

Empowerment and Family Supports Bulletin, 1(1), October 1989.

Evolving roles: self-help and the professional. *The Self-Helper* 2(2):3-4, 1985.

Executive Summary: Report to the Steering Committee for the Surgeon General's Workshop on Self-Help and Public Health, 1987. (Available from Barbara Giloth, Division of Ambulatory Care and Health Promotion, American Hospital Association, 480 N. Lake Shore Drive, Chicago, IL 60611.)

Ferguson, T. Sharing the uncertainty. *Whole Earth Review,* Winter 1987, pp. 130-133.

_____. Running a self-help group by computer. *Med. Self-Care* November/December 1987, p. 80.

French, G.A. Self-help groups: more than a Band-Aid treatment? *Chicago Med.* 92(18): 10-13, 1989.

Gaioni, K. "RX: self-help." *The New Physician,* July/August 1988, pp. 31-32.

Gerber, L.A. *JAMA,* 259(16):2461, 1988.

Giloth, B. Hospital Involvement with Self-Help Support Groups. Presented at the meeting of the American Public Health Association, Los Angeles, November 2, 1981.

Goldberg, G. Preventing the risk of another stroke. *Stroke Connection* 10(2):1-2, 1988.

_____. Reducing your risk of stroke. *Stroke Connection* 12(3):1-3, 1990.

Goldsmith, M. *JAMA* 261(17):2474-2475, 1989.

Growald, E.R., and A. Luks. Beyond self: the immunity of samaritans. *Am. Health* 7(2):51-71, 1988.

Growing Up and Getting Medical Care: Youth with Special Health Care Needs. Washington, DC: National Center for Networking Community Based Services, 1989.

Hafey, J., G. Hildebrand, and C. Spain. Emerging Players in the New Public Health. In *California's Response to the Institute of Medicine's Report on "The Future of Public Health": Policy Papers.* Berkeley, CA: California Coalition for the Future of Public Health, 1990.

Harris, L. Communication to the National Council on Self-Help and Public Health, July 1990.

The Health Policy Agenda for the American People. Chicago: American Medical Association, 1987.

Hedrick H.L. Allied health professionals and patients with life-threatening illness: a holy alliance. *J. Allied Health* 16(2):189-93, 1987.

_____. Increasing access to self-help groups. *J. Allied Health* 17(3):165-69, 1988.

_____. Expanded roles in holistic prevention for allied health professionals. *J. Allied Health* 14(4):455-61, 1985.

_____. Involvement in mutual aid/self-help activities. *J. Allied Health* 15(3):268-69, 1986.

Hinz, C.A. *AMN,* April 14, 1989, p. 10 ff.

_____. Physicians can't shut eyes to drug, alcohol abuse, MD, former addict, says. *AMN,* July 3/10, 1987, pp. 51-52.

Hurley, D. Getting help from helping others. *Psychology Today* 21(2):63-67, 1988.

Hyde, G.L. How to recognize and help an impaired surgeon. *Bull. Am. Coll. Surgeons* 73(4):4-6, 1988.

Jacobs, M.K., and G. Goodman. Psychology and self-help groups: predictions on a partnership. *Am. Psychologist* 44(3):536-545, 1989.

Katz, A.H. Self-Help Groups. In *Encyclopedia of Social Work,* Vol. 15. New York: National Association of Social Workers, 1965.

_____. *Partners in Wellness.* Los Angeles: California Department of Public Health, 1987.

_____. Professional/Self-Help Group Relationships—General Issues. Presentation at the *Symposium on the Impact of Life-Threatening Conditions,* Chicago, 1989.

Katz, A.H., and E.I. Bender. *Helping One Another: Self-Help in a Changing World.* Oakland, CA: Third Party Publishers, 1988.

Kempe, C.H., and R.E. Helfer, eds. *The Battered Child.* Chicago: University of Chicago Press, 1980.

Khantzian, E.J. The injured self, addiction and our call to medicine: understanding and managing addicted physicians. *JAMA* 254(2):249-252, 1985.

Koop, C.E. Foreword. In J.M. Romeder, ed., *The Self-Help Way: Mutual Aid and Health.* Ottawa: Canadian Council on Social Development, 1990.

Kushnick, H. A Mother's Viewpoint. In *Report of the Surgeon General's Workshop on Children with HIV Infection and Their Families.* Rockville, MD: U.S. Department of Health and Human Services, Public Health Service, 1987.

Kurtz, L.F., and T.J. Powell. Three approaches to understanding self-help groups. *Social Work with Groups,* Fall 1987.

Lavoie, F. Evaluating Self-Help Groups. In J.M. Romeder, ed., *The Self-Help Way: Mutual Aid and Health.* Ottawa: Canadian Council on Social Development, 1990.

Lieberman, M.A. Self-help groups and psychiatry. *Am. Psychiatric Ann. Rev.* 5:744-760, 1986.

_____. The role of self-help groups in helping patients and families cope with cancer. *CA-A Cancer J. Clinicians* 38(3):162-168, 1988.

Madara, E.J. Maximizing the Potential for Community Self-Help through Clearinghouse Approaches. In *Prevention in Community Health Centers.* New York: Haworth Press, 1990.

Madara, E.J., J. Kalafat, and B.N. Miller. The computerized self-help clearinghouse: using 'high tech' to promote 'high touch' support networks. *Computers in Human Services* 3(3/4):39-52, 1988.

Manber, M.M. Patient resource groups: a natural resource for physicians. *Medical World News* 25(23):51-75, 1984.

McEwen, J., C.J.M. Martini, and N. Wilkins. *Participation in Health.* London: Croom Helm, 1983.

McPheeters, H.L. The Professional and Family Caregiver: Medical/Psychiatric Issues. In J. Nottingham and J. Nottingham, eds., *The Professional and Family*

Caregiver—Dilemmas, Rewards and New Directions. Americus, GA: Georgia Southwestern College, 1990.

MD workaholics speak up, *Med. World News,* March 10, 1986, pp. 112-113.

Micozzi, M. Letter to Carlos J.M. Martini, November 8, 1989.

Monaco, G.P. Parent self-help groups for the families of children with cancer. *CA-A Cancer J. Clinicians* 38(3):169-175, 1988.

Mowrer, O.H. Peer groups and medication: the best 'therapy' for professionals and laymen alike. *Psychotherapy Theory Res. Practice* 8:44-54, 1971.

National Conference on Phobias and Related Anxiety Disorders (Program). Phobia Society of America, Rockville, MD, 1990.

Nottingham, J., and J. Nottingham. *The Professional and Family Caregiver—Dilemmas, Rewards, and New Directions.* Americus, GA: Georgia Southwestern College, 1990.

On Being Alone: AARP Guide for Widowed Persons. Washington, DC: American Association of Retired Persons, 1987.

Osterholm, M.T., and K.L. MacDonald. Facing the complex issues of pediatric AIDS: a public health perspective. *JAMA* 258(19):2736-37, 1987.

Owen, W.F., Jr. Healthcare Programs for Patients with Endstage HIV Infection. *Med. Aspects Human Sexuality* 22(2):18-33, 1988.

Post-Polio Directory. St. Louis: International Polio Network, 1990.

Powell, T.J. *Self-Help Organizations and Professional Practice.* Silver Spring, MD: National Association of Social Workers, 1987.

_____. *Working with Self-Help.* Silver Spring, MD: National Association of Social Workers, 1990.

The Prevention of Mental-Emotional Disabilities. Alexandria, VA: National Mental Health Association, 1986.

Rappaport, J. The Power of Empowerment Language. *Social Policy* 15(4):15-21, 1985.

Rehabilitation Gazette. St. Louis: Gazette International Network Institute, 1990.

Report of the Surgeon General's Workshop on Self-Help and Public Health. Rockville, MD. U.S. Public Health Service, 1988.

Riklefs, R. Bleak prognosis: the specter of AIDS is haunting the lives of the thousands who test 'HIV positive.' *The Wall Street Journal,* February 11, 1988, p. 17.

Riessman, F. The helper therapy principle. *Social Work* 10(2):27-32, 1965.

_____. New dimensions in self-help. *Social Policy* 15(3):2-4, 1985.

_____. The Surgeon General and the self-help ethos. *Social Policy* 17:23-25, 1987.

_____. Professional/self-help group relationships. *The Self-Help Reporter* 3, Summer/Fall 1989.

Riordan, R.J., and M.S. Beggs. Counselors and self-help groups. *J. Counseling Development* 65:427-429, 1987.

Robinson, D. Self-help groups in primary health care. *World Health Forum* 2(2):185-191, 1981.

Rogers, P.D. To Mr. Gambini: a physician makes his final amends. *AMN,* May 13, 1988, p. 66 ff.

Romeder, J.M. *The Self-Help Way: Mutual Aid and Health.* Ottawa: Canadian Council on Social Development, 1990.

Samples, P. A place to go to talk about the pain. *AMN,* August 1988, pp. 41-47.

Secunda, V. The 12-stepping of America. *New Woman,* June 1990, pp. 49-54.

Self-Help Groups. In *The Psychiatric Therapies.* Washington, DC: American Psychiatric Association, 1984.

Self-Help Through the Looking Glass. Leicester, England: Leicester Council for Voluntary Service, 1985.

Sharing Caring: A Communications Kit to Assist Hospitals in Their Involvement with Self-Help Groups. Chicago: American Hospital Association, 1987.

Skelly, F.J. Permission granted. *AMN*, May 25, 1990, pp. 37-39.

Squires, S. A Group for all reasons: why millions are turning to self-help organizations. *Washington Post*, May 17, 1988, pp. 14-17.

Staver, S. AIDS MDs cope with frustrations in support groups. *AMN*, June 5, 1987, pp. 34-35.

_____. MDs' responses aggravate battered women's plight, researchers say. *AMN*, August 23/30, 1985, pp. 9-10.

_____. Support group helps mothers share grief. *AMN*, January 22/29, 1988, pp. 3, 26-29.

Surgeon General's Workshop on Health Promotion and Aging Proceedings. Rockville, MD: U.S. Public Health Service, 1988.

Tavris, C. Self-help or therapy? *Vogue*, February 1987.

Thiers, N. Self-help movement gains strength, offers hope. *Guidepost* 30(9):1, 8, 16, 1987.

Vandermeulen, A. The Flemish Clearinghouse: An Information and Documentation Centre on Self-Help. Unpublished manuscript. Leuven, 1988.

Williams, R.M. The wave of self-help. *Foundation News*, July/August 1988, pp. 28-32.

Wollert, R.W. Human services and the self-help clearinghouse concept. *Canad. J. Community Mental Health* 6(1):79-90, 1987.

_____. *A Survey of Self-Help Clearinghouses in North America: A Special Report for the U.S. Surgeon General's Workshop on Self-Help and Public Health*, 1987. (Available from Department of Psychology, University of Saskatchewan, Saskatoon S7N 0W0.)

Year 2000 National Health Objectives: Comments from the National Council on Self-Help and Public Health, 1989. (Available from Hannah L. Hedrick, 515 North State Street, Chicago, IL 60610.)

Your Guide to Healthy Living. New York: Metropolitan Life Insurance Company, 1990.

2

Professional/Self-Help Group Relationships: General Issues

Alfred H. Katz, DSW

Just as we have reached a new stage in the recognition by government of the importance and contributions of self-help groups in the health field, so have we also reached a new potential stage in understanding and facilitating the relationships between professional providers and agencies and the tremendous social resource represented by self-help groups and their members. We are now at a stage where theoretical formulations of possible or right ways to go in this relationship are no longer appropriate, needed or useful. We are rather at a point of being able to evaluate experiences, of being able to test viewpoints, of analyzing attitudes and actions that work, and those that don't work. We can now speak with some authority from experience, instead of what were once just opinions.

It is important to point out that the self-help movement has grown up by itself, largely without professional guidance and help. It has been chiefly a self-starting, spontaneous, grassroots movement that has created its own culture, its own traditions, its own ways of doing things, mostly independently of professionals. Of course, it has captured the sympathy and help of some professionals, including physicians, nurses, social workers, psychologists, clergy and academics like myself who have been excited, even bowled over by the dynamic growth, creativeness and usefulness of the movement.

But largely it has made it on its own. The various meetings called by units of the federal government—by the National Institute of Mental Health and the National Heart Institute in 1985 and the Surgeon General in 1987, among others, along with the establishment of support for clearinghouses by various state governments since the early 1980s—these were recognition of a reality that had grown up outside government, a recognition that self-help groups are a resource that can be used. I think the same thing applies to the professional fields. When they have held meetings to discuss self-help groups and how to work with them, this has been because the groups are an inescapable reality with which professionals have to come to terms, and which they have to learn to work and live with.

Unlike some of my colleagues, I believe that self-help groups have mostly been self-created in response to specific needs and that by and large they do not reflect the initiatives of professionals. There are of course exceptions, in which some professionals—usually clinicians—have been more perceptive and far-seeing than the majority. Out of conviction they have dug in and contributed to the hard organizational tasks of helping to create self-help structures and programs that have endured and grown. We are now in the happy situation, unlike 10 or 15 years ago, that many professionals and the agencies in which they work are actively prompting the growth of specific self-help organizations and the growth of understanding in their own disciplines of what the groups have to offer.

OBSTACLES TO UNDERSTANDING

This situation is not yet a general one—there are still obstacles ahead. These lie both in the paucity of knowledge about self-help included in professional education and literature, and in the continuing dilemmas, conflicts and disagreements about how professionals, agencies and self-help groups should relate to each other.

Some of these conflicts are "turf" problems. As an example, there was the January 1988 issue of *Psychology Today,* at that time published by the American Psychological Association. Several articles presented information on self-help—some favorably, some critically—but the general tone was patronizing and even condescending. The conclusion was that if they accept the guidance of professional psychologists, "self-help groups may become a legitimate and accepted part of mental health services." *May* become? Tell that to the thousands of members at Recovery, AA and its affiliates, GROW and countless other groups who have already decided that they are and have been for some time "legitimate" members of the mental health movement, just as much as the professionals within it. Legitimacy is not conferred on a group by professionals; it is decided on by the members and consumers of services. I wrote a letter to the magazine, pointing out these things; not surprisingly, it was never published.

In a recent issue of *Social Work,* the journal of the National Association of Social Workers, an article by two academics discussed some newer approaches in social work, among them self-help. While generally positive, this article stated that self-help was not competent to deal with the psychological problems of laid-off and chronically unemployed workers, with pregnancy in unmarried teenagers and with other important social issues, and that in fact there was no hard evidence from research that self-help works. Again I wrote a reply correcting some of these misstatements and misunderstandings. I supplied factual examples of effective self-help programs in the very fields in which self-help was supposed to be incompetent, and I listed research that showed positive outcomes. This time the letter was published.

In social work, the field I know best, just as in clinical psychology, there is a strong drive toward private practice. Some of the reasons for this are understandable—agency rigidities, low salaries and the drive for greater independence—but it is an inescapable reality that private practitioners often see the operations of self-help groups as competitive, and therefore a "turf" and a "pocketbook" threat.

What is needed to bring about what Mort Lieberman and the late Leonard Borman referred to as a "paradigm shift" that would create a much larger corps of educated and dedicated professional workers? First of all, a revised approach in education is needed for the various human service professions. This is not easy to accomplish, but it is essential. It is well known that many medical and social work students enter training with a big fund of idealism. They want to serve people in need and are not concerned at first with money and status. But often because of the narrowness of curricula and the professional role models and rewards they see, the social idealism of these students dies away. They concentrate on the need to acquire the technical knowledge, skills and attitudes that they think will make them successful practitioners. These attitudes emphasize the critical, monopolistic role that professionals play in diagnosis and therapy, so that students soon acquire the belief that they have most of the answers and that patients or clients should listen, comply and not be too self-assertive.

To counter this view it is necessary to have materials in professional curricula that show what lay people know, what they can do for themselves, what lay self-help groups can accomplish for patients and their families, and that also show that true professionalism involves respect for and partnership with these lay resources. One way of doing this is to build into professional education at many levels the participation of former and present patients and their organizations—in classes, in field contacts, even in research studies. A few medical educators are doing just that, and I hope such an approach is penetrating social work, public health and nursing education, too.

One of the things I first learned from my study of handicapped children's and parents' groups 35 years ago was how important the parents were in educating professionals about the daily problems their children faced and what their children could actually do. The parents showed us then that education is a two-way street, that the "experiential" knowledge of group participants, acquired not from books or classes but first-hand from hard and bitter experiences, should be made available to professionals as a prime component in their understanding of what illness means to patients and their loved ones.

We obviously can't wait till a new generation of doctors, nurses, social workers and psychologists gets out of school, even if some magic wand would accomplish a revolution in professional education in these disciplines. We live in the here-and-now. We have a big cadre of already-trained professionals who somehow have to unlearn some of the attitudes and assumptions they picked up in their training, many of which are still bolstered by the health care delivery system in which they operate. This unlearning might better be called retraining, or reconversion, not unlike the changed skills needed when industrial workers have to take on new functions.

One of the other major things self-help groups can teach professionals is what it is like to be a group member—to participate in the group process, to be respectful of other people's opinions even when you think you know better, and not to attempt to dominate them or the discussion. Being a member and sharing in a group also means to be ready to admit one's own mistakes, weaknesses, inadequacies, fears and hostilities. In their training and their work-lives, professionals are not often called upon to expose to others their weaknesses and their vulnerabilities. They do not usually experience a self-help process that at once accepts, supports, instructs and does not stigmatize them for leveling with others about themselves. These are some of the reasons that I and others have advocated that every professional who works with self-help groups should be a member of one to experience the benefits of peer mutual aid. Whether related to overcoming burnout, bureaucracy, or some other common problem, professionals can best understand what happens in self-help groups by experiencing it themselves.

OWNERSHIP

The most prevalent fear of self-help groups is the fear of co-optation, of being taken over by professionals or agencies. This feeling of ownership by the group members is a key factor that professionals have to learn to appreciate in working with self-help groups. Professionals must learn to evaluate their own motives and actions in working with groups to make sure that, consciously or unconsciously, they are not pushing toward a takeover, perhaps in the interest of what they see as efficiency.

In my opinion, ownership by the members is the key to defining a true self-help group. We all know of the many support, discussion, self-exploration and therapy groups set up by hospitals and by people in private practice. Some of them use professionals as the chief active leader in all the sessions. These can't be called true self-help groups because the participants don't decide on the program or agenda—the professional does. Where the professional has the role of facilitator or resource person and decisions are actually thrashed out by and within the group, then I think we have a true self-help group situation, no matter what its structure and origins are or what it is called.

The professional facilitator or resource person has to be very conscious about motives and styles of working with the group. Groups with inexperienced, weak or frequently ill and absent leaders may tend to depend too much on the professional advisor or facilitator. The latter's task is to work toward stepping out as soon as the group has stabilized and has a consistent, competent roster of leaders to carry on the organization's various tasks. The professional's contact is best when it lasts for the shortest time.

SOME CONCLUSIONS

Theories and concepts of professional self-help group relationships, which are usually put forward by professionals, are not particularly useful— experience is. But it is worth mentioning some mistaken ideas or theories from the past to help guard against new versions of them turning up again. One of these ideas is that self-help groups and professionals are ''made for each other'' and that they do essentially identical things. Another idea is that self-help groups and professionals are ''two wings of the same bird''—which suggests that the bird can't fly without both.

The first idea, that self-help group help and professional help are identical, is just plain wrong in my opinion. It ignores several key factors: the powerful element of peer support, the effects of individual role models in the group, exchange of experience, and the interactions involved in both giving and receiving help. As compared with the socially isolated and isolating experience of individual therapy, group experience is closer to everyday life with its give and take, its concern with the present and not with digging into the past, and its potential to provide freer and more spontaneous personal relationships. These elements give self-help its distinctiveness from professional help, which, however competent, sensitive and well-meaning, cannot supply these things.

Are both wings needed for this bird to fly? There are many situations where the self-help group can supply everything and where professional help is simply not needed or is irrelevant. In other situations, the two can be useful complements, each providing what the other does not. And of course there are medical and psychiatric situations where technical professional knowledge, skills and care are the need of the moment, and group involvement may come later.

Above all I believe we must recognize that there is no simple blueprint or pattern for the ways professionals and self-helpers can relate to one another and cooperate in helping individuals, families and communities. Flexibility, pluralism, mutual respect, openness on both sides, and trying out new things are the keys to success.

We are in an exciting period of great change, growth and creativeness. At such a time, we will all make mistakes and learn how to correct them. Given that we will learn from our pooled experiences, the road ahead could not look more promising.

3

Rewriting the Social Contract in Health

Fitzhugh Mullan, MD

As a physician, as a practitioner of public health, and as a cancer patient, I have benefited both personally and organizationally from self-help groups. Such benefits are reported in a number of books, including my own *Vital Signs*. I frequently use the following story when I speak to groups, both professional and community, who are concerned with either cancer or self-help. I got it from reading some material two or three years ago from the Illinois Self-Help Center, which has been a galvanizing force for the self-help movement in general.

The story is one Leonard Borman attributed to Woody Guthrie's widow, and is about two rabbits hopping through the woods. Chased and surrounded by a group of dogs, they hopped under a log, where they got momentary protection. One rabbit said to the other "Looks like we're done for." The other rabbit said "What do you mean? We'll just stay under here until we outnumber them." Although Len is no longer with us, the story indicates what I think the self-help movement is all about.

FROM HEALER TO PATIENT

In 1975, I was a physician practicing in New Mexico, 32 years old, in good health and in full stride in my personal and professional life, when I discovered a cancer deep in my own chest. I will not dwell on the dramatic story, but it transformed me, rather rapidly, from a provider to a receiver of medical care. I was in the United States Public Health Service then, as I am now. A week or so after my discovery, when I was back in the National Naval Medical Center in Washington, I was treated with a certain amount of pain and deference from the medical and nursing staff. I was one of them, and of an age and a profession that was close to many of them, yet I was obviously very sick. The surgeon who was going to do the diagnostic procedure on the following day wanted to bronchoscope me, that is, to place a tube down my bronchus, to attempt to find out whether the tumor was impinging on my air passages. He had what is called a fiberoptic scope, which means that the physics of light allow you to bend the beam. He identified the area and did indeed see the tumor impinging on the bronchus and said, "You might be interested in this." For those of you who have never been bronchoscoped, it feels like you have a flexible automobile muffler down your throat. The physician bent the scope at 180 degrees, and there I was looking down this tube, looking at my own tumor.

For that one moment I was both healer and patient. A progressive transition occurred, both physically and mentally, because whatever I thought before about being a physician, we are all patients, all the time. I use that word not in the sense of being at the mercy of, but in the sense of being fragile—the sense of being ill, of being less strong than the others are now, in any number of ways. That process was being proved to me rather dramatically and quickly.

One day later, I was on my way to surgery. In my case, the rigorous process that goes along with military hospitals involved more than the standard scrubs. I was stripped nude and put on the gurney and was wheeled to the operating room with only a sheet over me, and then they did the final thing. They took away my glasses. I experienced the total vulnerability of being nude, prone and semi-blind, being wheeled through the chilly halls of the hospital, with people looking at me and not being able to see them. I knew that I was a patient at that point.

This is the vulnerability we all have to keep in mind. This is part of the experience for all those who suffer from illnesses and problems. My experience was a difficult one. The surgery went okay. The tumor was a nasty one. After surgery, I went through chemotherapy and radiation complications. Happily, there were no metastases, and happily, the several years of treatments were successful, at least in regard to arresting the tumor. I was fortunate enough to get back on my feet, go back to work and continue my family life. A few years later, I set down my story in the book *Vital Signs,* which generated more discussion and an opportunity to give lectures. I wrote an article in the *New England Journal of Medicine* entitled "The Seasons of Survival," in which I tried to describe what it was like to go through survivorship.

FROM PATIENT TO SELF-HELPER

Those two publications stimulated a lot of talk about cancer survivorship, and in 1986 a group founded the National Coalition for Cancer Survivorship (NCCS). We focused on independent, grassroots cancer groups, which are now networking with cancer centers, the National Cancer Institute, the American Cancer Society, local groups and anyone else willing to get on the grapevine. The principles of the NCCS, which are like those of many self-help and survivor groups, are to provide a voice, to let people know that we are here and we are vibrant, and while we are fighting with a potentially fatal disease, many of us are beating it. Those of us who are struggling with it are indeed struggling; we are not taking it lying down. We are also reaching out, as a model for other organizations, to the local, state and national scenes, to deal with the laws, the budgets, the corporate decisions and everything else that governs our lives. While we are promoting research in cancer survivorship in our area, we are also promoting the ongoing use of our collective minds to achieve better insight on how to deal with this illness.

Thus, I got interested in self-help through the back door. During the bleakest period of my struggle, in 1975, my wife commented that there must be somebody else out there who had gone through this. We had moved from New Mexico to Washington, D.C.; we were new in the community, and we didn't really have a lot of friends. So I felt particularly isolated. My wife suggested that we try to find some sort of group. A secretary at the American Cancer Society had heard about a doctor who ran group sessions for his patients. Every second Thursday, for two or three months, my wife and I went to a meeting held in his office, with the chairs pushed back. This was a very important experience for me and gave me the sense that there was something out there that could begin to deal with this isolation.

But it was only after coming back and revisiting my experience through my opportunity to talk about it that the notion of the generic concept of self-help began to firm up in my mind. The fruit of this concept came from six or seven years of traveling and talking in the area of self-help (with the slant that my experience has had toward cancer), and from the writings that have been so very helpful in crystalizing my concept. In particular, the *Report of the Surgeon General's Workshop on Self-Help and Public Health,* which I read in great detail, brought the movement into focus.

It is estimated that there are half a million self-help groups that involve between 10 and 15 million people in this country. It is in the great American tradition: people getting together, putting their shoulders to a common problem, getting that beam off the floor and up into the air. There are many different types of self-help groups, which the Surgeon General's Workshop has boiled down to three: physical and mental health groups, recovery (or addiction) groups, and minority groups (including underrepresented populations, such as persons with disabilities).

THE VETERAN HELPING THE ROOKIE

What are the important common elements of self-help groups? First and foremost is the concept of the veteran helping the rookie. There is an experience out there that you have had. It very well may have been a terrible experience, but it is an experience you have coped with, you have struggled with, you have hit your head against—and you have now gotten some wisdom, some maturity. You have some scars, God knows, and what are they? Are they going to be an ongoing dilemma, an ongoing pain, or are they going to be something that you can use in some positive way to help someone else? From the other perspective, you are the rookie. You are somebody who has just been diagnosed with disease X, or just realized you have problem Y, just had a child born with condition Z. Suddenly, you are on this new terrain, where terms are confusing, where directions are unclear. You get a lot of different people giving you advice. Then something better comes along—someone who has been there before, who says "don't worry, be happy." That is the idea of the veteran helping the rookie.

It goes without saying that the helping process also helps the veteran. It gives us something we can do with that pain, with that wasted limb, with that destroyed vision, with that compromised circulation, with that problem we bear. It allows us to reprocess it in some way that is useful and meaningful to us.

INSTANT IDENTITY

A second common element of self-help groups is fighting isolation or providing emotional support. Borman calls it "instant identity," when you are that rookie, when you are out there struggling and have been at it for a week or a month, and someone comes along who has an ostomy or is dealing with AIDS. All of a sudden, you have an instant identity with that person, an instant kinship, a feeling of community. As I dealt with my cancer, with my wife and small children alone in a new community, we said, "My God, we don't know anybody." In this case, I was 32 years old; we didn't know anybody who was sick, let alone one who had cancer or who might be dying. Now this may be an extreme, but we live in a society that by and large is fairly healthy. If you are not fairly healthy, then there is something wrong, and you tend to get isolated. So self-help groups provide an instant sense of community that is terribly important.

ADVOCACY

A third element of self-help groups is advocacy. I think groups have varying levels of focus and varying levels of concern on advocacy. First, you have to get your own act together before you can be strong enough to step out and say you are going to visit the state legislature, or you are going to Washington to testify, or you are going to take on an insurance company. Obviously, that is more of a second level, but it is crucial to move beyond the day-to-day concerns of the immediate creation of community and identity. These are important, but the next think to do—and many groups have begun to do it—is to talk about advocacy and empowerment, to get into the legal, vocational and political arenas.

EDUCATED CONSUMERISM

Another self-help group theme is consumerism. There is a lot of consumerism in what we are doing, but we ought to go further. We should look at the

National Consumers League and at *Consumer Reports,* at groups that have gotten down the last bit of strategy for how to buy a needed appliance. We should be equally clear on how to pick a physician or a psychotherapist, or how to select orthodox and nonorthodox treatments. At least, we should be struggling toward that. Elements of consumerism include our relationship to professionals as consumers, as patients and as clients. This relationship should be quality-monitored. Is the standard being provided in cancer care adequate? Are we being sufficiently vigilant about secondary tumors and long-term effects? We are finding out that there is a flip side, that there are longer-term problems to some of the chemotherapy and even to radiation. That is the kind of thing consumers should be monitoring. If the research scientists are not on top of these problems, we should be urging them to get going. Therefore, quality monitoring and quality control are important elements of consumerism.

Of course information exchange underlies most of these elements. We need to be informed, instructed, smart participants in our particular self-help area, and that means knowing the field—not just from the patient's point of view, but from a professional standpoint. You have to be able to read the literature, or at least have it interpreted for you.

BENEFITS PROVIDED BY SELF-HELP GROUPS

Let us turn to the question, Why self-help? Why is it important? Why have groups hung together? Why do so many people participate? I would call this the creation of a "new neighborhood." For you, as an individual, could be dealing as a patient, as a family member or loved one, as somebody with a condition or illness that is new, or even as a professional interested in how your patients are coping. Why is this new neighborhood so important to so many people? One influence is what one might call the impersonality of high-tech medicine.

Personal Touch

Particularly on the physical side, the same medical center that can perform high-tech procedures and is salvaging more people, is a pretty impersonal place. It is a hard place, speaking for both patient and physician, to practice caring and humane service. This is not impossible, and it is very important that we struggle on both sides to keep it as humane as possible. The sense of impersonality makes people look for ways to get into a community where people can really talk over the long term, in a language they understand, with supportive people. Second, many of the diseases or conditions we are dealing with are a product of life extension. We are living longer and encountering more illnesses. Some of the illnesses are a product of the kind of society we live in and the particular compulsions we are driven to; thus, we can speak of these as life-style diseases. A lot of us are engaged in lethal life styles and we create conditions, whether psychological or physical or both, that can be well addressed by self-help groups.

Cost-Effectiveness

There is a good argument for the cost-effectiveness of self-help groups. The veteran helping the rookie—the mutuality of it—is a lot less expensive than a psychiatrist at one hundred dollars an hour, or a surgeon at several times that amount, and that has appeal on both sides. Cost containment is an undeniably important element.

Empowerment

The information revolution we are living in also makes self-help more viable, because the information that is available to professionals is also available to the consumer, to the self- and mutual-help advocate. There seems to be a growing take-charge attitude in people's feelings about their own lives, about coming out of their closets. Two or three decades ago, people tended to be very reluctant to acknowledge that they had cancer. Today, while nobody is eager to have it or to trumpet it (other than those few of us who write books about it), people are far less reluctant to be open about it and to seek help in public ways than they were in the past. There is a frankness about health in general that it is very much a part of American life today—it is a spirit friendly to the growth of self-help groups.

REDEFINING THE DOCTOR/PATIENT RELATIONSHIP

So where does all of this lead us? I believe that what we are about is rewriting the social contract in health. We are redefining the doctor/patient relationship in the broadest of senses. We are moving away from the highly circumscribed relationship in which the patient thinks, ''Oh, I've got a pain. I don't know what it is—it's sort of in there. I'm not sure what the name of it is, but I am going to go to a doctor and he will give me some pills. I don't know what they are called or what they do, but he will write down whether it is twice a day or three times a day, and then I will take them and maybe I'll get better.'' That is the old-fashioned way of the patient complaining to the doctor, who knows what is best because he wears a white coat and uses a lot of Latin words.

We have now progressed a long way from that view. I don't mean to characterize my profession as standing on that ground. It has moved a great deal and there are large numbers of physicians, healers, therapists and providers across the spectrum who are much more prone to new and more mutualistic ways of providing care. The revolution, I think, is underway, but it is not yet where it is going to be. We need to help get it there because it is a good and a necessary revolution.

What are the elements of this new social contract? The first and most important element is the one I have already touched upon. The consumer/patient, instead of simply going to that white-coated doctor and medical establishment, will be turning to people who have already "been there" in some way. There is no highly specified model for what the contract will be, but it will include people who have already had the condition, or who are coping with it, as part of the basic formula, the basic prescription on how we care for people in need.

4

Illness, Professional Caregivers and Self-Helpers

Michael K. Bartalos, MD

Self-help groups and health care professionals share a common goal: to relieve suffering caused by illness. Medicine traditionally tries to accomplish this by preventing the occurrence of illness, promoting recovery from an illness or, if recovery is not likely, facilitating adjustment to the illness. Public welfare dictates that there be a complementarity between the services provided by self-help groups and health care providers. In order to pave the way for a fruitful cooperation between these entities, an attempt will be made to circumscribe the domain of the healing professions and propose a role for self-help/support groups in promoting healing and wellness. To this end we will discuss present concepts of wellness, illness and healing, try to identify possible candidates for self-help groups and point out the societal benefits of the self-help group movement.

THE CONCEPT OF ILLNESS

Interaction with the Environment

Our bodies are in constant interaction with the environment. We sense the outside temperature and adjust our body temperature to it. We sense variations in light intensity and our pupils vary in size accordingly. Every time we breathe, we interact with the environment by removing oxygen and releasing carbon dioxide into the environment. Taking in nutrients and releasing their by-products is an interaction with the environment; so are our defense mechanisms fighting off the invasion of bacteria or the varied chemical reactions that occur in response to stress, whether physical or psychological. In the process of interacting with the environment we change it, and while adapting to the ever-changing environment we too undergo changes.

68

Adaptation and Maladaptation

In its interaction with the environment our bodily functions are regulated by complex feedback mechanisms. Every perceived change in our environment is responded to in a way that ensures optimum functioning of the body. If the temperature increases around us, the body's regulatory mechanism goes into action to keep the temperature constant. In order to maintain the temperature at the most desirable level, we start sweating and thereby release heat. If the environmental challenge is greater than the body's adaptive capacity, a maladaptation or inappropriate coping ensues, leading to a state commonly referred to as illness. Heat exhaustion and heat stroke are examples. Extremes of temperature can overwhelm the body, causing tissue destruction as in case of burns. Similarly, many bacterial invasions are responded to by our bodies without our being aware of them. In other instances, however, we might experience a febrile illness with various somatic manifestations and recover in a few days. In still other instances infective organisms are able to overpower the body's defenses, leading to shock and death (Bartalos 1988).

Injurious Agents

The normal functioning of the body can be altered by agents that are physical in nature and act in direct contact with the body—examples are poisoning, trauma, radiation injury, microbial invasion, deficiency of key nutrients in the diet or imbalance in the composition of nutrients—or by circumstances that overwhelm orderly psychological functioning. Due to the integrated nature of physical and psychological functioning, physical trauma can have psychological sequelae, and psychological trauma can lead to changes in physical structure.

The Sick Role

In our complex society we are assuming different roles at different times and in different situations (Parson 1951). We can have the role of a breadwinner, a father, a lover, a patriot, a sportsman or a sick person. In all of these roles we are expected to act according to societal norms. For an individual to assume the sick role, he must fulfill the following criteria: (1) inability to achieve wellness simply by decision or will, (2) obligation to seek wellness and (3) responsibility to seek and cooperate with technically competent personnel. In return society provides him with assistance and exemption from social responsibility for the duration of the illness (May 1983).

Illness as Maladaptation

Persisting negative alterations in bodily functioning affect the physical state, the psychological state and the social state of the person, and thus illness possesses physiological as well as psychosocial aspects. Minor aches, pains, discomforts, labored bodily functioning and states of anxiety or depression are signs of maladaptation to the environment.

More severe maladaptation can be perceived by the individual as alteration in bodily function (such as diarrhea and visual disturbances), alteration in bodily appearance (swelling, change in color, bleeding) and alteration in perception (dizziness, disorientation, lethargy, severe pain, excitation, malaise, chills). Moderate maladaptation can remain unchanged for a prolonged period of time or it can progress to severe maladaptation or even revert to normal.

In the psychological realm a persisting negative alteration in a bodily function is perceived by the individual as a form of loss. (Other forms of loss include losing a loved person, losing property and losing bodily features.) In addition to symptoms that might be directly attributable to physical changes, the perception of loss can contribute to suffering by causing mental pain, anxiety and depression.

MECHANISMS OF COPING

Correction of the Maladaptive State

Corrective change can occur spontaneously or it may require assistance in the form of altered life style (such as altered nutrition, altered physical activity, cessation of smoking, increased recreational activity), performance of therapeutic exercises, taking of medications, undergoing surgical interventions and receiving psychological help. Corrective measures also can be directed to the environment in an attempt to eliminate, neutralize or mitigate the effect of offending environmental agents.

At the psychological level successful coping with loss—including illness—usually involves a passage through the stages of repudiation (denial/ questioning, anger/hostility, suspicion), recognition (ambivalence/ bargaining, loneliness/rejection, low self-esteem, regression) and reconciliation (Lambert and Lambert 1979).

Coping ability is determined by the "hardiness" of the individual and by the availability of a social support system. Hardiness, in this context, refers to psychosocial vigor. This term is applied to persons who feel in control of their destiny, who are committed to a goal and who view life experiences as challenges rather than as crises (Kobasa, Maddi and Kahn 1982). Major social support resources can be subsumed under the acronym SCREEEM, standing for seven descriptive categories: social, cultural, religious, educational, economic, environmental and medical. Of these the most critical is social support (Smilkstein 1988). High-quality relationships with family and friends are components of an effective social support system, as are self-help groups.

INTERPERSONAL SUPPORT

Self-Help Groups vs. Support Groups

The terms *self-help groups* and *support groups* sometimes are used interchangeably. Indeed, the phrase self-help group might at first sight appear contradictory. "Self-help" refers to personal initiative directed to benefit the individual himself, while "group" refers to a collection of individuals.

Self-help is a term that recalls our pioneer heritage with its encouragement and praise of individualism. In the early years of our country, to quote from Robert B. Reich's book, *The Next American Frontier* (1983), "American notions of civic virtue came to center less on cooperating with the neighbors than on leaving them alone." The apparent contradiction of the term self-help group is resolved when we look at the group as a collection of individuals who all exhibit initiative on their own behalf, assuming responsibility for themselves in the best American tradition, but act in tandem to assure greater benefits for themselves. Group action magnifies the effect of individual effort.

The term "support group" appears to emphasize the actions of others on behalf of an individual. It sounds almost like a rescue mission as contrasted with a break-out attempt. I believe that both terms have validity provided that in their usage attention is paid to their different meanings.

Benefits of Self-Help Groups

The primary beneficiaries of a self-help group are the members of the group themselves. They formed and maintain the group because they derive benefits from it. Interacting with others who have the same problem lessens the feeling of isolation, allows for the exchange of practical information and facilitates joint actions for attaining common objectives. The physician's work is made easier because greater insight into the nature of the illness by the patient or caregiver translates into a healthier attitude toward the illness and better compliance with therapeutic recommendations.

Society is likewise a beneficiary; better compliance translates into better health care, which in turn leads to faster recovery or, in cases of chronic illness, better adaptation to the illness and improved integration into society. If the services provided by self-help groups were administered by government agencies, they would be delivered at greater cost, with lesser speed and with less adaptability to local needs. Thus reduced expenditures in the care of the ill are a further benefit for society. Still another benefit ensues from the propagation of the spirit of self-responsibility, initiative, compassion, generosity and mutual assistance. These attributes are the ingredients of a well-functioning self-help group (Borman 1988) and, indeed, of a humane society.

Who Are the Potential Members of Self-Help Groups?

In order to be an effective member of a self-help group, one has to have adequate perception and judgment, ability to interact meaningfully with others and a reasonable chance to benefit from such interactions. One group of persons who could benefit from participation in a self-help group include handicapped individuals whose perception, judgment and interacting ability is not severely compromised. Other candidates are persons facing traumatic medical or surgical interventions, those at risk of developing a disease (such as carriers of a deleterious gene or of an infectious microorganism) and individuals attempting to break a harmful habit.

Individuals who take care of or regularly interact with patients who suffer from a severe, chronic, incurable, life-threatening or severely disfiguring illness are subjected to deep and prolonged stress. Such individuals include family members, health providers and friends of affected persons, all of whom would likewise benefit from joining a self-help group.

The current AIDS epidemic has brought to light another group of individuals who are potential candidates for self-help group participation: these are sometimes called the "worried well." There are, of course, many healthy people who are worried about having a disease other than AIDS or HIV infection. However, it was as a result of AIDS phobia that this group was subjected to detailed analysis resulting in the identification of seven subgroups: (1) those with a past history of homosexuality or IV drug use, (2) those with relationship problems, (3) the partners and spouses of those at risk, (4) couples in individual and family life-cycle transitions, (5) those with a past history of psychological problems, (6) those with a misunderstanding of health education material and (7) those with factitious or "pseudo" AIDS (Bor et al. 1989). Members of these subgroups, with the exception of number six, could probably benefit from participation in self-help groups composed of individuals belonging to the same subgroup.

A similar approach could be used for well persons who are worried about contracting other maladies, such as breast cancer. Within this group the identification of subgroups sharing similar concerns, such as having a family history of breast cancer or having undergone a biopsy for a lump in the breast, could lead to the formation of more effective support groups than if everyone who fears the development of breast cancer were placed in one group.

The Left-Outs

The formation of self-help groups presupposes attributes that are not present in many sick members of our society who are nevertheless in need of assistance in their adjustment to the environment, in articulating their needs, in mapping strategies to satisfy these needs and in translating their strategies into action.

The severely handicapped with impaired perception, impaired mental functioning or impaired communicative ability belong in this category. The very rich and the very poor both appear to belong in this category, but for differing reasons.

The very rich are isolated. They are constantly defending themselves from people who barrage them with requests for donations, often for dubious purposes, or who seek to take advantage of them by proposing shaky business deals. They have to scrutinize everybody new with whom they come into contact and monitor the actions of their older acquaintances who do not enjoy their complete confidence. Caution is exercised also in their interactions with those who belong to the same or a higher socioeconomic stratum. They are careful not to reveal any potential vulnerability, whether it be a health problem, a character defect or a financial misstep, as it could affect their respectability or become a means for their exploitation. The high degree of isolation, secretiveness and mutual mistrust that permeates the interpersonal relations of the very rich creates a barrier to the formation of self-help groups. Thus, when it comes to the availability of support to cope with health problems, the very rich belong to a disadvantaged group. The old adage thus applies: money does not buy everything.

The problems of the very poor are quite different. Their main problem is to survive from one day to the next, to have enough food for tomorrow, to have enough money for the rent (if they have been lucky enough to hold on to an apartment) and to escape the cruelties of scoundrels continuously appearing in different disguises. The very poor suffer from exposure to the elements, from the effects of overcrowding, from malnutrition, infestations by lice and other parasites, vitamin deficiency states and stress and have a high incidence of drug abuse and alcoholism (*Emergency Med.* 1989), causing great ravages to their enfeebled bodies. The very poor also are not likely candidates for self-help group formation. Their struggle for survival does not allow time and energy for organizing, their lack of education prevents them from articulating their needs effectively, they are not familiar with the machinery of government and their interaction with others is dominated by mistrust, a characteristic we have also observed among the very rich.

Two other groups that come to mind are the very young and the very old. They both tend to be dependent on others, whether living in the parental home or in a nursing home. Their dependent status prevents them from acting effectively on their own behalf. Unborn children, dying persons and those on death row might also be included in this category. In terms of forming self-help groups the latter two suffer from a shortage of time, while the presence of confining circumstances is readily appreciated in the first.

SOCIETAL RAMIFICATIONS OF INDIVIDUAL SUFFERING

Support Groups and Advocacy

Members of our society who are unable to fend for themselves, who cannot assure themselves of the rights that are theirs according to the Constitution, who have difficulty in adjusting to the environment, who are sick, who have difficulty coping, and all those who need help but are unable to get it deserve our society's support. The formation of support groups and acting as advocates are ways by which we can help our less fortunate fellow citizens.

Individuals can be motivated to help others by many factors: these include a sense of charity, compassion and fairness, a sense of social justice or a desire to become an agent of positive social change.

Additional reasons to help those in need have been given recently by Emily Friedman in an article published in the *Journal of the American Medical Association* (1989). She points out that our security is threatened by untreated conditions that can spread in the population and by the untreated mentally ill who can bring destruction on themselves and others. The large number of people who are without adequate health insurance (in early 1987, 23.1 percent of the self-employed, 23 percent of part-time workers and 12.8 percent of full-time workers were uninsured) hamper the productivity and competitiveness of our work force. Finally she reminds us that "We are at risk of forgetting a basic rule: most fabrics unravel at the edges first. In dismissing the medically indigent as though they belong to another species, we dismiss the fact that the barrier between us and them is movable—and that it is moving closer to the rest of us all the time."

I have a pet theory that misery circulates, it diffuses, it radiates and is propagated in society. Personal misery is transmitted to others in a variety of ways and is perpetuated in society by a ripple effect. Consider for instance an individual who has been under severe stress for a prolonged period of time and develops what is referred to in the scientific literature as "attitudinal, emotional and physical exhaustion" (Taylor 1987). He becomes irritable, impatient and his ability to concentrate is diminished. In his interaction with others such an individual is likely to be abrupt, argumentative and explosive and will generate hostility around him, which in turn will make him more irritable, more impatient, and the cycle goes on until civilized interaction ceases to exist between him and others. In the workplace such an individual will produce poor quality work, which in turn will irritate those who utilize his product. Such irritated people will treat others with impatience and abruptness. Thus the process is continual.

Misery creates hostility and hostility will radiate from the individual in every direction at all times. Some persons around such individuals will act as conduits of hostility (they will transmit hostility in the manner outlined above), others will act as amplifiers by responding to hostility with heightened vigor and emitting more hostility than they were exposed to, and still others will remain immune to the impudence of those around them and thus will act as barriers to further propagation of incivility. (This mechanism very likely applies also to the intrasocietal propagation of goodwill and civility. I have the suspicion, however, that members of our society are more efficient in propagating hostility and incivility than they are in spreading tolerance and mutual aid.)

The conclusion appears inescapable that it is in the best interests of society to reduce suffering among all layers of the population and to encourage the propagation of such values and attitudes as sensitivity, rectitude, generosity, tenderness, resoluteness, compassion, tolerance, cooperation and understanding.

Society is a collection of individuals; it changes when its members change. If we want society to change, we have to change ourselves first. We have to become sources, conduits and amplifiers of positive values and barriers to the diffusion of negative influences. The creation of a more workable society depends on the rightness of our convictions, on the strength of our resolution and on the decisiveness of our actions. It requires a personal commitment from all of us and our numbers must be in the millions. We must form a gigantic self-help group with all of us bent on the improvement of society and united by the conviction that our goals are more likely to be realized by acting in unison.

REFERENCES

Bartalos, M.K.: Disease and the Role of the Physician. In S.G. Wolf, Jr., M.W. Hamolsky, A.H. Kutscher, and K. Muraszko (eds.), *The Responsible Physician: Standards of Excellence and the Critically Ill Patient.* New York: The Foundation of Thanatology, 1988.

Bor, R., C. Perry, R. Miller and J. Jackson: Strategies for counselling the 'worried well' in relation to AIDS: discussion paper. *J. Roy. Soc. Med. (Lond.)* 82:218-220, 1989.

Borman, L.D.: Self-help/mutual aid groups: strategies for prevention. In *Directory of Self-Help/Mutual Aid Groups.* Evanston, IL: The Self-Help Center, 1988.

Friedman, E.: The torturer's horse. *J.A.M.A.* 261 (10):1481-1482, 1989.

Kobasa, S.C., S.R. Maddi and S. Kahn: Hardiness and health: a prospective study. *J. Pers. Soc. Psychol.* 42:168-177, 1982.

Lambert, V.A., and C.E. Lambert, Jr.: *The Impact of Physical Illness and Related Mental Health Concepts.* Englewood Cliffs, NJ: Prentice-Hall, 1979.

May, W.F.: *The Physician's Covenant: Images of the Healer in Medical Ethics.* Philadelphia: Westminster Press, 1983.

Parsons, T.: *The Social System.* New York: Free Press, 1951.

Reich, R. B.: *The Next American Frontier.* New York: Times Books, 1983.

Smilkstein, G.: Health benefits of helping patients cope. *Consultant,* 28 (1):56-67, 1988.

Taylor, R.B.: What are the best ways to handle stress? *Physician's Management,* May 1987, pp. 153-167.

With neither home nor health. *Emergency Med.* February 28, 1989, pp. 21-46.

5

Critical Aspects of the
Mutual Help Experience

Phyllis R. Silverman, PhD

This chapter is concerned with three issues that relate to the helping process in mutual help organizations. The first issue is that of understanding personal change as the goal of the interventions offered by mutual help organizations; the second is the nature of the help provided in these settings; and the third reflects on the nature of collaboration between mutual help systems and professional systems.

CHANGE

A major theme of this book is responses to life-threatening illnesses. However, I do not see bereavement as a life-threatening illness. Nevertheless, life-threatening illnesses invariably involve loss and grief. What can we learn from looking at the bereavement process about what people who have a life-threatening illness experience? What happens when people experience a loss, be it a person who has died, the loss of a relationship, or the loss of use of part of the body? Not only do they experience pain and sadness, but their lives are so changed that they cannot live as before. They experience a period of critical transition.

Transitions are periods of disruption in people's lives during which their prior coping techniques may be ineffectual. Typically in any critical transition, individuals have to give up a way of life, and usually the role associated with that way of life (Rappaport 1963). This role can often be quite central to their very sense of self and how they make meaning of their world. It is possible to talk about the end of a transition when individuals reenter society and reshape their lives to be consistent with their new roles. This holds true whether the new definition of self has become that of a recovering alcoholic, a person with cancer, or a widow or widower now living a single life. The shift may be not only in their physical situation, but in their sense of self as well. It is essential to understand some of the dimensions and qualities of this change to understand what the loss means and how people will cope. An example from the experience of the widowed points to their need to move from the acute stage of grief to a place where they can accept the loss and learn the needed skills to reshape their lives. I think of bereavement not as a period of illness but as a time of change and transition (Silverman 1966, 1982, 1986).

In conceptualizing loss often the focus is on the affective aspects of the experience. Professional intervention often centers on how people feel, ignoring the larger social context in which people live and how this context changes to effect people's very sense of self. After a loss, using the example of the experience of a woman when her husband dies, the woman cannot reconstitute herself and her world as it was before. A way of life is lost. She does not recover. She makes an accommodation:

> I've gotten used to being alone. I've never learned to like it, but I enjoy my freedom. I really like coming and going as I please.

People are wiser, more aware of both life's joys and sorrows. And in many ways they become quite different than the way they were before:

> I've changed in almost every way. I went back to school, I became active in educational organizations, I travel more, and I take the lead in these organizations.

These examples come from a study I did with two mutual help groups for the widowed. I was interested in documenting whether there is a change in people as a result of their affiliating with such organizations and if so, what this change looks like (Silverman 1987, 1988a, 1988b).

Change can simply mean exchanging one mode of doing things for another. It can involve limited aspects of people's lives or it can extend to all the parameters of their lives. Change can also be associated with the concept of development as we go from one stage in the life cycle to another. On what dimensions can we characterize social and psychological change during a critical transition? This question is important regardless of what led to this transition. I will continue to exemplify this process from my data on what happens after a spouse dies.

We used to think that people were basically formed in the first five or ten years of life, but now it is very clear that we continue to change and grow as we move through the life cycle. While we can talk of biological change, can we also talk about change in terms of the way we relate to ourselves and to others as we move through the life cycle? One of the women in my study remarked, "I intend to wear out, not rust out." She was 83, and I think that's a nice way of putting it.

In the face of adversity there are always at least two choices: to go ahead or to go down. The question is, how does "ahead" look? Can we talk of growing more empathic, of increased mutuality, of a new flexibility to respond to changing life conditions (Levinson 1978; Keegan 1983)? Are these aspects of a new sense of self that is needed to cope with the circumstances of a new phase in the life cycle that begins when a spouse dies? To live as a formerly married person, now single, what new patterns of behavior and thought do the widowed need to develop? If they develop new ways of seeing themselves and of living in the world, widowhood can be seen as a next stage in the life cycle—not simply an ending, but a beginning as well (Silverman 1987).

As I looked at the data, I asked if men and women changed in the same way. I assumed that marriage had a different meaning for each. Recent studies of the psychology of women have pointed to the fact that women's identity is framed by their relationships and their involvement with others (Gilligan 1983; Baker 1986). Men have traditionally been more concerned with maintaining their autonomy and getting the job done. To the extent that these views of men and women hold true, each would approach the marriage differently and would also experience the loss differently. Subsequent changes would obviously differ as well in these men and women (Silverman 1981, 1986).

As I looked at the data controlling for gender, I noticed that change in the way men and women react does not become apparent immediately. Initially, both men and women focus on their pain, on their loneliness and their feelings of aloneness. Both report a profound disruption in how they see themselves. What does this mean in terms of their day-to-day lives? Here their differences were obvious but were in response to the past and how they had lived their lives. Some women found coping with household chores and with household business and finances very difficult. Other women were concerned with their ability to support themselves. Men were primarily concerned with cooking and shopping for themselves, not with doing work to maintain their homes or with self-support. Most men and women, in fact, seemed comforted by routines that allowed them to carry on without much thought.

Differences began to emerge when they had to make necessary decisions 3 to 4 months after the death. None of the widowers questioned their decision-making ability. For widows, making decisions was very difficult:

> At first, I did not want to choose to do anything alone. I fought against making any choices.

In contrast, the widowers felt,

> I was quiet, but very strong in coping, in handling financial affairs and making decisions.

A widow said,

> Making a decision for myself was a new concept for me. I now voice my own opinions and I'm still kind of surprised I'm doing this, right or wrong.

For most women sharing their ideas and not acting on their own seemed important. Support and feedback seemed necessary as they came to a decision. For the men an exchange may have been pleasant but not necessary. If there was no opportunity for an exchange, they acted as they saw the need. Women seemed more accustomed to acting on behalf of someone else, as a daughter, a wife or a mother. Their new situation required that they act as they saw fit.

As I looked at the data, a very interesting pattern of change was reflected. The men began to recognize their need for relationships. They characterized their wives as "the person who held the family together." She was the focal point of their social life. They had to learn how to go out and meet people, and if they wanted to have relationships, how to nourish them. For the first time men found themselves in friendship relationships with other men. They found themselves in situations where people not only cared about how they felt, but worried about how they felt and expected them to reciprocate in a way they had not known. In the past their wives had done the caring for them.

Women slowly began to recognize that if they didn't act on their own behalf, no one was going to. One woman said that she was very sad to think that she was liberated as a result of her husband's death; she might be willing to go back if he could be alive again, but since that's not possible, she was delighted to go ahead in a new direction that involved a new way of seeing herself. In fact the men and women seemed to switch positions and some place in the middle, they developed a new kind of mutuality and a different way of looking at themselves in relationships. I concluded that often the change that had occurred was very subtle and that people often could only talk about it from the perspective of 3 or 4 years after the precipitating event occurred.

Change in self-esteem, in self-confidence, in empathic ability and in the ability to help oneself and others seemed to be the end product of membership in a mutual help organization for this study population. They reported that as a result of their affiliation they learned to cope with their grief and to develop a new sense of self that enabled them to live with the altered circumstances of their lives. How did affiliation in a mutual help group bring about these changes?

Facilitating Change: Helping in a Mutual Help Organization

Elsewhere I have written that people are attracted to mutual help associations at times of critical transitions in their lives (Silverman 1966, 1978,

1980, 1982). We are concerned with the impact of mutual help experiences on the participants during such periods of stress and change in their lives. I suggest that the goal of the help offered in a mutual help experience is to help people deal not only with their pain and sadness, but with the changes—the shifts that the loss brings to their lives—whether because of the loss of a person or the loss of a body function. To make help more effective it is necessary to respond to the shifts and to the dimensions and qualities of the changes involved.

Help therefore needs to be available over time to enable the individual to "get from here to there"—from one sense of self to another (Lennenberg, in Silverman 1976). We are talking about a dynamic helping process that involves teaching as well as learning—much more than simply providing· support to people involved.

Mutual help organizations do more than sustain and support their members. They help in many ways to enable their members to deal more effectively with their situation. People who participate in such exchanges usually develop qualities in themselves that did not exist before. They learn to recognize their own power to help themselves and each other. I want to look at how the experience impacts on the participants so that they not only behave and feel differently about themselves, but also appreciate their own power in the face of the adversity with which they are coping.

This process is exemplified in an experience I had several years ago. I was on a program with a widow who was in "bereavement counseling" with a therapist in a large urban city. I was representing the mutual help approach as we discussed interventions for the widowed. We went out afterwards for lunch. I asked the widow about her own networks and the kind of people she socializes with. She described a group of formerly married women with whom she was very involved. I asked, "When you're in trouble or have problems, you then have a support system to turn to?" And she replied, "Oh, no. I'm not qualified. I go to talk to my therapist."

I thought about this for a long time and realized that the women I was accustomed to meeting in mutual help groups were very different. They would never say, "I'm not qualified." They would understand their own power and what they had to teach, and they would indeed turn to each other. The key question is, how do people who get involved with a group feel legitimated so that they can appreciate their power to act on their own behalf as well as on that of others? It seems to me that the question of who chooses to join is more than a matter of self-selection. I want to describe what I see as the rhythm of helping that brings people to this point.

It is critical to clarify that being in a mutual help organization does not mean that each of these people had the same helping experience. In this chapter, "group" and "organization" are used synonymously. Most organizations provide a range of help to their members. Some people were helped by coming to information meetings, others by reading a newsletter and still others by partaking in social activities; sometimes members sat in a group with a leader to share their feelings, problems and solutions. Some people were helped in the process of helping others. As a result of their affiliation, they were exposed to new ideas and new directions. They were helped by peers who served as role models and teachers, and they were helped when they were not locked into the role of recipient but could offer help in return.

I think there is a rhythm to this help. If we talk about a transition, we need to realize that change takes place over time and that the nature of the help must be different as time passes. My thinking is largely influenced by situations in which the need to change arose from an identified event (such as a death, an illness or an accident) for which one's typical coping patterns were insufficient, and as a result one could no longer live one's life as before. For many people born with handicapping conditions, their sense of self is formed around this aspect of themselves. They do not experience themselves as defective or in transition. This is who they are. I am primarily talking about people who have had some kind of trauma that has caused a disruption in how they see themselves. For people who have always had a given condition, the trauma may come when they realize that they are not like everyone else in at least this one aspect.

If we examine a transition over time, we note that people experience the trauma differently as time passes. We can talk about phases of the transition. Tyhurst provides three: impact, recoil and accommodation (Silverman 1966, 1982, 1986).

In impact the initial reaction is often one of numbness or denial so that there is no reality to what has happened—it seems like a dream. Often at this point, seeing someone in the same situation is not helpful. I remember talking to a woman who got a letter from us in the original Widow-to-Widow project. She remembered her initial reaction to this letter sent to her one month after her husband died. She thought that "widow" was an awful thing to call her and did not see how anything to do with widows could apply to her. Two months later she went looking for the letter. For reasons not at all clear to her at the time, she had put it in a drawer instead of throwing it away. Two months later she realized that she was indeed a widow and wanted to find someone to talk with.

We need to acknowledge this early stage of disbelief in our interventions. I remember consulting with a group of physical therapists who presented the case of a young man who had had a recent spinal cord injury and was left a paraplegic. They were very concerned about him because he was denying his situation and was not willing to learn to "transfer." The concern was that he could not go home until he learned how to get into a wheelchair. He kept saying, "I'm going to walk; I don't need to learn how to do that." I suggested that instead of confronting him with his "denial," they offer to teach him to "transfer" so he could go home for a visit. This young man could not imagine himself not walking. It would be awhile before he could allow this reality to enter his consciousness and adjust his sense of self to this new situation. Rather than looking at his current behavior as pathological, the staff had to recognize that this was a normal part of his trying to make sense of a new world. They needed to give him space and time, and maybe even excuses, while he tried to negotiate where he was and what it meant. He was at a very early point in the transition process.

The critical question here is, how does one help someone begin to personally accept a problem, to allow that "this could be me"? Affiliation or even seeking out a mutual help experience depends on the individual's being able to recognize the similarity between himself and the group's members. Those organizations who do outreach to potential members find that meeting veteran members eases newly afflicted people's acceptance of their situation (Silverman 1976, 1984). Robert Lifton (1973) talks of developing an affinity with the condition. In Alcoholics Anonymous they talk about recovery. Recovery begins with saying, "I am an alcoholic." This is something that people do with great reluctance and resistance. Acceptance is made easier if the individual meets someone who is a credible role model. The individual reaching out makes a statement that this is a condition that can be lived with—there is a future, there is hope. While the individual may not be able to say, "I am like them," at some level a sense of unity or affinity with this person begins to form and then the process of moving through the transition can begin.

In a study I conducted (Silverman 1981) of birthmothers (women who have had untimely pregnancies and surrendered their children for adoption), one woman said that there were no reunions of people who lived in homes for unwed mothers. It was as if no one looked at another's face. Twenty years after the surrender, she learned of a new organization from a newspaper advertisement inviting anyone who had surrendered a child for adoption to come to a meeting. For the first time since the surrender, she had opened up this issue with a therapist. She cried all the way to the meeting, never dreaming that another woman had ever surrendered a child for adoption. She was terrified and almost needed to be pushed across the threshold of the meeting room. She found it incredible that these other women had the same experience of closing off their feelings of loss after giving up a child (Silverman et al. 1988). Only then was she able to acknowledge the sense of loss and even depression she had been avoiding all these years.

Once people feel safe and accept their new status, they can allow themselves to feel the pain and anxiety they may have. This is the second phase of the transition—recoil. In Alcoholics Anonymous they talk about a growing sense of unity, and Lifton talks about a sense of presence. The individual has to allow the group, at that point, to embrace him and to recognize his need for them. The group can legitimize feelings and normalize them under the circumstances. Tears are acceptable as is rage and panic. If people are terrified about the future, they are surrounded by others who have managed and by sharing their experience help in finding a new way.

At this point group members have to have information available, but what kind of information? If you have a spinal cord injury, for example, you need to learn that you can live alone if you choose and that there is help in reorganizing your home. If you are badly arthritic and feel you can never go out to eat because you can't manage both knife and fork, you must learn that you can ask to have your food cut in the kitchen. As a widow, you may need to learn how to balance your own budget. You may need to know what kinds of jobs are available; you may need to find out that there are other types of work you can do that could be more gratifying. You may need to discover that it doesn't matter that your kitchen floor is dirty and that there are dishes in the sink if there's something else you really want to do. You know you don't have to run home to supper; you can go out if you like. Members need the information that makes it possible for them to go on with their daily lives. It is not necessarily information of world-shaking significance, but knowing where to buy shoes that fit the brace your child must wear, for example, can open up many other avenues. It's not necessarily a profound processing of feelings either. There are people who don't like to talk—that should be all right. The question is not whether you talk about it, it is what you are doing about it, how you are living with it, how you are learning. And you don't always learn in one way. People learn in many different ways.

We also know that we learn better from people like ourselves (Reisman 1963). We put a lot of emphasis on peer influence during adolescence, but in fact we learn from peers all through our lives. When one of my children was little, I remember watching another woman restrain her child who was doing something inappropriate. It was the kind of situation I didn't handle well. As I observed her, I thought, "Oh, I have to try that." It didn't work with my son, but at least I had an option I hadn't considered before. Maybe it didn't work because I wasn't like her, and he wasn't like her little boy, but the point was that I expanded my repertoire and had some other thoughts about how I could manage a difficult situation. I was able to learn this, not in a lecture from someone who knew more than I did, but from another mother who was struggling with the same issue. This kind of exchange of information is easier to hear. In the words of a colleague of mine, it's the "older sibling" syndrome (Lennenberg, in Silverman 1976). They've been there before, they've negotiated the relationship with the parents and they can teach the younger child. It's easier to learn from the sibling, who is a peer, than from the parent, who is in a more authoritative position. The critical aspect of the mutual help process is to learn how someone else dealt with the problem; this learning is possible when there is someone with whom the sufferer can identify and who thereby provides a role model. The helper also provides hope and has the necessary information for successful living as a member of a new social category.

The final phase of a transition begins as people consider making an accommodation; that is, trying to live differently. This is a period when people's feelings have "quieted down" and they are beginning to integrate all the knowledge they have obtained into a new identity. This is the time to practice new behavior patterns, new ways of dealing with a new self in a different world. The making of an accommodation can be likened to an active apprenticeship period. During this time the moral support of the group may be essential for success as members integrate the past with the present.

It is at about this time that new members are able to be responsive to other people's needs and often take up the option of becoming a helper. By helping others they find one way of consolidating what they have been learning. In this way new helpers are available on a continuing basis, providing the group with new energy and vitality. Not everyone proceeds from the role of recipient to helper. In making the transition, some people want to move on. Lifton refers to this period as one of self-generation. When Alcoholics Anonymous speaks of service, the focus is on the new people becoming helpers and thereby providing new energy and life to the organization so that it can continue its work.

In the study I reported on earlier, the widowed members of these organizations talked of helping themselves by helping others as a brand-new experience in their lives:

> It's the secret. By helping others, you help yourself. Other than my children, 'To Live Again'—and the work I do with it—is the most important thing I do in my life. I feel I am really doing something worthwhile; it makes me feel a real sense of accomplishment.

I think that at this point this widower is empowering himself as well as others. The rhythm in this helping process moves from offering potential members someone to identify with, which makes it possible to at least acknowledge that this new status may apply to them, to providing a safe place to release feelings and to learn how to deal with the new situation, and finally to integrating this new knowledge and offering it to others.

COLLABORATION BETWEEN PROFESSIONAL AND MUTUAL HELP SYSTEMS

Can people in different helping modes work together? I have heard professionals at these meetings talk about taking in mutual help groups as their allies. Implicit in this statement is an assumption that the professional controls the system and that others who come into it will work at the professional's bidding. Many professionals have a very inflated view of their power to help people. They take people in and make them their patients or clients and assume that they can provide what is needed. This assumption of expertise can be very inappropriate, especially in the face of the disabilities and human pain represented here.

We need to look at the limitations of professional knowledge (Borkman 1976). We may have more to learn about the human condition from people in mutual help organizations than they from us. I can use an example from my own experience. When I first began to work with the widowed women who were the helpers in the original Widow to Widow program, I thought people got over their grief in several months. The widowed women I was working with laughed when I said this. First of all they said you don't get over it. They felt that there would always be a part of themselves that would be sad, but they have learned to live with this. The second thing they told me is that at the end of several months they hardly knew where they were and that it takes at least 2 years before a widow has her head "screwed on" so she can begin to look ahead instead of back. This information flew in the face of what I was learning from the literature at that time. As this project proceeded, I came to see that the experience of these women was indeed a more accurate and legitimate source of knowledge than the books I had been reading.

Professionals also need to see the whole person, not simply an illness or a condition. The role of patient occupies a very small part of most people's lives, and being handicapped or bereaved does not automatically mean that we become a patient or client and lose our ability to think critically and to understand our own needs. When the mutual help and the professional domains meet, professionals need to recognize that they are one among equals. We need to look at ourselves in terms of our common humanity as part of the human community. We need to learn to work together as collaborators in this community. We need to recognize that there is a great deal for all of us to learn from each other. Below I describe a model for collaboration that I developed in which this kind of mutuality and learning was enhanced.

This model was developed in a project funded by the National Institute of Mental Health. The purpose of the project was to look at the type of technical assistance mutual help organizations needed from professionals and then to provide this assistance. We identified a group of organizations that we were going to work with. These included a group of Haitians who were trying to deal with immigration problems, an organization of ex-convicts, an organization of birthmothers, a group of widows, a branch of a national organization for the elderly and a service program for battered women. Our project staff was concerned that in providing assistance we do nothing to weaken the integrity and independence of the groups. We defined our role as that of facilitators or consultants. We developed the following guidelines that would be respectful of the group while permitting a good working relationship to develop:

- The relationship between consultant and consultee is that of colleagues.
- Consultants must appreciate that groups have value systems of their own by which they judge their own work and whether or not they have achieved their goals.
- The consultant cannot tell the consultee how to integrate into the group's functioning the additional information provided.

- The consultant is a visitor, not a group member, and can take no responsibility to see that suggested ideas are implemented.
- The consultant can be dismissed at any time.

In trying to identify who the consultees would be in each organization, the flexibility of these organizations became very apparent. While in most situations the primary relationship was with the president, chairperson or designated leader (where groups rotated leadership), with some groups the entire steering committee wanted to meet with us. At some meetings we could be asked to react to events that were taking place at that moment or about our own personal situation as it related to what the group was discussing, or be asked to meet with an ad hoc committee to work on a particular problem. The informality of most settings made it impossible to have a clear delineation of roles. We could be asked to help serve coffee or share in a potluck supper. Membership in these groups changed frequently as people's needs were met or other pressures took precedence. We needed to be flexible and to match our activity with the uneven rhythm of the organization. The problems they wanted help with included questions on how to increase the involvement of members in the organizational life of the group, how to expand their helping program, and what organizational structure would be most effective in achieving their goals.

Professional literature on these subjects did not always seem relevant. We sought other sources of information from which to find solutions to these problems. We began to look at the literature developed by the mutual help groups themselves and found that there was a good deal of excellent and appropriate material. We began to report on this literature to the groups. None of them had any knowledge of the experiences of other mutual help organizations. They tended to idealize those organizations that seemed to them to be functioning well and presumed themselves to be unique in their difficulties.

The groups also became interested in what was happening in the other organizations involved in the study. The main thrust of the consultation became the sharing of this material and of our observations about what other groups were doing. Because the same process was being repeated within each group, it seemed appropriate to bring them together. When the groups came together, they discovered that the differences between them were less important than their shared interest in strengthening their respective organizations.

They formed themselves into a working group and decided to plan a meeting with leaders of exemplary mutual help groups, such as La Leche League, Parents Without Partners and Movement for a New Society, to discuss with them how their groups solved the problems of leadership, expanding the involvement of members and enhancing their helping programs. La Leche League and Parents Without Partners are hierarchical organizations, while the Movement for a New Society follows a consensus model. This workshop was very successful. In the course of planning this day and evaluating it afterward, the working group discovered that they had within themselves hidden resources to help solve each other's problems. They convened several subsequent meetings to provide a forum for sharing their own expertise with each other (Silverman 1979, 1980).

We found that what we were doing involved several phases that applied to the activities of individual groups as well as those of joint mutual help group ventures:

- There was a need to develop mutual trust, understanding and respect.
- The group was able to identify its problem and to reveal difficulties it could not deal with alone.
- The consultant was able to point out that other groups had the same problems, thus legitimating the group and its concerns.
- Ideas, experiences and written materials from other groups were presented to indicate how they approached similar problems.
- There was a review on how to use the new data.

By the end of the project it became clear that our primary function was that of linking agents—that is, "middle men" between groups in need and available resources—which would help solve their problems.

The concept of consultant as linking agent, discussed by Havelock and coworkers (1971), most accurately describes this activity. Generally, linkers stand between two parties, and the way they are seen may have considerable effect on their ability to introduce users to information or services. A linking agent has the task of building awareness and understanding of a body of information for the potential user of that information. The consultant's primary task is to link groups with each other or to provide them with relevant information gathered from groups with whom they have no direct contact. From the consultant's point of view, three stages can be identified in this process:

1. Discovering that the group's problems are not unique, members find that there are commonalities across diverse organizations.
2. Sharing respective experiences of successful and unsuccessful solutions, members engage in a mutual learning exchange, identify with each other and provide models for implementing new knowledge.
3. Searching for additional answers, solutions and techniques together, group members help each other.

We can see that this is a replica of the mutual help experience that takes place for individual members in their organizations. In an atmosphere in which people can identify with each other, they find their dilemma typical rather than unusual and learning is enhanced. In duplicating the mutual help experience, some of the institutional barriers that exist between the two systems are taken down. The role of the professional is (1) to legitimate the groups' learning from each other using experiential rather than professional knowledge, (2) to facilitate groups meeting each other, (3) to help mobilize resources and (4) to share skills in group process. Above all the professional has to know when to step back as groups take over this process for themselves.

CONCLUSION

The three issues discussed in this chapter focus on three critical aspects of the mutual help experience. Mutual help is a modality that all of us use in response to stress. When faced with a need to find a new direction, the importance of peers cannot be underestimated. The dynamic of help offered by peers applies not only to the individual relationship of members in an organization, but also to the relationship between organizations and different helping systems. As we learn to value experience learned from living and to apply it in solving problems, we enrich all our lives.

REFERENCES

Borkman, T. Experiential knowledge: a new concept for the analysis of self-help groups. *Social Services Rev.* 50:445-456, 1976.

Gilligan, C. *In a Different Voice.* Cambridge, MA: Harvard University Press, 1982.

Havelock, R., et al. *Planning for Innovation Through the Dissemination and Utilization of Knowledge.* Ann Arbor: Institute for Social Research, University of Michigan, 1971.

Kegan, R. *The Evolving Self: Problem and Process in Human Development.* Cambridge, MA: Harvard University Press, 1982.

Lennenberg, E., and J.L. Rowbotham. *The Ileostomy Patient.* Springfield, IL: Charles C Thomas, 1970.

Levinson, D.J. *The Seasons of Man's Life.* New York: Alfred A. Knopf, 1978.

Lifton, R.J. *Home from the War.* New York: Simon & Schuster, 1973.

Miller, J.B. *Toward a New Psychology of Women,* Ed. 2. Boston: Beacon Press, 1986.

Rappaport, R. Normal crises, family structure, and mental health. *Family Process* 2(1):73-87, 1963.

Riesman, F. The "helper-therapy" principle. *Social Work* 10:27-32, 1965.

Silverman, P.R. Services for the widowed during the period of bereavement. In *Social Work Practice.* New York: Columbia University Press, 1986.

_____. The widow as caregiver in a program of preventive intervention with other widows. In G.D. Caplan & M. Killilea, eds., *Support Systems and Mutual Help.* New York: Grune & Stratton, 1976.

_____. *Mutual Help Groups and the Role of the Mental Health Professional.* Washington, DC: National Institute of Mental Health. DHEW Publication No. (ADM) 78-646, 1978.

_____. *Mutual Help: Organization and Development.* Beverly Hills, CA: Sage, 1980.

_____. *Helping Women Cope with Grief.* Beverly Hills, CA: Sage, 1981.

_____. The mental health consultant as a linking agent. In D.E. Biegel and A.J. Naparstek, eds., *Community Support Systems and Mental Health.* New York, 1982.

_____. *Widow to Widow*. New York: Springer, 1986.

_____. The impact of parental death on college-age women. *Psychiatric Clin. North Am.* 10:387-404, 1987.

_____. In search of new selves: accommodating to widowhood. In L.A. Bond, ed., *Families in Transition: Primary Prevention Programs That Work*. Beverly Hills, CA: Sage, 1988.

Silverman, P.R., L. Campbell, P. Patti and C.B. Style. Reunions between adoptees and birth parents: the birth parents' experience. *Social Work* 33(6):523-528, 1988.

Silverman, P.R., and D. Smith. "Helping" in mutual help groups for the physically disabled. In F. Gartner and F. Reisman, eds., *The Self-Help Revolution*. New York: Human Sciences Press, 1984.

Silverman, S.M., and P.R. Silverman. Parent-child communication in widowed families. *Am. J. Psychotherapy* 33:428-441, 1979.

6

Physicians, Patients and Self-Help Groups

Joanne G. Schwartzberg, MD

The changing worlds of medical knowledge, scientific capability and technology, and health care delivery are often discussed in the medical and health policy literature. What is not addressed is how these changes alter the roles of physician, patient and family. We live in a time of very rapid change, and nowhere is that more evident than in the field of health care. Science and technology changes come so swiftly that 50 percent of what physicians learn in their medical training is obsolete within 10 years. It is a continuous struggle for physicians to try to keep up-to-date, even in narrow specialty areas, and to know how to translate the new information gleaned from as many as 40 journals a month into patient care.

Consider, for example, the radical changes in the care of patients with heart attacks. Twenty years ago accepted treatment was to keep the patient at bedrest in the hospital for 6 weeks, with a long, slow recuperation following that because the patient had become so weak and debilitated. Since that time there has been an explosion of new diagnostic techniques, new surgical procedures, new drug therapies—and now we see patients leaving the hospital in less than a week, sometimes having undergone stress testing before they left! Today cardiac patients don't become disabled from prolonged bedrest; it takes much less effort to rehabilitate them, and we are so successful at cardiac rehabilitation that "cardiac cripples" are only a specter of the past.

We've come to expect more and more from medical science, which puts an even greater burden on physicians to keep up. Faced with a complex problem extending outside their area of expertise, physicians have to ask for consultations from other physicians in order to be assured that they have the most current information. They must absorb the available information and differing viewpoints and come up with a recommendation for the care of the patient. But even when they have established a plan of action, physicians may not be able to implement the plan as they used to. This is the age of "informed consent" where we believe the patient has the right to know and to choose the treatment to be provided. This is a uniquely American approach to health care—there is no informed consent in Great Britain, for example.

It is difficult to translate medical information from technical language into everyday speech and be sure that the information is presented in a way the patient and family can understand. Moreover, there is always the worry that the method of presenting the information biases the patient's response. It's hard to be truly objective, particularly if the physician has strong, personal feelings about one choice over the other.

Science is changing, the physician's role is changing, hospital utilization is changing, but the greatest changes are occurring in the patients themselves. The very word patient is changing: from patient to consumer. The person who is ill no longer has to be passive and completely dependent on others who provide him with tender loving care. In the old days TLC and a few drugs were all we had to offer the acutely ill patient who either got better or died.

Nowadays science can keep seriously ill people alive, returning many to full health, but leaving many others with long-term medical problems that necessitate continuing interaction with health professionals, and with permanent disabilities that interfere with normal living.

It becomes an intolerable situation if we continue to think of such survivors as patients, as *the* disabled or *the* sick. We need to learn to think of them as people who happen to have a medical problem, a disability, an illness. They are people first, and as such have rights to be in control of their lives and to find a way to function independently and to participate fully in society. These are the days when we speak of living in the mainstream, in the least restrictive environment.

One major difficulty for persons with a disability comes with success— the closer they come to overcoming their handicap and living successfully in the mainstream, the less emotional support they get from people around them. After all, they've proved their point that they can function independently, so families and co-workers go on to think about something else. People with disabilities don't want pity, but they would like some recognition of the sheer courage it takes to go on struggling to live a normal life. It takes courage and it takes effort—2 or 3 hours of preparation to get ready for each day that an "able-bodied" person just wakes up to. It is a lonely life— and the only people who can really share the feelings and frustrations are other people in the same situation, who can often be found in a self-help group.

Among the first things shared are feelings of deep anger: anger at the illness, so well expressed in the name of one self-help group, Y-Me—anger at society for providing so many barriers to overcome—anger at physicians for not diagnosing the problem earlier when prompt treatment might have prevented the disability or the sentence of death.

One of the real challenges for self-help groups is how they can deal with this anger and channel it into productive activity, rather than letting it take over the group and poison relationships with families and health professionals. It is very easy to take bits of information from the group back to the physicians and say, "Why don't you put me on medication X? It seems to be helping Mrs. Brown and she is doing much better than I am." There are ways of asking that can produce helpful responses and ways of asking that can only produce anger.

Physicians have a lot of anger to deal with, too, particularly when people won't follow the advice they are given. Some physicians have become so angry they refuse to treat certain patients—for example, the many cardiologists who refuse to accept patients unless they stop smoking. If the patients insist on following a self-destructive life style, these doctors feel they are justified in refusing any involvement, rather than prescribing stop-gap toxic medications and treatments, with the knowledge that eventually the doctor will end up in the ICU one night, desperately trying to save the life of someone who wouldn't take the first step to help himself.

My own involvement with self-help groups came as a parent of a deaf child who is now 24. Starting 24 years ago as a quiet observer in the back row, ready to dash out the door if anyone looked at me twice, I've participated in many different groups, in many different roles. In all those years I've never met a parent who went back on her own to the doctor who missed the diagnosis.

Deafness is an invisible handicap and easily overlooked. Doctors tend to offer reassurance to nervous parents until after the child is two and still not talking. Then the testing begins and children often aren't placed in the necessary educational programs until they are almost 3. Then the parents join a parents' group where they find another parent whose child was diagnosed at 2 months, got hearing aids at 3 months, and now, at age 3, is talking and communicating with her family, while their child has no language, no communication skills, and probably has a behavior problem to overcome before education can begin! So the parents are really angry. They don't talk to their old pediatrician, they go out and get a new one—and they remain angry for years. Their child may be in high school and they are still talking about that terrible first pediatrician.

Meanwhile, that first pediatrician doesn't know what happened, why they are no longer patients—perhaps they moved away. The parents may become very active in the self-help group, they may work hard to raise money for medical research and education of physicians about deafness, but they don't educate the one physician they have direct access to. If they would go back and tell him, they would change his future behavior. Physicians don't forget their mistakes.

More important than educating physicians, it is essential for the parents to go back and talk in order to deal with their anger and provide closure. They need to say, "This is what happened to us and our child has suffered greatly because you failed to make the diagnosis and help us—and we are hurt and angry." They need to give the physician the opportunity to say, "I'm very sorry this happened to you. I didn't know and I can promise you that I've learned from what you have told me and will make sure this doesn't happen again."

With whatever words we can find, we need to learn how to talk to each other because all of us—patients and families, self-help groups and physicians—share the same goal, that of helping people with disabilities and illnesses learn to deal with their problem, to take control and enjoy their lives.

7

Self-Help Groups: Self-Healing and Ethical Responsibilities

Jeffrey M. Kauffman, PhD

Self-help groups are peer and mutual support groups. The word *self-help* is apt and appropriate to the purpose of these groups. Self-help is reflexive. The verb is not transitive to an external object. The action of the group is directed toward itself. The group as a whole functions for the purpose of helping itself. The therapeutic value of the self-help group is primarily in the self-recognition of private pains and burdens in each other. The relationship of the professional to the self-help group must be based, in the first place, on fulfilling this purpose in the life of the group. The professional needs to allow and enable the group to use him or her in ways that maximize the group's autonomy. The basic principle of self-help is the mutuality of peer relationships.

I recall giving a talk for a self-help group where I was surprised to discover a member whom I knew from a professional hospice team support group. In this group, personal feelings were present and opened up, but were filtered and framed by her professional role identity. In the self-help group she was virtually a different person in her vulnerability, in the parts of herself that were identified with her pain and her personal needs, and in the private issues that she shared with the group members. The group self is the core commonality in which members are bonded to each other and in which parts of themselves from which they have been alienated are found. This common bond is the touchstone of meaningfulness and of the healing power of the self-help group.

What is the place of the professional here? Whatever his specific tasks are in providing support for the self-help group, in his role as a professional he is outside the healing mutual identity bond of group membership. He is adjunctive to the common reality that secures, protects and heals members. The simple validation of experience and sense of belongingness in one's struggling and pain that is provided in the mutuality of persons helping each other characterizes the therapeutic matrix of the self-help group. This distinguishes it from the asymmetrical therapeutic relationship in which one party is the agent of care based on specialized knowledge.

Today there is a special need for such peer support structures. The reason for this appears to be the lack of adequate support within the traditional and conventional societal structures. Persons tend to seek out the most homogeneous group composition possible. The specificity of need for common experience may reflect the need to be able to see oneself, as much as possible, in the other. It may also be a reflection of specialized problems, needs and experiences that relate to specificity of medical procedures and uniqueness of experiences. The need to find oneself in the other—for the others in a self-help group to be other selves—is a very powerful need that seeks realization in self-help groups. Not only are the conditions that prompt the function of self-help groups conditions that threaten one's sense of identity, but in conjunction with this there is a profoundly disturbing sense of being different and isolated and not understood by others. This cluster of feelings is particularly heightened by a societal condition that does not sanction the grief and suffering or accept the differences of the ill and their families. A basic underlying need of members of self-help groups is not to feel different, isolated and misunderstood, and is simply the need for a context for social sanctioning of their pain and grief. "There are others who understand what I am going through . . . I am not alone" is a common refrain of group members. The professional, especially one operating in the medical model, is treating and caring for pathologies. In the self-help group, the differences that enable one to be a member are normal. The self-help group bond normalizes members. Our generalized societal intolerance of pain, especially prolonged suffering, complicates the coping ability and further burdens person with life-threatening illnesses and their families.

Professionals may be able to provide meaningful support to organizers and to those entrusted with managing the group boundaries and process to help secure the safety and helpfulness of the group, especially when they are confronted with complicated or special problems. They may also be expert speakers or provide information in other ways. However, professionals tend to arrogate to themselves two privileges that run counter to their basic ethical responsibilities in regard to self-help groups. One is that professionals tend to operate from the principle that their skills and knowledge are private property. Responsibility and social obligation are subordinated to personal gain and power. Some professionals believe otherwise—namely, that they have an ethical responsibility to the community. This is an important consideration of which self-help groups remind us—for our contribution to such groups is a community service and is basically without profit. I have repeatedly had the experience of having to account to my colleagues for contributing time to self-help groups. Some of them will say, "Well, is it paying off? Are you getting referrals?" Making money is usually taken as a principle of self-respect and good sense. The spiritual and ethical poverty of our time (reflected in another way in the general failure of traditional means of social support) renders the "sacred trust" to our community an alien concept to many. Mental health professionals divorced from the humane foundations of their work are technicians who do not recognize or understand the source of the powers socially invested in them.

The second major ethical issue for professionals is based on a topic already discussed—that the healing of the self-help group is the *self-healing* of the group. The mental health professional is ethically obligated to respect and foster the autonomy and autonomous growth of the group, protecting the mutuality of peer support as the healing matrix and heart of the group's life. The privilege of initiating interventions, as an authority with responsibility for containing and guiding, needs to be completely subordinated to respecting and enabling the self-help structures of the group. The professional ought not to arrogate to himself the rights and powers he experiences in asymmetrical and more or less hierarchical relationships he contracts in his usual professional responsibilities with patients or clients.

These principles of professional responsibility to the community and of respecting the peer mutuality of self-help group healing ought to be more meaningfully integrated into educational and practice standards.

8

The Impact of a Self-Help Group on Nurses and Their Dying Patients

Sr. Alice L. Cullinan, PhD

Nursing personnel are becoming increasingly aware of the pressures inherent in their work with seriously ill and dying patients. Most nurses are committed to caring and deep concern for these patients and their treatment, and they struggle to maintain a personal integrity and professionalism. It has been found that a nearly universal feeling of defenselessness and helplessness assails nurses who care for dying patients. This vulnerability seems to relate partially to conflicts between doing "too much" to keep patients alive and trying to reverse the inexorable course toward death. Added anxiety centers more on waiting for "lingering to die" than on emergency situations that demand immediate and urgent responses (Price and Bergen 1977).

Nursing literature is replete with articles about the social and psychological dysfunction of nurses trying to be compassionate and understanding in the face of repeated exposure to suffering and death (Vachon 1979). Yanik (1984) described how nurses and their coworkers seemed especially susceptible to the disruptive consequences of strain resulting from frequent intensely pressured situations, the expectation that they perform in certain high-level ways and the unrealistic expectations of patients and their families. Staff reactions to debilitating and life-threatening illness can become more intense and complex the longer a patient lives and the more familiar the patient's personal life becomes. Even very seasoned nurses can experience an enormous sense of helplessness when a well-known patient deteriorates. They can tend to become involved in the family's emotional distress, can experience ambivalence about continuing aggressive treatment and may feel conflicted about the priorities of meeting a patient's physical needs as against providing emotional support. They may want to withdraw from the situation, thus generating guilt. Adding to the stress is a dominant trend in nursing today for institutions to reward those willing to move away from

97

direct patient care (Stephenson 1985). Another burden of the job can be emotional flooding, which occurs when too many patients are dying at the same time. The staff lacks the time to grieve and experience affective closure with one patient before becoming involved with another. Given the limited capacity to reduce suffering and death among patients, caring nurses caught in these situations have little time and emotional energy left over to work through separation and mourning issues. It can become more difficult to make sense out of one's relationship to death. Anger can then erupt and be projected at doctors, other staff and the institution, and even at the patient and family. All this stress often results in such negative consequences as job turnover, absenteeism, physical illnesses and burnout, which is "a progressive loss of idealism, energy and purpose experienced by people in the helping professions as a result of the conditions of their work" (Edelwich 1980, p. 14) and which can be as hazardous to the welfare of patients as it is to professionals. Signs of burnout include insensitivity and lack of concern for colleagues and patients, negative self-concepts, loss of self-esteem and dissatisfaction with the job.

The stress experienced by nurses is "endemic in our time, both in and out of medicine" (Price and Bergen 1977, p. 235). Structures and values of the institution of medicine are strongly involved in reinforcing the unconscious role conflict between trying to control death and being responsible for its occurrence (by not doing enough), in not being aware of or responsive to the emotional needs of nurses working in thanatological areas and in not providing educational and therapeutic opportunities for nurses to deal effectively with these procedures.

SELF-HELP SUPPORT GROUPS

One way in which nurses in such situations can be aided is through self-help support groups (Moynihan and Outlaw 1984). An example of how a need for such groups arises occurs when nurses perceive job-related situations as harmful, threatening or over-challenging and consequently feel overwhelmed and isolated (Scott, Oberst and Dropkin 1980). Support groups can provide for ventilation and alternative perceptions of feelings, problems and circumstances, increase the understanding of psychological and systems issues, facilitate and model the learning of new ways of problem-solving, aid in coping with stress and the gaining of a greater sense of cohesiveness and emotional support with other staff, and provide support for changes in attitudes toward oneself, one's behavior and one's work environment (Levy 1979).

Lieberman (1979) found that impelling those seeking aid through self-help groups was the overall amount of accumulated life strain encountered. Membership in such groups is determined by a common condition, situation, heritage, symptom or experience. They are largely self-governing and regulating; they emphasize peer solidarity rather than hierarchical governance; they prefer controls of consensus rather than coercion; they advocate self-reliance; and they require equally intense commitment and responsibility of other actual or potential members. Dorman (1979) wrote of how, in many self-help groups, "a professional played a key role in the founding, giving a major early boost or an instrumental role at various stages of an organization's development" (p. 21). Cohesive groups offer almost unconditional acceptance, generating a sense of belongingness and nurturing among participants, and provide a supportive atmosphere for taking the risks involved in sharing of personal material. Small face-to-face groups have a capacity to induce powerful affective states in participants and provide a context for comparing their own approach to particular problems with that of others to gain new perspectives (Lieberman 1979).

The use of support groups for dealing with work-related stress in caregivers has been one of the most commonly prescribed techniques for dealing with this stress and yet was the least commonly mentioned technique in Vachon's (1987) comprehensive study of stress and nurses. Two-thirds of those mentioning self-help groups believed them to be an effective technique, but not a panacea for all stress reactions. The support groups studied seemed to work optimally if the caregivers involved had asked for the group and had input into its format. The best model seemed to be that of meetings in which patient issues or specific management problems could be discussed and feelings addressed only as people were ready to do so.

A SELF-HELP GROUP FOR NURSES IN A PSYCHIATRIC CENTER ACUTE MEDICAL CARE UNIT

Prelude

The director of the medical care unit of a large state psychiatric center was concerned that many of her professional employees were being stressed by caring for many terminally ill and dying patients. She asked that an educational program be organized for the staff on coping with the needs of the terminally ill and dying. Because of the large number of participants involved, three separate groups were formed, each meeting three times. During the sessions, participants were exposed to theories of death, dying, grief and bereavement, alternately struggling with their own unresolved grief and existential issues. They learned of anticipatory grief, which is an emotional reaction spawned by knowledge of impending death. Though tempered with hope, sadness and anger are usually present in its initial stage, along with much disorganization and reorganization, and a strong feeling of relief at the time of death with an accompanying surge of energy (Stephenson 1985). Participants were taught that the grief process should not be encouraged during the anticipatory phase because this can lead to withdrawal from the dying person, but rather that it was best to be aware of the disorganization and to live with it.

Among the topics discussed was how almost all grieving involves elements of both existential and reactive grief, and that to fully understand our grief and that of others, we must become aware of the degree to which grieving can be reactive or existential. In existential grief, death is a dramatic reminder of its reality in life, with an accompanying turmoil and sense of disorganization. Grief over a loss is accompanied by a realization that all life, even one's own, ultimately involves death. Life's meaning is often called into doubt as one is thrown back on inner convictions as providing meanings for existence. Another's death may awaken dormant death anxieties, and a fear of death may return to haunt or unsettle. Roots of existential grief issues can usually be found in childhood. Lifton (1976) viewed the development of a sense of integrity (personal wholeness) and a fear of annihilation (disintegration) as part of early development and wrote that when this sense of organization or wholeness is lacking, one will seek out ways of shielding against the reality of death. When a meaningful death occurs, this defending is difficult and existential grief is experienced, rooted in primary issues involving the reality of death itself. This struggle (of mastering the polar realities of life and death) engages us all, probably on a repressed unconscious level all our lives (Stephenson 1985).

Reactive grief is concerned with the loss that death represents to survivors. The severity and extent of reactive grief experienced by the caretaker/survivor will depend on factors such as the social reality of the griever's world, which sanctions acceptable modes of grieving, the degree to which death is seen as preventable, feelings of guilt or anger at the needless or inappropriate death, the basic personality and emotional makeup of the caregiver/survivor, past losses and one's experience in resolving them.

After spending time working through their own unresolved existential and reactive grief issues, the grief process was then presented from the perspective of its relevancy for work with the dying. The frequent early reaction of numbness was discussed and participants learned how initial functioning often occurs only on an intellectual level and how feelings strongly repressed may be a life-preserving adaptation to some emergency situations. However, if one permanently numbs oneself to preserve integrity and maintain a sense of personal organization, the cost can be exceedingly high. Vitality can be impaired; the very things that mean life, such as spontaneity, open and emotionally satisfying relationships and a sense of wholeness, can be sacrificed to anesthetize the awful reality of death. One stops feeling to stay alive.

The idea was introduced that an early stage of bewilderment can be an attempt to assign meaning to the loss event. The more inappropriate the loss (such as a young person dying), the greater the challenge to make sense out of the event. As the reality begins to be accepted, a great urge (often unconscious) to recover the lost object can well up. Nurses reported that weeks after a death, they would still look to a particular patient's bed, expecting to see the patient there. Anger at the deceased or at God or the attending physicians can often occur during this early phase. If a disorganization and reorganization with deep and sometimes incapacitating despair sets in, there may be no place to focus one's thoughts or maintain organized activity; often purposeful activity ceases. This can lead to a strong (if temporary) dependency on others.

With reorientation and recovery, loss takes on different meanings. The memory no longer elicits strong grieving reactions. One's symbolic world is reorganized, and the dead person may be given a new image and identity. "The grief is mastered, not by ceasing to care for the dead, but by abstracting what was fundamentally important in the relationship and rehabilitating it" (Marris 1958). Connection and personal integration are regained, and one can now redirect and take charge of life. Life moves forward, and the ability to interact openly with others is regained. "Healthy grieving should end with new avenues for creative living" (Simos 1979; Stephenson 1985).

As the seminar drew to an end, the experience was discussed and the participants felt that the new understandings and tools learned would serve them well. However, within a few weeks, it seemed as if an avalanche of deaths was occurring, and the staff started floundering. On the female ward, four deaths occurred in a single week. One of these was a beloved 34-year-old woman who had been in the ward for several years as she deteriorated from a rare, congenital disease. Another was "Grandma," a gentle person who, even as she suffered from dementia, could easily evoke love and humor from the staff. That same week on the male ward, one young man suffering from AIDS left to go the general hospital with the words: "Thanks for all you've done—remember me." He died the next week away from his home of 4 months. The staff was overwhelmed and had great difficulty addressing their grief individually or jointly.

Group Beginning

The nurses asked if a self-help support group could be started. An announcement was posted, and at the first meeting it was decided that the group would be open-ended in membership and duration. It was not to be a forum for unproductive complaining, but supportive, therapeutic and positive in its focus. The group agreed to meet weekly for an hour, pledged confidentially, promised to work to develop trust in one another and decided to have a main focus of providing mutual support. Initially, the building of trust proved difficult because of the immense level of psychic pain in the group. Gradually, this pain subsided as members allowed themselves to trust the group and to experience each other's caring and support.

Ongoing Process

The group has now been operating for 6 months. A main focus continues to be on issues concerned with the plethora of patients dying. Debate about the ethics of resuscitation of elderly and debilitated patients who cease breathing is an occasional topic. Problems related to sharing, supporting and working closely with nursing colleagues are discussed, as are ways of relating to personal problems that affect the collective effort. Learning how to handle positive and negative feeings in a way that maintains staff cohesiveness has been a consistent focus.

Early on the group raised the topic of the cost that an unconscious feeling of being responsible for the occurrence of death had on them. They remain ambiguous about knowing "how much to do to save a life," and the nurses struggle at times with "whether I (or we) did the right thing." Trying to construct a meaningful relationship to death—"my own," "my loved ones'" and "my patients'"—remains a challenge to be confronted and resolved each time another death occurs.

Group discussions have included the nurses' professional identity and relationship to the hierarchical, multidisciplinary hospital structure. Better ways of addressing the emotional needs of patients and group members are discussed. Tears flow as a nurse reads a poem about the death of a beloved patient; anger explodes at the irrationality of young patient's dying, and caring love for each other is evoked with open, honest sharing. Recently a staff nurse and group member's child developed cancer that was initially thought to be terminal. Many of the members identified with her fear and anxiety, and worked together over several weeks to give her support.

Results

As group cohesiveness grew, the participants began to experience less stress and greater confidence in their ability to give not only good nursing care, but also compassion and caring. Emphasis has switched from teams "doing nursing" to "helping patients die well" or "accompanying them on the way." Staff turnover has diminished as has the incidence of sick days; group members have come in on days off just to participate in group.

The group now finds itself better able to draw upon and integrate what was learned and experienced in the symposium they participated in. Anticipatory grief is being acknowledged and discussed individually and by the team. Both the existential and reactive grief dealt with so extensively during the seminar is being recognized and dealt with more realistically. Time is now taken for grieving after a death, and although the work with the seriously ill and dying patients is still experienced as stressful and demanding, it is now more rewarding and less frustrating to the group participants.

Patient care also has benefited from the nurses' positive experiences with the self-help group. The terminally ill and dying seem to sense the increased capacity and ability of their caretakers to be more available to them and to be more accepting of the process they are going through. Because "being with the patient" in the process of dying comes easier, more time is spent by the professional in attending to emotional needs. It is now not an infrequent occurrence for patients to reach out for emotional help and to express their feelings spontaneously, whereas previously they were more reticent and passive. Patients die more easily and peacefully now.

Recently, the members of the group were polled to determine whether the overall group experience was helpful. Each said it was. Comments included: "I never realized just one hour a week could make such a difference in my life"; "Just knowing I will be coming here gets me through sometimes" and "It's been so good learning that others feel the way I do and that I'm not a weirdo!"

CONCLUSION

This chapter first described some of the stresses that nurses experience in working with the terminally ill and dying. It then presented a rationale for the use of self-help groups to help nurses doing this work. Finally, the prelude, development, ongoing functioning, results and informal survey of results thus far were offered. The use of a self-help group by nurses to cope with the occupational stress of working with the dying is a method that can be recommended for relieving tension, facilitating grieving, providing support, stimulating emotional growth and bringing about a more rewarding and life-giving career experience. In addition, as nurses translate these gains into their work of helping their patients to die well, the emotional, spiritual and even physical well-being of the patient is enhanced.

REFERENCES

Dorman, L.D. Characteristics of Development and Growth. In M.A. Lieberman and L.D. Borman, eds., *Self-Help Groups for Dealing with Crisis*. San Francisco: Jossey-Bass, 1979.

Edelwich, J. *Burn-out: Stages of Disillusionment in the Helping Professions*. New York: Human Sciences Press, 1980.

Levy, L.H. Processes and Activities in Groups. In M.A. Lieberman and L.D. Borman, eds., *Self-Help Groups for Dealing with Crisis*. San Francisco: Jossey-Bass, 1979.

Lieberman, M.A. Help Seeking and Self-Help Groups. In M.A. Lieberman and L.D. Borman, eds., *Self-Help Groups for Dealing with Crisis*. San Francisco: Jossey-Bass, 1979.

Lifton, R.J. A Sense of Immortality. In R. Fulton, ed., *Death and Identity*. Bowie, MD: The Charles Press, 1976.

Marris, P. *Widows and Their Families*. London: Routledge & Kegan Paul, 1958.

Moynihan, R.T., and E. Outlaw. Nursing support groups in a cancer center. *J. Psychosocial Oncology* 2:33-48, 1984.

Price, T.R., and B.J. Bergen. The relationship to death as a source of stress for nurses on a coronary care unit. *Omega* 8:229-238, 1977.

Scott, D.W., M.T. Oberst, and M.J. Dropkin. A stress-coping model. *Ann. Nursing Sci.* 3:9-23, 1980.

Simos, B. *A Time to Grieve*. New York: Family Service Association of America, 1979.

Stephenson, J.S. *Death, Grief and Mourning*. New York: Free Press, 1985.

Vachon, M.L. Staff stress in care of the terminally ill. *Quality Rev. Bull.*, May 1979, pp. 13-17.

——————. *Occupational Stress in Care of Critically Ill, Dying and Bereaved.* New York: Hemisphere, 1987.

Yanik, R. Sources of work stress for hospice staff. *J. Psychosocial Oncology* 2:21-31, 1984.

9

Self-Help and High-Tech Home Health Care

Allen I. Goldberg, MD, MM, Ann Hughes and Steve Hughes

Persons who depend upon prolonged use of medical technology for optimal wellness represent major management challenges for health care providers and members of their families. The ventilator-assisted child is a good example. A small but increasing number of such infants and children today can be found in neonatal and pediatric intensive care units. These patients are survivors of modern acute care who have been successfully treated for a variety of congenital and acquired conditions and can be made medically stable with the assistance of technology. When this occurs, the hospital is no longer the appropriate setting for optimal growth and development, or for the health of the patient and family.

This chapter will focus on a recent case that will demonstrate how valuable the self-help concept can be in extending the benefits of home care. It will be presented from the perspectives of both the home care physician and the family.

HIGH-TECH HOME HEALTH CARE: A CASE EXAMPLE

The Physician's Perspective

A 15-month-old child was first seen in consultation by the home care physician while still in the hospital in an unstable medical condition. The child had been born prematurely and subsequently developed severe respiratory distress syndrome and bronchopulmonary dysplasia. At the time of the first physician visit, attempts were being made to wean the infant from mechanical support. The consultant recommended that it would be preferable to maintain optimal mechanical ventilation. This was described as a necessary prerequisite for home health care planning. Two reasons were given. Medically, optimal support would provide a degree of functional reserve that would result in a medically stable condition and the greatest potential for health, growth and development. Logistically, a health care plan could only be designed and financed when the prescriptions for equipment and supplies could be determined over time.

When medical stability was accomplished, home care planning was initiated by an integrated professional care team coordinated by an extraordinary primary care nurse and a core team of home care experts who served as resource consultants. The center of the team was the family. By this time, this highly motivated family had already demonstrated expertise as observers and care providers. They provided important input into health care management decisions and participated in management changes. By involvement in home care planning, preparation, training and education, the family members gained insights, improved skills and became highly committed to a plan of action. The medical management at home was transferred from the attending physician to the home care physician, who was the medical consultant of the core team. During this planning process, the home care physician could evaluate the capabilities, readiness and appropriateness of this family for self-help. This would take the form of family-centered care with a high-degree of family involvement in decision-making and case management. By the time the patient was discharged home, the family was as knowledgeable and skillful as the professional home health care providers.

The child remained at home for many months on optimal mechanical and pharmacological support. This was a mutual decision of the physician and family. The overall approach to management and each individual aspect were the result of an interchange of observations and a mutual continuing education process. The physician encouraged and fostered an independence in clinical management up to the limits preferred and well-tolerated by the family. When decisions were made that were contrary to the judgment of the physician, they were revised by means of explanations that gave the family greater insights.

Routine evaluations were done in the home and by telephone communication on a regular basis, and technical support was coordinated with primary medical care provided by the community-based primary care pediatrician. This permitted the child and family to remain at home for minor adjustments in the overall support plan and even during periods of mild decompensation requiring acute care, such as infections acquired from siblings or neighbors. Expensive and unnecessary hospitalizations were avoided for long-term care management as well as acute needs.

The home care physician played both a case management and a managed care role. Because of continuous involvement and evaluation of what was clinically necessary, there was ample documentation for communication. The third party payors were satisfied that the required care and services were medically appropriate. Because of the excellent observational and technical skills of the family members, a home care plan revision could be accomplished on a regular basis that resulted in a planned, safe withdrawal of support without the pressures of time or funding.

The Family's Perspective

In the hospital, parents are often frustrated because of their inability to go directly to primary sources of information, obtain medical information needed to understand the status of their child, and affect decision-making. A parent is the primary advocate for their child; yet doctors often do not explain the child's treatment plan. Parents sometimes feel that professionals are ignoring their rights. In addition, they often are angry about the way they are handled:

> The games played were horror stories. There were different approaches to dealing with us depending upon the hospital and individuals involved. There was a major effort by professionals to show who was in control and this led to major power struggles.

For parents the home care experience can be a frightening one:

> At home, we felt a sense of fear even though we were very well prepared. Without this preparation, home care would have been impossible. After everyone leaves, being home alone with your [ventilator-assisted] child is an awesome, frightening experience. However, the alternative [re-hospitalization] was far worse. We were amazed at our resourcefulness; you'd be surprised what you can do if given the chance. It was essential to have a home care physician who said, 'you're doing OK' even if we screwed up. We were always afraid. Given a boost, 'now I can do it!'

Discussion

Home care for children with special needs has been an option for over a decade. Home care in general is not appropriate for everyone, and success depends upon the proper selection and preparation of each family. The success factors for such an approach include the following:

1. *Medical:* The child must be medically stable on optimal pharmacologic or technical support. It is essential that no major diagnostic decisions or therapeutic alterations are necessary over a period of time that is predetermined as appropriate to the medical condition. It is not possible to discharge home or logistically plan and fund a home care plan for a patient who requires frequent management decisions or changes. Furthermore, a patient who receives optimal support must have the degree of functional reserve required for activity, growth, development and extraordinary circumstances.

2. *Environmental:* Home care requires an informed family that is aware of the magnitude of the undertaking and willingly accepts the challenge. Furthermore, the home setting must be appropriate to the unique care needs of the child, and the community must have the available support services that the family will require.

3. *Organizational:* A comprehensive, written home care plan must be developed that meets the unique needs of each child and family. This is best done by an integrated, interdisciplinary team approach that includes the hospital-based primary caregivers, community-based health care service providers, and other involved and concerned persons as appropriate to the individual case, such as educators and third party payors. The home care planning process must be family-centered and include a component of case management. All efforts must be made to involve the family in clinical management decisions prior to and during home care planning. The family and all home caregivers must be fully prepared by a complete education and training program that is documented and evaluated by all participants.

4. *Financial:* The health and safety of a technology-dependent child at home requires complete funding of those components that are considered clinically necessary and medically appropriate. Supplemental home care and related incidental costs that are not covered by reimbursement sources are beyond the financial means of most families. Creative funding solutions and innovative managed care can result in safety, quality and cost-containment.

This case demonstrates the ultimate self-help goal for persons at home who require prolonged use of life-supportive medical technology: the ability of the patient and family members to make independent, informed decisions regarding their own health management. Although only an infant, the patient dramatically communicated his desires and intentions. Little doubt was present when it was time to proceed with withdrawal of therapy. His input was augmented by the keen observation skills and informal clinical judgment of his parents. With the family and physician working collaboratively in the home and by telephone, management decisions and changes were determined by negotiation and persuasion.

It is essential that physicians and other health care providers employ the self-help concept to enable users of medical technology and their families to understand their medical conditions and equipment. To assure the successful outcome of self-help and professional collaboration, the home care candidate (both patient and family) must be properly selected by rigorous criteria. While in the hospital, great attention must be paid to the details of preparation. However, education is an ongoing process. Home care physicians and other service providers extend training into the home initially during an extension of the orientation period. Thereafter, continued education is a by-product of the co-management.

BENEFICIAL OUTCOMES

Collaborative home health care provides a number of important benefits. For one thing, medical decisions are made easier for physicians. When they develop confidence in the judgment of the patient and family, the physician has a continuous source of accurate information from an interested group that takes charge of its own health needs. Medical management is safer since the care is provided by persons who are properly prepared, trained and educated. Families are sensitive to mechanical problems with equipment and often devise creative solutions. Medical liability risk is reduced due to the participation and involvement of the family in planning. Family members have a sense of ownership of their own program.

Wellness is promoted as a result of a more health-promoting environment that eliminates medical complications of prolonged hospitalization, such as nosocomial infections. In the home setting, a different "culture" (attitudes, behaviors, beliefs) prevails with a mindset toward patient- and family-centered influence over their own outcomes.

Cost containment is possible when a case management approach is utilized that features a case manager (often the family) who is accountable for coordination and communication. Optimal cost savings result from integrated systems management that operationally links suppliers, distributors, providers, payors and consumers.

SUMMARY

Well-prepared, technology-dependent people and motivated family members are very capable of making appropriate decisions regarding their own health management. They have the insights and make the continuous observations to best understand their own needs and requirements for technological adjustments. If they are given the adequate professional encouragement, their perspectives can be invaluable for decision-making. By offering them the opportunity to co-participate in decisions and self-management, the care plan can be modified in the home setting where optimal adjustments can be made that fit current living patterns. Needless costly hospitalizations can be avoided for both long-term management adjustments and acute care. Finally, co-management in informed decision-making reduces the risk of medical liability.

There are new roles for physicians in home care and new opportunities for families to apply the concept of self-help. Through collaboration, patients and family members can be empowered with skills and knowledge to permit involvement and participation in their own care. The result is a commitment to wellness. The outcome is a degree of health that cannot be accomplished in an institution and that cannot necessarily be explained by current scientific methodology.

10

The Old and the Ill: Application of Self-Regulation Theory to Chronic Sorrow

Virginia B. Newbern, PhD, RN

The concept of chronic sorrow, though not new, is rarely understood by caregivers and seldom applied to their interactions with people suffering ongoing losses. Yet their practices are often top-heavy with older persons and people with chronic conditions—that is, people with diverse and complex problems who are never going to be cured and will never recoup their losses. This chapter focuses on these people and their chronic grief and applies self-regulation theory to them and to the responses of caregivers.

THE CONCEPT OF CHRONIC SORROW

Long-lasting, static grief was first described as chronic sorrow by Olshansky (1963), who documented the inability of parents of developmentally disabled children with whom he worked to bring closure to their grief. He saw these parents as facing a crisis, a "critical life event" that is a "continuing event, not one that happens and then is over and ended" (Garrison 1965). As Borsh puts it:

> If a metabolic error, an extra chromosome, a viral infection, a congenital anomaly, a lack of oxygen, or some other vague agent adventitiously introduces a handicapped child on the terrain of parenthood, the business of parenthood continues. The obligations remain the same (1968, p. 7).

Wolfensberger (1967) sums up the findings of many writers when he speaks of "an intense and chronic emotionality [that] may be understood as an outcome of grief and mourning . . . as a chronic sorrow" which "even the passage of years has done little to ameliorate" (p. 333).

Bowlby (1969) studies the responses of children to prolonged or permanent separation from their parents. He sees grief as a normal mourning reaction to the loss of an object of attachment. Bowlby's attachment theory emphasizes that a person operates most effectively in his own environment. Becoming adapted, according to Bowlby, occurs through one of two distinct kinds of change:

> First, a structure can be changed so that it continues to attain the same outcome but in a different environment. Secondly, a structure can be changed so that it attains a different outcome in the same or a similar environment (p. 51).

Werner-Beland (1980) takes exception to Bowlby's contention that attachment behaviors are repressed after about age 3, becoming evident in later life only when a loss threatens. She contends that the attachment process becomes increasingly inner-directed as maturation occurs so that one's self becomes an important object of attachment. Thus, illness or disability threatens that sense of self as a trustworthy object and the self is forced to regress to an outside attachment (p. 23).

The reactions observed in persons caught in the chronic grief process are often very like those delineated by Lindemann (1944) in his description of unresolved or delayed grief: (1) overactivity without a sense of loss; (2) acquisition of symptoms belonging to the last illness of the deceased; (3) a recognized medical disease; (4) alteration in relationships with friends and relatives; (5) furious hostility against specific persons; (6) hiding hostility so that affect and conduct become wooden and formal; (7) a lasting loss of patterns of social interaction; (8) activity detrimental to social and economic well being; and (9) agitated depression. The antecedents, however, are very different. In unresolved grief the mourner refuses to deal with the grief response for extended periods; in chronic sorrow the mourner cannot get the grief work done because the event or condition continues.

What might be called the noninfluence of time should not be surprising, for "What might have been and what has been point to one end which is always present" (Eliot 1951, p. 1301). And what is present is the critical life event, the ongoing crisis, the certainty of daily stress. In our society it is not socially acceptable to mourn aloud, and grief work cannot be completed until the event is over and ended, and that ending may lie far in the future.

AGING, CHRONIC ILLNESS AND CHRONIC SORROW

By the middle of this century, medical science had almost vanquished infectious diseases. Improved nutrition, access to prenatal care and other preventive measures had lowered maternal and infant death rates and survivors were generally healthier. Average life spans—especially for females—have therefore increased dramatically.

Moreover, the population is aging. In 1980 there were 25.5 million Americans aged 65 or older. Projections are that this number will increase to 30.2 million by the year 2000. In addition, the proportion of those aged 75 or older is increasing rapidly. By 2020 this group, particularly vulnerable to chronic health problems and to the normal losses of old age, is expected to number almost as many people as the entire population of those over 65 today (Siegel 1980). This ever greater proportion of the total American population is now suffering and will continue to suffer the losses that attend advancing age *plus* the losses that are part of any chronic health problem.

At the same time, the increasing sophistication of medical technology has resulted in the continuation of life for many younger people who, even 20 years ago, could not have survived. These are people with chronic illnesses such as diabetes, chronic obstructive pulmonary disease, hypertension and end-stage renal disease.

Both the elderly and the chronically ill sustain loss after loss, sometimes slow and insidious, sometimes multiplying in geometric progression. With each loss they grieve and their families grieve so that sorrow becomes a part of daily living.

Caregivers seldom think in terms of chronic sorrow when they interact with the elderly and with those with chronic conditions. Their mindset is still oriented in terms of acute, episodic illness and cure. They concentrate on managing the acute flare-ups or complications that are associated with the patient's chronic condition (Diamond and Jones 1983).

Losses are temporary, they say (or imply), and reversible, or really not so bad, now that this new prosthesis—crutch, plastic breast, dialysis machine, respirator—is available to replace the loss. If the lost part is found there is no reason to grieve, caregivers imply. They are impatient with the patient who mourns the lost object, ignoring the effect of the loss on the patient's sense of self and urging the patient to embrace the latest technological substitute (Newbern 1984). They demonstrate little understanding of the concept of chronic sorrow and show little interest in seeking out and applying theoretical concepts such as self-regulation that hold great potential for working with the old and the chronically ill.

The message the patient and the family get is that they are wrong to mourn. There is nothing to mourn about and, even if there is, the time is not now. So the grief responses of patients and their families are ignored or disparaged and the grief work, left undone, feeds their despair (Werner-Beland 1980).

SELF-REGULATION THEORY

Nerentz and Levinthal (1983) were the first to apply self-regulation theory to chronic disease. Their explication would seem to apply to the aged, too, since they are more likely to be trying to deal with one or more chronic conditions and certainly are trying to cope with the multiple losses that attend the process of aging.

Nerentz and Levinthal analyzed three varieties of self-illness relationships:

The first is total: the self is the disease, the disease is the self. The second is encapsulated: a component of the self is diseased but large areas of the self are disease-free. The third is risk: the self (total or part) faces a constant threat of outbursts of acute, symptomatic illness (p. 28).

They saw the patient as striving to treat the illness as episodic and not really a part of self at all.

There are three features of the self-regulation model, according to Nerentz and Levinthal. The first is composed of a series of stages for guiding adaptive action: reception and interpretation of a health risk, action planning or coping, and evaluation. The second is the assumption of two feedback loops, one for regulation of danger, the other for regulation of emotion. The third is that each stage is hierarchically organized, ranging from highly abstract material to concrete, situation-specific material.

In adapting this model to chronic illness, Nerentz and Levinthal postulated that the self is the determinant of regulation; that is:

The organization of the self, how it relates to the environment and to its own emotional reactions, is critical in determining whether the illness is integrated with or remains alien to the self, and whether the links of illness to self take on the characteristics of a total, encapsulated, or at-risk model (p. 33).

They analyzed the self in terms of its hierarchical differentiation. At its most abstract is overall self-worth, where a good sense of self-esteem enables one to isolate the impact of the illness.

If this coping mechanism is successful, the patient goes about his activities of daily living. When coping efforts fail, the patient struggles to apply new strategies for dealing with the problems. If the feedback continues to be negative—if none of the problem-solving works—the patient is reduced to a sense of failure, with loss of self-esteem and destruction of the self.

Carver and Scheir (1981), from whose work Nerentz and Levinthal drew heavily, developed a model of self-regulation that sees people as active information processors who set standards that are used to measure subsequent behavior. According to this model, people give and receive information from their internal and external environments, modifying their concept of self and their standards accordingly. From this, Nerentz and Levinthal concluded that the coping abilities of the patient with a chronic condition depend on whether the links of illness to self are consistent with a total, encapsulated or at-risk model.

But chronic conditions, by their very nature, progress downhill. As the disease, the disability, or the normal act of aging incorporates more of the physical self, the patient senses that the self is, in fact, changing. Therefore, the characteristics of the links of illness displayed by the patient need to be seen within the context of the state of the illness. For example, the diabetic in end-stage renal disease who still treats the illness as episodic is not facing reality and has not changed the standards to meet that reality.

APPLICATION

A newly diagnosed diabetic man may treat his illness as alien to the self. Finding himself more susceptible to colds and flu, he can treat these episodes as acute. He may see his illness as occupying a fair amount of his life since he must take daily injections, maintain a rigid diet and exercise program, and no longer go barefoot. He may see the disease and the treatment regimen as taking over his whole life, annihilating his sense of himself as a whole, strong, virile, indestructible male.

When he sees himself as separate from the illness, he has no difficulty in meeting his standards. He also meets the expectations of the caregiver who is comfortable dealing with episodic illness.

When this patient perceives the illness as encapsulated, the standard can still very often be met or modified to reflect the changes the patient sees in his self, changes that reflect the losses he perceives he has sustained. The caregiver who ignores those losses or who insists they never occurred insults the patient's sense of reality and impedes his progress toward standard redefinition.

When the disease becomes the self, and the self the disease, the patient believes that there is no hope of meeting the original standard. The patient may refuse to follow treatment regimens, feeling that if his life cannot be lived according to his expectations, then it is not worth living at all. He may refuse to modify the standard, thereby not coping with the disease. Too often, the caregiver labels him "noncompliant" and reacts to him with anger and frustration rather than seeing him as bereft, mourning his lost self-esteem and his dreams for the future.

When self-regulation theory is used as a framework to help caregivers deal effectively with the old and the chronically ill, understanding the patient's behavior becomes easier. Once the behaviors are understood, caregivers can begin to help patients express their grief, to evaluate the standards and to redefine self when necessary, and to cope.

Where patients and their families are in terms of self-regulation provides a clue to where they are in terms of accepting their losses. If they can isolate the illness from their essential selves or, in Werner-Beland's words, "Resolve the distance between what is a fantasized image of self (as based upon an image of self as what once was, as well as values related to perfection) and what now is" (p. 172), then they can cope with their ongoing sorrow. The caregiver who can meet that patient and that family where they are and join in the grief work helps them to hope and to face each day with courage.

REFERENCES

Borsch, R.H. *The Parent of the Handicapped Child.* Springfield, IL: Charles C Thomas, 1968.

Bowlby, J. *Attachment and Loss, Volume 1: Attachment.* New York: Basic Books, 1969.

Carver, C., and M. Scheir. *Attention and Self-Regulation: A Control Theory Approach to Human Behavior.* New York: Springer-Verlag, 1981.

Diamond, M., and S. Jones. Ethics and the Quality of Life in Chronic Illness. In *Chronic Illness Across the Life Span.* Norwalk, CT: Appleton-Century-Crofts, 1983.

Eliot, T.S. "Burnt Norton." In A. Witherspoon, ed., *The College Survey of English Literature.* New York: Harcourt, Brace & World, 1951.

Garrison, K., and D. Force. *The Psychology of Exceptional Children.* New York: The Ronald Press, 1965.

Lindemann, E. Symptomatology and management of acute grief. *Am J. Psychiatry* 101:141, 1944.

Nerentz, D., and H. Levinthal. Self-Regulation Theory in Chronic Illness. In T. Burish and L. Bradley, eds., *Coping with Chronic Illness.* New York: Academic Press, 1983.

Newbern, V. The year of denouement for an insulin-dependent female and application of self-regulation theory. *Proceedings of the First International Congress on Women's Health Issues,* Halifax, Nova Scotia, October 1984.

Olshansky, S. Chronic sorrow: a response to having a defective child. *Social Casework* 1/2:190-193, 1963.

Siegel, J. Recent and Prospective Demographic Trends for the Elderly Population and Some Implications for Health Care. In S.G. Haynes and M. Feinlich, eds., *Second Conference on the Epidemiology of Aging.* Washington, DC: U.S. Department of Health and Human Services, 1980.

Werner-Beland, J. *Grief Responses in Long-term Illness and Disability.* Reston, VA: Reston Publishing, 1980.

Wolfensberger, W. Counseling the Parents of the Retarded. In A. Baumeister, ed., *Mental Retardation Appraisal, Education and Rehabilitation.* Chicago: Aldine, 1967.

11

The Primary Value of a
Self-Help Clearinghouse

Edward J. Madara, MS

DEVELOPING NEW COMMUNITIES: IGNITING SPARKS AND FEEDING FLAMES

Perhaps the most important variable to the increased development of self-help groups is encouragement. Persons who recognize the need and contemplate the possibility often face discouragement from different sides, from family friends who say, "What, you start a group? You've never even served on a church committee before, and you think you can take this on with the problems you face?" But there are many ways that individuals can be encouraged to start a group—by word, example, education and positive feedback. We need to examine how encouragement sparks and nurtures motivation if we want to motivate more people to start more self-help groups to fulfill unmet needs.

In 1978, as a staff member of our hospital's community mental health center and with the help of a student intern, I began to compile a listing of local self-help groups for the referral use of our clinical staff. In the course of that research work, I initially came in contact with a number of people who had at one time considered starting a self-help group, but were either unsure of how to proceed or were discouraged in their early efforts. In my initial discussions with them, I discovered the importance of my having information on an existing national group or a one-of-a-kind model self-help group for their issue of concern. If I could provide that information, especially newspaper articles that described how the group was started, it would usually rekindle their interest in starting a group, giving a powerful "demonstrational effect" (Madara 1985) wherein people are more prone to start a new self-help group in their community if they can be provided with just one example of how others with similar problems have actually succeeded in starting a self-help group elsewhere. Therefore, I added national or demon-strational groups, which had no local state chapters or counterparts, to my listing in order to provide that encouragement.

With the publication of the listing in 1980, I began to receive more inquiries from professionals and lay persons alike who were simply seeking a specific support group. In cases where no group was available, I would ask the caller, "Would you be interested in joining with others to develop a group?" Those who said yes had their names recorded so that future callers, who might be similarly interested in developing a group, could be referred to them. Like rubbing two sticks of wood together to start a fire, those link-ages with subsequent callers often resulted in the establishment of new groups. It became clear that a unique and powerful potential, inherent to the self-help field, was that a significant number of "help seekers" who were calling simply for a group referral could actually be turned into "community resource developers" who would eventually start a local resource group in their community. It became clear that having the information on any national or model group also provided significant encouragement, reassur-ance and the practical information that came with knowing that one did not have to "re-invent the wheel."

In following up and expanding that work statewide since its official start in 1981, the New Jersey Self-Help Clearinghouse has helped to develop more than 520 new self-help groups in the state through its consultation and networking services. Over that time the Clearinghouse has also worked with a variety of individuals in efforts to help start new types of national and international self-help groups. These have included new groups for post-partum depression, osteoporosis, Lyme disease, phobias, histiocytosis, Addison's disease, Sturge-Weber syndrome and TMJ syndrome, among others. In addition to newsletters and directories, the Clearinghouse has printed a variety of how-to materials that address general issues pertaining to the development of a group, stressing shared leadership from the start, so that the responsibility and work of starting and running a group never falls on any one person's shoulders. Emphasizing the need for shared responsibil-ity encourages more people to take on the challenge of starting a new group since they understand from the outset that they won't have to do it alone.

The Clearinghouse currently provides self-help group referrals to over 14,000 professional and lay callers annually over its toll-free statewide help-line. The resources to which they are referred include a national and model group database for over 3,600 self-help group meetings in New Jersey. A directory of the national and model self-help groups (Madara and Meese 1988) is published every 2 years. That same database is shared and updated with a dozen other self-help clearinghouses who use MASHnet, a computer software program developed just for self-help clearinghouse operations and reporting (Madara, Kalafat and Miller 1988). The database also includes information on some unique types of self-help groups in other countries. Several major self-help group models were first imported to the United

States from abroad: from England, Compassionate Friends, for those who have lost a child, and Let's Face It, for the facially disfigured; from Australia, GROW, for mental health clients.

Traditionally, mutual aid self-help organizations have been started when a person or a family—buffeted by a trauma, disability, loss or life-disrupting problem—seeks help, but finds no local agency or support organization available to meet their needs. If their problem has a high prevalence rate (e.g., arthritis, single parenting, or widowhood), there will usually be at least one existing national self-help organization that can assist them in starting a local self-help group focusing on that problem. Such face-to-face groups meet a need that is as old as mankind itself—the need to ease burdens by sharing them with others. However, if the disorder or problem is an uncommon one, it is unlikely that the individual or family will be able to find enough people to actually hold a group meeting, or a national organization that can assist them. It is for this reason that we should learn more about alternatives to the traditional face-to-face self-help group meetings.

THE VALUE OF GROUPS FOR LIFE-THREATENING ILLNESS

Mutual aid self-help groups have become better recognized as an important segment of the natural caregiving system. Member-run mutual help groups meet the need for new sources of support and coping skills to help individuals deal with the hardship and pain accompanying many illnesses, disabilities, addictions, losses, parenting concerns, and other stressful life problems, thus decreasing the intensity of suffering and isolation.

These self-help support networks also reach out to large numbers of "hidden patients," the families and friends of persons with these problems. Such mutual help networks are uniquely suited to reducing social isolation, promoting needed research, advocating for new community-based health care services, finding new solutions to problems, and fostering new collaboration between people in general and the professional health care community in particular. The proliferation of self-help groups over the last decade represents a major new social phenomenon that has shown the potential to meet emotional and health needs unmet by professional services.

A basic human need that we all share is our desire for feedback as to how well we are doing in our lives—whether in our work, our close relationships, or in handling our daily problems. We do this by comparing our experiences to those of others and thereby come to learn what the norms are. But when facing a life-threatening disorder, it is difficult for persons to find others with whom they can share experiences, coping skills and information on resources, and from whom they can obtain needed and valuable feedback as to what is "normal" for living and coping with that illness or situation. People are more inclined to enter into a group for the purposes of self-education than they are to seek treatment at a mental health center. In their own ways, self-help groups help to normalize, rather than psychopathologize, individuals facing stressful life problems. By providing help that is more psychologically as well as financially accessible, more people can receive the help they need and learn about additional services available to them.

Over the last two decades an increasing amount of research has reflected the positive impact of social supports on health and the health care system. Dimsdale and his colleagues (1979) have pointed out how "Much research suggests that social supports have a direct effect on health . . . Recent authors have argued that the influence of social supports on health can best be understood by considering their role in modifying the deleterious effects of stress, either reducing the stress itself or by strengthening the individual's coping efforts."

Mutual aid self-help groups and networks are an important segment of the lay social support system in that they can be purposely organized and provide a unique form of "instant community" or support born of common experience at a time when traditional social supports (e.g., extended family, neighborhood or church) are less available or less approachable on specific health problems (e.g., venereal disease, mental illness or other stigma-laden disorders). The health care system is not set up to provide such social support. Self-help groups, however, provide that support in many different ways, serving very much like a family in that they can provide support 24 hours a day through buddy systems and telephone listings, all without forms or fees.

THE NEED FOR ALTERNATIVE SELF-HELP NETWORKS

Given the value of self-help groups to support, educate and advocate, what then is a major problem in developing new types of groups for people who experience those needs the most? To begin with, it has become obvious that the problems faced by persons wanting to start new types of groups are quite different from the problems associated with starting local chapters of existing groups for more well-known afflictions. In starting a local group of an existing national organization, one has the built-in support of other group founders and leaders (Julien 1988). Different means must be found to provide mutual support and information-sharing for persons who have no national support and whose condition is relatively rare, since many geographic areas do not have a sufficiently large affected population to permit even the smallest of meetings within an affordable travel distance for members. Development of specialized resource materials could address this problem by exploring, articulating and disseminating information on the alternative and most appropriate ways that such support networks may be started and operated (e.g., through development of correspondence, telephone, home computer, and other communication networks).

Telephone and correspondence networks have allowed people with similar problems to share common concerns, support and information without the traditional face-to-face meetings that typify self-help groups. These "alternative community networks," largely unrecognized as a distinctive form of the mutual aid self-help group movement, offer similar benefits of social support, education, and often advocacy. There is a long history of these types of alternative community mutual help networks, from the early exchanges of the "Committees of Correspondence" leading to the Revolutionary War, to the "Loners Clubs" correspondence of Alcoholics Anonymous; from the more recent telephone networks such as the Tay-Sachs Parents' Telephone Network, to the government-funded Mental Health Consumers' national telephone conferences.

Key to the development and success of such phone, correspondence and computer networks is their special ability to reach out and support previously unserved populations, to include those who are isolated by geographic location, concern or disability. We believe that these model networks need to be better identified and described. Their development strategies and resource materials could be very helpful to those interested in starting new networks. Such alternative self-help networks can increase the linkage of people, ideas and concerns. They can also relieve social isolation, helping people by providing innovative ways for them to find and develop the mutual aid and support they need.

Home computer networks are becoming more common. There are free local computer bulletin boards (BBS) that one can call, computer-to-computer, to leave or respond to messages, as well as to obtain extensive files on topics of interest. There are already more than 200 BBSs across the country that specialize in health, mental health or disability issues. There are also national computer information systems, like CompuServe, that for a charge provide these services, plus on-line conferencing capabilities. The result has been regular meetings of Alcoholics Anonymous, persons with disabilities and others, with most of the members "attending" from their homes. A third system, BBSs that share their specialty message databases on an international basis daily, is called FidoNet. FidoNet special sections include those for disability, AIDS, alcoholism and spinal cord injury, among others. As computers become as common as telephones, more people will "meet" and access needed information and support through their home computers.

Another factor contributing to the need for support networks for rare disorders is that more and more persons and families suffer with these conditions. According to estimates by the National Organization for Rare Disorders, more than 20 million Americans are afflicted. There are a number of factors that are contributing to the increase in the number of people with new health problems or new diagnoses for which there are few or no self-help groups. These include but are not limited to:

- improved medical technology that continues to increase the survival and prevalence rates for previously life-threatening disorders, resulting in populations such as patients on hemodialysis, laryngectomees, ventilator-dependent families and coma recovery families.

- improved research and technology to save babies born prematurely, resulting in an increase in the number of children born with birth defects or special syndromes.
- children whom medical technology has saved over the last two decades, who are now growing into adulthood to face new problems, including hydrocephalic children with shunts, children with short bowel syndrome and adult polio survivors facing post-polio syndrome.
- increases in longevity and the "graying" of the population, resulting in a proportionate increase in prevalence of chronic and disabling conditions, some of which are rare.

It is also important to note that some conditions that appear at first to be rare may subsequently reflect a high incidence (e.g. Alzheimer's disease, AIDS, Lyme disease). By supporting the development of self-help networks for new or rare health disorders, our clearinghouse seeks to accelerate the natural cycle of social change that may hasten the identification of new or growing health problems. Advocacy efforts of these self-help organizations often lead to the development of responsive services and, with time, sometimes evolve into more formal health service organizations. Better understanding of how to nurture the development of these networks might actually accelerate the natural cycle of social change for many new problems—helping people to network, organize, educate or advocate more readily and quickly.

PROFESSIONAL ROLES AND PARTNERSHIPS

We should remember that the history of self-help groups illustrates how a few individual professionals have played major roles in developing several international self-help organizations (e.g., a psychiatrist starting Recovery Inc., a social worker linking clients to form Parents Anonymous, a physician starting Mended Hearts, and a clergyman introducing two grieving couples to spark Compassionate Friends). Key to their efforts was their ability to encourage and network people, recognizing the potential that their clients had to help one another.

On the other hand, we know that some professionals, instead of providing needed encouragement, actually discourage lay persons from starting groups. A major problem expressed by a few of our consultees, who first turned to professionals for initial support in their development of a self-help group, was that they were told they could not and should not start such a group because it could only be started by professionals. As another example, Susan Charney, the founder of what is today the International Turner's Syndrome Society, first asked her college professor for help when she was considering starting such a network. She was told by him that she would have to wait until she had at least a master's degree, because only skilled professionals have the expertise to develop support groups.

It was Woody Allen who once commented that if the day comes when the lion and the lamb lie down together, "the lamb won't get a lot of sleep." Some self-help groups are indeed suspicious of professional calls to partnership, often because of past experience with professionals who either attempt to control and co-opt, or benignly and "implicitly assert the professional's superiority" (Wollert, Knight and Levy 1980). Alfred Katz has cautioned that there are still many obstacles and pitfalls to professionl understanding, especially with regard to the continued lack of professional knowledge and education about self-help groups. If true partnerships are to be built, it is vitally important that both parties have a true sense of equality and respect for one another's values and knowledge, whether that knowledge is experiential or professional. Professionals often lack knowledge about self-help groups because they are in large part not being educated to them, their principles and their value (Black and Drachman 1985; see also Recommendation No. 14, *The Surgeon General's Workshop on Self-Help and Public Health* 1988). Self-help clearinghouses serve as primary resources for providing and promoting such training.

There are also fears that incorporation of self-help groups into the dominant health care delivery system, along with possible government funding, could result in pressures for their accommodation, leading to potential co-option and a weakening of their advocacy efforts and vitality. For example, a quite separate but related movement, the hospice movement, shared in its early development a number of experiences and goals similar to those of many self-help groups: dissatisfaction with bureaucratic and authoritarian institutions, a desire to humanize services and relationships, and a determination to avoid domination by experts (Abel 1986). However, there is now concern on the part of some proponents that while government funding may have "been facilitated by increased support for hospice ideals, the government views hospices primarily as a way to save money. Paradoxically, as hospices have grown in popularity, the critical force of the movement has been blunted . . . and [they] have lost their uniqueness" (Abel 1986, p. 71). Both self-help groups and professionals need to examine how such dangers may be avoided, whether through negotiated mutual agreements or the groups' adaptation of principles or "traditions" similar to those used by Alcoholics Anonymous.

For many illnesses and disorders there is a clear need for partnerships between professionals and self-help group representatives. This is especially true for rare conditions. Abbey Meyers, Executive Director of the National Organization for Rare Disorders, recently articulated this need:

> I must be candid when I say that I don't think a partnership between consumers and professionals exists today; but it will . . . because it must. Professionals haven't learned how much they need consumers, and consumers haven't learned that professionals are human, with frailties just as real as our own. When we finally come to these realizations, we will unite together in a strong bond in order to defeat a common enemy. The enemy is here, and has

been here for some time. Instead of fighting it together, we've launched our own individual battles, and in the end we have defeated ourselves (Meyers 1988, p. 4)..

In summary, a self-help clearinghouse can serve a very important and very real community development function beyond its other information, referral, education, research and training services. The dreams and hopes of self-help group founders and members have been the driving force behind the dramatic growth of self-help groups. For the ultimate realization of those hopes and dreams, we must continue to identify and share those ways by which we can better encourage, accelerate and improve the networking of individuals into new self-help groups and organizations, while also preserving and respecting self-help autonomy and principles.

REFERENCES

Abel, E.K. The hospice movement: institutionalizing innovation. *Int. J. Health Services* 16(1):71-85, 1986.

Black, R.B., and D. Drachman. Hospital social workers and self-help groups. *Health and Social Work* 10(2):95-103, 1985.

Dimsdale, J.E. et al. The role of social supports in medical care. *Social Psychiatry* 14, 1979.

Julien, T.M. The Relationship Between Self-Help Groups and the Community Organizations that Provide their Resources. Doctoral dissertation, Teachers College, Columbia University, 1988.

Madara, E.J. The self-help clearinghouse operation: tapping the resource development potential of I & R services. *Information and Referral* 8(1):42-58, 1985.

Madara, E.J., J. Kalafat, and B.N. Miller. The computerized self-help clearinghouse: using "high tech" to promote "high tough" support networks. *Computers in Human Services* 3(3/4):39-54, 1988.

Madara, E.J., and A. Meese. *The Self-Help Sourcebook: Finding and Forming Mutual Aid Self-Aid Groups.* Denville, NJ: St. Clares-Riverside Medical Center, 1988.

Meyers, A. "Network Building for Empowerment: A Consumer and Professional Partnership." Alliance of Genetic Support Groups, Washington, DC, November 4, 1988.

U.S. Department of Health and Human Services. *The Surgeon General's Workshop on Self-Help and Public Health.* Washington, DC: U.S. Government Printing Office, 1988.

Wollert, R.W., B. Knight and L.H. Levy. Make today count: a collaborative model for professionals and self-help groups. *Professional Psychology* 11(1):130-138, 1980.

12

Self-Help: What a Congregation Can Do

Rev. Perry T. Fuller, MDiv, DMin and
Rev. Lewis R. Bigler, MDiv, MA

The material contained in this chapter is a special gift, a pearl of great price. For it comes not from books and researchers, but from hard-won wisdom out of the lives of a group of families who have endured and surmounted life-threatening illness themselves.

First, they are white, middle-class folk, which is nothing more or less than a recognition that our society is a pluralistic one, and not everyone's experience is alike. The church in which Perry Fuller carried out his ministry has that cultural heritage. However, if one concurs with Harry Stack Sullivan's "one-genus postulate," then we are all more alike than we are different. As he puts it, "everyone is much more simply human than otherwise" (Sullivan 1953, p. 32). It is our hope that people of differing cultural backgrounds will find it striking a resonant chord with them as well.

Second, they are a great mixture of people—Caucasian American, Afro-American and others. They are the many patients that Lew Bigler has worked with over the last 17 years at Roswell Park Cancer Institute in Buffalo, New York. They are the many brave people and families who have had their children, their parents and their most significant others live and die with cancer.

The privilege it has been for us to be associated with these people is enormous. It would be difficult to measure the admiration—indeed awe— we feel in their achievement, although none of them would allow such talk to go on for long in their presence. Unless one has experienced the pain and anguish illness can introduce into a family, it is not possible to imagine the full impact. Time after time it has been our privilege to hear and to watch these stories unfold from devastation to coping, to surviving, to rising above, with evidence of growth and depth in their lives no matter what the outcome of the illness may have been.

Most of these people are intentional Christians, and all consider themselves to have a religious dimension to their lives. They have found comfort, guidance and strength from their faith, although, by their own admission, sometimes just barely enough. Their story is one of the majesty of the human spirit in general and the glory of the faithful human spirit in particular.

THE FAMILY UNIT

As much work as has been done in the area of family relationships in the past two decades, it is not an easy task to find a definition of "family." There are almost as many ideas as there are commentators on family life. For that matter there is a multitude of family constellations to be considered. For our purposes here, when "family" is referred to, it means those people who are related by blood, marriage, divorce (divorce doesn't end relationships, it just changes them), or by virtue of sharing a household, who were continuously involved with each other during an illness.

Fourteen families are represented in the church planning element of this program, with as many members interviewed as were willing and able to be. The individuals involved in the families numbered 54. The interviews, with one exception, were conducted in their homes and were recorded when permission was granted.

Several thousand visits were made to the Roswell Park patients and their families. These families are as vast and different as the sands of the sea, and almost as numerous. None of them can be identified by name, but all of them are identified by their courage and their resolutions of faith and life that are herein reflected.

The initial thesis proposed for this self-help project was that it is possible to discover ways in which a local congregation can support and help families who suffer life-threatening illness in their midst. To the extent such things have been determined, the thesis was fulfilled. A larger sampling of families might be necessary to prove a hypothesis. However, the number of families on one hand, and the number of individuals on the other, is consistent with samplings used in many of the studies represented in the review of literature.

At the time when most of the interviews in the church project were completed, Perry Fuller had the opportunity to present the initial findings to a cancer support group for their comment and discussion. About 40 patients, family members and interested professionals were present. This discussion helped elaborate and refine some of the items. No new aspects were added, nor was any indication given that any of them were inappropriate. This group of people represented, by and large, the same population out of which the findings have been drawn.

The ideas presented here as possibilities for concrete congregational support of families are ones that had a good deal of consensus about their value. One or two came as single offerings but make such grand common sense as things for which a congregation is ideal.

These proposals probably could not all be carried out by any individual congregation. The intent is to offer a smorgasbord of possibilities from which a congregation can pick and choose on the basis of available energy, time and talent of the members. It is probably true that the larger the church, the larger the pool of workers and resources available. However, it is certainly conceivable that a joint effort among several small churches in a community could achieve as much as a single larger congregation and serve a broader constituency.

The material in this chapter is the raw material out of which a concerned congregation can fashion a serious, concerted effort to support families in which life-threatening illness has intruded.

THE ONGOING EDUCATIONAL PROGRAM

One usually has to look no further than the professionals in an institution to find a ready-made body of critics. The church is no exception. However, for all its foibles, and for all the pervasive secularization of western culture, the church must not be undervalued in its role within society. It is a singular institution. As J.C. Wynn has written, "the church—and perhaps the church alone—touches people at every possible age. . . . Its intergenerational composition makes possible programs and emphasis often overlooked" (Wynn 1981, pp. 13, 14). It is certainly the place where at least a large minority of the population can be reached with various educational programs, religious and otherwise.

Health education is one of these programs. When one is presented with the idea of self-help, it is the church that shines forth in the American culture as such a self-help model. It seemed only natural to us to turn to the church as a model for self-help success. If any place should foster the development of physical and mental health, it is the church. Programs for prevention of illness and maintenance of health could easily be programmed into the educational ministry of a congregation often starved for study topics.

More particularly, the church could be a source of basic information for its members in regard to major health concerns such as cancer, stroke and heart attack. When illness strikes, many people feel ill-prepared to deal with it even on the most elementary informational level. Denial and fear are the two main reasons that many people do not have basic knowledge about serious illness. In itself, no educational program can do away with them. However, when illness strikes, ignorance is not bliss, and an organized attempt at education can help.

We suggest that this project of education could take place in adult forums and in special units of the church school. An area could be set aside in the church for display of pamphlets and books to be taken or borrowed. It is important that such an undertaking have someone who will assume responsibility for keeping it current and well-stocked.

Units of the associations related to serious illness, such as the American Cancer Society and Heart Association, are set up on a county, and often a local level. These organizations often have speaker's bureaus that provide programs of basic information, such as explanations of chemotherapy and radiation therapy for cancer. Many people have heard of these treatments and their unwelcome side effects, but they have no idea how the treatment works and why. Often this knowledge alone reduces anxiety. These associations also publish a great deal of material directly related to the illnesses, which they make available for distribution.

THE SELF-HELP PROGRAM

No attempt is made to duplicate medically based or hospital-based resources. Yet discharge planners in hospitals with an oncology unit will concede that the greatest problem they face is providing a discharge support system for patients. Second is dealing with the family's concerns while they are hospitalized. This church-based program is simple and direct; its aim is to address the needs of families of patients with a chronic disease.

The details of the self-help program were worked out by Perry Fuller, in his church organization outside a large metropolitan area, with the support and supervision of Lew Bigler and his program at the Roswell Park Cancer Institute. The Roswell Park program includes a three-times-yearly residency for clergy in working in a holistic manner with cancer patients and their families. This self-help approach could represent a starting point for similar programs under consideration in other churches and communities.

A PLANNED APPROACH TO FOOD ASSISTANCE

Perry Fuller's interest in families and illness developed over a relatively short period of time. Several families in his congregation were struck with serious illnesses. As a result of his work with the Roswell Park Cancer Institute and Lew Bigler, he began to develop some of the resources that these families could use. In doing so, he uncovered many special needs.

It should be noted that some organizational structure must be set up in advance of the provision of assistance. No more than one person should be in contact with the family about their food needs. The cooks and providers coordinate their efforts through that person. Although it is possible that food for every meal may be welcome during the first days of an illness, none may be required during that time because the family is likely to be eating at the hospital. Later, one dinner a week may be enough to give the cook of the household a night's break from the struggle of "scraping something together" at the end of a difficult day.

Another practical consideration is bringing the food in throwaway containers as often as possible. In the midst of all the other things that must be dealt with by the family, having to wash, keep track of and return dishes and pans to those who prepared the food can often be a difficult and burdensome detail.

The coordinator of food should keep a record of who gave what and when it was given, and should make it known that such a list is being kept. In this way, families who wish to thank those who offered help will be able to do so. Some of our families felt cheated by anonymous help. They had received so much from so many that they were overwhelmed by a sense of obligation that they felt was best discharged by being able to thank people individually.

On the other hand, personal expressions of gratitude may be more than some families are able to undertake. Their thanks can be conveyed in a more general way through the church newsletter or bulletin. Either way, when the coordinator keeps the food-giver list, it is available for those who want to thank individuals. Eliminating names on donated dishes relieves the sense of obligation from those who are not able to respond with thanks immediately.

TRANSPORTATION NEEDS

The daily transportation necessary in many treatment and rehabilitation programs can be a difficult thing to manage. Researcher Mary F. Bozeman has discussed this problem in connection with her work with young leukemia patients and their families. Transportation is one of the greatest anxieties for parents of ill children. They are concerned with the child's condition, particularly after treatment. Even if a driver is available in the family, it may be of more value for the family member simply to go along while someone else does the driving. Sometimes patients suffer anticipatory symptoms related to treatment side effects prior to their going for the treatment. It is difficult to drive and to assist someone who is ill at the same time.

The cost of transportation is something to be considered in the congregational budgeting process. Often there are people in a congregation who are willing and able to drive patients and families to treatment, but who cannot afford the added cost of the gasoline. A driver who listens well can be a great asset. Someone who is able to capitalize on an opening and to be an active listener may give more to a patient than simply a ride.

RESPITE TIME

This is the age of "burnout." The popular psychology bookshelves groan with self-help volumes about coping with this condition. Essentially it is a general exhaustion of personal resources after an intense period of involvement and concentration.

Families of persons with life-threatening illness are highly susceptible to burnout. A congregation may help the family by providing time off, such as mornings or afternoons for shopping, going out to eat, or simply some time alone. There may be young children or grandparents to be tended, household responsibilities and chores, and even patient care, assuming that professional medical attention is not required. These things can be provided by a team of volunteers, giving family members a time of respite.

As will be urged all along the way, no more than one or two people should serve as primary contacts with the family for those services that the congregation is able to provide. The family should not have to deal with the chairpersons and coordinators of every unit that may be called in to assist. The family has many new people to deal with under circumstances that are stressful at best. More people simply add to the strain.

It is important to keep in mind that there are dynamics working beneath the surface that may resist the kind of help that a "respite day" implies. If there are strong underlying themes of guilt within the family, it may be that family members are unwilling to have a day off, preferring to spend all their time at the hospital or with the patient at home in an attempt to relieve the guilt they feel. Taking time out would only intensify their feelings of guilt.

In all these possible areas of support, the family's felt and expressed needs should be the guideline. A family can be made aware of what is available through the pastor or the coordinator of the helping team. Long before the need ever arises, there should be ongoing publicity about the program in the church newsletter and in educational events at the church. Once the family knows what is available, it is up to them to decide which services they wish to use. Service providers should avoid appearing like the cartoon image of the Boy Scout dragging the woman across the street only to find out she didn't want to cross. Let the family be responsible for determining their own needs. Some families will gratefully use as much help as they can get; others will resist help. A family's sense of themselves should be honored at all times.

HOSPITALITY HOUSES

After World War II, one of the dramatic changes that occurred in American society was mobility. Until that time, many Americans had an extended group of relatives living in the same town or locality. Now family members live all over the country. They may wish to make a visit to the ill relative, either to see that person for what may be the last time, or to be there for help and support.

This raises the question of their accommodation. Whether or not the family members are happy to have the visiting friend or relative on hand, the basic issues remain: privacy, alone time and together time for the immediate family, and the matter of feeding and housing additional people.

A volunteer home offering an extra room and a meal, especially breakfast, is a very helpful resource. Hospitality houses make good common sense. The difference between a common-sense idea and an attempt to lend support to families with serious illness lies first in having the idea, and second in organizing it into a concrete reality. Some of the most compelling contemporary photographs are of the most ordinary kind of object or setting, so much so that we are tempted to think, "I could have taken that picture." The point is that we didn't. These families point out needs to us, and in retrospect they may seem obvious. While we may not have thought of them, we can see to it that they are met.

MEDICAL LISTENERS

In talking with families who have had to have a great deal to do with the medical community under conditions of enormous stress, one finds a wide range of response, from love and deep appreciation to bitter hostility. One of the difficulties families and medical personnel face is communicating with each other under highly charged conditions. A common block is that the doctors have to tell people what they don't want to hear. In the worst case, when a doctor who does not report bad news well is paired with a family that is used to communicating in oblique and obfuscated messages, there is bound to be trouble.

Even if families and doctors communicate well, the forces of denial are at work. One of the common problems in all communications is that people do not "hear" everything that is said. They are hesitant, if not resistant, about having a non-family member monitoring the conferences. One of their reasons for reluctance is the idea of yet another person to deal with in a life that is already full of such encounters.

Here are two countering suggestions. In the first place, both in workshops for clergy and physicians and in the practice of hospital pastoral care, doctors are more apt to be open to overtures of assistance with families than closed to it. The resistant minority should not deter us from our own tasks of ministry. Second, if it can be shown that the presence of a medical listener in a conference can help the position of the physician by reporting accurately to the family outside the immediate and most threatening circumstance of the interview, it may be welcomed by many.

During a recent hospitalization, recognizing the difficulty people often have in "hearing" what doctors tell them, a member of Perry Fuller's congregation took a small tape recorder with him to the hospital. Whenever the doctors came in to talk, he would indicate that he was taping the conversation. Later he would replay the tape for himself and any family member who wanted to know what the doctor said.

A tape recorder has the advantage of absolute recall. However, there is an additional advantage in having a medical listener accompany the family if they desire it. A family therapist, reflecting on the idea of medical listeners, remarked that it suggested to her the natural desire to have an ally along for security rather than the desire for factual recall of the conversation with the medical team. The advantage the medical listener has over the tape recorder is the human connection. One can have a conversation with the medical listener—something a tape recorder does not provide.

The context of life-threatening illness is a difficult one for everyone involved, including the medical personnel. The medical listener, although posing some difficult and sensitive issues, offers assistance and support to the whole process of communications in the midst of adverse circumstances.

What does the medical listener listen for? We have developed a checklist of material likely to be most helpful to a patient and family. It is an organizational outline that volunteer listeners use to make certain that they have asked all the questions that will be helpful.

First, it is important to hear what the diagnosis means. To hear only the words is not enough. After writing down the diagnosis, it is wise to ask the meaning of all unfamiliar words. Medical personnel tend to use a specialized jargon that must be digested into common, everyday language.

Second, it is helpful to ask about the prognosis. The prognosis tells us what can be expected to happen as the disease progresses. The third consideration involves options for treatment. The physician will probably be proposing one form of treatment. It is important to know not only what that treatment is all about, but also what other treatments might be employed. There may also be a desire for a second opinion. Patients and families need to know about other treatments that have been used and about where to get those treatments or to learn more about them.

The fourth consideration concerns the risks and benefits faced by the patient and family if they choose the recommended treatment. What are the steps for treatment? How long will the patient be in the hospital, in the operating room, in chemotherapy or radiation therapy? What rehabilitation will be necessary and how long will it take? What has been the experience of other patients receiving this treatment? How many people have been treated and what has happened to them?

It is important to retain the option to have no more treatment, but to be provided instead with supportive care. This means that patients can elect to have no further aggressive treatment and ask their caretakers to work with them and their families to make life as enjoyable as possible.

In all treatments there are things we want to happen and things we don't. Any time surgery, chemicals, radiation or other interventions are used, there is a chance that unpleasant things may happen to us. These are the side effects of treatment. It is important for patients and families to understand the things that could happen as a result of the treatment—not just the good things but the uncomfortable things as well. We recognize that not all the things that could happen will, in fact, happen. We have found it helpful to create a three-category description of "very probable," "somewhat probable" and "not likely." The idea is to indicate not only the side effects, but also the probability of the various outcomes.

It is essential to check with the physician to determine whether the treatment is standard or experimental. It is important to find out which procedure will be most efficient if the patient wishes to stop treatment at any time. The patient must understand that all treatment is voluntary.

It is always helpful to have the physician's name, address and telephone number. It is equally helpful to know who to contact if the patient or family is not able to reach the physician. Phone numbers and addresses should be readily available to the family at all times.

SURROGATE RELATIVES

The children of a sick parent or the siblings of a sick child are a group with special needs. Attention is automatically focused on the sick individual. The energy, both psychic and physical, soon begins to wane for doing anything but attending that person. This could leave the children of the family in a difficult spot.

There are dancing lessons to be kept, soccer games to be watched, Saturday matinees to see with friends, school functions in need of an appreciative audience, and so on through the whole long list of activities that make up the life of a young person. If parents are taking care of a sick brother or sister, or if a parent is focused on an ill parent, these things often go unnoticed.

The response to the needs of the well children could come on two levels. One is simply being sure that a reasonably normal activity schedule is kept for the well children. Parents who have children on athletic teams should be sure to pick up the well child on the way to the game or play practice. The child should not have to miss out on basic normal activities.

The big brother/big sister or surrogate relative approach is the second level. This goes a step further than simply being sure that the children keep up their routines. It involves more nurturing and support. Instead of just taking the child to an athletic event, the surrogate could also stay to watch, as a parent or older sibling would, and talk over the game on the way home. Special trips could be arranged to a museum or the zoo, or perhaps an afternoon of fishing, swimming or skiing.

The depth of this relationship can develop as far as both the surrogate and child wish it to. This is one of the helping areas that is always unique. Because children invest almost all of their feelings in their parents, the death of a parent affects a child's total life experience. As a result, the role of the parent surrogate is a challenging but vital one.

Below are some of the insights that we have learned and wish to share with parent surrogates in their training and supervision. The loss of a parent creates profound reactions in children. Among these reactions are the following:

1. denial
2. reversal of affect
3. identification with the parent
4. an intense attachment to the lost parent
5. fantasies of the parent's return
6. idealization of the parent
7. persistent demand to be cared for
8. vindictive rage against the world

9. effort to force the parent to return by suffering
10. self-inflicted repetition of loss via other relationships

We must remember that these children are, in fact, left without a parent and must take whatever adaptive steps are possible in order to cope with the loss. There are at least two phases to this process: (1) the painful acceptance of the loss in reality, and (2) the beginning of losing the love relationship, which has been invested in the parent, and the parent's love relationship invested in the child, which is also painful. This is a process whereby the child's inner-world representations or images of the parent must gradually go through a process of change.

There are at least three major factors that seem to contribute to a child's ability to cope with the parental death. The first is directly related to the level of maturity that the child has achieved and also the child's ability to understand or comprehend the death itself. The second factor is directly related to the child's previous experiences with the loss of a valued object or person. The third contributing factor to good adjustment is directly related to the educational and supportive help given by the surviving parent. This is especially useful when the parent takes time to recognize and be tolerant of the feelings of the child, to hear and accept those feelings.

It is important for the child to be able to face the fact of the death, but of equal importance is the dying and surviving parents' ability to accept the feelings of the child (even though these feelings may differ from those of the parents). It is very important that the home remain stable and that the parent does everything possible to encourage the development of the well child.

A SUPPORTIVE NETWORK OUTSIDE THE HOME

In the case of the impending death of one parent, the surviving parent and the surrogate parent must do everything possible to see that the relationship between the child and the life-threatened parent is a stable one. All these factors—a stable home relationship; a supportive network, such as a church community and friends; and a good relationship with the dying parent before death—can combine to give the child a tolerance for separation and the grief expressions that are to be encouraged afterward.

It is of utmost importance that the child have a realistic concept of death. When we say realistic, we mean a specific, concrete understanding of the death event, such as experienced through the death of a pet or another member of the family. With this background an understanding of the death of a parent is much more realistically conceived.

DEPENDENCY

The child who has been highly dependent upon a parent who is now lost will have a less well developed self-concept and will need more help in differentiating himself from the parent's death. This can cause enormous complexity in dealing with the child's ability to understand death and is further complicated if the child is very young. Therefore, a sense of abandonment will result in the loss of some of the basic aspects of the child's ego-functioning, as well as a narcissistic depletion.

FRIGHTENING EXPERIENCES

It is frightening for a child to realize that death can be even more powerful than the loving parent. In this respect, they feel directly threatened themselves. If the parent, who is so powerful, can be destroyed by death, certainly they, being so much weaker, could be destroyed as well. Some of these children actually consider living on in death as living in a changed circumstance. Their reasoning is characterized by fantasy and magical thinking. Quite often a child is able to articulate that a person is dead and buried, and yet wonder about that person's feelings, whether they are hungry or cold or wet. Many children believe, either consciously or unconsciously, that death is reversible. They may become quite angry at the surviving parent for not reversing the process and returning the dead parent to life.

We must never forget that children often see death as a punishing act. We must be very careful that our words and images do not suggest a threat of punishment. It may not be only in threatening terms that we express it, but that if we inject normal human functions into discussions of death, those functions will become things of which the child will be fearful. For instance, if we suggest that the dead person is only sleeping, we could make a preschool child fearful of sleep.

RELIGIOUS BENEFITS

Although religious beliefs are very comforting to older children and adults, young children may become quite confused by the idea of "heaven," and certainly of "hell," and may be fearful that they are being watched or looked after in everything they do with the threat of death hanging over them. Out of this may develop a feeling of anger at a God who is presented as loving, but who they now perceive as someone who takes away parents and makes others cry, seemingly at will. As these children begin to develop a conscience and feel responsible for the events in their lives, they will need much reassurance that illness and death are not a result of their thoughts, their feelings or their wishes.

In our culture, many adults directly connect death with punishment and bad things that will happen to us as a result of bad conduct in life. It has been suggested that school-age children are much more involved in understanding and mastering the world outside the home than within it. Younger children may identify with death or may attempt to keep death at a distance to allow themselves time to escape from its impact. Death to them is external, frightening and dangerous. Sometimes they will speak of death in terms of the "devil" or the "grim-reaper" or some other personification of a monster, a skeleton, or even a dark angel.

As children approach early adolescence, they begin to search for causes and effects to understand the biology and physiology of human beings. In fact, children over the age of 8 have some comprehension of death and are able to understand some of the explanations of its causes. As these children grow up, they are able to learn a great deal from the cultural rituals associated with death.

Children younger than 8 still generally personify death, but by age 12 they have come to understand that death is permanent and irreversible. The child of 13 or 14 is able to understand the abstract qualities of death and the emotions that are associated with the dying process. Our experience is that symptoms of school refusal or daydreaming, and even moodiness and conflicts with peers and teachers, ought to be recognized as possible signs of children's difficulty in relating to the intellectual content concerning the illness that has intruded into their lives.

TEENS

The older adolescent is able to do some abstract thinking about illness and death, and to understand the process of deterioration, old age and disease. Therefore, older teenagers are much better able to initiate mourning than are young children. They have a real sense of the past and their own history and are able to experience a yearning for the future and even to understand its limitations. Adolescents are certainly able to experience a true sense of loss at the death of a parent.

Sometimes the conflicts built up around normal life patterns are not well tolerated by teens and they respond by acting out. Many teens try to recapture earlier and happier experiences; their basic attitude is that if they don't feel bad, nothing bad has really happened.

On the positive side, our work seems to indicate that most teenagers enjoy being a young adult in the family and respond to an opportunity to help manage a situation no matter how challenging it may be. They are quite capable of assuming responsibility in times of crisis. Surrogates, as parents, need to be careful that they do not place too much of a burden upon teens at any one time. Surrogate parents should make sure that adolescents who are attempting to help their families in times of pressure are also setting aside enough time to maintain the activities that they as teenagers need for themselves. They should not feel guilty for hoping to have a date for the school dance, or lie awake worrying how they can raise the younger brother or sister in case a family member should die.

We found it very helpful to talk with teens to encourage them to identify with their parents' positive aspects. Often they can use abstractions, such as peace or beauty, and understand the function of these symbols much better than do most adults. Young people often make use of religious beliefs to help themselves sustain a sense of universal order in the midst of the chaos they are experiencing.

A thorough understanding of the progressive order of child development can assist us in working with children as they face the death of a significant other. These children have several identifiable needs:

1. To obtain information that is clear and comprehensible at their age level.
2. To feel importantly involved in the process of handling the stress of the death event.
3. To have reassurance about the grief of the adults around them; that it is all right, that this is healthy and normal.
4. To be able to share their own thoughts and feelings and know that these are healthy and appropriate.
5. To maintain their own age-appropriate interests and activities.

The needs children have for opportunities to mourn and to grow in their perceptions of illness and death must always be kept in focus.

In our experience, families felt keenly the needs of their well children and expressed guilt and sadness over the lack of attention they may have had to suffer while the ill person was being tended. Assisting in the nurturance of the well children, as thorny as it may be emotionally for the helper, needs careful consideration in the development of the helping teams.

FINANCIAL ADVISORS

Extensive and prolonged medical treatment of serious illness is enormously costly. Families struggling with the implications of a life-threatening illness have still another burden to add to their overloaded energy reserves. There is an avalanche of paperwork that inevitably accompanies the financial liabilities of illness. One family saved all of their bills, statements, forms and papers; it made a stack nearly two feet high! Every treatment, every test, every service is billed to the family and must be dealt with in relation to the medical plans and insurance companies. Very shortly after treatment commences, these papers begin to arrive. One can imagine arriving home late at night, after a long and emotional day at the hospital, and finding in the mail a stack of bills and forms to be confronted. For many, the reaction is simply to throw them aside in an ever-growing pile for another time, but postponing work on the bills simply adds another element of stress.

It is very important to appraise the needs of each family. There are some people for whom such a task may be therapeutic. Wading into a sheaf of papers can help to objectify what is happening and lend, like liniment, a counter-irritant that masks the more basic pain. For others, having access to someone familiar with accounting and finance, who is also acquainted with medical paperwork and billing, would be most welcome. This person would have to be someone with a sense of discretion and confidentiality. A whole range of services would be needed, from a simple sorting of bills and reimbursement statements to actual financial planning.

The degree of help needed is a matter for the family to decide. It cannot be emphasized enough that the family must be encouraged to be as much in control of their situation as possible, and this includes the amount of help they receive. Catastrophic illness is an out-of-control situation, and the more control that can be fostered in other aspects of the family's life the better. Well-meaning but unwanted help is of little or no value. A helping team in a local congregation exists for the purpose of helping families, not to exercise its need to be helpful.

FINANCIAL ASSISTANCE

Even families who are well-insured soon find that not every cost associated with an illness is covered even by the best of policies. For instance, if out-of-town treatment is indicated, a host of things arise that otherwise would not be included in the family budget.

People who are undergoing chemotherapy often gain and lose several sizes during the treatment and remain at the various levels of weight long enough for clothes with a range of sizes to be necessary. People sensitive about their appearance may also require a wig or toupee.

A congregation should seriously consider establishing an emergency fund for serious illness from which grants may be made to families for unanticipated and unreimbursed costs. I.C. Lewis, in his study of families with leukemic children, found that financial assistance was among the most basic needs (Lewis 1967). The pastor is a key person in determining with the family the availability and extent of financial help. Provision could be made for the fund through special gifts given by members to initiate the fund. Giving could be encouraged during the course of the church year, and, once established, the fund could become a regular part of the church budget.

EXTENDED THOUGHTFULNESS

"Other people were through dealing with this long before I was." So said one person who has successfully recovered from grave surgery. If they are not personally and daily involved with a serious illness, caring people may not be able to sustain constant concern for someone who is ill and not a family member. This is even more of a problem at a group level. It is a lovely, if romantic, notion that truly caring people respond out of instinct and spontaneous motivation to the needs of others. It is not a criticism of the human condition to say that this may not be possible on a large and extended scale. People outside of a situation simply do not have the same stake in it as those who are directly involved. One answer is to start with the care people are willing and able to provide and place it in an ordered, organized setting so that it can be most effective.

In many congregations there are people who cannot be involved in church activities, but who may be able to write notes, send cards and make telephone calls. These people may be recruited along with others who wish to make it their personal ministry. They can see to it that patients and their families have continued evidence of the congregation's support well past the first few weeks of intense interest.

The expression of concern need not be some major effort. People often express their consternation at not knowing what to say. By this is often meant, "What can I say to make things all better for this person?" So far, no such ideal set of words has been discovered. A note that says nothing more than "I am thinking about you today, and you are in my prayers" speaks volumes more than a potentially awkward attempt at reassurance. A contact such as this, two or three times a week, can be very sustaining.

HOUSE AND FRIEND SITTERS

In the early days of an illness, family members may worry about leaving their houses unattended overnight. This may dissipate after the initial anxiety level recedes. Nevertheless, it might be a real concern, depending on location. A team of people who are willing to stay overnight in a family's house that has had to be left vacant can be a source of reassurance. If that is not possible, there may be people who would make it a point to keep a watch on the house.

Some people find it difficult to stay alone, particularly when a loved one is seriously ill in the hospital. Persons who are free to stay overnight with someone who could use this support can be of very practical service. The attended person should not feel the need to entertain this overnight companion as a guest.

HOUSEWORK BRIGADE

Most people have times in their lives when coping with the ordinary matters of everyday living seems a major challenge. When serious illness enters a family's life, routine activities can seem impossible. Much of the help needed by people who have experienced this trauma is of a very practical nature. The congregation's role may be seen as helping to reduce the number and intensity of things that must be attended to, so that the family can have some "breathing space" and can concentrate on some of the more pressing aspects of their situation. We ought not to underestimate the value of simply lightening the load.

Sensitivity to the family's feelings must prevail in all circumstances. Something as basic as housecleaning may be welcomed by some and not others. When it is desired, a time should be arranged at the convenience of the family. The areas to be cleaned should be indicated by the family. For those who obtain this help, it is a pleasure to return to a clean house where they can spend a few moments relaxing without seeing evidence of all there is to be done.

HELPERS WITH PERSONAL EXPERIENCE

It was frequently mentioned by those we interviewed that it would be of great benefit to have people who had dealt with serious illness in their family available to those recently faced with the prospect. There were a variety of suggestions as to how these people could be employed. There could be one such resource person on the committees or teams representing the areas of help the congregation was able to offer. Others felt these persons should just be available in case family members wanted to talk. Still others felt that the more experienced persons could make special contacts with the family independent of any specific assistance the rest of the helping team was carrying out. Perhaps just the knowledge that such people are around and surviving is in itself encouraging for those coming to terms with critical illness. Of course, people with personal experience in their own families would have to indicate the extent of the assistance they were willing to offer.

It would be helpful to encourage the experienced people to avoid saying such things as, "I know just how you feel. That's what we went through." None of us knows precisely how another person feels, even if our experiences have been similar. The family may want to hear how others handled certain situations, but not necessarily how they felt about them. It would not be helpful to give unsolicited descriptions of the various problems that may occur or the modes and results of treatments. People in the circumstances of life-threatening illness are likely to feel that they are being governed by forces beyond their control. Those who seek to help must not allow their aid to become one more thing that is out of control.

REFERENCES

Adams, M.A. Helping the parents of children with malignancy. *J. Pediatrics* 93(5):734-738, 1978.

Aquitera, D.C., and J.M. Messick. *Crisis Intervention: Theory and Methodology.* St. Louis: C.V. Mosby, 1974.

Anderson, M.J. *Help for Families of Stroke Victims.* St. Louis: Concordia, 1981.

Anthony, E.J. The impact of mental and physical illness on family life. *Am. J. Psychiatry* 107(2):138-146, 1970.

Arndt, W.F., and F.W. Gingrich. *A Greek-English Lexicon of The New Testament and Other Early Christian Literature.* Chicago: University of Chicago Press, 1957.

Benjamin, P.Y. Psychological problems following recovery from acute life-threatening illness. *Am. J. Orthopsychiatry* 48(2):284-290, 1978.

Bertalanffy, L. von. *General Systems Theory.* New York: George Braziller, 1968.

Bilodeau, C.B., and T.P. Hackett. Issues raised in a group setting by patients recovering from myocardial infarction. *Am. J. Psychiatry* 128(1):73-78, 1971.

Binger, C.M., et al. Childhood leukemia: emotional impact on patient and family. *N. Engl. J. Med.* 280:7:414-418.

Bunn, T.A., and A.M. Clarke. Crisis intervention: an experimental study in the effects of a brief period of counseling on the anxiety of relatives of seriously injured or ill hospital patients. *Br. J. Med. Psychology* 52:191-195, 1979.

Burton, L. *The Family Life of Sick Children.* Boston: Rutledge & Kegan Paul, 1970.

Cadden, V. Crisis in the Family. In G. Caplan, ed., *Principles of Preventive Psychiatry.* New York: Basic Books, 1964.

Cassem, N.H., and T.P. Hackett. Psychiatric consultation in a coronary care unit. *Ann. Intern. Med.* 75(1):9-14, 1971.

Chodoff, P., S. Friedman, and D.A. Hamburg. Stress, defenses and coping behavior: observations in parents of children with malignant disease. *Am. J. Psychiatry* 120(7):743-749, 1964.

Drotar, D., et al. The adaptation of parents to the birth of an infant with a congenital malformation: a hypothetical model. *Pediatrics* 56(5):710-717, 1975.

Freud, S. A General Introduction to Psychoanalysis. In E. Jones, ed., *The Collected Papers of Sigmund Freud* (The International Psycho-Analytical Library, No. 8). New York: Basic Books, 1959.

Friedman, S.B. Care of the family of the child with cancer. *Pediatrics* 40(3):498-507, 1967.

Goldenberg, I., and H. Goldenberg. *Family Therapy: An Overview.* Monterey, CA: Brooks/Cole, 1980.

Goldson, E. Parents' reactions in the birth of a sick infant. *Children Today,* July-August 1979, pp. 13-17.

Gourevitch, M. A Survey of Family Reactions to Disease and Death in a Family Member. In E.J. Anthony and C. Koupernick, eds., *The Child in His Family.* New York: John Wiley & Sons, 1988.

Haley, J. *Problem-Solving Therapy.* New York: Harper/Colophon Books, 1976.

_____. *Uncommon Therapy: The Psychiatric Techniques of Milton H. Erickson, M.D.* New York: W.W. Norton, 1973.

Hamburg, D.A. Coping behavior in life-threatening circumstances. *Psychother. Psychosomatic Illness* 23:13-25, 1974.

Hill, R. Generic Features of Families Under Stress. In H.J. Parad, ed., *Crisis Intervention.* New York: Family Service Association of America, 1965.

Hoff, L. A. *People in Crisis: Understanding and Helping.* Reading, MA: Addison-Wesley, 1978.

Howells, J.G. *Principles of Family Psychiatry.* New York: Brunner/Mazel, 1975.

Jackson, D.D. Family practice: a comprehensive medical approach. *Comprehensive Psychiatry* 7:338-344, 1956.

Janetkos, J.D. *Psychosocial Needs of the Cancer Patient.* New York: American Cancer Society, 1974.

Johnson, F.L., L.A. Rudolph, and J. Hartman. Helping the family cope with childhood cancer. *J. Psychosomatic Illness* 20(4):241-251, 1979.

Kaplan, D. and J.S. Mearing. A community support system for a family coping with chronic illness. *Rehab. Lit.* 38(3):79-82, 96, 1977.

Klagsbrun, S.C. Communications in the treatment of cancer. *Am. J. Nursing* 71(5):944-948, 1971.

Kübler-Ross, E. *Conjoint Family Therapy.* Palo Alto, CA: Science and Behavior Books, 1967.

_____. Hope and the Dying Patient. In B. Schoenberg et al., eds., *Psychosocial Aspects of Terminal Care.* New York: Columbia University Press, 1972.

_____. *On Death and Dying.* New York: Macmillan, 1969.

Küng, H. *On Being a Christian.* New York: Doubleday, 1976.

Kupst, M.J., and J.L. Schulman. Family Coping with Leukemia in a Child: Initial Reaction. In J.L. Schulman and M.J. Kupst, eds., *The Child with Cancer.* Springfield, IL: Charles C Thomas, 1980.

Kupst, M.J., et al. Family coping with childhood leukemia: one year after diagnosis. *J. Pediatric Psychol.* 7(2):157-174, 1982.

Lewis, I.C. Leukemia in childhood: its effects on the family. *Austral. Pediatric J.* 3:244-247, 1967.

Livsey, C.G. Physical Illness and Family Dynamics. In Z.J. Lipowski, ed., *Advances in Psychosomatic Medicine,* Vol. 8. Basel: S. Karger, 1972.

Lukton, R.C. Crisis theory: review and critique. *Social Service Rev.* 48(3):384-402, 1974.

Maddison, D., and B. Raphael. The Family of the Dying Patient. In B. Schoenberg et al., eds., *Psychosocial Aspects of Terminal Care.* New York: Columbia University Press, 1972.

Mandanes, C. *Strategic Family Therapy.* San Francisco: Jossey-Bass, 1982.

Marston, K. *Communication . . . or "I Want to Tell You What I Don't Want to Say."* Buffalo, NY: Roswell Park Memorial Institute, 1978.

Miller, J.G. *Living Systems.* New York: McGraw-Hill, 1978.

Minuchin, S. *Families and Family Therapy.* Cambridge, MA: Harvard University Press, 1974.

Molter, N.C. Needs of relatives of critically ill patients: a descriptive study. *Heart and Lung* 8(2):332-339, 1979.

Moos, R.H., ed. *Coping with Physical Illness.* New York: Plenum, 1977.

Parkes, C.M. The emotional impact of cancer on patients and their families. *J. Laryngol. Otol.* 89(12):1271-1279, 1975.

Peck, M.S. *The Road Less Traveled.* New York: Simon & Schuster, 1978.

Perrault, C., J. Collinge, and E.W. Outerbridge. Family support in the neonatal intensive care unit. *Dimensions in Health Service* 56(5):16-18, 1979.

Porteus, N.W. Soul. In G.A. Buttrick, ed., *The Interpreter's Dictionary of the Bible,* Vol. 4. New York: Abingdon Press, 1962.

Racker, E. *Transference and Countertransference.* New York: International Universities Press, 1968.

Rabjohn, E.K. Richard. Unpublished paper, 1982.

Rapoport, L. Crisis-oriented short-term casework. *Social Service Rev.* 41(1):31-43, 1967.

Satir, V. *Peoplemaking.* Palo Alto, CA: Science and Behavior Books, 1972.

Satterwhite, B.B. Impact of chronic illness on child and family: an overview based on five surveys with implications for management. *Int. J. Rehab. Res.* 1(1):7-17, 1978.

Scherzer, C.J. *The Church and Healing.* Philadelphia: Westminster Press, 1950.

Schulman, J.L. *Coping with Tragedy: Successfully Facing the Problem of a Seriously Ill Child.* Chicago: Follett, 1976.

Speedling, E.J. Social structure and social behavior in an intensive care unit: patient-family perspectives. *Social Work in Health Care* 6(2):1-22, 1980.

Stewart, C.W. *The Minister as Family Counselor.* Nashville, TN: Abingdon, 1979.

Sullivan, H.S. In H.S. Perry and M.L. Gawel, eds., *The Interpersonal Theory of Psychiatry.* New York: W.W. Norton, 1953.

Tillich, P. *The Courage to Be.* New Haven, CT: Yale University Press, 1952.

_____. *The Meaning of Health.* Richmond, CA: North Atlantic Books, 1981.

Travis, G. *Chronic Illness in Children: Its Impact on Child and Family.* Stanford, CA: Stanford University Press, 1976.

Wellisch, D.K., M. Mosher, and C. van Scoy. Management of family emotion stress: family group therapy in a private oncology practice. *Int. J. Group Psychotherapy* 28(2):225-231, 1978.

Wells, R. Family stroke education. *Stroke* 5(3):393-396, 1974.

Westberg, G. *Congregations in Health Care.* Care Cassettes, The College of Chaplains, 1974.

_____. *The Holistic Accent.* Care Cassettes, The College of Chaplains, 1974.

Whitehead, A.N. *Religion in the Making.* New York: Macmillan, 1957.

Williams, C.C. The intensive care unit: social work intervention with the families of critically ill patients. *Social Work in Health Care* 2(4):391-398, 1977.

Wishnie, H.A., T.P. Hackett, and N. Cassem. Psychological hazards of convalescense following myocardial infarction. *J.A.M.A.* 215(8):1292-1296, 1971.

Wynn, J.C. *Family Therapy in Pastoral Ministery.* New York: Harper & Row, 1981.

13

Self-Help Group Models: An Ecological Conceptualization

Kathryn D. Kramer, PhD and Kermit B. Nash, PhD

This chapter will discuss the conceptualization and design issues surrounding self-help research. Studies in this area are fraught with methodological problems that are not easy to overcome. However, given that anywhere from 6.5 million (Jacobs and Goodman 1987) to 14 million (Lieberman 1986) individuals participate annually in self-help groups, research efforts must continue. What can be gleaned from past research efforts can be applied to present evaluation strategies conducted in both university and community settings.

Despite the growth of self-help groups in recent decades, surprisingly little is known about various group processes and outcomes. In addition, much of the work on self-help and mutual support has been atheoretical (Briscoe 1986). Due to the nature of self-help groups, where members are both the tools for and objects of change, tightly controlled research studies of this phenomenon are almost impossible to achieve. Therefore, methodological problems in the studies on self-help groups abound. In light of this, only a few researchers (e.g., Levy 1976; Lieberman 1986; Rappaport et al. 1985) have embarked on large-scale examinations of self-help groups.

In the process of developing an evaluation strategy for a five-year longitudinal study examining the impact of self-help groups on adults with sickle cell disease (funded by the National Heart, Lung, and Blood Institute of the National Institutes of Health), methodological issues in the self-help literature had to be tackled. A dearth of information was encountered with regard to conceptualization and design. Drawing on the literature in various areas (including medicine, psychology, public health, social work and sociology), a conceptualization of the dynamic, transactional interplay of individual and environmental factors was formulated as were procedures for evaluation.

A TRANSACTIONAL/ECOLOGICAL CONCEPTUAL MODEL

At the core of quality, interpretable and generalizable research findings is a solid theoretical base. Although theories can be data-driven, it is preferable if research designs are theory-driven.

The conceptual model used in the study examining the impact of self-help group participation on adults with sickle cell disease relied on two basic assumptions that were first outlined by Bandura (1977) and then later expanded (1986). First, individual behavior and the environmental context are reciprocal systems, interacting with one another. Second, the interactions are dynamic and transactional. These assumptions also have been documented in the developmental psychology literature (Sameroff 1975).

To examine these processes, a careful multilevel analysis must be undertaken to understand the dynamic interplay between individuals and the environmental context in which they operate (Bronfenbrenner 1977). This type of multilevel analysis can influence the design of interventions and can aid programmatic work (e.g., helping to anticipate and understand the potential impacts of interventions). One can explore (1) individual factors (age, disease severity, social skills); (2) family factors (social support, size, interaction styles) or (3) community factors (availability and accessibility of services such as hospitals or self-help groups, rural versus urban status, funding). These factors interrelate with individual factors to influence physical, psychological, social and behavioral dimensions, which in turn impact on family and community factors—thus, the transactional, dynamic dimensions of the model.

A person with sickle cell disease, for example, may experience severe pain that results in hospitalization. This experience influences and is influenced by a number of factors. The experience of being hospitalized may be influenced by the availability and accessibility of hospital services (community level). Furthermore, children may be affected psychologically when someone in the family is hospitalized (family level). Ultimately, the employer may end up firing the person (community level). This can disrupt family income (family level) and can cause the person to become depressed (individual level). The individual may end up turning to a self-help group for support and guidance (community level).

This example illustrates the complexity of an ecological model where one views the sickle cell disease experience as part of a larger dynamic. From this perspective, one looks beyond the physical, biological level and examines psychological and social factors as well. In researching the impact of self-help groups on adults with sickle cell disease, the ecological model served as the basis for delineating factors to be studied.

This complex theoretical construct can cause even the most sophisticated researchers to take pause. However, it mirrors the real world and is comprehensive. To apply the theory requires a program of research, and not a one-shot approach. The complexity is challenging and expands the approach to research design.

METHODOLOGICAL ISSUES

In self-help group settings, designing interventions and testing impacts are problematic. Self-help groups are naturally occurring, and the intrinsic processes are automatically altered if interventions are implemented. The processes that make self-help groups unique naturally occur when members come together and become the help givers and help receivers, simultaneously being the targets of change and the change agents. Manipulating these processes changes the exact functions one wants to examine and undermines the essential nature of self-help groups.

If testing interventions in self-help settings are deemed inappropriate, this severely limits the ability of researchers to conduct tightly controlled studies where confidence in outcomes is more assured. Herein lies the problem. Experimental designs rely on random assignment to interventions so that judgments can be made regarding cause and effect. Thus, two core methodological problems exist for self-help researchers: an inability to randomly assign and an inability to manipulate interventions. These methodological problems in turn affect external validity—the generalizability of findings.

Since experimental designs are difficult, if not impossible, to implement, researchers turn to quasi-experimental designs. However the major difficulty with quasi-experimental designs revolves around sampling bias. If random selection or assignment cannot occur, one has to study intact groups and individual members. Self-help group members are inherently different from non-members by virtue of their participation in groups, frequently being active in a variety of organizations (Videka-Sherman 1986). In addition, groups will contain more members who are benefiting from participation than those who are not, assuming that those who are not benefiting have dropped out (Levy 1976). Issues regarding sampling bias are not easy to overcome. Thus, quasi-experimental designs pose further difficulties for self-help researchers.

Based on the limitations that have been discussed regarding applications of experimental and quasi-experimental designs in the self-help area, outcome studies on self-help groups are uncertain at best. Scientists have struggled for years to overcome the limitations of design and analysis in the self-help field. It is frequently heard that the current status of self-help literature is similar to the status 20 years ago of psychotherapy literature. Based on these observations, it is evident that one should be extremely cautious in making interpretations from the present body of material on self-help groups.

One solution to the methodological concerns that have been raised would be longitudinal designs and extensive direct observation of group processes and outcomes. Rappaport and colleagues (1985) have come close to achieving this type of design and analysis. However, few researchers have the luxury of time or the finds to conduct such complex studies. Furthermore, many groups would not allow such close scrutiny over a long period of time. Therefore, applications of longitudinal designs and direct observations of self-help groups remain limited.

FORMATIVE RESEARCH STRATEGIES

Based on the previous discussion, researching self-help groups may seem futile. However, many are still committed to research in this area, as the number of self-help groups and of individuals participating in them continues to climb. Currently, little is really known about self-help groups and although experimental and quasi-experimental applications (outcome research) may be limited, much work remains to be done in formative research strategies and descriptive analyses.

Formative research strategies are borrowed from social marketing frameworks and are quite applicable to self-help. Formative research can tell us a great deal about how groups are structured, who attends and how they function. For example, in sickle cell self-help groups, no evaluation was made prior to the present study being conducted through the Psychosocial Research Division of the Duke University Comprehensive Sickle Cell Center. Through formative evaluation we have (1) located approximately 100 sickle cell groups in the United States; (2) determined estimates of total membership; (3) estimated rates of attendance at meetings; (4) collected demographic data on individual members and (5) assessed level of professional involvement.

Formative research and descriptive analyses of this nature can provide the groundwork for correlation and regression analyses. Moreover, following groups longitudinally can provide information about the various dynamic structures of groups and their birth and mortality. Data collection on a national scale can be a cumbersome and costly task. In our study, for example, it took approximately one year and numerous hours, mailings and telephone interviews to locate sickle cell groups throughout the United States. One result of this task has been the formation of a sickle cell mutual help directory (available from the Duke Comprehensive Sickle Cell Center). Furthermore, this task is ongoing, as groups spring up and become defunct on an almost daily basis.

In conclusion, rigorous outcome studies on self-help groups are difficult to achieve. However, much can be gained through formative evaluation strategies. One can use an ecological conceptualization to determine factors to be examined and data can be collected. Correlation and regression analyses can follow. Qualitative data such as this can provide the basis for future studies, as outcome studies and methodological issues continue to be tackled.

Another avenue for data collection is through the groups themselves. Researchers could work as consultants and train group leaders or members to collect historical and archival data on structural variables. This type of collaborative work with self-help groups (where professionals aid the group process and phase out their own involvement over time) is in harmony with the basic philosophy of self-help and could result in data collection that contributes greatly to the knowledge base.

REFERENCES

Bandura, A. *Social Learning Theory*. Englewood Cliffs, NJ: Prentice-Hall, 1977.
_____. *Social Foundations of Thought and Action: A Social Cognitive Theory*. Englewood Cliffs, NJ: Prentice-Hall, 1986.
Briscoe, G. The Psychosocial Impact of Sickle Cell Anemia: A Review. Unpublished manuscript, 1986.
Bronfenbrenner, U. Toward an experimental ecology of human development. *Am. Psychologist* 32:413-531, 1977.
Jacobs, M.K., and G. Goodman. Psychology and Self-Help Groups. Unpublished manuscript, 1987.
Levy, L.H. Self-help groups: types and psychological processes. *J. Appl. Behav. Sci.* 12:310-322, 1976.
Lieberman, M.A. Self-help groups and psychiatry. *Am. Psychiatric Assoc. Ann. Rev.* 5:744-760, 1986.
Rappaport, J., E. Seidman, P. A. Toro et al. Finishing the unfinished business: collaborative research with a mutual help organization. *Social Policy* 15:12-25, 1985.
Sameroff, A. Early influences on development: fact or fancy? *Merill-Palmer Q.* 21:267-293, 1975.
Videka-Sherman, L., and M. Lieberman. The effects of self-help and psychotherapy intervention on child loss: the limits of recovery. *Am. J. Orthopsychiatry* 55(1):70-82, 1985.

Self-Help
Applications

14

Learned Helplessness, Self-Help and AIDS

Leslie M. Thompson, PhD

The concept of learned helplessness, first postulated by Martin E.P. Seligman, has special relevance for victims of AIDS, for their families and friends, and for the self-help personnel who work with AIDS patients. In his initial research, Seligman observed that dogs conditioned to a state of help-lessness would later fail to avoid painful shock even when afforded a ready means of escape. Subsequent studies indicated that human beings also develop conditioned helplessness. In his book *Helplessness: On Depression, Development, and Death* (1975), Seligman discussed the profound and widespread implications of learned helplessness as a possible means of understanding depression and as a major influence on death-related behav-ior. Numerous subsequent studies have modified, refined and challenged this theory, and new studies crop up daily. Researchers now debate the implications of this theory for matters ranging from depression and suicide to group behavior. In this chapter I will call attention to the implications of the learned helplessness theory for self-help groups who deal with life-threatening illness such as AIDS.

In the late 1950s Richter published his series of now-classic papers sug-gesting the possibility that a psychological state—hopelessness—could induce sudden death in wild rats (Richter 1957). This seminal research strongly influenced Seligman, who saw analogies between Richter's research on sudden death and what Seligman himself called conditioned helpless-ness. Operating from this theory, Seligman postulated that "when animals and men learn that their actions are futile and that there is no hope, they become more susceptible to death" (1975, p. 168). Seligman defines helpless-ness as a psychological state that frequently results when events are uncon-trollable.

Seligman first demonstrated this theory in a series of experiments involving dogs. He placed the dogs in a shuttle box with a barrier over which it was possible for them to cross. Seligman observed that when subjected to electric shock, dogs would eventually leap over the barrier in order to escape. On subsequent trials the dog would cross the barrier more quickly until with a few trials it would become very efficient at escaping and would soon learn to avoid shock altogether. Seligman noted that "after about 50 trials the dog becomes nonchalant and stands in front of the barrier; at the onset of the signal for shock it leaps gracefully across and never gets shocked again" (1975, p. 22).

Using the same apparatus for the next part of his experiment, Seligman used dogs who had been conditioned by receiving shock from which they could not escape. At first the reactions of these dogs to shocks were much the same as those of the earlier dogs. They would run around frantically for about 30 seconds, but then to the surprise of Seligman and his fellow researchers, the dogs would simply lie down and softly whine. He further noted, "After one minute of this we turned the shock off; the dog had failed to cross the barrier and had not escaped from shock. On the next trial, the dog did it again; at first it struggled a bit, and then, after a few seconds, it seemed to give up and to accept the shock passively. On all succeeding trials, the dog failed to escape. This is a paradigmatic learned-helplessness finding" (Seligman 1975, p. 22). From these and other experiments Seligman deduced that "when an organism has experienced trauma it cannot control, its motivation to respond in the face of later trauma wanes. Moreover, even if it does respond, and the response succeeds in producing relief, it has trouble learning, perceiving, and believing that the response worked. Finally, its emotional balance is disturbed: depression and anxiety, measured in various ways, predominate" (1975, pp. 22-23).

Seligman observed that "helplessness is a disaster for organisms capable of learning they are helpless. Three types of disruption are caused by uncontrollability in the laboratory: the motivation to respond is sapped, the ability to perceive success is undermined, and emotionality is heightened" (1975, p. 44). In summary, Seligman's theory of helplessness claims that organisms, when exposed to uncontrollable events, learn the futility of responding. Such learning, in fact, undermines the incentive to respond and "produces profound interference with the motivation of instrumental behavior." Seligman further points out:

> It also proactively interferes with learning that responding works when events become controllable, and so produces cognitive distortions. The fear of an organism faced with trauma is reduced if it learns that responding controls trauma; fear persists if the organism remains uncertain about whether trauma is controllable; if the organism learns that trauma is uncontrollable, fear gives way to depression (1975, p. 74).

Seligman's work sparked widespread interest and the next few years witnessed a broad range of studies using rats and subsequently experiments dealing with learned helplessness in human beings (Hiroto and Seligman 1975; Maier and Seligman 1976; Peterson 1982; Roth and Kubal 1975;

Rowland 1977; Tennen, Eller 1977). These and other works extended and verified many aspects of Seligman's original theory, but they also raised some relevant questions that the original theory could not answer. Abramson, Seligman and Teasdale (1978), who published a critique and reformulation of the helplessness model, proposed to address the following three inadequacies of the initial proposition: its failure to provide an adequate explanation as to why lowered self-esteem is a common symptom of depression; its inability to account for the frequently observed phenomenon that depressives commonly make internal attributions for their failures; and its lack of ability to account for the generality of helplessness across situations, or chronicity over time (Munton 1985-86).

To solve these and other problems with the original theory, Abramson and his colleagues turned to attribution theory. This theory describes the set of theoretical principles proposed to account for the way in which individuals draw casual inferences about one another's behavior (Munton 1985-86). In the reformulated model of learned helplessness, Abramson and his coworkers observed that the kinds of casual attributions individuals make for their lack of control over events determine whether or not the individual's self-esteem will be lowered and also the extent to which the individual's symptoms of helplessness and depression will generalize across situations and time (Munton 1985-86).

The reformulated theory attributes and dimensions of internal–external, stable–unstable and global–specific as being crucial to the explanation of helplessness and depression. The internal–external factor deals with the premise of whether an individual believes outcomes are most likely to be influenced by factors within or by external environmental factors. Weiner (1974) identified the stable–unstable dimension as being independent of the internal–external dimension. He further defined this dimension as either a long-lived and recurrent causal factor (stable) or a short-lived and intermittent causal factor (unstable). The global–specific dimension refers to either a wide variety of outcome situations (global) or one particular situation (specific). Peterson and Seligman (1987) assert:

> An internal, stable, and global causal explanation is the most debilitating account of bad events. Characterological self-blame (e.g., 'I'm a wretched and flawed excuse for a human being') is the paradigm case of such an explanation (Janoff-Bulman 1977). To blame one's character for a bad event is to expect future bad events, since one's 'character' by definition is consistent and general. In contrast, an external, unstable, and specific causal explanation (e.g., 'It was a fluke') is the least troublesome interpretation of bad events. To explain a bad event in this way is to minimize one's expectation of future bad events (pp. 240-241).

The reformulated theory of learned helplessness itself has been the subject of extensive research during the past few years (Alloy, Peterson, Abramson and Seligman 1984; Brown and Siegel 1988; Danker-Brown and Baucom

1982; Oakes and Curtis 1982; Tennen, Drum, Gillen and Stanton 1982; Fincham and Cain 1985; Peterson 1985). This work has demonstrated some weaknesses in the reformulated theory, but it has also strengthened and broadened the original hypothesis and has also shown the potential relevance of this theory for many areas of human interaction and psychology aside from depression. Flannery (1986) notes that research on learned helplessness with differing populations, including humans, reveals four common themes: no perceived control or mastery of the environment, no task involvement, disrupted normal routines, and the avoidance of social support.

The more general research on learned helplessness has also involved descriptions of how lay persons describe the concept. Van Kaam (1966) noted that feelings reported by lay persons regarding their experience of helplessness can be described by the following categories: (1) belief in the outcome's uncontrollability, (2) desire to cope with the situation, (3) desire to surrender, (4) loss of self-control, (5) hope for finding a solution, (6) belief in personal inability, (7) desire to escape from the situation, (8) self-anger and (9) anger against external objects (Mikulincer and Caspy 1986).

The growing research in the human population has broadened and intensified the potential factors involved in learned helplessness and has also demonstrated the relevance of this theory to a broad range of conditions and circumstances. This general research has also enhanced the potential linkages between such situations as death and dying, illness, hospitalization and the concept of learned helplessness. Simkin and coworkers demonstrated that learned helplessness can be produced in groups. Flannery (1986) hypothesized that adult children of alcoholics are psychological trauma victims with learned helplessness and that this helplessness can be resolved by utilizing stress management interventions. Wieland and associates (1986) demonstrated the strong possibility of a genetic component of susceptibility to helplessness in rats, a finding particularly important in view of the strong evidence for a genetic transmission of certain varieties of human depressive disorders. Baum and his colleagues (1986) make use of the concept of learned helplessness to demonstrate connections and the processes by which unemployment is translated into psychological, behavioral and physiological changes. In particular their study relates this experience to the loss of control, a concept very prevalent for victims of AIDS.

The applications of research on learned helplessness from animal and human laboratory experiments to research involving human beings outside the laboratory have been fraught with difficulty. In the first place, the necessary restrictions on the kinds of experiments that can be done with humans, inside or outside the laboratory, have limited the range of possible research. Lennerlof (1988) cautions that "it is of course very valuable if we can find mechanisms in the laboratory that help us to understand people's reactions in 'real life.' But there is a risk of believing that the experiences in a laboratory and in real life are similar and have similar effects when we try to study the graver effects of learned helplessness" (p. 215). Lennerlof also notes that many of the studies from real life deal with traumatic events, whereas the general circumstances of so-called normal life may be of far greater long-term importance than single, traumatic events.

In this respect Lennerlof poses the question—raised by numerous other researchers and by the popular press—whether people are made helpless in old-age institutions, in hospitals and in prisons, and whether the unemployed learn helplessness. We must also determine whether the organization of modern society itself fosters helplessness and whether the impact of computerization and automation and the influence of the media also condition people to be passive. And if people learn to be helpless in daily life, what are the consequences of this condition for them and for the society in which they live? Lennerlof notes that serious consequences may result from having to live in a situation in which one cannot control important aspects of his daily life and in which he may have little influence over future events.

The current level of research on learned helplessness will not permit conclusive proof to demonstrate the extent to which this concept operates throughout society. Nor will current research prove beyond a doubt the influence of learned helplessness in death-related situations. Nevertheless, laboratory research, studies with human beings, empirical evidence, feedback from patients, studies by popular writers such as Cousins and Siegel, and numerous other sources demonstrate the significant potential of the concept of learned helplessness for the victims of disease, disfigurement or other trauma, and the self-help workers and allied health professionals who care for these persons. In the balance of this chapter I will discuss the potential importance of learned helplessness for victims of AIDS and for the self-help volunteers and allied personnel who work with these patients. The nature of AIDS itself and the intense public reaction to this disease suggest strong affinities to the concept of learned helplessness for all parties concerned.

Victims of AIDS must undergo a series of dramatic changes that alter their entire concept of self and their perception of the world as a whole. The so-called sick role affords patients certain freedoms from responsibility or expectation, but it also places the patient under powerful physiological and psychological constricting influences and limitations. Under these circumstances the patient must develop new life roles, establish new priorities, rethink relationships and frequently develop a new life style. Of necessity the sick role for persons with a life-threatening illness contributes to an overwhelming sense of powerlessness and loss of control, particularly as the physical onslaughts of the disease progress. The bureaucratization of medical practice in large hospitals, the increasing reliance on technological gadgetry and technical thinking dramatically intensify this sense of powerlessness.

While hospitalized, the victim of a serious illness is in a low power position, subject to the routines of the institution and often ignorant about the nature of the disease and the physical limitations imposed by it. In addition, patients often unwittingly succumb to societal expectations about the disease. In fact, allied health personnel, and friends and loved ones as well, tend to applaud and support those patients who passively submit to institutional routines, who unquestionably follow orders, and who in general make no fuss. There is reason to believe, to the contrary, that so-called "bad patients" who challenge authority, who expect, demand and receive information about their disease, and who in other ways attempt to deal with and control their disease are much better in overcoming the disease or learning to live with it in the event that complete recovery does not occur.

The sense of powerlessness associated with a disease does not end once a patient leaves the hospital. The patient's own attitudes concerning the nature of the disease, social conditioning concerning acceptable behavior for sick people, the natural physical limitations imposed by the disease, and a variety of other factors combine to deny most people the full range of possible alternatives under their new life-threatened condition. These problems are exacerbated for AIDS victims who must deal not only with the deadly ravages of the disease itself, but also with the attendant social stigma and the pervasive fears of this disease that permeate all areas of society.

On the one hand, allied health personnel and self-helpers must realistically apprise the patient of the potential for continued growth and development and the potential for control over one's own life. On the other hand, all parties to the patient's situation must deal with widespread views that AIDS victims are receiving a well-deserved punishment from God, that they are a threat to the life style of the healthy, that they will create a financial disaster for the health care delivery system, that they pose a significant health threat to anyone coming near them and that they are incapable of being productive members of society. Such physical, psychological and social factors can easily produce an overwhelming sense of powerlessness that could ultimately condition AIDS patients and those who work with them to succumb to a sense of helplessness.

In discussing the possible implications of the learned helplessness theory (LHT) for social work practice, J.G. Barber makes an observation equally relevant to all those persons who work with AIDS patients:

> LHT is a psychology of the powerless. It provides an insight into the world of the poor, the oppressed, and the handicapped; indeed, all who are regularly confronted by events beyond their control. For the powerless choice is limited and (by definition) control over valued outcomes resides with someone else. Among the helping professions, social work has always had a unique commitment to marginalized and powerless members of society . . . and for this reason LHT must be seen as an important new practice theory. It is a theory which may prove capable not only of describing but also of mitigating the psychological effects of powerlessness (1986, p. 560).

According to the reformulated learned helplessness theory, aversive, surprising or unusual events elicit an attributional search (Wong and Weiner

1981). Peterson and Seligman (1987) note that "these are exactly the kind of events that produce learned helplessness in and out of the laboratory." As philosopher C.S. Peirce observed, "the purpose of thought is to allay doubt." Suffering from the physical limitations of the disease itself as well as from a socially conditioned sense of unworthiness, it would be very easy for AIDS victims to succumb to a condition of learned helplessness. This situation would not only enhance the likelihood of a death sooner than that predicted by the physiological symptoms of the disease, but one in which the quality of life during the dying process would be unduly impoverished.

Seligman (1977) noted the similarity between learned helplessness and the phenomenon of sudden death, and Peterson and Seligman (1987) underscore Engel's (1971) research, which studied numerous cases of stress-induced death and noted that in many instances the particular stress involved such loss of control as (1) collapse or death of a loved one, (2) acute grief, (3) threatened loss of a loved one, (4) mourning or anniversary of mourning and (5) loss of status and self-esteem. Sklar and Anisman (1979) point out that cancerous tumors grew more rapidly in mice exposed in inescapable shock than in mice exposed to escapable shock or no shock at all. Seligman and Peterson refer to an investigation by Laudenslager and coworkers (1983) that demonstrated that uncontrollable shocks disrupted lymphocyte proliferation in rats to a greater degree than controllable shocks. This research suggests that uncontrollability may lead to illness and death by interfering with the immune system (Jemmott and Locke 1984).

The potential link between uncontrollability and the immune system offers profound implications for AIDS, a disease brought on by an attack on the immune system itself. If, as increasing research evidence suggests, stressful life events such as bereavement, family pressures, financial concerns and other factors lead to increased vulnerability to infection and disease, then people who are already fighting the physical dimensions of AIDS face the additional difficulty of an explanatory style that would further weaken the immune system. Peterson and Seligman (1987) assert:

A pessimistic explanatory style may affect the individual's physiology. By analogy to animal studies (Laudenslager et al., 1983), perhaps helpless people have *less competent immune systems.* Rodin et al. (1985) reported preliminary results from a longitudinal study of immune functioning among the aged. The strongest correlates of immunosuppression were stressful life events and the individuals' sense of no control over these events. Explanatory style of these subjects may further determine the degree to which the efficiency of the immune system is compromised by stress (pp. 258-259).

Health care providers and self-help personnel should always keep in mind that AIDS patients must deal not only with disease, loss, disfigurement or some other significant trauma, but also that these persons—under the worst of circumstances—must adjust to dramatic new life roles and life styles and, in some instances, to a whole new set of priorities. Facing life from a new perspective is no easy matter. Patients find themselves confronting new physiological and psychological circumstances while also involved in a new life drama that often presents dramatically new conditions and scripts from those to which one had been accustomed. Siegel (1986) quotes Dostoyevski as saying: "A new philosophy, a way of life, is not given for nothing. It has to be paid dearly for and only acquired with much patience and great effort" (p. 11). Patience and sacrifice to achieve a new life philosophy do not come easily in a society prone to quick fixes and simplistic solutions to complex problems Without special insight and effort, caregivers and patients alike can easily succumb to a state of helpless frustration and depression.

AIDS victims, like those suffering from cancer, serious disfigurements and certain other diseases, face an additional burden because of the high premium placed on appearances in American society. Abetted by pervasive hedonism, Americans lavish massive attention upon the physical body. To a large extent, the body becomes the visible essence of the individual. Consequently, disfigurement, atrophy, or any other significant alteration in the body can easily lead to dramatic psychological consequences. AIDS is not a pretty disease, and this fact easily leads to lowered self-esteem for patients and diminished support by professional staff and self-help personnel alike.

What, then, can self-help workers and health care providers do to avoid contributing to or inducing learned helplessness in AIDS patients with their special needs? The most obvious thing is to become as familiar as possible with the general characteristics of grief, bereavement, and the other psychological factors that accompany any serious illness or loss. It is equally important for self-help personnel to become familiar with the particular characteristics of AIDS, for ignorance of such matters frequently contributes to the exacerbation rather than the alleviation of the patient's problems. By focusing on AIDS and learned helplessness, I hope to provide a paradigm of the ways that patients, self-helpers and allied health personnel might deal not only with this disease, but with related situations as well.

Even specialists in the field would have difficulty mastering all the intricacies of the concept of learned helplessness, as new research is generated daily. The same might be said about AIDS itself. Nevertheless, a general knowledge of the concept of learned helplessness and of AIDS and its physiological and psychological characteristics can go a long way in permitting self-help personnel to deal more effectively with AIDS patients.

It seems to me that we must become increasingly sensitive to the relationship of the mind and the body in both the physical and the psychological healing processes. Stress, for example, plays a major role in potentiating disease, and stress likewise subverts the healing process. The intense emphasis in the United States on individualism and competition dramatically enhances the level of stress while effectively minimizing the role of compassion and love in caregiving and self-helping. Siegel (1986) points out that "a panel set up by the Association of American Medical Colleges recently concluded that technological specialization is driving out the 'exquisite regard for human needs' essential to a doctor's prime goal, the relief of suffering (p. 57). An undue reliance on technology and bureaucracy enhance stress and likewise foster a deadly sense of helplessness.

Siegel (1986) emphasizes the role that hope and compassion play in healing by underscoring the importance that medical personnel and others often place on statistics. In dealing with people with serious illnesses like AIDS with little likelihood of long-term survival, Siegel truthfully lets each individual know the particular probability of recovery but encourages each person to believe that he or she might be the one to survive. Siegel maintains that patients do not have to behave like statistics, and he further asserts: "I became convinced that statistics rarely alter deeply held beliefs. Numbers can be manipulated to make bias seem like logic. Rather than dwell on statistics, I now concentrate on individual experiences. To change the mind one must often speak to the heart . . . and listen. Beliefs are a matter of faith not logic" (p. 32). Siegel also says, "Physicians must stop letting statistics determine their beliefs. Statistics are important when one is choosing the best therapy for a certain illness, but once that choice is made, they no longer apply to the individual" (p. 39).

The important point here for self-helpers is that they must not only be knowledgeable about the concept of learned helplessness and the nature of the situation of the people with whom they are working, but they must also become keenly aware of the American penchant for relying on science and technology and consequently the squeezing out of the emotional aspects of treatment and help.

The overview above should give some indication of the concept of learned helplessness and its potentially devastating effects on AIDS patients, their families, allied health personnel and self-help workers. I have also briefly pointed out some of the most compelling difficulties faced by AIDS patients. I will now call attention to possible approaches that might be made to permit patients and self-help providers to deal more effectively with AIDS. For the most experienced self-helpers, a major way of countering learned helplessness is to make use of existing research that suggests ways to develop strategies for modifying the causal attributions that people make. Fosterling (1985) identified the following strategies that might be employed by counselors to help modify causal attributions: (1) using *social reinforcement* for appropriate causal ascriptions; (2) using *persuasion* via modeling and group pressure; and (3) introducing *information* that is incompatible with existing attributions. Many of those involved with self-help may lack the expertise, time and knowledge to make full use of such theories, but this work does provide significant insights for those qualified to use it.

Self-help groups inherently recognize the major role played by social support groups. AIDS victims in particular can benefit from such groups, which afford an opportunity for the sharing of anger, frustration, love, hope and other powerful emotions. Such groups provide ample opportunity for touching, caring, listening, empathizing and other hallmarks of effective counseling and self-help. Social support groups can also play a significant role in promoting self-esteem, a well-known antidote to learned helplessness. Seligman has observed:

> I suggest that what produces self-esteem and a sense of competence, and protects against depression, is not only the absolute quality of experience, but the perception that one's own actions controlled the experience. To the degree that uncontrollable events occur, either traumatic or positive, depression will be predisposed and ego strength undermined. To the degree that controllable events occur, a sense of mastery and resistance to depression will result (1975, p. 99).

To be the most effective, self-help support groups should also include systematic and ongoing training and education for all participants. This training could focus on the potentially devastating effects of learned helplessness, the physiological and psychological problems faced by AIDS victims and the unique social stresses induced by this disease. As noted above, stress figures largely in American society, and stress also plays a prominent role in conditioned helplessness. Baum and associates (1986) assert: "Chronic stress appears to be mediated by several psychosocial factors, including social support and coping style" (p. 511). It should also be remembered that increasing evidence indicates that stress may also weaken the immune system itself. Obviously, such stress would literally be deadly for AIDS victims, persons already suffering from immunodeficiency.

There are thousands of books on the market dealing with matters ranging from biofeedback to Far Eastern religions, all of which might have some potential positive impact on developing self-help techniques and approaches. I would, however, like to call attention to a few specific techniques that have proven effective in other areas of counseling and mental health and that hold significant potential for self-help approaches for AIDS patients.

In speaking of the horrendous helplessness felt by suicidal individuals, Rosenthal (1986) calls attention to the following techniques that can help the person regain a feeling of control over his environment: (1) have the suicidal person sign a written contract; (2) do something to manipulate the individual's environment; (3) have the client chart self-defeating thoughts and feelings; (4) examine the individual's ability to express anger in a socially acceptable manner; and (5) give the person the message that additional help is forthcoming. These techniques might prove to be effectively helpful for AIDS patients who are gripped by an overpowering sense of physiological, psychological and social powerlessness. In speaking of the learned helplessness theory for social practice, Barber says that one option might be what Abramson and coworkers (1978) call resignation training. This theory postulates that when a client correctly assumes that an event cannot be controlled, then it becomes important to reduce the aversiveness of the uncontrollable event. This can be achieved by counseling the client to the view that life goes on and that the quality of life need not be irreparably damaged by it. This approach likewise could have significant relevance for AIDS patients, many of whom will eventually die. Use of this technique would permit AIDS patients to come to psychological terms with the nature of their illness while also allowing them to realize that they can have significant control over their attitudes and to a large extent over the quality of their lives and their personal relations with others. Nevertheless, there are limitations to the use of this approach.

Abramson and his colleagues (1978) advocate the concept of "environmental enrichment" to indicate the importance of aiding potentially helpless people in realizing the role they can play in attaining some valued outcomes while avoiding potentially negative ones. Obviously, not all negative outcomes can be eliminated, nor can all positive outcomes be overcome. The AIDS patient can, however, search for potential intervention strategies that would prevent many of the conditioned helpless responses that might ensue from AIDS.

There are obviously many other techniques that might be employed by those involved with self-help, but the suggestions above give some indication of the variety of tested and emerging theories likely to prove beneficial in addressing the psychological and other needs of AIDS patients and support groups who work with them. Perhaps the most important approach, however, is that of creating meaning from adversity. All people long for meaning and for a sense of purpose in life. Unfortunately, the philosophy of many people will not allow them to deal with life's happy moments much less with its difficulties. Dying people have constantly revealed, however, that meaning can be forged from adversity and that even persons suffering from AIDS do not have to give in to hopelessness but can take responsibility for their lives and seek meaning even in trying circumstances. They may even achieve a sense of control over their lives.

Such a possibility can be seen in the life and writing of the Austrian psychiatrist, Viktor Frankl, who spent three terrifying years in a Nazi concentration camp. In his gripping book *Man's Search for Meaning* (1963), Frankl recounts the humiliation and terror that he and other prisoners experienced. Frankl also relates the means by which he and others psychologically survived the brutalizing conditions of the concentration camps. In large measure Frankl attributes his success to his ability to find meaning in his suffering by relating it to his spiritual life. He later developed a psychotherapeutic approach called *logotherapy* to help others develop such an approach to extreme adversity and to life's traumas. Davison and Neale (1986) comment on this approach by noting:

> The task of logotherapy is to restore meaning to the client's life. This is accomplished first by accepting in an empathic way the subjective experience of the client's suffering, rather than conveying the message that suffering is sick and wrong and should therefore not be regarded as normal. The logotherapist then helps the client make some sense out of his or her suffering by placing it within

a larger context, a philosophy of life in which the individual assumes responsibility for his or her existence and for pursuing the values inherent in life. Nietzsche has said, 'He who has a why to live for can bear with almost any how' (p. 216).

While not everyone may possess Frankl's particular ability, there is reason to believe that most people can benefit from his insights and wisdom. This approach, like that of most others dealing with such difficult problems as AIDS, will not permit a simple or painless solution. Developing a philosophy of life and facing adversity are never easy or painless, but they can be done, even by AIDS patients.

I began this chapter by introducing the concept of a learned helplessness, a theory which had its origins in the laboratory and whose most significant early work dealt with dogs and rats. I traced the development, refinement and reformulation of this theory, and I then indicated its movement from the laboratory to the world where each of us live and breathe. The limitations concerning research on human beings and the myriad uncontrollable factors of daily life obviously limit the kind and nature of research that can be conducted on this concept in "real life." Consequently, many scientifically oriented people would cast doubts on the applicability or at least validity of this theory for numerous human interactions. I contend, however, that increasingly sophisticated and widespread research coupled with mounting empirical and other evidence will demonstrate the significant role that learned helplessness plays in society as a whole and the particular relevance of this theory to those persons involved with self-help. Future research will likely demonstrate the important role that attitude, hope, love and old-fashioned compassion play in helping AIDS patients and others develop the positive attitude necessary to enhance their chances for survival and to improve the quality of their life.

Siegel (1986) notes that Carl and Stephanie Matthews-Simonton characterize exceptional patients—those with a survival personality—as follows: "They are generally successful at careers they like, and they remain employed during illness or return to work soon. They are receptive and creative, but sometimes hostile, having strong egos and a sense of their own adequacy. They have a high degree of self-esteem and self-love. They are rarely docile. They retain control of their lives. They are intelligent, with a strong sense of reality" (p. 162). Siegel also notes that psychologist Al Sibert, based on years of research, has concluded that a survivor personality can be learned, although it cannot be "taught" the way algebra or chemistry can. This view gives considerable hope to AIDS patients, for the way in which most people face such traumas merely reflects in exaggerated form the way in which these people encounter the frustrations of daily living. In fact, those persons most afraid to take chances and strike out in new directions under the threat of death seem to be precisely the ones most indecisive about making decisions and taking risks in daily living.

To overcome the possibility of learned helplessness and to encounter the difficulties that confront them, AIDS patients, and those involved in supporting and helping them, must realistically face the circumstances and begin the development of an appropriate, positive philosophy. As Siegel asserts, "Most of us want God to change the external aspects of our lives so we do not have to change internally. We want to be exempt from the responsibility for our own happiness. We often find it easier to resent and suffer in the role of victim than to love, forgive, accept and find inner peace" (p. 176). I have outlined above that an understanding of learned helplessness, an awareness of the circumstances confronted by AIDS victims, and the use of various intervention techniques, psychological approaches and other theories can all play a significant role in improving the quality of life for AIDS victims. I further postulate that compassion, caring, love and the cultivation of a positive life attitude will be equally helpful. I close with a comment from Siegel that has particular relevance to the discussion above and to the physiological and psychological aspects of AIDS: "I am convinced that unconditional love is the most powerful known stimulant of the immune system. If I told patients to raise their blood levels of immune globulins or killer T cells, no one would know how. But if I can teach them to love themselves and others fully, the same changes happen automatically. The truth is: love heals" (p. 181).

REFERENCES

Abramson, L.Y., M.E.P. Seligman, and J. Teasdale. Learned helplessness in humans: critique and reformulation. *J. Abnormal Psychol.* 87:49-74, 1978.

Alloy, L.B., C. Peterson, L.Y. Abramson, and M.E.P. Seligman. Attributional style and the generality of learned helplessness. *J. Personality Social Psychol.* 46: 681-687, 1984.

Barber, J.G. The promise and pitfalls of learned helplessness theory for social work practice. *Br. J. Social Work* 16:557-570, 1986.

Baum, A., F. Fleming, and D.M. Reddy. Unemployment stress: loss of control, reactance and learned helplessness. *Soc. Sci. Med.* 22:509-516, 1986.

Brown, D.B., and J.M. Siegel. Attributions for negative life events and depression: the role of perceived control. *J. Personality Social Psychol.* 54:316-322, 1988.

Danker-Brown, P. and D.H. Baucom. Cognitive influences on the development of learned helplessness. *J. Personality Social Psychol.* 43:793-801, 1982.

Davison, G., and J. Neal. *Abnormal Psychology: An Experimental Clinical Approach.* New York: Wiley, 1986.

Engel, G.L. Sudden and rapid death during psychological stress, folklore or folkwisdom? *Ann. Intern. Med.* 74:771-782, 1971.

Fincham, F.D., and K.M. Cain. Laboratory induced learned helplessness: a critique. *J. Social Clinical Psychol.* 3:228-243, 1985.

Flannery, R.B. The adult children of alcoholics: are they trauma victims with learned helplessness? *J. Social Behav. Personality* 1:497-504, 1986.

Fosterling, F. Attributional retraining: a review. *Psychol. Bull.* 98:495-512, 1985.

Frankl, V. *Man's Search for Meaning.* New York: Washington Square Press, 1963.

Hiroto, D.S., and M.E.P. Seligman. Generality of learned helplessness in man. *J. Personality Social Psychol.* 31:311-327, 1975.

Janoff-Bulman, R. Characterlogical versus behavioral self-blame: inquiries into depression and rape. *J. Personality Social Psychol.* 37:1798-1809, 1977.

Jemmott, J.B., and S.E. Locke. Psychosocial factors, immunologic meditation, and human susceptibility to infectious diseases: how much do we know? *Psychol. Bull.* 95:78-108, 1984.

Laudenslager, M.L., et al. Coping and immunosuppression: inexcapable but not escapable shock suppresses, lymphocyte proliferation. *Science* 221:568-570, 1983.

Lennerlof, L. Learned helplessness at work. *Int. J. Health Serv.* 18:207-224, 1988.

Maier, S.F., and M.E.P. Seligman. Learned helplessness: theory and evidence. *J. Exp. Psychol.* 105:3-46, 1976.

Mikulincer, M., and T. Caspy. The conceptualization of helplessness: II. laboratory correlates of the phenomenoloigical definition of helplessness. *Motiv. Emotion* 10:279-294, 1986.

Munton, A.G. Learned helplessness, attribution theory, and the nature of cognitions: a critical evaluation. *Current Psychol. Res. Rev.* 4:341-346, 1985-86.

Oakes, W.F., and N. Curtis. Learned helplessness: not dependent upon cognitions, attributions, or other such phenomenal experiences. *J. Personality* 50:387-408, 1982.

Peterson, C. Learned helplessness and health psychology. *Health Psychol.* 1:153-168, 1982.

————. Learned helplessness: fundamental issues in theory and research. *J. Social Clin. Psychol.* 3:248-254, 1985.

Peterson, C., and M.E.P. Seligman. Explanatory style and illness. *J. Personality* 55:237-265, 1987.

Richter, C.P. On the phenomenon of sudden death in animals and man. *Psychosom. Med.* 19:191-198, 1957.

Rodin, J., C. Timko, and S. Anderson. The construct of control. In P. Lawton and G. Maddox (eds.), *Annual Review of Gerontology and Geriatrics, Vol. 5.* New York: Springer, 1985.

Roth, S., and L. Kubal. The effects of noncontingent reinforcement on tasks of differing importance: facilitation and learned helplessness effects. *J. Personality Social Psychol.* 32:680-691, 1975.

Rosenthal, H. The learned helplessness syndrome: specific strategies for crisis intervention with the suicidal sufferer. *Emotional First Aid* 3:5-8, 1986.

Rowland, K.F. Environmental events predicting death for the elderly. *Psychol. Bull.* 84:349-372, 1977.

Seligman, M.E.P. *Helplessness: On Depression, Development and Death.* San Francisco: W.H. Freeman, 1975.

Siegel, B.S. *Love, Medicine and Miracles.* New York: Harper & Row, 1986.

Sklar, L.S., and H. Anisman. Stress and coping factors influence tumor growth. *Science* 105:513-551, 1979.

Simkin, K.D., J.P. Lederer, and M.E.P. Seligman. Learned helplessness in groups. *Behav. Res. Theory* 21:613-622, 1983.

Tennen, H., P.E. Drum, R. Gillen, and A. Stanton. Learned helplessness and the detection of contingency: a direct test. *J. Personality,* 50:426-442, 1982.

Tennen, H., and S.J. Eller. Attributional components of learned helplessness and facilitation. *J. Personality Social Psychol.* 35:265-271, 1977.

Trotter, R.J. Stop blaming yourself: how you explain unfortunate events to yourself may influence your achievements as well as your health. *Psychology Today* 21:31-39, 1987.

Van Kaam, A.L. *Existential Foundation of Psychology.* Pittsburgh: Duquesne University Press, 1966.

Weiner, B. (ed.). *Achievement Motivation and Attribution Theory.* Morristown, NJ: General Learning Press, 1974.

Wieland, S., J.L. Boren, P.F. Consroe, and A. Masters. Stock differences in the susceptibility of rats to learned helplessness training. *Life Sciences* 39:937-944, 1986.

Wong, P.T.P., and B. Weiner. When people ask "why" questions, and the heuristics of attribution research. *J. Personality Social Psychol.* 40:649-663, 1981.

15

Self-Help, Social Networks and Social Adaptation in Lupus

Carl A. Maida, PhD, Alfred H. Katz, DSW, Gayle Strauss, EdD and Cecelia Kwa, MB, BS, MPH

This chapter reports on a pilot study of sociopsychological problems and adaptations of patients suffering from a rather common and serious but little-studied chronic disease—systemic lupus erythematosus (SLE), usually referred to simply as lupus. The overall goals of the study were (1) to investigate the "natural history" of SLE from perspective of the effects of its biomedical processes upon sociopsychological problems and coping strategies to meet them; (2) to study the effects of peer self-help support groups of patients' perceptions of, and coping behavior around, problems related to the illness; and (3) to compare this group using lay or self-care resources with controls from a teaching hospital rheumatology clinic and a population of chronic renal patients who use the continuous ambulatory peritoneal dialysis (CAPD) technique.

THE DISEASE

Systemic lupus erythometosus is estimated to affect more than 500,000 people in the United States (Phillips 1984). A chronic, inflammatory, autoimmune disease of unknown etiology, it damages the connective tissues and can affect any organ of the body. People with SLE develop blood-cell abnormalities, including overproduction of the antibodies that normally help pro-

This study was supported by grants from the Kroc Foundation and the Spencer Foundation. We would like to thank the following people for their support and assistance during various stages of the research: Sally Gardner, Norman Cousins, Bevra Hahn, Kenneth Kalunian, Suzanne Westman, Rima Rackauskas, Ingrid McReynolds, Julie Copon, Cathy Friedman and Ella Pennington.

tect the body against infectious environmental bacteria and viruses. In the absence of environmental infectious agents, these antibodies attack the body's own healthy cells, setting off an allergy-like reaction. In effect, the body's immune system turns against the body itself, attacking and sometimes destroying bodily tissue (Dubois 1976).

Lupus occurs in all races and ethnic groups and is more prevalent than such diseases as muscular dystrophy, cystic fibrosis and multiple sclerosis. It is far more common in women than men, with women representing 80 to 90 percent of known cases. Typically, the onset of the disease occurs during the childbearing years, from ages 15 to 40. More than 55,000 new cases are diagnosed annually in the United States, and approximately 6,000 lupus-related deaths occur each year (Dubois 1976).

SLE attacks body systems and can damage or destroy internal organs. Like arthritis, it causes swelling and inflammation of muscles and joints. It most commonly affects the kidneys, but may involve the heart, lungs, central nervous system, liver, or other organs or systems. Patients experience extreme fatique, lose hair, develop mouth sores and run a low-grade fever. Swelling of hands and feet, joint pains, and sensitivity to the sun, heat and cold are also common.

To date no cause of SLE has been established. Because there is no single pattern of onset and no single set of symptoms, the diagnosis of SLE may take several years. The difficulty of definitive diagnosis occurs because early indications may be vague and diffuse and often simulate syndromes of other diseases. Recently, an updated list of 11 criteria has been established for diagnosing SLE. The list includes both blood test results and physical symptoms. If a patient has four or more of the signs and symptoms on the list, a diagnosis of lupus is made (Phillips 1984).

The symptoms and course of lupus are unpredictable and erratic, and the severity of its manifestations varies widely over time. This "vicious circle" can make lupus life-threatening and can prevent its victims from achieving relatively normal modes of life.

SLE usually creates profound psychosocial stresses for its victims. The uncertainty and chronic stress with which most SLE patients live create periodic "flare-ups" of the disease and is a factor in their symptomatic discomfort. Frequent physical pain can result in severe fatigue, interrupted sleep and inability to perform the usual activities of daily living. The conventional medications—usually corticosteroids—relieve pain but often produce distressing physiological and emotional side-effects.

Psychosocial Aspects and Prognosis

SLE is a serious and presently incurable chronic illness. The prognosis is usually guarded and uncertain. State of mind, emotional stress and immunological factors seem to be closely linked in the disease process (Blumenfield 1978). SLE patients frequently have psychological or technically psychiatric symptoms. As in other chronic conditions, depression is a pervasive accompaniment of SLE. The steroid medications used in its treatment may also have depressive effects.

SLE may produce some specific neuropsychiatric manifestations (Rogers 1983). Damage to nerve cells in the brain can occur. Possible consequences of such damage include psychosis, cerebrovascular accidents, seizures and organic brain syndrome.

BACKGROUND OF THE STUDY

To indicate the conceptual background of this study, we will briefly comment on the relevant literature and the nature of the sociopsychological issues in chronic illness. Recent studies have addressed the role of socioenvironmental factors, such as stress and social support, in both heightening vulnerability and enhancing resistance and recovery in chronic illness. The critical short-term psychological and social consequences of chronic illness have received some research attention, but the longer-term, everyday reactions and problems of adjustment are less well studied and understood.

Studies of immediate psychological reactions that occur when a particular chronic illness has been diagnosed are abundant in the literature of the past 20 years. Much of the conceptualization of these studies reflects a crisis-theory orientation. From this standpoint, patient and family-member perceptions and fears regarding the illness, treatment regimens and prognosis, and their concerns to provide for medical care and other material problems are viewed as temporary reactions that disturb psychological homeostasis. Based on Selye's classical stress paradigm, patient/family responses to chronic illness are analyzed in terms of the processes of perception of threat, resource mobilization to meet it, and the diminution of the presenting crisis through adaptive behavior.

Only a few researchers have attended to the longer-term issues that arise once the immediate crisis has passed. These are issues of patient and family adaptation to changed circumstances and necessary changes in social roles and family organization; the patient's needed life-style alterations, including daily regimen and habits; and social interactions, including vocational activity. These longer-term sociopsychological consequences of chronic illness, taken together with the somatic factors, may be combined to give an account of the "natural history" of a given illness in its significance for those affected. Examples of such an analytic approach are found in Davis (1963) on parental reactions and adaptation to the occurrence of polio in a child. Similar but less extensive studies projecting a "natural history" for patients with muscular dystrophy and cerebral palsy are contained in the volume by Marinelli and Dell Orto (1977).

The conceptual and methodological approaches that underlie our research program have been piloted in previous studies of psychosocial factors in specific chronic diseases carried out by the investigators: end-stage renal disease (Katz 1970), hemophilia (Katz 1971), hypertension (Maida 1985) and CAPD for chronic renal disease (Nissenson et al. 1986).

The psychosocial aspects of most of these chronic disorders had been little studied previously, and the cited study reports include recommendations about needed services and pertinent psychosocial interventions, such as the differential effects on the coping strategies employed by patients at lower socioeconomic levels; the roles of vocational rehabilitation, public health and voluntary agencies in assisting chronically ill patients; and issues of genetic and family involvement.

Many writers have noted that in contrast to acute or short-term illnesses, chronic diseases significantly alter everyday behavior. Levietes (1974) states that the primary problem and requirement in chronic illness behavior is adjustment: the patient must adapt life style and daily functioning to a less-than-normal health status. Among the ensuing health and social problems are the management of medical crises and regimens, the control of symptoms including pain, the reordering of time, the management of social isolation, the processes of "normalization," the often changed relationships with family members and vocational status. For adaptation to be accomplished, psychosocial strategies to meet these problems must be continually worked on, tested and modified. Some recent studies of patient adaptation suggest how psychosocial strategies can facilitate the recovery process.

Taylor and his coworkers (1985) measured the impact of treadmill activity and explanatory medical counseling on perceptions of their physical and cardiac capabilities by noncomplicated post-infarction patients. The data indicated that patients' perceptions of their physical and cardiac capability were positively related to the workload and peak heart rates they were able to attain on their initial treadmill test; the higher they performed on the treadmill, the more they raised their perceptions of their capabilities. Wives who judged that their husbands had a robust heart were more likely to encourage them to resume an active life than were spouses who believed the heart was impaired and vulnerable to further damage. The investigators found that spousal encouragement during the recovery period may be a key mediator and predictor of a patient's level of cardiovascular functioning. Similarly, Lorig and his colleagues (1987) presented evidence for the significant role of perceived self-efficacy in mediating adaptive health outcomes in chronic arthritis.

Maida's study (1985) of mutual support groups for cardiovascular disease patients in a low-income urban community found that such intervention with recently diagnosed patients increased their understanding of the disease and its treatment, as well as their own responsibilities for health maintenance. The mutual aid groups provided a setting for participants who were experiencing treatment-related stress to discuss their problems and learn new forms of coping. Patients in these groups often did not have the spousal support that Taylor and coworkers found to be a key to treatment adherence and optimal outcome. The groups, however, placed these chronically ill patients in a network of peers where sustained communication and problem solving evolved and treatment and recovery were facilitated.

A study by Maida and his associates (1991) on social and psychological factors in the adaptation of dialysis patients found that patients on the self-care modality (CAPD) showed fewer problems in their general psychosocial adaptation than did hemodialysis patients. The CAPD patients indicated less disease/treatment stress on members of their intimate social networks and better relationships with physicians, nurses and their peers in the program. CAPD patients likewise showed lower levels of emotional distress and less distress from physical symptoms and the treatment regimen that hemodialysis patients. These findings point to the importance of mode and quality of life factors in treatment adherence and rehabilitation.

THE RESEARCH STUDY

In our study, we obtained demographic information and psychosocial measures on 41 SLE patients, a study group of 21 and a control group of 20. The subjects were recruited through the Rheumatology Division of the UCLA Department of Medicine and the local chapter of the Lupus Foundation of America, a self-help group. In-depth interviews were conducted with subjects and controls who met our eligibility requirements, including recent diagnosis (less than 24 months), willingness to participate in initial and follow-up interviews, a test battery and weekly or bi-weekly self-help group sessions (the experimental group). The test battery is discussed below.

The psychological status instruments used in the study were the Profile of Mood States (POMS), the Multidimensional Health Locus of Control (MHLOC) and the Antonovsky Sense of Coherence Scale.

The Profile of Mood Status is a 65-adjective self-report checklist of frequency of experienced feelings in the previous 7 days. POMS has subscales of tension/anxiety, depression, anger, fatigue, confusion/bewilderment and vigor. Scoring procedures and reference group norms are available. POMS has previously been used in research on medically ill patient groups (McNair, Lorr and Droppleman 1981).

The Multidimensional Health Locus of Control is an 18-item scale composed of three six-item subscales of internality, chance externality and powerful other dimensions. Extensive reliability and validity testing of the MHLOC has been reported (Wallston and Wallston 1981).

The Sense of Coherence Scale is a 35-item scale that assesses subjects' understanding of and reactions to their illness along dimensions of comprehensibility, manageability, meaningfulness and a global sense of coherence. The instrument has been tested for internal consistency, reliability and validity (Antonovsky 1984, 1987).

The social status instruments used were the Myers Social Resources and Social Supports Measure and portions of the interview questionnaire.

The Social Resources and Social Supports Measure provides information about the size and density of the subject's social network, the kinds of support exchanged with members of the network and the subject's satisfaction with these relationships. The instrument describes the subject's life space from a structural as well as a functional perspective. Other measures of social network have been limited by an emphasis on structural variables, such as network size and density. The Myers instrument measures structural features within a framework of behavioral expectations, perceived satisfaction and perceived reciprocity between the subject and the significant others within the network (Myers 1981).

Additionally, there was a semi-structured, open-ended questionnaire designed for this study and filled out by research staff in an interview session. The Social Adaptation and Psychosocial Coping Questionnaire covered eight areas of patient coping: (1) medical aspects of the illness, (2) social supports available, (3) advice to others, (4) summation of feelings, (5) well-being (6) relations with others, (7) perceived changes in the course of the illness, and (8) hope and optimism.

Psychosocial adaptation was therefore assessed in two ways: by a semi-structured interview and by psychosocial assessment scales. Detailed responses to the semi-structured interview were recorded in writing by the interviewers. These interviews were then read and scored separately by four raters—a physician, a medical anthropologist, an educational psychologist and a professor of public health. A global score was given of 3 for good adaptation, 2 for good adaptation with some problem areas, and 1 for poor adaptation. In 61 percent of the cases the four raters assigned the same score, and in the remaining cases three of the four raters agreed. The scores given by each rater were summed with patients having scores ranging from 4 to 12. The mean score for 39 subjects was 9.31 (SD = 2.8), indicating a high level of adaptation to the illness. Pearson correlation coefficients were calculated between the adaptation score derived from the interviews and selected subscales of the other research instruments.

Profile of Mood States

	r	p
Tension Anxiety Scale	−0.3	n.s.
Depression Scale	−0.4	<0.01
Anger-Hostility Scale	−0.34	<0.05
Vigor Scale	0.22	n.s.
Fatigue Scale	−0.50	<0.005
Confusion Scale	−0.54	<0.005

Good adaptation correlated negatively with depression ($p<0.01$) and anger ($p<0.05$) as well as fatigue and confusion ($p<0.005$). Thus the Profile of Mood States and the results of the semi-structured interview were consistent with each other.

Myers Social Support Scale

	r	*p*
Emotional Support	0.39	<0.05
Reciprocity	0.41	<0.01
Specific Help	0.33	<0.05
Socializing	0.33	<0.05
Praise/Criticism	0.15	n.s.
Advice	0.31	n.s.
Unidimensionalities	−0.02	n.s.
Multidimensional Ties	0.12	n.s.
(N = 39)		

Locus of Control

	r	*p*
Internal	0.34	<0.05
Chance	−0.07	n.s.
Powerful Others	0.03	n.s.
(N = 39)		

Good social adaptation correlated highly with emotional support, specific help, socializing and internal locus of control. The questionnaire correlated very highly with reciprocity in social relations as measured by the sociometric scale.

Antonovsky Sense of Coherence

	r	*p*
Manageability	0.45	<0.005
Meaningfulness	0.51	<0.001
Coherence	0.49	<0.005

The Social Adaptation and Psychosocial Coping Questionnaire correlated very highly with the clinical ratings of adaptation, suggesting that success in dealing with the areas of the interview questionnaire goes along with a sense of the illness and environment being manageable, having meaning to the patient, and with a sense of coherence. Taken together the qualitative clinical data gathered in the interview correlate strongly with more objective measures that have known psychometric properties.

RESULTS

Summarizing the data obtained through the psychosocial battery and detailed interviews with subjects in both the experimental and control groups, we may construct a profile of SLE patients in our sample, bearing in mind that the experimental group embodied a rather high socioeconomic level in terms both of income and education (see Table 1).

They are predominantly women of reproductive age. Their illness had taken a long time to diagnose definitively—a mean of 4.3 years since medical care was first sought. Their mean age at the time of study was 37 years. While a sizable percentage had never been married, the majority had been. However, 20 percent of those in marriage and in stable partnerships were

Table 1.

Demographic Characteristics of Lupus Patients

	Lupus Experimental Group (N = 21)	Lupus Control Group (N = 20)
Age:		
19–24	1	4
25–29	5	4
30–34	3	4
35–39	4	3
40–44	3	1
45–49	2	2
50–59	2	2
60–69	1	0
Mean	37.09	35.05
Education Level:		
graduated high school	6 (26%)	8 (40%)
some college	9 (42%)	5 (25%)
college degree	2 (11%)	5 (25%)
graduate work	4 (21%)	2 (10%)
Ethnicity:		
Caucasian	12 (57%)	12 (60%)
Black	4 (19%)	3 (15%)
Hispanic	4 (19%)	2 (10%)
Asian	1 (.5%)	3 (15%)
Marital Status:		
married	8 (38%)	10 (50%)
widowed		
divorced	4 (19%)	5 (25%)
separated		
never married	9 (43%)	5 (25%)
Number of Children:		
0	9 (42%)	10 (50%)
1–3	11 (58%)	10 (50%)
Income:		
less than $10,000	5 (24%)	
$10,000–25,000	8 (38%)	n.a.
over $25,000	8 (38%)	
Employed at time of interview:		
yes	14 (66%)	
no	7 (33%)	n.a.

divorced or separated after the onset of their illness; these breakups were usually attributed by patients to the stress of the disease.

Results from Psychosocial Instruments

Table 2 shows the results on the three subscales and the global coherence scores of the Antonovsky Sense of Coherence Scale. There were no statistically significant group differences; however, the experimental group scored slightly lower on all three subscales than did the control group and our previously studied CAPD patients. Their overall coherence score was thus lower than that of both the latter groups, and of a normal population (N = 311).

Table 2.

Data from the Antonovsky Sense of Coherence Scale

Means	Lupus Experimental Group (N = 21)	Lupus Control Group (N = 20)	CAPD (N = 16)	Norms
Comprehensibility	18.24	19.50	20.2	20.94
Manageability	18.42	18.75	18.9	18.25
Meaningfulness	14.90	16.75	16.6	15.23
Sense of Coherence	51.57	55.00	55.8	54.42

Table 3 shows the results on the three subscales of the Multidimensional Health Locus of Control. Although there were no statistically significant group differences, the experimental subjects scored lower than the control group and the CAPD patients on powerful other externality. This may be related in part to their differential pattern of coping with illness, namely through greater reliance on lay resources and participating in the self-help discussion groups. There were only slight differences between all three chronically ill patient groups and the norms for healthy adults (N = 1287).

Table 3.

Data from the Multidimensional Health Locus of Control Scales

Means	Lupus Experimental Group (N = 21)	Lupus Control Group (N = 20)	CAPD (N = 16)	Norms: Healthy Adults (N = 1287)
Internal	25.80	25.05	27.06	25.55
Chance	18.04	18.10	17.68	16.21
Powerful Others	20.95	23.20	25.87	19.16

Table 4 shows the group mean POMS subscale scores for the two groups of lupus patients and the CAPD subjects. The experimental group mean scores were higher than the controls on all five of the negative mood POMS subscales, and higher than the CAPD subjects on four of these subscales.

The mean POMS subscale scores of all three chronically ill patient groups were within one standard deviation of the group mean scores of the college student reference group (N = 856) on all six subscales. POMS did not appear sensitive enough to reveal indicators of psychopathology that had been disclosed in our initial interviews with lupus patients in the experimental group, who reported a higher proportion of central nervous system symptoms (22 percent) and behavioral problems (40 percent) than previously reported in the literature. Depression occurred in 58 percent of them. It was associated with delays in diagnosis, sociopsychological stresses and the medications prescribed; 26 percent of the patients had experienced seizure disorders or neuropathies. Including depression and headaches, fully 73 percent of the patients thus experienced neuropsychiatric disorders, and 30 percent were currently taking medications prescribed for them.

Table 4.

Data from the Profile of Mood States

T Scores*	Lupus Experimental Group (N = 21)	Lupus Control Group (N = 20)	CAPD (N = 16)
Tension/Anxiety	52	48	47
Depression-Rejection	55	47	48
Anger-Hostility	56	51	49
Vigor	46	49	46
Fatigue	57	52	49
Confusion	50	46	39

*T score:
  Mean = 50
  SD = 10

This inconsistency of findings may reflect both the inadequacies of the POMS instrument as a tool for assessing a chronically ill patient population and the circumstances under which the instrument was administered (i.e., the subjects' expectations about responses the interviewers might prefer to receive).

Regarding the small but apparent differences between the lupus (experimental and control) and CAPD groups on Tables 2, 3 and 4, we may speculate that the differences in mood state, locus of control and sense of coherence arise from the CAPD patients' having to perform a daily, specific self-care regimen to assure their survival. In contrast, the lupus patients have no regular physical act of self-regulation or self-care to perform.

Table 5 shows the results of the social support variables. The experimental and control lupus groups were similar in their patterns of relationships, the satisfactions with the support they received from significant others and the reciprocity within their networks. There were statistically significant differences in the structural characteristics of the social networks, as indicated by the mean number of available supports and, consequently, the dimensionality and density of the networks. This may be the results of the experimental group members' participation in the regular self-help group sessions, which served as a medium for instrumental and affective support. The experimental group and the CAPD patients were similar in support network size, dimensionality and density. The lupus patients, however, attached greater importance to the forms of support received from significant others and reported greater satisfaction with all forms of support received from those in their networks than did chronically ill patients in the CAPD comparison group.

Table 5.

Data from the Myers Social Resources and Social Supports Measure

Means	Lupus Experimental Group (N = 21)	Lupus Control Group (N = 20)	CAPD (N = 16)
Number of Available Supports	13.3	9.9*	11.2
Pattern of Relations:[1]			
spouse	0.5	0.5	0.4
nuclear family	3.8	3.4	3.2
relative	0.7	0.4	0.9
in-law	0.6	0.4	0.4
medical	0.2	0.3	0.2
all other	1.6	0.4	2.2
Dimensionality of the Network:			
unidimensional ties	3.2	1.6*	3.6
multidimensinal ties	10.1	8.3	7.6
Satisfaction with Support:			
advice	15.1	15.9	11.5
praise/criticism	15.1	14.2	11.2
socializing	15.1	14.3	13.2
specific help	17.0	17.9	15.0
emotional support	18.2	18.8	14.9
Network Density	6.2	3.8*	5.4
Reciprocity	− 0.05	0.5	0.8

*p < 0.05.
[1]May not add up to 100 percent because a person may be a member of more than one category.

Results from Interviews

In contrast to reports concerning other chronic diseases, initial reactions to the diagnosis of lupus in our patients were of relief rather than shock or fear. The relief expressed is understandable when it is realized that these women went through an average 4.3-year period in their lives in which they experienced self-doubts about their symptoms and were often told by physicians that they were neurotic and hypochrondriacal.

PROBLEMS OF LIVING

More than 50 percent of patients reported a decrease in their social activities. This was most frequently attributed to fatigue, but changes in physical appearance such as dermatitis and weight gain were cited as associated problems. Life-style changes involved protection from the sun's ultraviolet rays, including the use of sun screen, hats and long-sleeved clothing, and refraining from excessive exposure. Changes in dietary habits were common; cooking less and eating more fast foods were also reported. Subjects' abilities to carry out household tasks were restricted; these included vacuuming, cleaning floors and ironing. For some subjects, just getting out of bed was occasionally difficult; others reported physical difficulties including sitting or standing, opening a toothpaste tube, buttoning a blouse, participating in a child's baseball practice and going on a family picnic.

VOCATIONAL ACTIVITIES

Twenty-five percent of the patients had to accept full work incapacitation as a result of their illness. Another 25 percent were forced to interrupt school or find a less stressful job.

RELATIONSHIPS

About 20 percent of the study group reported that their partnerships (marriages or long-term unions) dissolved within 6 months of the initial diagnosis of SLE. Neither financial reasons nor tensions concerning having children were cited as factors, but spousal disbelief in the illness was frequently mentioned. In fact, many lupus patients look healthy and appear to be well. Some patients expressed a good deal of anger about their partner's insensitivity to their true situation. Other frequently cited sources of tension were the male partner's inability to change his conceptions of marriage or to provide emotional support after the diagnosis. Spouses were reported to resent lack of nurturing by the incapacitated partner, or not understanding why the patients could not engage in normal social activities. Black and Latino partnerships seemed particularly vulnerable, perhaps because of a greater adherence to traditional spousal roles than was observed among their Anglo counterparts. Almost all respondents noted a decrease in sexual activities and cited this as a cause of strain in their relationships. Single women reported that their depression, lethargy and self-perceived unattractiveness kept them from dating, let alone seeking sexual intimacy.

Social Support

The reported changes in relationships of the patients and family, partners and friends are summarized in Table 6. In the experimental group, 42 percent of the patients talk to their friends when they have a problem, as compared to 30 percent in the control group. Of the patients in the experimental group, 15.8 percent talk to their husbands when they have a problem, while 40 percent in the control group do so. Of the experimental group, 42 percent will talk to other family members—mother, sister, brother, daughter or other close relatives. However, about one-half of these expressed reluctance to share their problems, not wanting to burden or upset their family members. In the control group, 40 percent mentioned a family member as someone they would talk to.

Table 6.

Patients in Experimental and Control Groups
Who Reported Changes in Their Relationships

	Lupus Experimental Group (N = 19)	Lupus Control Group (N = 20)
Family:		
no change	18.8%	63.2%
negative change	12.5	15.8
positive change	68.8	21.1
Friends:		
no change	27.8	68.4
negative change	44.4	15.8
positive change	27.7	15.8
Partner:		
no change	13.3	46.2
negative change*	53.3	38.5
positive change†	33.4	15.4
Sexual feeling and activity		
no change	29.4	92.8
decrease	70.5	7.2

*Negative changes include worsening or severed relationships.
†Positive changes include closer or more supportive relationships.

In the experimental group, 11 percent of the patients have no one to talk to, as compared with 5 percent in the control group. Only 1 and 5 percent of the patients in the experimental group and control groups would talk to their physician or psychiatrist.

In both the experimental and control group, nearly all the patients feel that the persons to whom they talk are helpful. However, most of them still look for additional support (77.1 percent in the experimental group and 63 percent in the control group). Those looking for additional support nearly all want to join a support group with persons having similar problems.

When patients from both groups were asked what things they need most from people close to them, the majority expressed a need for "understanding." Other responses included love, support, nonjudgmental and positive attitude, help with daily activities and allowing patients to set their own limits.

Hope and Optimism

Over 60 percent of patients were very or moderately positive about their future, 20 percent could not forecast it, and 18 percent expressed little hope. The latter group all had major organ involvements and were severely depressed. One-third of the respondents reported relief through escape behavior such as increased reading, television viewing or listening to music. Twenty-five percent sought more social interactions, but an equal number were passive in this regard.

THE SELF-HELP INTERVENTION

Groups were set up in two locations, consisting of both study subjects and other lupus patients. The latter, who did not meet the formal criterion of recent diagnosis, were included to add experience and variety to the groups. The groups met regularly for 8 months. Table 7 summarizes data on participant characteristics.

In order to record, assess and compare the general character, contents and degree of participation of group sessions, an instrument was devised for completion by research observers after individual group sessions. The instrument has five parts:

1. Characterization of session as a whole, with subcategories for "flow of discussion" (easy or difficult start-up, continuous or halting) proportions of "small" talk and "significant" content; breadth of participation; mood at end of session ("involved, indifferent, antagonistic").
2. Description of three significant exchanges during the session: emotional weighing, reception by group, identity of and effect on initiator.

3. Types of social support occurring in session: advice, praise/
   criticism, help with specific issue or problem, emotional empathy,
   socialization.
4. Checklist of 15 content themes ranging from illness etiology and
   symptoms to significant others, work and aspirations; including
   checks for extent of theme discussion and positive or negative references.
5. Observer's comments about session as compared to others, and
   additional observations.

Table 7.
Summary of Data on Participant Characteristics

	Group A	Group B
Number Initially Participating	24	18
Sex	22 female 2 male	18 female
Age Range	25–60 years	24–42
Ethnicity	16 Caucasian 5 Black 3 Hispanic	17 Caucasian 1 Hispanic
Marital Status	4 married 20 single, 　separated or 　divorced	11 married 9 single 　separated or 　divorced
Employment Status	16 full-time	12 working
Residence	Urban	Suburban

This easy-to-use instrument enabled us to keep an accurate summary and to
compare the functioning and content of the sessions of the two groups.
Some selected data regarding the group sessions are presented in Table 8.
The instrument seems to have provided an effective means of recording
group data. Despite small numbers of participants, the composition of the
groups reflected socioeconomic differences, as well as marital status and
ethnicity. As Table 8 indicates, the group data reveal variations in breadth of
participation, content of discussions, participant satisfactions and other
aspects. These differences seem best explained in terms of group composition.

Our preliminary observations had suggested that SLE patient groups
may be divided into two main types that function differently according to
the characteristics and needs of their members. The first, which may be
termed "primary support" groups, are made up of members who, for a variety of reasons, are experiencing lack of support from other social systems,

Table 8.

Characteristics of Group Sessions

	Group A	*Group B*
Number of Groups Sessions:	18	14
Number of Participants:		
1–5	15	6
6–9	1	5
10 +	2	3
Flow of Discussion:		
easy start-up	14	14
difficult	4	0
continuous	16	13
halting/pauses	2	1
Content of Discussion: (Proportion of Small talk to Significant Comment)		
1:1	5	1
1:2	2	2
1:3	1	8
1:4	0	1
2:1	8	2
3:1	2	0
Breadth of Participation:		
most members participated	14	12
few members participated	4	2
General Mood at End of Session:		
involved	13	13
indifferent/bored	1	1
antagonistic/critical	4	0

such as immediate family and intimate friends. The second type, which may be termed "supplementary support" groups, consist of people with relatively intact and satisfying primary supports, but for whom contacts with peers experiencing a similar problem are desirable.

The data from group sessions indicate that this dichotomy may be a useful conceptualization, since group A was largely a primary support and group B largely a supplementary support entity. Differences were found among the two groups in such aspects as the breadth of participation, proportion of trivia to significant content and the frequency of conflicts or disagreements. Table 8 indicates that the suburban group, probably because of the greater homogeneity and personal security of its members, allowed for rapid and intense discussion of significant issues surrounding the illness, rather than focusing on procedural and status questions, as was observed in the urban group. Relatedly, there was a more positive mood at the end of the sessions and greater member satisfaction with the group process in the suburban than in the urban group.

From Table 8 it is clear that group A had a high proportion of "small," rather than "significant," talk during its sessions compared to group B. Group procedure was in fact the second most frequent topic of significant interchanges in group A (see Table 9). These "procedural" issues, nonsubstantive so far as the disease is concerned, involved such questions as who should be invited to address the group, who should do the inviting, and the frequency of meetings. Group A discussions had more difficult start-ups than those of group B, and group A had more sessions where few members participated. Antagonistic, critical or indifferent moods were manifest at the end of 25 percent of group A's sessions, but not at all in group B.

Table 9.
Significant Interchanges and Content

Group A (N = 54)	Group B (N = 42)
13 Significant Others	11 Significant Others
11 Group Procedures	6 Symptoms
5 Drugs (Rx)	5 Physical Activity
3 Socializing	3 Rest
3 Legal/Entitlements	3 Stress
3 Etiology of Illness	3 Work
3 Change in Habits	2 Etiology of Illness
2 Symptoms	2 Drugs (Rx)
2 Physical Activity	2 Change in Habits
2 Fears	2 Group Protocol
2 Peer Counseling	1 Sexuality
1 Stress	1 Stigma
1 Work	
1 Hopes/Aspirations	
1 Alternative Healing	

We speculate that such differences in the content, level and intensity of group discussions and group functioning, as recorded by the instrument, are related to factors in group composition. The majority of group A's members were single, separated or divorced women, most of whom had to work. Their various kinds and levels of situational life stresses were substantial and continuous, and this was reflected in often acrimonious group sessions. In contrast, group B's members were mostly married, lived in middle-class suburbs and generally had supportive husbands; fewer of them worked, as a matter of choice, not necessity. Thus, from our data, differences in group composition seem to affect the content and intensity of discussions as well as the general climate of the group meetings. The implications of this factor for group creation do not seem to have been explored in the literature, but seem important and suggestive for further study.

SUMMARY AND CONCLUSIONS

SLE is a prevalent chronic disease largely affecting women of reproductive age, about which little is known except for its clinical manifestations. It has potentially severe medical sequelae and can be life-threatening. It affects all areas of psychosocial functioning: family and intimate relationships, vocational status, finances, self-esteem, sense of personal control, psychological mood and morale.

The sociopsychological aspects of this chronic disorder have been only minimally investigated by clinicians and social science researchers. Greatest attention to them has been paid by self-help groups organized by patients, such as the Lupus Foundation of America. From the anecdotal experience of such groups and data from patients' participation in the self-help discussion groups, which was the treatment intervention in the present study, there are indications that participation in regular group meetings with other lupus patients is beneficial to the morale, self-esteem and coping abilities of patients who either lack a satisfying and intact social support network, or who, possessing one, nevertheless seek additional emotional help through interactional sharing with fellow patients.

If confirmed through further studies, these indications suggest that health professionals who deal with lupus patients should recognize that the severe sociopsychological problems accompanying the disease can be partially alleviated through participation in a lupus patient self-help group.

This conclusion also necessitates a brief discussion of the related area of self-care in lupus. Self-care describes activities carried out by an individual, sometimes with the help of others, to deal with somatic/psychological problems arising from illness, to improve health status or to prevent illness from occurring.

Fry listed the major constituents of self-care as health maintenance, disease prevention, self-diagnosis, self-medication and other forms of self-treatment and patients' participation in professional care (Fry 1975). In their later account of self-care, Levin, Katz and Holst (1976) added a different form of action that individuals may take to meet self-care objectives, namely by participating in health-oriented self-help groups. The purposes of such participation are several: to get information from fellow sufferers about effective coping with somatopsychic difficulties; to obtain social and emotional support by sharing problems in a group setting; and to bolster self-esteem and self-reliance, both in understanding one's illness and in relationships with the health care system and its professionals. The effects of this form of self-care through participation in self-help groups have been increasingly studied in recent years.

For lupus patients, while conscious self-care in the form of life-style changes is necessary to improve their physical and social adaptations, the major problems seem to be in the mental health sphere. Specific self-care actions cannot "cure" the disease or even change its course, but participation with other sufferers in self-help groups seems to alleviate its psychosocial stresses and improve patients' ability to cope with them. While not a substitute for needed medical interventions, self-help participation is a desirable form of parallel social treatment in this severe, often disabling and life-threatening chronic illness.

Our study also disclosed that many questions require further research: the differential effects on and coping strategies employed by patients at lower socioeconomic levels; the roles of vocational rehabilitation, public health departments, and community agencies vis-à-vis lupus patients; possible genetic aspects and other family issues.

The present study appears to have significance for health behavior theory and practice. The results add to knowledge of factors in patient adaptation, the effects of self-help as a treatment intervention, and the role of such cognitive factors as Bandura's concept of self-efficacy (Bandura 1982, 1986) and Antonovsky's sense of coherence concept (Antonovsky 1979). These foster *empowerment*—the individual's sense of mastery of the skills necessary for a return to productive living.

Self-help research is thus important for public and mental health theory and practice as testing and adding to knowledge of the aspects of self-care and peer self-help support groups in chronic illness, generally believed to underlie their stress-buffering, supportive and socializing effects. These are the processes they embody of empowerment and role modeling, and the effects of their action orientation. The application of such concepts in the planning of preventive health intervention has been rarely attended to or attempted. It is hoped that the present research provides data on these alternative treatment processes so that health professionals will be motivated to recognize, encourage and consciously employ informal and lay resources in helping chronically ill people learn effective strategies to cope with life pressures and crises.

REFERENCES

Antonovsky, A. *Health, Stress and Coping*. San Francisco: Jossey-Bass, 1979.
_____. The Sense of Coherence as a Determinant of Health. In J.D. Matarazzo et al. (eds.), *Behavioral Health*. New York: Wiley, 1984.
_____. *Unraveling the Mystery of Health*. San Francisco: Jossey-Bass, 1987.
Bandura, A. Self-efficacy mechanism in human agency. *Am. Psychol.* 37:122-147, 1982.
_____. *Social Foundations of Thought and Action*. Englewood Cliffs, NJ: Prentice Hall, 1986.

Blumenfield, M. Psychosocial concepts of systemic lupus erythematosus. *Primary Care* 5(1):159-171, 1978.

Davis, P. *Passage Through Crisis.* Indianapolis: Bobbs-Merrill, 1963.

Dubois, E. *Lupus Erythematosus,* Ed. 2. Los Angeles: University of Southern California Press, 1976.

Fry, J. Role of the Patient in Primary Health Care: The Viewpoint of the Medical Practitioner. Paper presented to the Symposium on the Role of the Individual in Primary Health Care, Institute of Social Medicine, University of Copenhagen, 1975.

Katz, A.H. Patients on chronic hemodialysis in the United States. *Soc. Sci. Med.* 3:669-677, 1970.

_____. *Hemophilia: A Study in Hope and Reality.* Springfield, IL: Charles C Thomas, 1971.

Levietes, P. The problem of chronic disease. *Am. J. Hosp. Pharm.* 31:1048-1052, 1974.

Levin, L., A.H. Katz, and E. Holst. *Self-Care: Lay Initiatives in Health.* New York: Prodist, 1976.

Lorig, K., et al. Development and Evaluation of a Scale to Measure the Perceived Self-efficacy of People with Arthritis. Unpublished manuscript, Department of Medicine, Stanford University, 1987.

Maida, C.A. Social support and learning in preventive health care. *Soc. Sci. Med.* 21:335-339, 1985.

Maida, C.A., et al. Psychological and social adaptation. *Loss Grief Care* 5(1-2):47-69, 1991.

Marinelli, R.P., and A.E. Dell Orto. *The Psychological and Social Impact of Physical Disability.* New York: Springer, 1977.

McNair, D.M., M. Lorr, and L.F. Droppleman. *Manual for the Profile of Mood States.* San Diego: Educational and Industrial Testing Service, 1981.

Myers, H.F. *The Social Resources and Social Supports Questionnaire.* Los Angeles: Department of Psychology, UCLA and Charles R. Drew Medical School, 1981.

Phillips, R. *Coping with Lupus.* Wayne, NJ: Avery, 1984.

Rogers, M. *Psychiatric Aspects in Clinical Management of Systemic Lupus Erythematosus.* New York: Grune & Stratton, 1983.

Taylor, C.B., et al. Raising spouse's and patient's perception of his cardiac capabilities after clinically uncomplicated myocardial infarction. *Am. J. Cardiol.* 55(6):635-638, 1985.

Wallston, K.A., and B.S. Wallston. Health Locus of Control Scales. In H.M. Lefcourt (ed.), *Research with the Locus of Control Construct, Vol. 1: Assessment Methods.* New York: Academic Press, 1981.

16

Loss, Mourning and Suffering: The "Ongoing Funeral" of Dementia

Carol J. Farran, DNSc, Geraldine Monbrod-Framburg and Cynthia Russell, DNSc

Existing research and literature have identified caregivers' stress and burden in great detail, but much less attention has been given to understanding the process of caregiving from the perspective of loss, mourning and suffering. This process has been acknowledged by some, however, who have suggested that caring for a person with dementia can be described as an "ongoing funeral."

To more fully understand the process of loss, mourning and suffering, first it is necessary to define these terms and examine how they apply both to the impaired family member with dementia and to their caregivers. Second, it is essential to look at the context of caregiving as the experience of loss, mourning and suffering occurs within the framework of the caregiver and impaired family member's past, present and future. Third, it is necessary to examine the mourning process and to compare and contrast this process with the experience of losing someone by death. Finally, it is essential to identify the practical approaches that caregivers can take to work through their experience of loss, mourning and suffering.

DEFINITION OF TERMS

Loss involves the act or experience of losing something significant. Losses may be physical or tangible, such as losing a person to death, but they may also be symbolic or psychological (Rando 1984).

Mourning, while often viewed as synonymous with grief, describes the lengthy process that follows a loss. Mourning or grieving is a process whereby an individual separates from a significant loss, dream, fantasy, illusion or projection into the future (Moses 1988). This process extends beyond the first reactions to a loss to include the period of reorganization, resolution and reattachment (Das 1971; Simos 1979). For the purposes of this chapter, mourning is differentiated from grieving because of the lengthy process that caregivers experience in caring for their impaired family member.

Powerlessness, or the inability to change one's external circumstances, has been identified as a fundamental element in *suffering*. Essential dimensions associated with suffering have been defined as afflictions at four levels—physical, psychological, social and spiritual. Pain in one or two of these dimensions is easier to overcome and forget, but afflictions at all four levels constitute suffering in its truest sense (Frankl 1978; Missinne 1984; Soelle 1975).

The diagnosis of dementia spares nothing—both the impaired family member and the caregiver experience loss, mourning and suffering. Both experience losses at physical, psychological, social and spiritual levels. The loss experienced by impaired family members has been aptly referred to as *the loss of self* (Cohen and Eisdorfer 1986). Physical losses experienced by an impaired family member include the eventual loss of body functioning. Psychological losses include the loss of the ability to express one's thoughts or feelings as the dementia progresses. Social losses also occur as impaired persons experience changes in the ability to communicate in the same way as they have done in the past. Spiritual losses occur when impaired persons can no longer comprehend and express the meaning that this whole experience has for them.

The losses experienced by family caregivers have been described as stress, burden and changes in well-being (Chenowith and Spencer 1986; George and Gwyther 1986; Mace and Rabins 1981; Zarit, Orr and Zarit 1985), but these can be further categorized as physical, psychological, social and spiritual losses. Physical losses may include those changes in physical health often associated with the additional responsibilities of caregiving. Psychological losses incorporate emotional responses experienced by caregivers as a result of losing their family member to dementia, while social losses focus on the inevitable changes in relationships, not only with the person who has dementia, but also with others within the caregivers' social world. Spiritual losses for the caregivers may also focus on the fact that because of the occurrence of dementia in their family, they must now reorganize their thought patterns, their way of ordering their world and, subsequently, the manner in which they find meaning in life.

Both the impaired family member and the caregiver mourn. It is likely that the impaired family member begins to mourn long before the caregiver and other family members are aware that changes are taking place. It is also likely that the impaired family member's early mourning may be camouflaged by anger, irritation or other strange behaviors. As the dementia progresses, it is likely that the impaired family member's mourning is trapped in a body that can no longer express these feelings in an understandable manner.

Caregiver's mourning may be derailed by the fluctuating functioning of their impaired family member and the need to assume additional tasks that the impaired family member can no longer complete. Like the impaired family member, the caregiver mourns in isolation. While both can see the daily decrements, loss of language skills in the impaired family member may prohibit an ability to share these thoughts and feelings with the caregiver so that both could mourn together.

Both the impaired family member and caregiver suffer—both are powerless to change their external situation, and both likely would not have chosen this set of circumstances. However, as the disease progresses, the impaired family member is unable to take the initiative to make changes that might ameliorate the situation. Thus the caregiver is abandoned, in a sense, and left in isolation to structure the environment around the impaired family member. Some have described the suffering of spouses of persons with dementia as one in which they "live in a prison, struggle on a battlefield, and languish in a concentration camp" (Levine et al. 1984, p.222).

THE CONTEXT OF MOURNING

While both the impaired family member and the caregiver may experience isolation throughout the mourning process, their mourning does not occur in isolation. The mourning process of impaired family members and caregivers is sociologically shaped by their cultural/ethic and religious/philosophical mores and customs (Averill 1975; Simos 1979); it is demographically shaped by such things as age and gender, psychologically shaped by personal characteristics, and temporally shaped by past and present events, as well as future prospects.

Past experiences in the lives of impaired family members and caregivers affect both present and future experiences. Answers to the following questions shape the past context of mourning: Was the past relationship between the impaired family member and caregiver built upon love and commitment or upon duty and obligation? What roles did each assume in the past? Were these roles fixed or flexible? What types of stressors or crises challenged the impaired family member/caregiver dyad in the past? And what coping strategies did they develop through these earlier difficult experiences?

The present mourning context is shaped by answers to other kinds of questions: What does the diagnosis of dementia mean to both the impaired family member and the caregiver at the present time? What are the secondary losses, such as role and status, associated with the current situation? What unfinished business exists between the impaired family member and the caregiver?What kinds of changes has the caregiver needed to make as a result of the impaired family member's deterioration? How long has the dyad been affected by the diagnosis of dementia? And what concurrent stressors or competing events face the family caregiver?

Future issues also affect the context of mourning and revolve around such questions as these: Will the caregiver have the physical and emotional energy to re-establish, reorganize and reattach to others in the future? And how will the caregiver be affected by the financial aspects of providing long-term care to the impaired family member? Past experiences, present situations and future anticipations all work interactively to shape the caregiving context.

THE GRIEF AND MOURNING PROCESS

Much of the literature that discusses loss and grief revolves primarily around the experience of losing someone by death. Different stages of grief have been identified and can be organized into five general phases. However, it is important to recognize that these phases do not occur in lock-step fashion and may be re-experienced in different ways throughout the grieving process (Bowlby 1969, 1973; Kübler Ross 1969; Lindemann 1979; Parkes 1972). One of the first reactions to grief has been defined as a sense of numbness, shock, disbelief, or denial of what has happened.

A second phase of the grieving process has been described as one in which persons express yearning/searching behaviors involving a strong desire to be reunited with the lost person. During this phase individuals experience emotional, physical and social reactions. Emotional responses may include weeping and expressions of anger and guilt. Grieving persons may have a sense of worthlessness, helplessness and depression. Physical reactions may include changes in appetite and sleep patterns, as well as loss of strength, physical exhaustion, emptiness, heaviness and shortness of breath. Persons who grieve will often sigh as a way of expressing the emotional and physical pain of their loss. Social reactions are also experienced. Persons may have difficulty initiating and maintaining organized activities, and may withdraw from social situations.

A third phase commonly identified with grief is a sense of disorganization and despair. Here persons begin to realize that their attempts to search for the deceased will not be rewarded. This realization can contribute to feelings of depression and a sense of hopelessness about the future. A fourth phase has been referred to as restitution. The funeral and family rituals following death begin this process of emphasizing the reality of the loss. These rituals also facilitate the expression of support and caring from other persons. Restitution continues on a daily basis as grieving persons come to grips with the meaning of a death.

A fifth phase of reorganization/resolution/reinvestment has been identified as one in which the grieving person begins to acknowledge the loss, "withdraw" from the lost relationship and reinvest in other activities or persons. The grieving process is a very individual experience, and while it has commonly been thought to take at least a year, the necessary time span varies from person to person.

While there are many similarities between losing someone to death and losing someone to dementia, there are also numerous differences. One of the major differences in losing someone to dementia is that it is an ongoing process that may last for many years. What is lost is a moving image and is ever-changing. Because of this lengthy process, "mourning" is selected as a more appropriate term than "grieving" in order to differentiate this experience from the loss of someone by death.

Another major difference between grieving over someone's death and mourning the loss of someone to dementia is that the stages associated with grieving become more amorphous in the mourning process. There are no clear demarcations in the first phase of losing someone to dementia. The numbness, shock or disbelief associated with the loss of someone to death is experienced in small, subtle, incremental doses by the person losing someone to dementia. Because the onset of dementia is gradual and insidious, families may live for several years with "troubling symptoms" (Kuhn 1989). The diagnosis of dementia may also be revealed in stages, so that even before a definite diagnosis is reached, the family knows that "something is wrong." This protracted period of time between an awareness of "troubling symptoms" and the announcement of the diagnosis provides a fertile field for denial both on the part of the impaired family member and the caregiver (Russell 1988).

The second and third phases of the grieving process—awareness/ yearning/searching and disorganization/despair—are superimposed upon the daily demands already placed on the family caregiver and may become indistinguishable as such. The emotional, physical and social reactions associated with the grieving process may instead be interpreted as stress and burden in the caregiving context. This blurring between the stressors of providing care and the experience of mourning may short-change family caregivers because they themselves (as well as other family members, friends and professionals) may not recognize that if the mourning process can be attended to, some of the other stressors associated with the caregiving context may be minimized.

The fourth phase of the grieving process—restitution and rituals—is also distorted in the process of mourning someone with dementia. The funeral rituals available to persons mourning a death are not provided to those who are mourning the loss of someone with dementia. Society does not have a way to deal with the "ongoing funeral." The comfort and support provided by others immediately following death are not readily given to the still-struggling caregiver. Family and friends may be available sporadically, but the ever-changing and lengthy process of caring for someone with dementia generally results in a dwindling social world for the caregiver.

Reorganization and resolution, the fifth phase associated with grieving, also varies in this process of mourning. It is difficult for the family caregiver to withdraw from the person with dementia because that person is still present and in need. It is also difficult for the caregiver to reinvest energies into other activities and persons, because the demands of providing care may limit the time available for this effort. In order to work through the phase of reorganization and resolution at some level, it is essential that caregivers recognize the context of their grief and suffering, and actively engage in the mourning process.

PRACTICAL APPROACHES TO DEALING WITH THE MOURNING PROCESS

Recognizing the Context of One's Loss, Mourning and Suffering

It is essential for caregivers to acknowledge that there two ever-present, simultaneous and ongoing processes, and that these two ongoing processes must be balanced against the caregivers' past and present experiences, as well as their future anticipations.

The first process involves the assumption of caregiving responsibilities, which has its own consuming nature. The ever-increasing physical, mental and emotional demands on caregivers are always present. Caregivers may be away from their caregiving responsibilities for a few hours of rest and relaxation, but they are still "there" mentally, with and for their family member. In addition to the ongoing caregiving tasks, in the back of their minds caregivers are also wondering about the long-term future and calculating how they might handle eventual emergencies (Farran et al. 1989).

The second ongoing process is the process of mourning. This is a daily, if not hourly, experience for the caregiver and involves intense, laborious inner and outer work. The caregivers' 24-hour/day, 365-day/year shift is one in which day by day, piece by piece and inch by inch, they helplessly and hopelessly watch as the "person" of their loved one disappears. The reality of the mourning process is that it impacts every aspect of caregivers' lives. All decisions, viewpoints, interactions and communications in the present and future are touched. How is it, then, that caregivers can engage and work through this process?

Allowing the Gift of Being Human

First, it is essential for caregivers to allow themselves the gift of being human. When they experience intense emotions, it is important that they *go with them.* Caregivers can say to themselves, "I'll go with this fear, anger, pain or grief for X minutes." This process is often feared and avoided by caregivers, but it is the single most effective action they can take to assist them in their healing process.

Healing can begin to occur when caregivers acknowledge these feelings, thereby releasing them from their memory pools of "repressed negativity" (Kübler-Ross 1969). Because mourning is a process, just as life is, this acknowledgment of feelings and their release must be frequently repeated. It is important for caregivers to realize that there are no short-cuts in the process of mourning and healing. Ultimately, the caregiver must be able to "Welcome the expression of strong, powerful emotions, as making peace with their pain is the essence of its resolution" (Hendel 1989).

Mourning with Others

Because society does not have rituals to deal with the "ongoing funeral," caregivers, in spite of their feelings of powerlessness, must develop their own rituals. It is important for caregivers to realize that significant grieving is done with others, and rituals for involving others in their mourning can be intentionally engineered in a number of ways. One way is to seek out a sincere, nonjudgmental person who can be trusted and who will simply *listen* to the caregiver. It is helpful if caregivers can arrange an up-front agreement to have this person listen to them *when they need it*. Then caregivers must *ask* for this time in order to express their emotions. Asking for help can be a tough and humbling step for those who have made it a life-long point to be independent, but it is an essential positive action toward caregiving survival. For some caregivers, this person may be a close friend, whereas other caregivers may wish to seek out a therapist who is especially trained in the area of grief and mourning.

A therapist who specializes in working with those in the grieving/ mourning process can be a critical tool for some caregivers, as this individual can offer tremendous support and guidance. It is important for caregivers to find an experienced grief therapist, as not all therapists specialize in this work. The caregiver may wish to interview several therapists before making a decision. It is essential for the therapist to "feel right" for the caregiver, as caring for a person with dementia will more than likely occur over an extended period of time. The care and skill of a trained professional, one who has the necessary vision, perspective and supportive stamina, can be invaluable to the caregiver.

Another way in which caregivers may involve others in their mourning process is by attending self-help support groups such as those provided by the Alzheimer's Association or professionally led educational support groups (Keane-Hagerty and Farran 1989). The general purpose of these groups is to help caregivers intellectually and emotionally to deal with their family member who has dementia. Meeting with others in similar situations helps caregivers to normalize their experience, as well as to find a sense of hope from others dealing with comparable problems. Support groups can help caregivers to develop their knowledge about dementia and caregiving, establish a supportive network for themselves, receive positive feedback from others who understand, and can provide opportunities to express shared feelings (Marks 1988). It is important for caregivers to realize that support groups may not be helpful for everyone, and that they themselves may benefit more from a support group at some times than at others. Caregivers should also be aware that groups vary depending upon the leader and group membership, so that if a variety of support groups is available, caregivers may wish to visit several of them to find the one that best meets their needs.

The Ritual of Balance

Developing and maintaining the ritual of balance in caregivers' lives will help facilitate the mourning process and ultimately nurture the caregiver toward the necessary goal of healing. Caregivers, who must cope with the needs of their impaired family member as well as their own, appear to develop a two-track life. One track is devoted to providing care for the impaired family member, while the second track is intended to take care of themselves. Generally, caregivers have obtained a great deal of knowledge and skill for implementing the caregiving track, but they have less experience in developing their self-care track. Often caregivers need permission and encouragement from others to develop this self-care track which is essential for their own healing.

The Ritual of Rest

It is important for caregivers to develop and maintain the ritual of rest from the physical and emotional fatigue that inevitably occurs as a result of both the caregiving and the mourning process. A full-body relaxation tape with nature sounds or music can be a welcome tool to facilitate this ritual. Caregivers may also wish to work on deep-breathing exercises such as the following:

> Inhale through the nose.
> Exhale through the mouth.
> Breathe in harmony and health.
> Breathe out anxieties and fear.

Engaging in the ritual of rest will help caregivers to develop the stamina for their continuing caregiving role, as well as assisting them through the undeniable, yet necessary, process of mourning.

The Ritual of Physical Exercise

While caregivers may get a great deal of exercise "chasing after" their impaired family member, what is most needed is time for play. Not only is this a must to keep the body and soul together, but it will help caregivers to gain a clearer sense of themselves and the tremendous load they are carrying in terms of the caregiving and the mourning process. Playing can be a life-giving process that touches the parts of the caregivers' lives that are still vibrant. One of the beauties about life's natural process of separation from losses is that caregivers are forced to see the parts of themselves that are very much alive, the parts sometimes referred to as blessings. One caregiver recalled her utter amazement on a short outing that she gave herself, of all places, to the zoo:

> Just seeing the families with children, lovers hand-holding, animals with their new offspring, made me acutely aware of just how long I'd been living with a catastrophically ill, dying human being. Perhaps I was not admitting this painful fact to myself daily—but just the same, it was and had been working on my psyche for over three years! This eye-opener reminded me that there could and would be life after Alzheimer's disease. Just that spark of hope renewed my energies (Monbrod-Framburg 1989).

The Ritual of Humor

While there is nothing humorous about caregiving and mourning, one caregiver remarked, "I choose to make this a humorous heartache." Finding a piece of humor in the rest of life provides caregivers the opportunity to step back and observe the incredibly hard work they have done through both the enmeshing and consuming caregiving and mourning processes. Healthy living depends a great deal on healthy thinking, and humor can remind caregivers that they are mortals and that there is more to this life than the tremendous work and pain involved in the caregiving experience.

The Ritual of Dreams

Caregivers are separated not only from their own dreams as their loved one's disease progresses, but also from the significant others who are attached to those dreams. Dreams, whether of the past, present or future, will not be released until caregivers dare to dream new dreams. One caregiver shared her view of this idea:

> It was not until I forced myself to go on a retreat (after finding respite care for my husband) that I began to realize that I was actually more than a caregiver, and that there were other parts of me to acknowledge. Acknowledgment of these parts encouraged me to continue my own self-development. I found additional meaning in life—a new dream. Just that small bit of new life made a world of difference for me. In fact that new outlook on life renewed my zest in the caregiving role as well (Monbrod-Framburg 1989).

It is by the caregivers' self-acknowledgment and engagement in the prolonged and complex process of loss, mourning and suffering that they can begin to open their hearts and minds to the insight that caregiving is not just a test of survival, but an actual experimental step in their own evolution—a will to thrive.

REFERENCES

Averill, J.R. Grief: Its Nature and Significance. In A.S. Carr et al. (eds.), *Grief: Selected Readings.* New York: Health Sciences Press, 1975.

Bowlby, J. *Attachment and Loss,* Vol. 1. New York: Basic Books, 1969.

_____. *Attachment and Loss,* Vol. 2. New York: Basic Books, 1969.

Chenowith, B., and B. Spencer. The experience of family caregivers. *Gerontologist* 26(3):267-292, 1986.

Cohen, D., and C. Eisdorfer. *The Loss of Self.* New York: New American Library/ Penquin, 1986.

Das, S.S. Grief and imminent threat of non-being. *Br. J. Psychiatry* 118:467-468, 1971.

Farran, C.J., E. Keane-Hagerty, S. Salloway, S. Kupferer and C. Wilken. Finding Meaning Through Caregiving (unpublished manuscript). Chicago: Rush University, 1989.

Frankl, V.E. *The Unheard Cry for Meaning.* New York: Washington Square Press, 1978.

George, L.K., and L.P. Gwyther. Caregiver well being: a multidimensional examination of family caregivers of demented adults. *Gerontologist* 26(3):253-259, 1986.

Hendel, J. Write away—thoughts on the art of writing to heal. *Bereavement,* February 1989, p. 41.

Keane-Hagerty, E., and C.J. Farran. An Educational Support Group for Caregivers of Persons with Dementia (unpublished manuscript). Chicago: Rush University, 1989.

Kübler-Ross, E. *On Death and Dying.* New York: Macmillan, 1969.

Kuhn, D. Addressing the Normative Crises of Families Caring for Dementia Patients (unpublished manuscript). Chicago: Rush Alzheimer's Disease Center, 1989.

Levine, N.B., C.E. Gendron, D.P. Dastoor, et al. Existential issues in the management of the demented elderly patient. *Am. J. Psychotherapy* 38(2);215-223, 1984.

Lindemann, E. *Beyond Grief: Studies in Crisis Intervention.* New York: Jason Aronson, 1979.

Mace, N.L., and P.V. Rabins. *The 36-Hour Day.* Baltimore: Johns Hopkins University Press, 1981.

Marks, J. Alzheimer Support Groups: A Framework for Survival. In M.K. Aronson, ed., *Understanding Alzheimer's Disease.* New York: Charles Scribner's Sons, 1988.

Missinne, L.E. Reflections on the meaning of suffering. *The Priest,* March 1984, pp. 11-13.

Monbrod-Framburg, G. A Caregiver's Reflections (unpublished manuscript). Chicago, 1989.

Moses, K.L. *Relating to the Parents of the Disabled,* Tape 1. Evanston, IL: Resource Networks, 1988.

Parkes, C.M. *Bereavement: Studies of Grief in Adult Life.* New York: International Universities Press, 1972.

Rando, T.A. *Grief, Dying and Death.* Champaign, IL: Research Press, 1984.

Russell, C. Loss, Grief and Depression: An Analysis of Caregivers of Persons with Dementia (unpublished manuscript). Chicago: Rush University, 1988.

Simos, B.G. *A Time to Grieve: Loss as a Universal Human Experience.* New York: Family Service Association of America, 1979.

Soelle, D. *Suffering.* (Translated by Everett R. Kalin.) Philadelphia: Fortress Press, 1975.

Zarit, S.H., N.K. Orr, and J.M. Zarit. *The Hidden Victims of Alzheimer's Disease.* New York: New York University Press, 1985.

17

The Relationship Between The Wellness Community and the Medical Profession

Harold H. Benjamin, PhD

The relationship between The Wellness Community and the medical profession is one of mutual respect and support. Almost all the physicians who are aware of our program of psychological support for cancer patients are enthusiastic supporters. Our program is not an alternative. It is in support and in addition to conventional medical treatment. While we do not require that our participants be under medical care, more than 95 percent of them are being treated by conventional physicians and health care teams. If the medical profession indicated to us that what we were doing was not in the best interests of their patients, we would stop. This has never happened in the 7 years of our existence during which we have been of service to over 8000 cancer patients and interacted with innumerable physicians. We constantly reiterate that our program of psychosocial support for cancer patients is exactly the same type of support that all physicians, nurses and other health care professionals would provide if they had the time.

We believe that medical care is primary and our function is supportive and adjunctive. While there are some physicians who believe that our program can be of no more than psychological help, there are at least as many who believe there is the possibility that it may have a beneficial physical effect. Because (1) we do not make any promises, (2) we do not interfere with and are supportive of the prescribed treatment and (3) we do not charge under any circumstances, to the best of my knowledge there are no physicians who believe that their patients would not benefit in some way by being part of our program.

To expand on the above and because of the relative newness of The Wellness Community, it will be best if I first describe very briefly what we do and a little of our history. A more complete description of our program and its methods appears in my book, *From Victim to Victor,* published in paperback by Dell.

The Wellness Community opened its doors to cancer patients in Santa Monica, California, in June 1982 without a participant or a physician. Since that time it has provided, without cost of any kind, psychosocial support to more than 8,000 cancer patients and now sees more than 500 each week, most of whom are referred by their physicians. Our second facility opened in Redondo Beach, California, in April 1987 and already sees over 150 cancer patients each week. Both facilities are growing at a dramatic rate and new facilities are being opened around the country. Norman Cousins is the honorary Chairman of the Board of The Wellness Community-Westside, and the Professional Advisory Boards include many prominent physicians such as Richard Steckel, Director of the Jonsson Comprehensive Cancer Center at UCLA, and Jimmie Holland, Chief of Psychiatry at Memorial Sloane Kettering.

The Wellness Community is not a hospice or a place where cancer patients learn to die from cancer or adapt their lives to the illness. It is a program where they learn whatever they need to know to participate in their fight for recovery along with their health care team rather than acting as hopeless, helpless, passive victims of the illness. I reiterate—it is a place to learn to fight for recovery. It is nonresidential and free. The mission of The Wellness Community is to be of as much help as possible to as many cancer patients as possible without permitting money or insurance forms to get in the way so that the largest number of cancer patients recover to the greatest extent they can. We provide every modality of psychosocial treatment for cancer accepted by the oncological and psychological community.

The Wellness Community program is based on the discoveries made by those working in the newly emerging field of psychoneuroimmunology. Their work has taught us that pleasant emotions enhance and unpleasant emotions suppress the power of the immune system. Of course, we do not as yet know, except by anecdotal evidence, whether such enhancement or suppression has any effect on the onset or recovery from the illness. However, despite this area of uncertainty, since it is possible that an enhanced immune system may have a beneficial effect on the course of the illness and since the immune system is enhanced by pleasant emotion and depressed by unpleasant emotions, it is appropriate for cancer patients to expend all reasonable effort to have as many pleasant emotions and as few unpleasant emotions as possible to improve the quality of their lives as a part of their fight for recovery. Our efforts to enhance the power of the immune system as a method of fighting for recovery are not very different from the efforts being made by those scientists who prescribe interferon and interleukin to strengthen the immune system, except that the effort to improve one's quality of life has no unpleasant side effects.

At The Wellness Community we are convinced that one of the best ways for most cancer patients to improve the quality of their lives, and thus enhance their immune systems, is to be a part of the fight for their recovery along with their health care team instead of acting passively. This conviction is supported, in substantial part, by the preliminary results of a study made at The Wellness Community under the auspices of the UCLA School of Public Health. That study, which spanned a period of 1 year, compared a group of cancer patients who involved themselves in The Wellness Community program to a similar group who had access to the program but decided against using it. The results were that, under certain circumstances, the involved group suffered less pain and depression and reported a higher quality of life than the uninvolved group—reason enough to be a part of the fight for recovery.

The philosophy and the modus operandi of The Wellness Community is well described in the following statement which has become the cornerstone of our program: "Cancer patients who participate in their fight for recovery along with their physicians instead of acting as hopeless, helpless, passive victims of the illness will improve the quality of their lives and just may enhance the possibility of recovery." Since it is the mission of The Wellness Community to help as many cancer patients recover to the greatest extent possible, and since the possibility of recovery may be improved by an enhanced immune system, and since pleasant emotions enhance the power of the immune system, all of our efforts are directed toward making it possible for cancer patients to improve their quality of life—to combat those psychosocial problems confronted by all of us and specifically those faced by cancer patients.

The literature concerning the effects of cancer is replete with evidence of the fact that the two most serious psychosocial problems cancer patients face are loss of control and unwanted aloneness. Therefore those are the two areas most directly attacked. That is why we use the following three C's as our guide: cancer, community and control.

It is important to understand that the assertion that the cancer patient is at fault for the onset or failure of the illness to progress as hoped, is nonsense. It is also ridiculous to believe that those cancer patients who become a part of the fight for recovery are the "good or strong guys" and that those who turn all control over to their physicians are somehow weak or wrong. I believe that each person knows what is best for him and that whatever he decides to do for himself is right and proper for him, no matter the results.

As I turn to the relationship between The Wellness Community and the medical profession, I must make it quite clear again, as I have to the medical community from the very beginning, that our program is not an alternative. It is in support and in addition to conventional medical treatment. When I started The Wellness Community, my "advisors" all advised against it for many reasons, not the least of which was their belief that the medical profession would "shoot it out of the sky." That's not what happened at all. The medical profession acted in exactly the way I hope I would act in similar circumstances. They were originally very suspicious—I would have been suspicious, too, if I heard that a lawyer was retiring to start a program for cancer patients. But after 6 months a large group of physicians in our area asked me to meet with them. After we spoke for about an hour and a half, they were convinced that we were not going to charge and that we were not going to interfere with the prescribed treatment, and they issued a bulletin suggesting that all physicians in the area send their cancer patients to us.

They were impressed, among other matters, that we were aware that the relationship between cancer patients and their physicians was of exquisite importance—that we knew that a good relationship enhances the quality of life and perhaps improves the possibility of recovery, while a bad one may impede recovery and make life miserable for everyone. From this point on I will consider the patient-physician relationship from the patient's point of view. It is the support of this concept that has made the relationship between The Wellness Community and the medical profession what it is.

Dr. Herbert Benson underscored the importance of the patient-physician relationship when he wrote that the placebo effect (the body's ability to heal itself) works when three elements are present: "One, the belief and expectation of the patient; two, the belief and expectation of the physician; and three, the interaction between the patient and the physician." Thus, the quality of the interaction between the patient and the physician is not a matter to be left to chance. But a rocky beginning for this relationship is not uncommon, because the cancer patient's first reaction after diagnosis is typically shock and disbelief, followed by the "why me?" syndrome, and then unreasoning anger. At that time, what the patient wants to hear more than anything else is that the diagnosis is a mistake, or at least that the illness will be of brief duration and leave no lasting effects. And the physician is the one who must disappoint the patient in this regard, while prescribing medications, procedures and tests that can have unpleasant side effects. As a result, it's not unusual for the patient's anger to land on the physician, setting up a delicate and sometimes uncomfortable situation.

Although the great majority of physicians respond as caring fellow human beings, there are a few who do eliminate all hope, who are distant, who won't answer questions, and who treat the patient like a not-too-bright employee. Even when the physician is sensitive and caring, a doctor-patient dance always ensues, with the physician doing the leading. If the physician can direct the patient's anger at the real enemy—the disease—the doctor and patient can fight that enemy as a team. If, on the other hand, the doctor is less than adroit at the psychological task of helping the patient, the relationship can be forever marred, much to the patient's detriment.

In the early stages of the illness, all the responsibility falls upon the physician, who is at no risk and has been in similar circumstances many times before. The doctor should be prepared for the reactions of the patient, and should have developed some way to transmit information to a frightened, bewildered person in a manner that is supportive, hopeful, positive, yet accurate. Any physician who acts and speaks in an uncaring or insensitive way that strips the patient of all hope is either not aware of the crucial importance of the patient-physician relationship or just doesn't care. Fortunately, such behavior is by far the exception. I reiterate that most cancer patients to whom I have spoken consider the withdrawal of hope by the physician one of the major sins a doctor can commit.

Of course, a medical degree does not bestow sainthood or unlimited patience, and a physician cannot be expected to act forever as a caring friend and confidant to an overly demanding, hostile and angry patient. As in every interaction, the patient-physician connection must be a two-way street.

In many respects, the patient-physician relationship is the same as a business relationship with any independent contractor, such as a lawyer, accountant, plumber or mechanic; each is paid for doing the best he or she can to accomplish the desired results. But physicians are special in several ways. They help us maintain or regain our most precious possession, our health. In no other situation do independent contractors have so much responsibility. In no other situation is it quite so important that their advice and ministrations be correct, and that errors of both judgment and performance be avoided. In few other situations is so much training required and such an obligation placed on the independent contractor. One of those obligations is to instill confidence and a feeling of security in a patient, while not appearing too authoritarian or remote. This is a very difficult role to play, and woe to the physician who fails in any way or does not perform as expected.

Because a good relationship with the right physician is of overriding importance to the cancer patient, the active patient commits as much time and energy as is necessary—and sometimes it takes quite a bit—to attain such a relationship. Choosing a medically competent physician is the first step. In most cases, this is done primarily by recommendation and reputation.

The next step is ensuring that the relationship is cordial. Patient-physician relationships are as numerous and varied as are patients and doctors. Some patients want every bit of information they can get. Others want to hear nothing but instructions. Some want to know what the alternatives are and want to make the final decisions themselves. Some want the doctor to decide what's best. Some consider sitting in a waiting room an acceptable inconvenience, while others find it intolerable. Some want to ask questions, write down answers and have other people in the examining room. Others don't.

Physicians also differ. Most look forward to having the patient act as a partner. Others, because of temperament or training, can only interact with patients as a parental figure.

In a paper discussing the importance of a good patient-physician relationship, Dr. Howard Leventhal and his colleagues at the University of Wisconsin discussed the necessity that each clearly understand the expectations of the other:

> Both patient and physician have specific expectations of and preferences for the type of relationship they will enjoy and the outcome they expect from their interaction. The expectations held by each party may differ considerably, and these differences may go unrecognized. Since the relationship places the physician in general control of the interaction, the substance of the relationship is likely to conform more closely to his or her expectations. Thus, to the extent that the patient's and physician's expectations differ, the patient may ultimately be unhappy with the care and may be less likely to remain in and comply with the treatment.

A frank discussion is therefore indicated, preferably after a reasonable breaking-in period during which patients become aware of what their needs are and how their doctors are responding to them. But patients should not put off the discussion too long; too much time must not be allowed to pass while the problems of cancer are exacerbated by petty annoyances.

Very often it is difficult for patients to start the conversation with their doctors. After all, physicians have always been authority figures. But patients should start it anyway: With very few exceptions, physicians are as anxious to have the conversation as is the patient. The dialogue should continue as long as necessary and should be reopened when any part of the relationship appears unsatisfactory. The discussion can range from how decisions regarding treatment will be made to questions as mundane as whether the patient and the physician will be on a first-name basis. If a physician calls his patient John, the patient is free to call his doctor Frank; it is unacceptable for a 42-year-old physician to call his 65-year-old patient by her first name and expect her to call him "doctor."

When the expectations of physicians are understood, patients can determine what accommodations to make if those expectations do not coincide with their own. If the patient's needs conflict seriously with the doctor's style, she should consider whether it's in her best interests to find another physician. Most people find it difficult and sometimes embarrassing to leave a physician. Although this rather drastic step should be taken only after serious consideration, it's not impossible or unthinkable. If the situation is irreparable, it's entirely appropriate.

Often cancer patients are treated by a group of physicians that may include an oncologist, a radiologist, a surgeon, and perhaps some other specialist, along with the family doctor. One of the patient's most frequent complaints is that no one is in charge—each physician acts almost independently—and there is no one to whom the patient can talk and get *all* the information needed to make a decision. Therefore, it's important that the patient try to get one of the doctors to be the coordinator of the team and the repository of all information. When patients are satisified that they have found the right physicians, the next step is nurturing the relationship. It does not have to blossom into a full-blown friendship in order to be effective and efficient. It is only necessary that it be agreeable.

One of our participants summed up his perception of his role in this relationship as follows:

> As a cancer patient, I cannot think of anyone whose approval I am more interested in than my oncologist's. I want him to think of me as a decent, reasonable man who wants to recover more than anything else in the world. While he may not look forward to the day he is scheduled to see me, I wouldn't want him to dread it.
>
> In order to be worthy of my doctor's respect, I am, within my own capabilities, courteous, friendly, and considerate of his time. I am careful that my demands on him are reasonable. I try to be constantly aware that he is not a god who can cure me with a wave of his hand, that he has other patients, and that his entire life does not revolve around me alone.

One admonition: Patients should not ask for a prognosis or inquire about longevity statistics unless they are actually ready to hear the answer. Most physicians refuse to make any prediction about longevity because they just don't know what an individual's life expectancy will be. If hard-pressed, they will discuss the statistics but will also describe patients who substantially outlived the statistics or who recovered completely. Also, patients should decide with their doctors how much they want to know and what part they want to play in the decision-making process. The patient should make sure that those issues are clear and that both agree.

Not long ago I had a discussion with about 60 participants of The Wellness Community. From that dialogue it became apparent that most of them had complete confidence in their physicians and were generally happy with their relationship. But there were also some horror stories, particularly about physicians stripping the patient of hope.

This interchange raised the question of what a cancer patient could reasonably expect from a physician. I decided to ask the experts, the oncologists on The Wellness Community's Professional Advisory Board: Laurence Heifetz, then co-director of the Department of Oncology at Cedars-Sinai Medical Center; Daniel Lieber, then director of the Oncology Unit at Santa Monica Hospital and Research Institute; Frank Rosenfelt, an oncologist in private practice in Los Angeles; Richard Steckel, director of the Jonsson Comprehensive Cancer Center at UCLA; and Michael B. Van Scoy-Mosher, an oncologist in private practice in West Los Angeles.

At that meeting, the oncologists concurred that some patients, while receiving proper medical care, had relationships with their physicians that were not the most conducive to recovery, and that many patients believed that insensitive treatment by their doctors was normal. Eventually, we prepared a statement (The Wellness Community Patient/Physician Statement) and tested it by distribution to 300 cancer patients. It is designed to help cancer patients judge whether their relationship with their oncologists is all it should be. We suggested that cancer patients might show it to their physicians and discuss it with them.

Now that it has become clear what five prominent oncologists believe cancer patients can expect, the following guidelines may be useful in that it will help them:

- Understand the instructions given more thoroughly and comply with them more precisely.
- Get the information needed quickly.
- Have greater peace of mind because they will be aware of the procedures being used and the hoped-for results.
- Have more confidence in their physicians because of their ability and willingness to explain the plan of treatment in language understandable to them.

The recommendations are as follows:

- Before the visit, patients should prepare a written list of the questions to ask the doctor. This will save office time and assure that all questions are asked.
- For the same reasons, before the visit, patients should prepare a written list of the information the doctor should know.
- If patients don't understand something the doctor says, they should say so. If they don't speak up, they may follow the wrong advice or take an improper amount of medication.
- Patients should take someone with them when they visit their doctors. Friends will not be as stressed as patients and will be able to listen to and understand the doctor with greater objectivity.
- Patients should get a second opinion when a major course of action is contemplated.
- The patient and the doctor should decide between them whether (1) the doctor will make all the decisions, (2) the decisions will be made jointly, or (3) the patient wants the right to make the final decision in all cases. Of course, whatever they decide is not carved in stone and can be changed as the situation evolves.

During recent decades there has been a marked change in the way people in our society, including health experts, view the role of the patient. No longer are patients seen as passive recipients of health care who are expected to do willingly whatever the doctor says. Rather, they are increasingly regarded as active decision-makers, making a series of crucial choices that can markedly affect the kind of treatments they receive and the outcome. According to Irving L. Janis of Yale University, it is quite usual these days for cancer patients to be informed as to the details of what is taking place and make the decisions as to treatment jointly with the physician.

Patients should do everything in their power to ensure that their relationships with their physicians are as trouble-free as possible. They should make certain that any problems between them are not their own fault and then discuss any problems with their physicians. If that doesn't work, the patient should find a new doctor.

The relationship between The Wellness Community and the medical profession is indeed a splendid one, and we will do everything in our power to keep it that way.

18

The Self-Help Approach to Sjögren's Syndrome

Elaine K. Harris, MA

WHAT IS SJÖGREN'S SYNDROME?

Sjögren's syndrome (SS) is an autoimmune disease in which the mucus-secreting exocrine glands are regarded as "foreign" and are therefore attacked by lymphocytes that destroy the glands, resulting in impaired or complete loss of function of the lacrimal, salivary and Bartholin's glands. It is characterized by dry eyes, dry nose, dry mouth and throat, and dry vagina. When accompanied by a form of arthritis, the disease is called secondary Sjögren's syndrome; otherwise, it is called primary SS.

The letters SSF, well known today to Sjögren's syndrome patients and the doctors who treat them, stand for Sjögren's Syndrome Foundation, Inc. The Foundation, which had its birth in December 1983 at the Long Island Jewish Medical Center (LIJMC) in New Hyde Park, New York, came into this world as "The Moisture Seekers." In 1985, when the Foundation was formally incorporated, the Board of Directors voted to use the name of the disease as the official name of the organization, so that both the public and medical professionals would be able to identify us immediately. Dolores Sciubba (wife of Dr. James J. Sciubba, the first chairman of our Medical Advisory Board) appreciated my reluctance to give up the name "Moisture Seekers," which I felt so aptly described our purpose. The name was retained for our monthly newsletter.

DOING SOMETHING POSITIVE

Like most SS sufferers, I was a lonely, desperate patient, both before my diagnosis and immediately thereafter. When I was diagnosed in 1982, there was no self-help group for SS patients, and I didn't know any other patients. During my frequent visits to LIJMC, I became friendly with a doctor's secretary, Flo Goldberg, who seemed to have problems similar to mine. Before the doctors figured out what she had, I remarked to her, "I think you have what I have." And she did. At this time (summer of 1983), I was feeling particularly desperate. Dr. Steven Carsons, my immunologist, told me, "Elaine, you either have to go for help or do something positive." Flo and I decided to do something positive. Flo, who also had rheumatoid arthritis, contacted the Arthritis Foundation in New York City about starting a self-help group at LIJMC. She was turned down because her primary concern was the rheumatoid arthritis, and LIJMC was too close to other arthritis self-help groups in the vicinity. I refused to give up. I informed the Arthritis Foundation that what I really wanted was a Sjögren's syndrome group. OK, they said, but a leader must be trained and their training course had just ended; I would have to wait until spring. But I was persistent. I impressed upon them all the community work I had done and the courses I had taken in group dynamics. As a result I was sent on to Carol Eisman, then associated with the New York City Self-Help Clearinghouse, for final approval and a private training session.

I was excited. Despite feeling like something "the cat wouldn't even want to drag out of the garbage can," I had important work to do and could not allow myself to give in to all the pain and fatigue. I had to pace myself. And I did. My visits to the three doctors at LIJMC responsible for my SS care must have thrown their schedules completely off because, as I discussed my ideas with them, they too became excited, very supportive and involved in starting a Sjögren's syndrome mutual aid group. These three doctors, Dr. Steven Carsons, Dr. James J. Sciubba and Dr. Ira Udell, a cornea specialist, did more than just talk to me about the group. They enlisted the interest and support of colleagues and urged them to help by serving on our Medical Advisory Board. We were on our way.

Dr. Sciubba, Chairman of the Department of Dentistry at LIJMC, arranged for a meeting room and informed his other SS patients about our group. The New York chapter of the Arthritis Foundation (AF) gave us seed money for our first two mailings and also put me in touch with the Long Island Division of the AF. Chickie Goldstein, Medical Director; Frances Mason, Self-Help Coordinator of the New York chapter; and Pat McAsey, Executive Director of the Long Island Division, have been wonderful counselors and supporters. Both groups, as well as the Patient Services Department at Arthritis Foundation headquarters in Atlanta, continue to help by referring their SS patient inquiries to us and by publicizing our symposium and local meetings.

At our first meeting, in December 1983, the small conference room that had been reserved was filled to overflowing. Fourteen frustrated patients and eleven family members attended. We decided to meet the following month in a larger room. It was exciting. We were learning and sharing.

That September, *The New York Times* printed my reply to a Jane Brody column about dry mouth. Thanks to the national and international circulation of *The Times,* inquiries started coming in from all over the country. The fall of 1984 also marked our first symposium, with Dr. Norman Talal as our guest speaker. In April 1984, the Long Island Weekly section of *The New York Times* carried an article about our self-help group. There is nothing that can equal a good story in print (regardless of how much more glamorous a TV or radio interview may seem). People can cut it out, xerox it, and send it to friends and relatives. And that is exactly what occurred as a result of that article. A woman in New York sent it to her friend in Los Angeles, because she remembered that her friend's daughter (who happened to be living in Seattle) had SS. This was the start of our Seattle chapter. And a doctor at the NIH told one of his "go-getter" patients about us, resulting in the start of our Washington, DC chapter.

At our January meeting, it was decided to "pass the cup" to offset future mailing costs. And by our third meeting, attendees were so enthusiastic that they suggested we have membership dues. Our problem became an administrative one, since we were not yet incorporated and therefore could not get an organization bank account in New York State. Dr. Sciubba came to the rescue by helping obtain a special hospital account for our group until our incorporation in the summer of 1985.

LAUNCHING THE NEWSLETTER

Our next big step forward came as a result of a meeting that had been arranged with some officers of the Lupus Foundation of America (LFA). Although we had arranged the meeting to learn more about bylaws and chapters, the most productive part of the meeting came when Fran Heims, an interested friend but not an SS patient, and I brought up the newsletter the LFA put out. We thought putting out a simple newsletter could serve a dual purpose—a report on the past meeting as well as a notice for the coming one. Fran offered to help edit the sheet. She drew our first masthead. I took the finished copy over to LIJMC, where Dr. Sciubba's secretary gave me permission to xerox the 30 copies we needed for our first issue in May 1984. Although Fran could not continue to help due to back surgery, *The Moisture Seekers Newsletter* owes its birth to her help. By October 1984, we had expanded to a four-page, professionally printed format. Once again, LIJMC came to our rescue and for the first two years helped with the mailing, which went out first class. Our current monthly circulation is 6500, with newsletters going to members all over the world. It is now translated into Japanese and Dutch.

PRO BONO SERVICES

Organizations such as ours are very dependent on personal friends and contacts for pro bono services. To Sherman Lawrence, Esq. we will always be indebted for filing the papers necessary for our incorporation as a nonprofit organization in the State of New York, and we will remember my dear departed friend Sylvan Gefen for serving as the Foundation's accountant and auditing our books for us from our start until he became critically ill. If you think filing a personal income tax is a bother, you should see the records and work necessary for nonprofit organizations such as ours. My dear husband, Herb, currently devotes the majority of his time to developing computer programs for the SSF so that labels for newsletters can come out in zip code order, records of new members for each chapter can be sent to the proper leaders, renewal notices can go out, and special letters can be sent to a targeted section of our mailing list.

THE SJÖGREN'S SYNDROME ANNUAL SYMPOSIUM

"Living with Sjögren's, Day-to-Day with a Chronic Disease" is the subtitle of our annual symposium. It aptly describes the focus of the program, which is to bring to patients and interested health professionals the latest news concerning treatment and practical ways of dealing with the various aspects of the disease. The program usually consists of a guest speaker noted for his work related to the diagnosis or treatment of a particular aspect of Sjögren's syndrome. Distinguished guest speakers have included Dr. Norman Talal, Dr. Harry Spiera, Dr. Philip Fox, Dr. Jan U. Prause and Dr. Haralampos Moutsopoulos. In addition to the guest speakers, the program also has a resource panel of specialists, usually clinicians in rheumatology or immunology, ophthalmology and dentistry. The 1988 symposium for the first time had a separate morning session devoted to "Living with Sjögren's in the Family," a discussion of the psychological implications of living with a chronic illness. The discussion was led by Dr. Robert Phillips, a clinical psychologist who, as Director of the Center for Coping with Chronic Conditions, is well known for his work with patients who have illnesses for which there is at present no cure. The symposium presentations are reported in *The Moisture Seekers* and tapes of the program are also available. We received so many requests from our members in various parts of the country for similar programs closer to their home base that we decided to hold the 1989 symposium at the Clinical Center of the National Institutes of Health in Bethesda, Maryland. Not only did this enable members and local health professionals who had not previously attended the symposium to do so, but it also gave us an opportunity to involve in the program several doctors in the Washington, DC area who, although closely identified with some aspect of Sjögren's syndrome, had not previously participated in the annual symposium. The Foundation does not pay its speakers and tries to avoid costly travel reimbursements by piggy-backing the date of the symposium and the special programs to a time when the desired speaker will be in the area. The symposium itself and the tremendous circulation of the symposium reports in the newsletter provide excellent exposure for the speakers' remarks. Doctors now regard it as an honor and privilege to be asked to participate in our annual symposium.

CHAPTER DEVELOPMENT

Growing is not all glorious, even if it is glamorous. The many chapters and contact leaders listed in each newsletter require a great deal of support and servicing, beginning with their initial request to serve as an "arm" of the Foundation. Contact leaders respond to local requests for information and are expected to attempt to increase local public awareness about SS. The Foundation forwards to the local contact, group and chapter leaders the names of local people who have contacted the Foundation. The next developmental step is an SSF group, which consists of a minimum of seven Foundation members. These SSF groups, usually quite informal, require a leader and a medical advisor. Their meetings may be no more than coffee hours and rap sessions. The Foundation reimburses the leader for expenses incidental to the functioning of the group, such as postage and telephone calls. Groups are encouraged to elect officers and become chapters. The chapter application must bear the signatures of 15 SSF members. Chapters must have a medical advisory board consisting of a rheumatologist or immunologist, an oral specialist, and a cornea and external eye disease specialist.

A tremendous amount of work is necessary to service our chapters and to make certain that all activities conform with the Foundation's standards and bylaws and the IRS regulations for nonprofit foundations. Many of our chapters are doing outstanding work in educating the public as well as their members. They participate in local health fairs, work hard to get the media to cover their meetings and write human interest articles about members. Our Twin Cities, Central Arizona and Southeast Florida chapters produce local newsletters that go to local doctors as well as the chapter members. Our high standards have resulted in recognition by many "networking" groups. The National Institute of Dental Research (NIDR), the Arthritis Foundation, health columnists, the American Academy of Ophthalmology (AAO), and the Office of Public Health Information Clearinghouse (OPHIC) of the National Institutes of Health (NIH) each refer SS patients to our organization for information and help on SS.

MEDICAL INTEREST

Increasing medical interest and awareness about Sjögren's syndrome is a most important function of the Foundation. As the number of diagnosed SS patients increases, so too does the interest of the medical community in responding to their need for knowledgeable and caring medical care. The 1989 conference on "The Many Faces of Sjögren's" was a direct result of testimony that Betsy Latiff, a member of the SSF Board of Directors, and I gave in 1987 before the National Commission on Orphan Diseases. That conference, which took place in January 1989, was without question one of the Foundation's most significant achievements. It was sponsored by the National Institute of Arthritis and Musculoskeletal and Skin Diseases

(NIAMS) and the Arthritis and Musculoskeletal Diseases Interagency Coordinating Committee. In addition to Conference Chairman Lawrence E. Shulman, Director of NIAMS, there were three co-chairmen, one from each of the three principal NIH Institutes involved in "the many faces of Sjögren's": Michael A. Lemp, MD, Professor and Chairman, Department of Ophthalmology, Georgetown University; Philip C. Fox, DDS, Head of the Clinical Studies Unit, National Institute of Dental Research; and Haralampos M. Moutsopoulos, MD, Professor and Chairman, Department of Internal Medicine, University of Ioannina, Greece. In conjunction with the conference, the National Library of Medicine prepared a special issue on Sjögren's syndrome for the Current Bibliographies in Medicine Series.

INTERNATIONAL AFFILIATES

In 1985, I received a call from Lyn Linse, an English woman who was in the United States visiting her family. She had heard of our existence from the Biosonics Company. We corresponded regularly, and on her next visit we met at JFK Airport in New York and discussed how Lyn could start a British affiliate of the SSF. The British Sjögren's Syndrome Association (BSSA) is the result of her efforts. Lyn and her husband moved to Scotland, and soon after Lyn made plans to start a group there. Lyn still edits the excellent *BSSA Newsletter,* and we have reprinted some of its articles in *The Moisture Seekers.*

As a result of my attending the First International Conference on Sjögren's Syndrome, which took place in May 1986 in Copenhagen, overseas awareness and interest in the Sjögren's Syndrome Foundation was greatly increased. I was able to personally explain our needs as patients, including the inadequacies of many of the palliatives prescribed for SS, as well as our need for more information about our disease. Many of the doctors attending that conference have not only become members of the Foundation, but are actively helping us. Jan Prause of Denmark and Harry Moutsopoulos of Greece have been guest speakers at our annual symposia, Dr. Prouse in 1987 and Dr. Moutsopoulos in 1988. Dr. Susumu Sugai of Japan heads the Japanese affiliate of the SSF, and he is planning to translate our handbook, *Sjögren's Syndrome: An authoritative guide for patients*, into Japanese. Several of our overseas medical friends are working with their local patients to start SSF affiliates. Dr. Daniele Goldberg, who became our "French Connection" as a result of her work with Dr. Talal, in addition to caring for her own patients, took on several of our members who wanted medical advice while visiting Paris.

At the Second International Conference on Sjögren's Syndrome, held in Austin, Texas in October 1988 under the chairmanship of Dr. Norman Talal, our national and international connections were strengthened and increased. Several of the doctors promised to write articles for *The Moisture Seekers* about the research they are doing. After completing their sabbatical, Doctors Jehudith and Yehuda Scharf returned to Israel and made plans to start an Israeli SSF connection. Our Dutch affiliate, the National Vereniging Sjögren-patienten, was already in existence when Mr. H. Lissenberg, their president, contacted us about joining our international network, which they did in 1987. Ruth Borah, one of their members, attended our 1987 symposium and translated the minutes of their meetings into English.

NETWORKING WITH OTHER ORGANIZATIONS

In September 1987, as President of the Sjögren's Syndrome Foundation, I was one of 160 self-help leaders chosen to attend Surgeon-General C. Everett Koop's Conference on Self-Help. Several times the discussion centered on improving the credibility of a group and its recognition by medical professionals. I felt proud that the Foundation has encountered no such difficulties and that we have been commended by medical professionals for the help we render our members.

NEED FOR PATIENT LITERATURE

When I was finally diagnosed as having Sjögren's syndrome (after a year of going from doctor to doctor with my medical complaints), I became aware of the acute need for patient literature and information about this hard-to-diagnose, poorly understood, massively ill-treated disease. As Abbey Meyers of the National Organization for Rare Disorders has stated, "Sjögren's syndrome is not really a rare disorder; it is simply massively undiagnosed." It is a sad situation when you know that according to professional estimates there are probably as many as 1 million people in the United States alone with SS. According to the Centers for Disease Control, Sjögren's syndrome doesn't even exist. They have no statistics on its incidence. However, we hope that will soon be remedied. Dr. Stephen Heyse, a member of Dr. Shulman's staff at NIAMS, has assured me that with an expanded staff in view, a priority task will be to gather statistics on the incidence of SS.

The Foundation responds to inquiries for information with a leaflet about SS, developed with physicians, plus a copy of our newsletter. We have a membership package of articles that are sent out upon receipt of an application. When doctors request information, we respond with a letter outlining the highlights of our programs and services, including the annual symposium, and a set of the membership materials. We have found that although the doctors themselves do not always become paying members of the Foundation, they do keep our materials to show their SS patients and encourage them to join the Foundation. Many doctors cannot afford the time necessary to cover all the information contained in our membership package; and rheumatologists usually cannot give new patients the detailed information on eye and mouth care contained in our membership material.

Our book, *The Sjögren's Syndrome Handbook: An authoritative guide for the patient,* represents the first time that a work on Sjögren's syndrome has been written by medical specialists expressly for patients and their families. This book is another example of the cooperation that exists between doctors and the Foundation. Each of the 26 authors, including physicians, dentists, psychologists, and nutritionists, has made valuable contributions. The three medical editors—Doctors Carsons, Talal, and Sciubba—have contributed their services. Published in June 1989, the first printing of 5000 copies quickly sold out and a second printing of 3000 was ordered. The acclaim accorded the book by both patients and doctors has been most gratifying. Many patients have sent in reorders for the book to give to their doctors. And many doctors have ordered copies to keep in their offices to show their patients.

The recently published medical textbook, *Sjögren's Syndrome: Clinical and Immunological Aspects,* edited by Doctors Talal, Moutsopoulos, and Kassan, contains a chapter on "The Patient's Perspective," which as SSF president and founder I was asked to write. According to Dr. Talal, this contribution by a patient to a medical textbook is unique. It once again demonstrates the high regard that medical experts on Sjögren's syndrome have for the Foundation.

For the past few years we have been exhibiting our literature and services at professional conferences such as those given by the American Rheumatism Association (now the American College of Rheumatology), the American Academy of Ophthalmology and the American Dental Association. Our exhibits and the materials we distribute to patients are increasing medical awareness about SS and helping to keep the medical professionals alert to our needs.

The history of the Sjögren's Syndrome Foundation would be incomplete without mention of the National Organization for Rare Disorders (NORD) and Abbey Meyers, its executive director. Abbey's counsel in directing our efforts to persuade Boehringer-Ingelheim to institute trials relating to bromhexine as a safe and effective medication for SS has been invaluable. Her help in introducing us to the proper people in the FDA and the Office for the Development of Orphan Drugs will never be forgotten. NORD's annual meeting is a great learning experience, and I wish each of our chapter, group and contact leaders could attend. In 1989, the Foundation underwrote the registration fees for leaders wishing to attend, with travel expenses being paid for out of chapter funds. The NORD meeting is an opportunity for sharing knowledge, learning new techniques, getting the latest information on how government actions will affect our organization and appreciating the problems of other groups.

Connective tissue diseases such as scleroderma, lupus and Raynaud's syndrome not only affect SS patients, but have several common manifestations. Networking among the organizations representing these diseases is important. We share patients, information and skills. Nancy and Harlan Hersey of the Scleroderma Information Exchange not only put us in touch with other scleroderma groups, but have twice traveled from Rhode Island to Long Island to videotape our symposium.

INCREASED PUBLIC AWARENESS

The Sjögren's Syndrome Foundation has turned Sjögren's syndrome from a disease that hardly anyone had even heard of into one that is receiving increasing attention and help from medical professionals. To all the people who have helped us reach this stage, only some of whom have been specifically mentioned here, go my personal thanks, plus those of every Sjögren's syndrome patient. They have helped us to help ourselves.

Despite the fact that public awareness about Sjögren's syndrome is on the increase, "Sjögren's" is still a very difficult name to pronounce, and we receive many calls from people who haltingly spell out each letter. (The pronunciation of Dr. Sjögren's name is "Show-gren.")

19

Hearing Loss: The Value of Self-Help

Patricia A. Clickener

The quality that makes us truly human is our ability to communicate with other humans. When communication is threatened or cut off, life itself is threatened. Even Helen Keller, both blind and deaf, believed that hearing is our major life sense. As she noted, blindness separates us from things; deafness separates us from people.

My purpose here is to give some insights into how hearing loss truly is life-threatening, and then to describe how the self-help concept implemented nationally has been successful in bringing hard-of-hearing persons to effective adjustment.

As hearing impairment strikes at the very essence of being human, it impacts in a myriad of ways. It restricts the ability to be productive, frequently manifested in lowered career expectations, lost jobs or early forced retirement; it limits social intercourse; it has a major impact on relationships with spouses and family members; it reduces constructive use of leisure time; it affects physical and mental health; it often leads to poor self-image, to isolation, to despair, and ultimately it can affect the will to live.

Over 19 million Americans have some degree of hearing impairment. Fewer than 2 million are deaf; over 17 million have mild to profound hearing losses. Many of these people have yet to seek out appropriate medical diagnosis or care. Hearing loss is no respecter of age, as there are many causes of hearing loss and they can affect the hearing mechanism at any time from birth onward. However, the heaviest incidence of hearing loss is among older persons. Under age 55, less than 10 percent of us have hearing problems. Between 55 and 64, that incidence moves up to 15 percent. From 65 to 74, 24 percent, and after 75, 39 percent have hearing losses of some magni-

This chapter was adapted from a paper presented by Howard E. Stone, Founder and Executive Director of SHHH, at Bristol University, Bristol, England.

tude. The situation worsens with the elderly in nursing homes, where 9 of 10 have significant hearing problems.

For many, hearing loss happens slowly and is progressive. For others, onset is rapid, giving the person little time to adjust to this new reality. No matter who, or when, or how—the loss of hearing creates a reaction not unlike that to any major loss. There is a natural history that appears to differ only in length of time and degree of reaction, not in its course. From shock, people typically move through stages of denial, anger and guilt to some level of adjustment. Although adjustment for some begins even prior to diagnosis, many persons seem to get stuck somewhere in the process. An estimate has been made, by those who work with hearing-impaired people, that on the average the denial phase extends for 7 years.

The path through the stages just outlined is lengthened by a variety of factors, the lead one being society's current perceptions of hearing loss. Although attitudes have improved over time—in 550 A.D. the Justinian Code barred from the rights of citizenship people who were deaf—the stigma of hearing loss is still quite pronounced. The desire to hide or deny hearing loss is very strong in our society, perhaps with good reason. Even today, people who are hearing-impaired are often viewed as incompetent, stupid and subject to ridicule. The costs to the individual and to society are high.

Reaching a level of adjustment is compounded by the many mini-adjustments required both physically and psychologically. An invisible condition without external evidence, without sign language as used by many deaf people, the hard-of-hearing are in limbo. They do not belong to deaf communities and they are often estranged from the hearing community of which they had been a part.

Uncertainty, anxiety and the development of chronic stress produce adverse perceptions that perpetuate a vicious circle. Fatigue, caused by the strain of concentrated listening and lip reading, reduces the hard-of-hearing person's physical and psychic capability to function and to cope. Isolation, a feeling of being alone—even in the middle of a crowd—develops the trend toward withdrawal. Perceived rejection sets in, accompanied by poor self-esteem. The process of socialization gradually shuts down. The telephone, one of the most basic tools in our civilization, becomes an instrument of torture for the hard-of-hearing person who no longer can decipher conversation without lip reading. Many activities that once enriched each day and were to enhance the "golden years" no longer are possible. Add to this the perceived and very real threats to physical safety experienced by the hard-of-hearing person, and you have an initial understanding of why hearing loss truly is life-threatening.

For a hard-of-hearing person to stay in effective communication requires tremendous physical and emotional energy, far beyond that required normally by a hearing person. The breakdown of communications causes intense stress, which hard-of-hearing people live with constantly.

Such unrelenting pressure produces changes in behavior and in emotional health. Isolation, despair, defeat—a downward spiral is in place for the person to lose the will to live.

A new field of study, psychoneuroimmunology, contends that the body's immune system can be affected behaviorally, leading to increased or decreased disease susceptibility. The point is that when we lose our will to live, we open ourselves to more terminal types of illness such as cancer, heart disease and leukemia. Medical science and psychology are working toward a comprehensive view of how our emotions directly affect our physical well-being. We are moving from the concept of separation of mind and body back to awareness of interaction between the two. Bernie Siegel makes some excellent points about this in his book *Love, Medicine and Miracles.*

If people are getting stuck in the denial, grief or guilt phases that precede adjustment, what becomes important is how to get them unstuck. Until 1979, no major mechanism existed to help people learn how to do this for themselves. Then, in November 1979, Self-Help for Hard-of-Hearing People, Inc. (SHHH) was founded. SHHH is a volunteer, international organization of hard-of-hearing people, their relatives and friends. It is a nonprofit, nonsectarian educational organization devoted to the welfare and interest of those who cannot hear well yet want to remain a part of the hearing world.

SHHH is an educational organization. As one definition has it, education is "leading forth the intellect and the emotional capacities of the learner; in short, his or her entire personality, enticing it out of its most secret retreats and challenging that personality to a sort of wrestling match, a full-scale struggle to understand and cope with all the complexities of being human." That is exactly what SHHH tries to do.

By publishing a journal about hearing loss (the only one of its kind in the U.S.), along with brochures, educational papers and training manuals, and by putting on workshops and conventions, SHHH educates its members.

There is nothing SHHH (or anyone else) can do for persons who are hearing-impaired until they make the decision to help themselves. However, a helping hand, expressions of encouragement, association with (or at least awareness of) hearing-impaired role models and education from an empathic source can all impact on that decision. Even if a positive decision has been made to help oneself, many people struggle to reach that goal of adjustment. Self-help and peer groups can facilitate the process of change.

Finisdore (1984) states that the adult who acquires a hearing loss has already forged a personal and social identity, but with the onset of hearing loss, many fears arise. The person fears ridicule, people, new situations, chance encounters, sudden noises, being slighted, and being avoided or made conspicuous.

Peer-support and self-help groups often are established for problems that are given low status by society. The central issue of these groups is acceptance of the disability and a new social identity. This type of group can help the hearing-impaired members learn how to integrate hearing loss into their lives. The groups will also allow family members and friends to meet and to learn about other families and their coping methods with hearing-impaired members.

SHHH does these things at the local chapter level. There are 240 chapters and groups of SHHH meeting in 46 states, with more continuously forming. The chapter focus is on education and self-help activities that foster growth and acceptance for each individual at a pace comfortable for that person. Opportunities are available for leadership roles, giving members chances to build self-confidence and self-esteem. As a result, we have seen dramatic changes in many members. Invariably, the very first reaction upon coming to a SHHH meeting near home is, "I never knew there were so many other hard-of-hearing people." In that flash of understanding, the glue in the adjustment process begins to unstick.

Life is lived in community. When something unintentional happens to isolate a member of any community, adjustment must be made, both by the individual and by the community, in order to bring about a new and satisfactory circumstance. In short, adjustment concerns the individual and his or her environment, as well as the interpersonal relationships peculiar to that individual.

For that reason, SHHH encourages families to attend meetings with the hearing-impaired person. Special programs are held to educate families, to sensitize them and to show them in practical terms how they can improve a situation that has deteriorated because of a member's hearing loss. Take the case of marriage. Using Sternberg's theory of love (Trotter 1986), the components of commitment, intimacy and passion are all affected by hearing loss. Both parties to the union (if there is anything left at this point) begin to understand through SHHH meetings that adjustments are practical and can save the marriage.

Perhaps the most important activity in which SHHH is engaged, for helping hard-of-hearing people move into an effective adjustment stage, is a training program of coping strategies. Developed in conjunction with Gallaudet University, the program is being offered to a number of SHHH chapters. Groups meet weekly for 8 weeks and focus on problem recognition and problem solving. Results from this program have been excellent.

Through national programs and local groups and chapters, SHHH has achieved an increased quality of life for its members, one not believed possible after hearing loss. We have arrived at a number of conclusions that tie together our broad base of experience with self-help and the disability of hearing loss:

1. While the burden of responsibility for adjustment to hearing loss rests with the hard-of-hearing person, support structures within the family and community share the challenge to successful adjustment.
2. Hearing loss affects people differently. Each person must determine what that loss means in the context of his or her experience, circum-

stances and perceptions of self. As Rocky Stone, founder of SHHH, has often said when speaking to hard-of-hearing people, "You have only lost your hearing, not your humanity."

3. Psychological problems prior to the onset of hearing loss probably will complicate successful adjustment. It is important to sort out what is and what is not caused by hearing loss.

4. In addition to detailed data regarding the hearing-impaired person, environment—including the people around that person—must be taken into consideration.

5. The hearing health delivery system has not yet accepted the need for much broader involvement by professionals in the area of rehabilitation.

6. Our members see themselves as part of the solution to their problems and demand participation, as equals, in the rehabilitative process.

On this latter point, we find that by taking responsibility for their health in its broadest sense, people discover new meaning and fulfillment as they participate along with the best of medical science in maximizing their health. The anxieties, the fears, the loneliness that we take to the physician's office are compounded if there is no personal interest, no rapport between our doctors and ourselves. With increased technology and specialization in medicine, it is all too possible that people may feel left out of the process. When that happens, we are treated like things. Frequently, too frequently, when doctors talk, they talk about us, not to us. Assertiveness, then, becomes a part of the holistic process consumers are finding themselves engaged in as they take charge of their own health. Through SHHH, hard-of-hearing people are developing the personal mechanisms to enter into intelligent and assertive partnerships with their doctors and audiologists.

It has been SHHH philosophy from its inception that we will work constructively with all facets of the hearing health care delivery system toward satisfying the needs of hard-of-hearing people. Issues of *Shhh Journal* have been distributed without charge to otolaryngologists, audiologists and hearing aid fitters throughout the country for several years. We know that two things are happening with those issues. The professionals are reading them and learning from them. They tell us that the insights into the psychological ramifications of hearing loss are keener in *Shhh Journal* than those they obtain from their own professional publications. Secondly, the journals are being placed in waiting rooms for patients to read and learn from.

As an organization, we have excellent working relationships with the American Academy of Otolaryngology, Head and Neck Surgery and the American Speech, Language, Hearing Association. Each SHHH chapter selects professional advisors—doctors, audiologists and others—from the local community to consult with them in their educational activities. We believe that this two-way interchange is mutually beneficial.

What is still needed, however, is additional outreach into the medical profession, particularly at the general or family practice level. The early signs of hearing loss should be, but commonly are not, picked up by the family physician as part of routine visits. If patients with beginning hearing losses were made aware of the fellowship, empathy and practical benefits of a self-help group, the pathway to acceptance and adjustment could be effectively shortened.

We look into a future in which the hearing health care team and hearing-impaired persons share equally in the rehabilitative process. Although gradual negative feelings may develop after diagnosis of hearing loss, SHHH members have demonstrated that change is possible and a better quality of life is the reward. Most importantly, they have learned that "We cannot do it alone—but we alone can do it."

REFERENCES

Finisdore, M. Self-help in the mainstream. *Volta Review* 86(5), 1984.
Ries, P.W. Hearing ability of persons by sociodemographic and health charateristics: United States. Vital and Health Statistics. Series 10, No. 140. DHHS Pub. No. (PHS) 82-1568. Washington, DC: U.S. Public Health Service, 1982.
Trotter, R.J. The three faces of love. *Psychology Today,* September 1986.

20

Multiple Sclerosis Telephone Self-Help Support Groups

Sharon Romness, PhD, Vicki Bruce, BA, RN and Catherine Smith-Wilson, MA

In our efforts to develop a general self-help strategy utilizing telephone conferencing for chronically disabled persons with multiple sclerosis (MS), we began by focusing on: (1) an examination of existing telephone self-help groups based on first-hand experience, (2) a review of the advantages of phone conferencing and (3) an assessment of the obstacles involved. Two populations were addressed in the telephone self-help groups being studied: homebound persons with MS and chronically ill persons with MS who had transportation and fatigue problems.

The duration of the groups ran from 2 to 5 months. Each group met weekly at a designated time for 1 hour on the phone. The size of the groups varied from 5 to 10 members. Termination of the groups was solely due to financial constraints. At this writing, the homebound group is still meeting weekly after 3 years.

The groups were initiated because of the results of a needs survey conducted by the agency. Over 40 percent of the respondents indicated that they relied upon others to be transported from place to place, and the most unmet need was talking with others who had the same illness. The society therefore budgeted monies to pay for conference calls for MS patients. The cost of each call averaged $150. The agency ran six groups the first year.

The advantages of having a self-help group meet by telephone are both obvious and obscure. The most obvious is the convenience of being in one's own home, comfortable and at ease. People can come from all areas of a county or state and not have to worry about the distance. Another positive aspect of the phone group is its anonymity. One does not have to be seen or see others in the same situation. (This can be a disadvantage, but if the alternative is no contact at all, it is clearly preferable.) One may share feelings on a sensitive topic without having to feel embarrassment. As a result, people in the group become open to sharing their thoughts at an early stage in the group process. The time element is an advantage. The meeting begins on time because the operator connects everyone simultaneously, and it ends with everyone hanging up in unison.

Among the disadvantages of using a telephone strategy that might inhibit the group process are the following:

1. Developing a level of trust seems to take longer without the aid of face-to-face contact.
2. Domination of a member of the group, without the assistance of body language, can develop into a major problem.
3. Inclusion and participation of all members is essential. The facilitator must always be aware of who has spoken. Some members could be excluded simply because they were never called upon; others may drop out or stop listening.
4. Identification of feelings is critical. A member may become upset, but the facilitator and other members would only know this by the person's words, since nonverbal clues such as body language cannot be observed.

DESCRIPTION OF ONE OF THE GROUPS

Seven people were contacted regarding a telephone counseling project because they had responded positively to a questionnaire sent to them by the Multiple Sclerosis Society. The telephone counseling project was then initiated with the six persons who expressed an interest in the evening group. These six reacted positively and have continued with the group since its inception. Five women and one man decided to become members.

The group started out using the format of a telephone support group sponsored by the Multiple Sclerosis Society. The group leader was then given the names of potential members who were contacted by the group leader. All the members expressed interest and the group ran on a weekly basis. The meetings were held every Thursday evening from 7:00 to 8:00 P.M. The system chosen was an AT&T conference call originating from Minneapolis. To arrange for such a call, the telephone company first contacts the group leader and then the other members are called. The conference call becomes a group session in which all members participate.

The group members have discussed several key psychological points about multiple sclerosis. The first session was spent introducing all the group members so they would be able to understand and learn a little about each other. This has led to great camaraderie. The most difficult part of this group has been lack of visual communication and identification; as a result, we have learned to recognize the voices of the individual group members.

Over time, the members have discussed some key issues that they feel are very important and with which they have had to struggle over the period of their illness.

The members of the group range in age from 25 to 57. The length of their illnesses ranges from 1 1/2 to 16 years. All of the group members went through a period of extreme stress during the initial onset of MS. This seems to be a factor that is consistent with all the members, and it appears that a period of stress precedes the onset of relapse as well.

All the group members have expressed appreciation for a self-help group because they feel that other people cannot really understand the emotional stress and the difficulties they have gone through with their illness. The two common psychological issues that seem to surface with each of the members are depression and anger. They are depressed because of the shock of the onset of their illness and the fact that it interferes with their "normal" life goals. The activities in which they were quite competent, such as walking and sports, have been curtailed because of the illness. Since MS affects the neurological system, many key personal issues have been thwarted. Moreover, a sense of depression and anxiety arises from such impediments as being incontinent. The other major psychological issue is anger. All of the group members have said that they have experienced a sense of anger because they cannot control their illness. Their family members have also experienced this kind of reaction.

A key issue brought up by the group members is that they have encountered problems with employment and job opportunities. Some people at work were observed to avoid their fellow employees when their illness became apparent. It was hypothesized by some members that some of their coworkers were actually afraid of developing an illness similar to MS, connecting an issue of helplessness and immobility.

Other members wondered whether they should tell the employer when they are applying for a position that they have MS. Several members said they did not think that was wise, especially if the symptoms were not apparent. One woman made a comment that some people with whom she works, including a physician, have recommended that she take it easy and watch her stress level because of the progression of the disease. She felt that possibly this physician was afraid that he might develop the illness himself, even though MS is not contagious. As a result, they are dealing with a lot of social pressures and biases about MS and about being disabled.

The other concern involved finances. Most of the group members were partially employed or on total disability. Only two members had full-time employment. The financial aspects of disability are very important and create a fair amount of stress and discomfort for those affected.

Finally, the group voted to hold their sessions during the Christmas and New Year's season. The reason for this decision was to help them cope with the potential anxiety, depression and feelings of sadness that they might experience because of the holidays. All the members have decided to continue the group indefinitely, and they realize that if they are not able to attend a session, they are expected to notify the conference call operator, using an 800 number. This arrangement has worked out very well.

Several members of the group have begun to discuss their physical symptoms. They have noted such symptoms as fatigue, ataxia, numbness, spasms of the legs, bladder control and jittery sensations of the hands. Three members have also mentioned that they frequently feel fine, even though others may question this because of the disease process. It is possible that since these people do not experience pain or any physical irritation, their sense of well-being is based on the lack of any specifically irritating symptoms. These individuals often cannot walk or function normally. Since they do not experience any disturbing symptoms, they consider themselves to be fine even though persons who are "normal" have a difficult time understanding the patients' descriptions of themselves as feeling good. Thus it appears that the absence of irritating symptoms indicated to MS patients that their health was acceptable.

SUMMARY

The groups quickly began to express their many feelings about their illness and their disabilities. These included rage, embarrassment, hurt, disrupted family and work relationships, stress and shock reactions, and feelings of depression and isolation.

Although the members could only communicate verbally, they opened up rapidly into a genuine self-help group, including strong evidence of rapport, understanding, inclusion, cohesion and openness about feelings. This matches the desirable components of a group process in which members can both see and hear each other.

There is little doubt that the telephone self-help group process can be further utilized to improve the psychological status of persons with a chronic illness such as multiple sclerosis.

21

Starting from Scratch:
Self-Help for Peroneal Muscular Atrophy

Howard K. Shapiro, PhD

Every self-help group program starts with one person. There is some special problem in that person's life that represents a daily and long-term dilemma. Information on the issue is not readily available; most people are unfamiliar with and largely uninterested in the issue. Competent professional advice is difficult to come by, yet misinformation on the subject may be far more common. And, unseen by the general public, many other people are facing the same issue in their lives, asking questions, frequently spending money for professional assistance of dubious value, misunderstood by family members and friends. Finally, some dissatisfied person decides the time has come to get organized and take the initiative, to attack the issue that has attacked that person's life. A self-help group is born.

But the question is, how does a self-help group grow? To a certain extent this depends on the specific nature of the issue. Personal issues such as bereavement, domestic violence and terminal or chronic illnesses each have specific needs. Yet there are many common challenges to be met and many common aspects to the successful development of self-help group programs.

Since the origin of the National Foundation for Peroneal Muscular Atrophy in 1983, our relationship with the medical community has evolved from my background as a medical research scientist. I have a doctorate in biochemistry and have done laboratory studies at the University of Pennsylvania School of Medicine. In addition I have Charcot-Marie-Tooth disease (CMT), a form of genetic peripheral neuropathy also known as peroneal muscular atrophy. As I found research grant support for CMT studies harder and harder to come by during the early 1980s, my thoughts turned to the need for a public program devoted to the issue. Where there is no public recognition of a medical issue there is no priority. In this chapter I would like to briefly describe CMT and the current scope of our program, then focus on our relationship with the medical community.

WHAT IS CHARCOT-MARIE-TOOTH SYNDROME?

The CMT patient experiences degeneration of the peripheral nerves that control muscles in the lower legs and forearms. Muscles atrophy as these nerve fibers slowly deteriorate, leading to impaired walking and loss of hand and forearm muscle control. The peroneal muscles are located below the knee on the lateral surface of the leg; they assist in walking and are quite adversely affected in CMT. This syndrome, by the way, has nothing to do with teeth. Its name refers to the three physicians who first described this disorder a century ago.

Typically, CMT becomes a clinical disability issue during the second decade of life. As lower leg muscles atrophy, foot bone positioning changes. High arches and hammertoes develop, foot alignment and width may be altered and more serious foot bone malalignment problems may occur. Frequently these problems necessitate corrective orthopedic surgery.

Peripheral sensory neurons also deteriorate, leading to peripheral loss of thermal sensation and loss of sense of touch. Less known within the medical community, the autonomic nervous system is also affected. Thus, for example, a patient may experience some difficulty in breathing (weakness of the diaphragm muscles) or swallowing. Life expectancy generally is normal. Visual and auditory function may also be diminished, sometimes to a quite serious extent. Several patterns of inheritance of CMT are known, including autosomal dominant, autosomal recessive and X-linked. Hence CMT is more than one disease at the genetic level.

Our best estimate, based in part on European demographic studies (Skre 1974; Combarros et al. 1987), is that there are approximately 125,000 CMT patients in the United States. Although still virtually unknown to the general public, CMT is the most common genetic neurological disorder. It is important to note that the degree of symptomology varies widely from one patient to another. Thus, even within one kindred, one patient may be severely disabled and wheelchair-bound during childhood, another may be moderately disabled during adulthood and a third may have only the slightest of symptoms appearing late in life. Clinical heterogeneity is a fundamental aspect of CMT.

AN OVERVIEW OF THE NFPMA PROGRAM

In developing our program several nonoptimal factors have had to be addressed. These include:

1. Confusion regarding the name of this syndrome. In the medical literature this disorder is referred to as Charcot-Marie-Tooth disease,

peroneal muscular atrophy or hereditary motor and sensory neuropathy, with several clinical subvarieties recognized.

2. Absence of information on this subject within the medical community. Very few medical texts mention CMT at all, even though approximately one of every 2000 people have this syndrome. Most of those texts that do mention CMT provide only a minimum of information.
3. Misinformation on this subject within the medical community, still a very common problem.
4. No public recognition of this class of genetic neuropathies.
5. Patients who frequently know virtually nothing about their disease, not even one of its names.
6. A patient community that has been completely disorganized up to this point.
7. No convenient systematic opportunities for establishing contact with patient families. Medical data bases usually do not include a term specific for this syndrome. When seeking medical attention, a CMT patient may consult a podiatrist, an orthopedic surgeon, a pediatrician, a physician rehabilitation specialist (physiatrist), a physical therapist, an occupational therapist, a chiropractor or a neurologist.
8. A very limited financial base.

In our experience, a successful community outreach program can be run on very limited financial resources. Each such local, regional or national effort must include one or more individuals who are exceptionally committed to the cause, have time available for the effort, are articulate, can write competently and, preferably, have at least some college education. Such programs may or may not be incorporated. Small local groups meeting in someone's home or a church basement need not be incorporated. However, programs that involve active charitable fund raising should be registered at the state level as not-for-profit corporations and should apply to the Internal Revenue Service for classification as section 501(c) (3) public charities. A helpful quarterly newsletter on the legal aspects of nonprofit organizations, the *Nonprofit Monitor,* is available at no cost.

Services for patient families provided by our program include:

1. Regularly scheduled regional support group meetings with informal discussions or speakers.
2. Reprints of medical journal literature on various aspects of CMT.
3. Referrals to credible local medical authorities familiar with this subject.
4. A newsletter, the *NFPMA Report.*
5. Access to other information services.
6. CMT information kits and pamphlets.
7. Patient family educational seminars organized by our national office.

Public information work is essential for the development of a program such as ours. This involves developing a mailing list of local newspapers. They should be sent meeting announcements, a draft of a suggested general public service announcement and press releases regarding special events or accomplishments such as notable medical advances. For similar reasons an effort should be made to develop a local mailing list for television and radio stations. At our headquarters in Philadelphia we maintain a national directory of newspapers, television and radio stations and professional publications, which we are constantly expanding.

Fund raising for organizations such as the NFPMA is typically handled on two levels. On the local level, support groups raise the funds required for their activities by literally passing the hat at meetings, holiday sales, lotteries or other such efforts. At the national level, funds are raised by semi-annual appeal letters to our newsletter readers; grants from private foundations, corporations, service organizations and the federal government; contributions from regional United Way programs; and by gifts made in honor of or in memory of designated individuals, which are privately acknowledged and also mentioned in the *NFPMA Report*. The backbone of any successful national fund-raising effort is a growing mailing list of people interested in one's particular cause. Basic textbooks and college-level continuing education courses on the basics of public relations and fund raising for nonprofit organizations are now readily available.

TOWARD A WORKING RELATIONSHIP WITH THE MEDICAL COMMUNITY

Each self-help group must build its own bridges to the medical community. This is an active process. As CMT patients consult many different types of medical specialists, this is an ongoing challenge for the NFPMA. Several basic aspects of this process may be summarized as follows:

1. Establish a regional and, if possible, a national directory of medical specialists familiar with your subject of interest. Some of these names will come from satisfied patients in your self-help group, as will the names of some medical specialists to be avoided. You can also consult the medical journal literature to see which professionals are publishing clinical reports. Medical school libraries are open to the public, complete with librarians eager to assist new visitors. Other medical centers such as nursing schools and large regional hospitals may also have libraries open to the public. Medical journal literature is organized by author and subject on a month-by-month basis in the *Index Medicus* reference system. This same information is available in a national computer system known as *Medlars,* which is available on request at medical libraries. The fees for such computer searches are surprisingly low. (A 1988-89 *Medlars* search for CMT articles done at the University of Pennsylvania Medical School

library cost $8.00.) As another approach for identifying medical specialists familiar with a particular subject, you can send out a questionnaire to targeted departments at medical schools and regional medical centers. A self-help group can also arrange for booth space at medical conferences, thus encouraging direct discussions, as well as distributing literature on your subject of interest.

2. As the names and addresses of appropriate medical specialists come to your attention, add them to your newsletter mailing list. Professional quality newsletters are appreciated by medical specialists as well as patients.

3. Working through medical libraries and computer data bases, find out who is doing research related to your special subject. Establish contact with those people.

4. Encourage additional medical specialists to start research studies on your subject. Even if you cannot provide any financial support for such research, which frequently is the case, one's self-help group can be a source of patients for research studies. Inability to find enough patients willing to participate in a research study is a common and costly source of delay.

5. Incorporated, well-established self-help groups frequently will sponsor research symposia to encourage interest in their particular medical priorities and to facilitate distribution of information. In 1987 the NFPMA sponsored the Second International Conference on Charcot-Marie-Tooth Disorders, which was held at Columbia University. This conference brought together approximately 100 leading authorities on CMT from around the world for three days of discussions. Financial support for this meeting was obtained from several sources: a grant from the National Institutes of Health, corporate grants, private donations specific for this event and general funds of the NFPMA. The total expenses for this conference were approximately $52,000, but smaller conferences can be held on smaller budgets.

6. Publication of a medical text. On relatively rare medical issues, information is hard to come by. The proceedings of the Second International Conference on Charcot-Marie-Tooth Disorders was published in book form (Alan R. Liss 1989). This was the first medical textbook devoted exclusively to this subject. Its chapters include information on the details of CMT clinical diagnosis, clinical heterogeneity, genetic heterogeneity, secondary symptomology, demographics, biochemical research studies, pharmacological research studies, corrective orthopedic surgery and physical therapy. A self-help group may also be able to bring together a smaller group of medical specialists for a more modest text project, one not necessarily based on the proceedings of a conference.

7. Invite medical specialists to address patient family support group meetings and to discuss the disorder with media reporters as opportunities permit. In general, speakers at support group meetings are not financially compensated.

8. Register with regional and national referral networks. There are many such programs in the United States. Some of these programs will forward patient information inquiries, some publish directories of self-help organizations, and some will send information about a self-help group back to the person making an inquiry. The following is an introductory sampling of such programs:

National Information Center for Orphan Drugs and Rare Diseases, P.O. Box 1133, Washington, DC 20013-1133

National Center for Education in Maternal and Child Health, 38th and R Streets, NW, Washington, DC 20057

National Information Center for Handicapped Children and Youth, P.O. Box 1492, Washington, DC 20013

World Institute on Disability, 1720 Oregon Street, Suite 4, Berkeley, CA 94703

National Organization for Rare Disorders, P.O. Box 8923, New Fairfield, CT 06812

Neurology Institute (NIH), Building 31, Room 8A-16, Bethesda, MD 20892

National Society of Genetic Counselors, 233 Canterbury Drive, Wallingford, PA 19086

Department of Information Analysis and Publications, American Medical Association, 515 North State Street, Chicago, IL 60610

Each self-help group should endeavor to establish its own collaborative links with the medical community. Although there is no cure for CMT, we know that maintaining physical activity is important. CMT patients involved in carefully defined, ongoing physical therapy programs can actually regain a certain degree of lost physical abilities. On the other hand, patients who mistakenly avoid physical activity may well encourage a worsening of their disabilities. Hence, we frequently discuss rehabilitation medicine in our newsletter, at patient family educational seminars and at support group meetings. We have also established an informal working relationship with the Pennsylvania College of Podiatric Medicine to help explore an experimental form of CMT rehabilitation medicine based on the use of functional electrical stimulation.

We have assisted in obtaining CMT blood samples for several molecular genetics studies and have brought these projects to the attention of the patient community. In addition, my own efforts as a research scientist have continued on a part-time basis. Funded in part by the NFPMA and in part directly by a CMT family, I have continued a research program of metabolic screening studies on this syndrome (Shapiro et al. 1986). Thus, the NFPMA may be described as part self-help program, part research program and part educational program. Our relationship with the medical community is quite active, and we look forward to its continued development in coming years.

REFERENCES

Combarros, O., J. Calleja, J.M. Polo, and J. Berciano. Prevalence of hereditary motor and sensory neuropathy in Cantabria. *Acta Neurol. Scand.* 75:9-12, 1987.

Shapiro, H.K., G.C. Kahn, and H. Goldfine. Metabolic screening of Charcot-Marie-Tooth disease patients by gas chromatography/mass spectrometry. *Muscle and Nerve* 9(5S):128, 1986.

Skre, H. Genetic and clinical aspects of Charcot-Marie-Tooth's disease. *Clin. Genetics* 6:98-118, 1974.

22

The Dynamics of Self-Help in Healing Parental Grief: The Role of The Compassionate Friends

Dennis Klass, PhD

The Compassionate Friends (TCF) functions as an effective intervention with bereaved parents because there is a congruence between the dynamics of parental grief and the dynamics in the processes of the group. TCF's organizational structure and interaction patterns have been molded by the needs of newly bereaved parents and by the processes within the resolution of those bereaved parents who affiliate. The rituals and traditions of the group and the psychic energy in the bonds between members grow from the particular quality of parental grief. Clearly there are common elements in all self-help groups, just as there are common elements in all human suffering. In this chapter, however, I want to focus on the particular quality of parental grief and the particular characteristics of TCF in order to show the fit between the dynamics in the group and the dynamics of parental bereavement.

THE NATURE OF THE RESOLUTION OF PARENTAL GRIEF

The death of a child creates two disequilibria. First, there is a disequilibrium between the self and the social world, for the death of a child radically changes the social environment in which the parent lives. Second, there is a disequilibrium in the inner life of the parent, for the child who died was part of the parent's self. The resolution of parental bereavement is achieved when bereaved parents reach new equilibria in these two areas. We will look at these two equilibria and then examine the self-help process in TCF to see how each is facilitated within TCF.

Achieving Social Equilibrium

To find a positive resolution to parental grief is not simply to return to the status quo ante. Parental bereavement is a permanent condition. One of the consistent themes we have heard from bereaved parents is that the resolution of their grief is not simply cutting the attachment to the child and going on with new attachments in their lives. Rather, they speak strongly of something about themselves that has changed. They are not the same person they were before the child died. As they reconstruct their model of the self, so too they reconstruct their way of interacting within the social environment. Parents do no "get over" the death of a child, but they do go on living.

The resolution of grief as a resolution of an equilibrium between the self and the social environment is the focus of a large body of scholarly work based on John Bowlby's attachment theory (Bowlby 1969-1980; Parkes 1972; Parkes and Weiss 1983; Raphael 1983; Worden 1982). In this literature, individuals "recover" from grief "in the sense that they replan their lives and achieve a new and independent level of functioning" (Parkes and Weiss 1983, p.5). For these writers, the resolution of grief is giving up old roles, patterns of interaction and sources of gratification and finding new ones:

> The longer term adjustments to the loss may involve many processes. The bereaved person may need to grieve, and mourn, and finally relinquish old roles, patterns of interaction, and sources of gratification that were once fulfilled by the person who has died. Only when these are relinquished may new and satisfying roles, interactions, and sources of gratification evolve (Raphael 1983, p. 57).

The process by which the new social equilibrium is achieved is multifaceted. It involves intellectual recognition of the death, emotional acceptance of the loss and a reorganization of the individual's model of the self and his social interactions to match the changed reality (Parkes and Weiss 1983). Each facet holds special difficulties for bereaved parents.

The resolution of parental bereavement is not simply replacing the investment in the child with other investments. Rather, it is a reorganization of the self and the self's interactions within the environment (Edelstein 1984). Parents need to master the practical issues of the role of bereaved parent. They must learn to live in a world in which their control and competence have been radically challenged.

Each element of the reorganized self puts the parents in a new relationship with those around them, for as they resolve their grief, they are not who they used to be. In the best of cases, significant people in the social environment will affirm the new self; just as often, however, others demand that the parent remain the same as before. The ability of the parents to resolve the grief and find a new equilibrium may depend on the degree of flexibility they find in the social world as much as on the degree of flexibility they can find within themselves.

In the months right after the death, the parents may have difficulty assimilating the reality of the child's death. Each new situation that would have included the child must be processed with the understanding that the child is not there. One of our interviewees reflected on the question of the hardest part of her grief:

> The hardest part—I think reality, realizing the finality of it. Realizing that it is real, it's true. Living day to day without her. Holidays.
>
> Q: How does that sense of reality come to you?
>
> One place is in my career planning. When I'm planning to do things I might stop and think, maybe I can't do that, but then I say, 'Oh, I can do that; I don't have to worry about how doing things like traveling will affect [her] anymore.' I moved into an apartment. It had two bedrooms, and I thought, 'this bedroom should be hers.'

Special days that would have included the child are difficult, for each of the days comes with the message that the child is dead. "I didn't know a year had so many holidays," said one bereaved mother, "Thanksgiving, Christmas, Valentine's Day, Easter, Mother's Day, Father's Day, and his birthday and my birthday. Every time I think that he is not here and it hurts all over again."

Most literature and research on grief assigns to the bereaved the primary responsibility for recognizing reality. Among bereaved parents, however, the majority of reports are that the community has difficulty recognizing the reality in everyday interactions. In the early months of grief, bereaved parents often find that their natural support system experiences the death and pain as so difficult the the topic becomes forbidden. One parent reported:

> There we were at my mother's house for Christmas three months after [my son] was killed, and not one person, not one of my brothers or my parents, mentioned his name all day. I just sat there boiling. It was like they didn't care and they wanted to go on as if nothing had happened. The next time I saw my mother, I told her how much that had hurt me. She said, 'Well, we didn't want to make you sad by bringing it up.' What else do they think I am thinking about?

One of the ways others use to protect themselves from the full reality of the pain the parent feels is to convince themselves that the parent is "strong" or "handling it so well."

> That always came back to me, that 'You handled it so well.' Well, I didn't handle it well. . . . The hurt was there, but I couldn't show it and I didn't know how to handle the loss. I was like a zombie and they took that to mean that I was strong.

Another frequent method others use to protect themselves from the parent's pain employs statements of compensatory consolation, such as:

"You're lucky you have other children." Parents whose newborn dies may be told: "It is good you don't have many memories to be sad about." And parents whose older children die might hear: "Well, at least you had her for a few years."

Because the reality is so strong inside, but not integrated into the social reality, some parents are confused about how they appear to others. Conversely, they have trouble in their views of others because the social reality in which others are acting is so different from the parents' inner reality.

EMOTIONAL PROCESSES

For bereaved parents the symptoms of grief can be extreme. Parents often have no energy for several months after the child's death, a problem characterized this way by one parent in an interview: "I just tried to make it through the hour; never mind trying to think about making it through a day." They feel listless, tired and unable to concentrate. This is especially difficult for those parents who must return to work a few days after the death. Bereaved parents report that they are unable to perform routine mental tasks such as checking lists of numbers or typing. There is often a loss of short-term memory. Several men in one support group shared that they had all been allowed about 2 months of below-par performance on the job, but then they were expected to return to their former standard.

Emotions seem out of control; at any moment the parent may begin to cry. At other times when the parent expects to cry, the feeling is apathy. Relationships between spouses tend to become strained. If surviving children are young, parents often report they have limited patience and find themselves out of control when they begin to respond to slight misbehavior.

Parents' ideation is often strange. They think gruesome thoughts trying to recreate the accident or to picture the body in the grave. They blame themselves for sins or imperfections that could have caused the death. They may contemplate suicide as a way to join the child.

For some bereaved parents, the entire effort is spent trying to control the pain. In those cases there is usually a tacit agreement within the household not to talk about the dead child or about the circumstances of the death. Evaluations about the self are expressed in terms of hurting or not hurting. Early in our work with the Compassionate Friends, we called several people who had attended one or two meetings, but had not returned thereafter. We found that the majority had good natural support systems and did not think they needed the group, though a few years later some did begin attending again. A few parents we called, however, found that sharing painful memories and experiences with others was very stressful. One mother reported that her family was making every effort to get back to normal, but that when they talked about the child everyone became upset, so they put away all reminders of the child and things returned to normal. After a few minutes she said that the conversation with us was difficult and she terminated the interview.

When there is good social support, the pain is shared and the emotions within the inner representation and the experience of loss can be expressed. Parents can thereby allow themselves to experience the pain of the loss.

SELF AND SOCIAL INTERACTIONS TO MATCH THE NEW REALITY

How do parents learn to live in a world that includes the fact that their child is dead? They must build a new life with a diminished self in a poorer world. As one mother we interviewed observed:

> It's not over after a year or two years. It's an ongoing thing. Your life has changed. It's like moving from one town to another. You can't go back. Even if you did go back, it's not going to be the same.

The parent is confronted with a series of practical problems that have existential implications. For example, what should the parent say when asked the common question, "How many children do you have?" Other experiential issues include how to celebrate holidays and birthdays, what to do with the child's belongings, and how to deal with siblings and spouses.

Bereaved parents move into a whole new world. In that new world they find new ways of being themselves. In those cases where they had been easily hurt by others, they protect themselves from the hurt. The sense of the tentativeness of life brings reordered priorities. As they have felt the hurt and known the social estrangement that comes with the death of a child, they have become acutely conscious of themselves and have made some decisions about the stance they take in their world.

The resolution of parental bereavement is not simply the cessation of the early symptoms of grief. The resolution of the disequilibrium between the parent's self and the social environment is the establishment of a new self within a changed world. There is more to the new self, however, than simply changed interaction patterns and new sources of gratification in the world. There is a more private and intrapsychic aspect to the new self, for the relationship with the child is not severed. The world of the bereaved parent is a far poorer place than it was before the death of the child. To live in a diminished world requires solace. We find that as part of the resolution of parental bereavement, the inner representation of the child is transformed in a way that gives solace.

Achieving Psychic Equilibrium

A child is part of the psychic structure of the parent. At the same time it is the task of mature parenting to maintain the child as a person distinct from the self in such a way that it is possible to empathize with the child's needs and desires separately from the needs and desires of the self.

Many parents use the metaphor of amputation to describe the death of a child. They feel as if a part of the self has been cut off. The sense of a missing part of the self is an ongoing aspect of parental bereavement. As an amputee learns to live without the missing limb, so the parent learns to live "as a one-armed man," as a bereaved parent.

What happens to the inner representation of the child after the child dies? How does a parent find solace after a wound so deep as the death of a child? The answer to both questions is in the process of internalization of the inner representation of the child. The inner representation is made part of the ongoing self in such a way that it provides consolation to the parent, even as the parent learns to function within a world made poorer by the death of the child.

This intrapsychic aspect of the recovery from grief has been the focus of grief theory considered from a psychoanalytic perspective. For Vamik Volkan (1981) the basic task of grief is to internalize the inner representation of the dead person. There are three elements to an inner representation: (1) those aspects of the self that existed before the child was born and that are identified with the child; (2) characterizations or thematic memories of the child; and (3) emotional states connected with those characterizations and memories (Fairbairn 1952). Volkan finds two kinds of internalizations of inner representations: identification and introjection. Identification is the integration of the inner representation into the self in such a way that the two are indistinguishable and the ego is enriched. Introjection is the process of maintaining the inner representation as a frozen entity in the psyche, one that is separate from the ego.

The function of internalization is solace. The defining characteristic of solace is the sense of soothing. The word *solace* means something that comforts, that alleviates sorrow or distress. It is that which brings pleasure, enjoyment or delight in the face of hopelessness and despair. Solace emerges within irreducible meaninglessness in our lives, that place in human life where chaos seems to outweigh order, where the absurd abyss opens before us, where the purpose for our living seems overwhelmed by purposelessness.

Paul Horton (1981) finds that the majority of people have a history of solace that they nurture. Solace, he says, has three characteristics: (1) it is experienced as blended inner and outer reality (that is, it feels as if it is both inside and outside the self); (2) it is derived from, but not reducible to, the internalized mother figure; and (3) the comfort of solace is not challengeable, for the experience of solace is self-validating (Horton 1981, p. 26). Art and religion have the quality of solace objects for many people, as do recurrent fantasies or dreams. The calming effects of music would seem to be solace to many. These adult objects are no longer transitional, for they are an ongoing part of the adult's life. Horton finds that solace is necessary for the individual to be a part of society. Psychopathic criminals, he says, have no solace in their lives.

An examination of the lives of bereaved parents shows that introjection of the dead child is a common feature of the resolution of parental bereavement, that those introjections bring solace, and that such solace is a healthy part of the ongoing life of the parent. The introjection changes over time, especially in the first few years after the death. But for many parents, the introjection is the permanent residue of their loss. Some inner representations may move toward identification, but even in those parents who meld an inner representation of the child into their ego, other inner representations of the child remain as solace-giving introjections.

SOLACE THROUGH INTROJECTION

We can see introjection in linking objects, in religious solace and in memories.

Linking objects are objects connected with the child's life that link the bereaved to the dead; in so doing, they evoke the presence of the dead. We find that many parents use physical artifacts as linking objects for extended periods after the death of their child. The biggest linking object we found in our study was a truck. When we asked a father whose daughter had died 5 years earlier if he had an object that helped him feel her presence, he replied:

> It's that old pickup truck. She used to ride around in it with me. She would lean against me on the seat. It has almost 200,000 miles on it, but I am not going to sell it. By now I probably couldn't get anything for it anyway. I told the boys they could work on it and use it if they got it going. But I'll never sell the truck because I can sit in there and feel my daughter. It's great.

In religious solace, the inner representation of the child is experienced within a culturally given symbol. Religious solace is diverse and complex, but two examples can stand for that diversity and complexity. The sense that the child is in heaven is a widely held belief among bereaved parents, even those for whom other aspects of their former faith have been unhelpful. Knapp (1986) found that his interviewees could not sustain a belief that there is no afterlife.

A sense of the religious as found in nature also is widespread in the culture. When bereaved parents have a naturalistic mystical experience (Hood 1977), they can feel the presence of the child within that experience. One mother reported that on her daily walks she could quietly feel a sense of communion with her son who had been dead for 10 years.

> I'm a walker. I remember I used to take long walks with [my son]. We would go at any time of the year. In the winter he would roll in the snow and make angels. In the fall he would gather leaves. In spring and summer he would watch the birds and pick wildflowers. Sometimes I remember those times when I walk, but sometimes it is just the beauty. Like the other day, I was out early and as the sun rose, I was at peace and [he] was a part of that.

Bereaved parents can find the space that is between the self and the other in memories that are cherished and nurtured. Unconflicted and peaceful memories are often at the endpoint of a difficult process within parental bereavement. Memories are at first very painful, for they are reminders of the loss. To remember is to cry. Indeed, a common phenomenon among bereaved parents is guilt at that point in their grief when they no longer feel sad all the time.

Once the memory comes, the solace time is often ritualized. In Jewish ritual the yearly memorial regularizes the memory to appropriate times in the mourners' ongoing lives. When ritual is made part of the community, the bond with the child may become part of the bond with the community. The candlelight memorial service is the largest gathering of our local Compassionate Friends chapter. For the most part, however, we find that the child is not publicly remembered for long, and parents must find quiet moments during which they retreat from the world and return to a time when life was better.

The inner representation becomes a memory held in that space in the psyche that is neither completely self nor completely other. As we listen to these reports of memories, the emotional states attached to the thematic memories seem to be the aspect of the inner representation that carries the quality of solace. Writing nearly 20 years after the death of her daughter, a mother reflected on her memory of a beginners' ballet recital:

> I can't remember the details of the afternoon. . . . But I remember the feeling, somewhere between laughter and tears. I remember loving that small, beautiful person, my child. I remember my sense of admiration for her, and a fittingly stifled flood of pride. . . . I have forgotten so many things, but I remember the feeling. Always the feeling.

SOLACE IN IDENTIFICATION

Linking objects, religious solace and memories are all introjections in Volkan's understanding of the resolution of grief, for all keep the child as a frozen entity in the psyche. The majority of the solace we find in bereaved parents comes from those introjections. We also find the other kind of internalization—identification (Miller, Pollock and Bernstein 1968). In identification, the inner representation of the child is integrated into the self in such a way that it is difficult to distinguish the two. Because the inner representation of the child is maintained less as a separate entity, solace has a somewhat different character. It is found in a sense of reinvigorated life, in renewed feelings of competence. This solace is less clearly defined, but it is solace, for it provides comfort in the face of potential meaninglessness.

Identification has its social aspect. With adequate social support pain is shared, and in that sharing the relationship with the child is shared within the supportive relationship. Thus the identification with the child is made a part of wider identifications. In that wider context the life of the child can be integrated into the whole self. This is the process Volkan called the enrichment of the ego. One parent described the self-help process in a Compassionate Friends meeting as a circle of weavers in which the bonds that were with the child now become attached and interwoven with those of other bereaved parents in the group. Thus, rather than having the child as a frozen entity in the psyche, the inner representation of the child becomes a part of the ongoing social relationship within the group. The sense of oneness with other bereaved parents is an enlargement of the self—or in Volkan's terms, an enrichment of the ego.

Often identification is found in a decision to live fully in spite of the death. One parent wrote:

> I came to the decision that I was going to try to use my gift of life to the utmost as my son had used his. . . . There is joy in my life now. . . . We have sought positive ways to remember [him]. Members of our family continue to give books to a memorial shelf of books [at the library] . . . started by [his] friends. . . . Members of our family periodically give blood to the Red Cross, hoping to help others who may need that gift in their struggle for life. . . . Life will never be the same. I will always be disappointed that [he] did not have a longer life, but I will always be proud of him and love him. I continue to search for ways to bring love, hope and meaning in my life as I try to make use of my one gift of life.

SOCIAL SUPPORT IN GRIEF

The most consistent finding of research on grief is that social support is central to the quality of the resolution. Most of the research has been done with widows (Arling 1976; Bowling and Cartwright 1982; Cary 1979-80; Lopata 1973, 1979; Maddison and Walker 1967; Parkes 1972; Parkes and Brown 1972; Parkes and Weiss 1983; Raphael 1983; Sanders 1980-81; Silverman 1986; Vachon et al. 1982). A number of studies on bereaved parents have shown similar results, though the studies were far less extensive (Bourne 1968; Carr and Knupp 1985; Forrest, Standish and Baum 1982; Kowalski 1984; Rando 1983; Spinetta, Swarner and Sheposh 1981).

TCF is a social support system that grew out of the dynamics of parental bereavement, for it is run by bereaved parents to help bereaved parents. The processes within TCF are specifically fitted to the processes we have seen within parental grief.

THE COMPASSIONATE FRIENDS PROCESS

We will examine the dynamics of TCF by exploring the sense of affiliation with TCF felt by parents; we will then briefly look at the transition made by group members, from being helped to both being helped and helping others. We will find within the TCF process two dimensions that correspond to the two equilibria toward which the resolution of parental grief strives. We will see an interpsychic dimension that facilitates the internalization of the inner representation of the child in a way that brings solace, and we will see an experimental dimension that helps the parent find a place in the changed social environment.

Affiliation

We define those who have affiliation with TCF simply as persons who return to the group four or more times within an 8-month period and who say that they find the processes within the group helpful in their grief. Yet obviously this simple definition points to some very complex matters in a person's life.

AFFILIATION A: INTERPSYCHIC DIMENSION

The newcomer asks, "Are these people like I want to be?" Those who have been there longer say, "I was like that, but I am different now." It is this sense of identification with fellow travelers on the road through the valley of the shadow of death that we have called the *interpsychic dimension*. One's identification with others in the same condition moves one toward transformation of the inner representation of the dead child in the ongoing life of the self.

In a study of professional therapies, the study of the interpsychic dimension would largely center on *transference*. Transerference is the emotional attachment to significant figures in one's past that is projected onto a person in the present and therefore is available for use in the therapeutic interactions. In TCF this interpsychic dimension remains in the present, for there is very little sense of continuity that the bereaved parents feel with their personal pasts as they try to come to terms with their loss. The time factor, which could be several decades in the transference of therapy, is in TCF a matter of months. The self that is brought to the TCF meeting is not the old familiar self for whom social skills and social position are well established. It is a new self, one that is not pleasant to behold and whose future is frightening to project. That new self is isolated from the interaction patterns of the familiar self. The discovery that the new self can be socially validated within a group of others who share the same condition provides a beginning place to rebuild.

In group psychotherapy the interpsychic dimension would be understood in terms of group cohesiveness (Yalom 1975), but in self-help groups of bereaved parents, the group will stand far less internal stress than do therapy groups. In the self-help group, positive identification of others in a similar life situation is part of the decision to affiliate, whereas it is discovered in the psychotherapeutic group as the process matures. The Dutch psychologists van der Avort and van Harberden (1985) found *identification resonance* as the central theoretic construct in understanding self-help. The investment of the energy formerly invested in the child seems unique to these self-help groups.

The parent-child bond is part of the interpsychic dimension. Not only have other members experienced the same life crisis, but the group is a place in the present that includes the attachment the parents still feel to the dead child. It is not that parents reach into the past for the significant figure they will bring to the new attachment. The child is real to the parents, and the child can be real within the group. Because other inner representation of the child is available within the TCF process, the inner representation can be transformed within the process.

Because everyone else in the group has lost a child, the child who is dead is the common ground in the bond between bereaved parents. Thus the identification can have some of the emotional energy that was part of the bond with the child. One of the activities that bonds members of TCF to each other is sharing pictures of the dead children. At the national conferences there are boards on which parents can pin a picture of their child. Those boards become a gathering place for many parents. Our chapter has a picture-sharing session. Photographs are brought and passed around while stories are told about the occasion for the picture—the summer camp, the family baptism, or even the body after life support had been removed.

In discussing their relationship to the group, parents show in their descriptions a sense of unity with those whose lives had also been shattered by the death of a child, the feeling of being in a family-like community, and the sense that the group is an appropriate place to which energy formerly attached to the child might now be attached. The TCF credo makes that mixture explicit:

> We reach out to each other with love, with understanding and with hope. Our children have died at all ages and from many different causes, but our love for our children unites us. . . .Whatever pain we bring to this gathering of The Compassionate Friends, it is pain we will share just as we share with each other our love for our children.

These words were read at a Christmas candlelight memorial service:

> We are here tonight as Compassionate Friends because our beloved children lived and because they died before us—their parents. As we light a candle in the memory of each of our children, we do so in eternal gratitude that they lived. They are no longer physically here on this earth, but they are still with us in spirit and will always be. They are here in spirit to give us the courage to go on with our lives in a positive stance. It has been said—'Compassion is not pity that looks down: it is love that shares and divides the poignancy of pain.' As we light the candles tonight in remembrance of our cherished children, we do so as Compassionate Friends who care, who share, and who remember.

Although the elements within that bond between bereaved parents seem disparate on first hearing, the relationship of parenting to social support shows that the parent-child bond is not an individual matter, but rather that it is embedded in the bonding within the larger social network. Just as having other people share the joy of parenting is important to the quality of the bond established between the parent and child, the sharing of parental grief is important to the quality of the resolution of parental bereavement (Anisfeld and Lipper 1983).

TCF is not a group in which the child is forgotten. Rather, TCF is a group in which the parent can develop a full life that includes the child. The sense of being accepted within a community that includes the dead child is seen in the social programs the group holds. We can see the child's place in the group in the report of the chairperson of the annual picnic. She said there would be good food and games, but

> These are the sidekicks of our picnic. The center, the best, the reason we come back year after year is simply to be together. Whether meeting new people, talking to old friends, playing or just being there, it is the gathering that makes this event so special for so many of us.
> If our gathering is the center, our children lost are the heart and soul of our picnic. It is for and because of them that we have come, and it is for them that we have our cherished balloon released, a time set aside in our day to remember and include our special children.
> Helium-filled balloons are passed out, along with markers, giving us all one more chance to tell our children the things we most long to say—mostly 'I Love You.' And then, oblivious to the world around us, we stand as one, but each involved in his own thoughts, prayer and emotions as we release hundreds of balloons to the sky and they disappear; to a destiny we are certain they will reach.

The children are the heart and soul of the group, for it is the shared inner representations of the dead children that bond the members to each other. The children are in the midst of the group, not simply in the memories of each of the individual parents. Yet the inner representations of the children are also beyond the trees behind which the balloons disappear. The children are wherever balloon messages are carried. The group validates and supports the tie that parents still have with their child, and the group provides the ritual expression by which parents can communicate with the child they have lost. They "stand as one, but each involved in his own thoughts, prayer and emotion." Because the bond with the child is shared within the group, the parents can be in touch privately with the individual inner representation of their child. They are not simply remembering; they are communicating, sending messages that they know are received. Because the members share in the strong bond with the child, there is a tremendous strength within the group. Because there is such strength within the group, the bond with the child feels surer. One balloon sent into the sky would seem a lonely and fragile message. Hundreds of balloons, each addressed to an individual child, are a message sure to get through.

For some members the identification with the group is heightened by finding very close models for behavior in the group. At the TCF national conventions, special sessions are held for parents on specific kinds of children's deaths. Informal networks form continually in TCF chapters as parents whose experiences are very similar seek each other out. The group attempts to foster subgrouping by occasionally offering meetings aimed at one specific group—for example, the parents of suicides. On occasion the group facilitates such hookups by having a meeting in which a panel of parents coping with different kinds of deaths presents short speeches, following which the audience breaks into smaller groups with a panelist leading each.

The sense of unity with those whose lives have been shattered, the sense of hope at seeing that others have made it, the sense of finding an appropriate object on which to attach the energy of the parent-child bond, the sense of family in a supportive community, the sense of the shared loss of the individual's child and the special relationship with someone very much like yourself but further along are all part of the interpsychic dimension. That dimension allows for great intimacy by which the healing process can work.

It seems, however, that for some individuals, the intimacy of the TCF process does not open up the self in identification. Rather, intimacy threatens the defenses by which the pain is kept at bay. Knapp (1986) refers to some bereaved families as *isolated families.* They are internally atomized and nonsupportive. An isolate family is a closed system that does not interact within the larger social environment. When we called those who did not return after attending one or two TCF meetings, some of them said they already had the intimate relationships that they saw in TCF. But a significant minority of those we called were isolate families. They said that they found attending the meetings to be stressful. They found no relief from their pain and reported that hearing of the experiences of others only made them feel worse. Characteristic of these people was that they did not communicate about the child's death even within the family. Several of these parents indicated that the conversation with us was stressful, one of them saying, "Why don't you call the Compassionate Friends? They like to talk about it there" (Hoeppner and Klass 1982). Without the interpsychic dimension, pain could not be shared, and others' pain could not be an occasion for expressing one's own pain. Instead of reaching out, the parents attempted to hold the self back from pain even if that entailed shutting off the self from potential healing relationships and from the inner representations of the dead child.

AFFILIATION B: EXPERIENTIAL DIMENSION

The temporal perspective of the interpsychic dimension in TCF is oriented to the present and future. As in all the interactions in TCF, the basis for that temporal orientation is complex. We have already noted the transference of the attachment from the child to the group. The sense of shattered self also contributes to the temporal perspective. In effect life starts over for the bereaved parent. How does one learn to live in this new world—in this new self? One must learn by experience, and from the experience of others, how to find one's way around. It is this learning that we called the experiential dimension of affiliation with TCF.

The experiential dimension is a sharing of solutions to concrete problems that confront bereaved parents (Borkman 1976). When the child died, the parent was cast into a world for which there are few role models. In the experiential dimension, bereaved parents help each other explore the pitfalls and possibilities of that world. The importance of the experiential seems to be one of the characteristics that differentiate this self-help process from professionally led group therapy in which "tools for action" are considered by group members to be far less important than other factors (Dickoff and Lakin 1963).

The experiential is concerned with grief as a disequilibrium in the social world of the bereaved. This can be understood as the loss of environmental psychobiologic regulators, as does Hofer (1984), or as the loss of habitual roles and the resultant dysfunction of the repertoire of responses, as does the Bowlby group (Bowlby 1961, 1969-80; Parkes 1972; Parkes and Weiss 1983). The task in the experiential dimension is to adapt to the environment by forming new attachments or finding new psychobiologic regulators within the existing field of attachments and social roles.

To an observer with a psychotherapeutic background, many of the interactions in a TCF meeting would appear rather directive. A person newly bereaved may cry and tell the story of the death. The group listens with little interruption. But after the emotions are drained out, a rather direct question is likely to be asked by one of the newcomers: "Does anyone else have problems going into the child's room?" or "What have other people done with the child's things?" After the emotional catharsis of the earlier part of the sharing, these practical and rather objective questions might appear, to the psychotherapeutically inclined listener, to be too simple. It seems that valuable group time should be spent on issues more central to the core of the self. Yet many TCF members see the practical advice they received as one of the most helpful parts of the process. One member reported:

> I came into TCF with all these blank problems that had no solutions. Such things like, do we hang the stockings? Do we have the Thanksgiving dinner? I was so relieved to hear people at the November meeting talking about the stockings and how they handled it. It was a big thing to me, yet you certainly don't go to a friend with this problem. They would think you were stupid, or nuts, or both. . . . I remember reading in Ann Landers about someone, after the death of a child, asking how many children the parents should tell people they had. To me it seemed foolish. I could not even see how this posed a problem for them, yet that turned out to be the biggest problem I had. I was always so proud of my five kids, and it absolutely broke my heart to ever speak the words, 'Four kids.'

The experiential first defines the problems as normal. Because the problem may not be seen as important by the larger society, many bereaved parents have difficulty because seemingly small matters are causing them major stress. The two issues that seem to recur most often in the group are what to say when asked "How many children do you have?" and how to celebrate the holidays. Often when the TCF members speak of there being no right way to grieve, they are not talking about emotional expression; rather they are talking about how to deal with the practical issues that the death of the child raises in this culture.

The holiday issue is probably clearer to the nonbereaved parent. Each year TCF has a meeting just before Thanksgiving at which the topic is "Getting Through the Holidays." Parents tell what they have done in the past that was helpful, and other parents try to make plans that will suit them. For example, one parent wanted to remember the child, but did not want to make the rest of the family more uncomfortable, so she attached a black bow among many colored bows on the wreath outside the door. Some parents find it helpful to put a Christmas tree on the grave. Parents often measure themselves by how well they are able to deal with the holidays, and the experiential advice given at TCF is central to that measuring.

The question about what to say when asked "How many children do you have?" seems at first a rather simple one. But in fact the question reaches deep into the nature of the parental bond. What does it mean when people say they "have" a child? After all, only under specific conditions do children understand that they "have" parents. Yet even if we were to "work through" the nature of that bond in therapy, the parent is still left with the problem of what to say in the social situation in which the question is asked. It is a casual question to the one who asks, while to the bereaved parent it is an issue of the degree of intimacy there must be in a relationship before the loss is shared. The issue of the degree of intimacy is related to factors in the culture that bring on discomfort in people when they hear about the death of the child; it raises the marginal social role of a bereaved parent in a death-denying society.

In the group are others who have faced the question and found answers. Not all the answers are the same. Each answer positions the parent differently toward the underlying nature of "having" a child and toward the problematic social role of bereaved parent. When TCF members say they listen to the information or opinions of others and then decide what might work best for them, they are saying that they are finding ways to position the new self in the world. The parent with the problem can thus choose a position from several available models in the group. At the point of choice, the underlying issues are understood clearly in a way that is both concrete to the social situation and congruent with other existential positions the person takes in life. It is interesting to watch the faces of the individuals who ask the question at a meeting, for very often when the option they will choose is mentioned, they nod and grin in a way that shows instant recognition of the issues involved and the solution that is now lined up. The problem is not that the parents need to understand what it means to "have" a child. They understand that all too well. They also understand deeply the marginal nature of their social role. The experiential dimension has given them options for existential action.

The experiential dimension does not provide answers set in stone, for different answers may work at different times. A newsletter on preparing for the holidays had the following report on hanging stockings:

What a torment! Funny how you worry what your friends will think. For days I worried and finally I hung three on the fireplace wall, and laid one gently on the mantle.

But that was last year! This year I shall hang all four above the fireplace. For this year the confusion of the mind has found new answers—with conviction! For it does not really matter whether my oldest daughter lives in Tucson, or my youngest son is dead—these are my children—our family—and as long as we hang the Christmas stockings, we shall hang them *all* . . . with love.

The experiential dimension of affiliation with TCF is thus not a decision to act in a particular way. Rather it is an understanding that TCF members have gathered some experience about the problems of being a bereaved parent, as well as a decision to use the experience of other TCF members as a starting point for learning to manage the new self in the world. As the affiliation develops, the experiential dimension is also a decision to share experience from one's own life with those who follow by a few months.

Transition to Helping

Does one get over being a bereaved parent? The answer seems to be no. What, then, is the continuing relationship with TCF? While parents do not get over it, neither do they remain in the condition that brought them into the group. A newsletter article comparing parental bereavement to the grief of an amputee concluded with these words:

In time, the pain in our hearts will gradually ease, and we can learn to live again without our beloved child. Our lives will never be whole, but they can become full once more.

The transition to fullness, if not to wholeness, is in part a transition in the relationship of the member to the self-help group. The transition within the group is a turn of energy toward others. Videka-Sherman (1982) identified "altruistic behavior" as the coping mechanism that characterized TCF participation. She found a positive relationship between altruism and lowered symptoms. The death of her subjects' children, however, had occurred no more than 30 months earlier, so the full resolution is not seen in her study. The experiential dimension is a part of the transition to the helper role, for just as members were given options for existential stances in relation to difficult problems, they now present the options to others. Sharing a solution can be as simple as a sentence in a meeting or over the phone or in a short newsletter article, so it is an easy step to take. By listening to others and offering possible solutions to their situation, TCF members put their own life experience in perspective, for the individual can see the self more clearly when it is reflected in the lives of others. The sense of competence is gained by showing others that own's own life experience is worthwhile.

The experiential resolution of grief is the general recognition of the changes in the social world and the decision to live in that changed world in as creative and positive a way as possible. Thus, in the resolution, the specific existential issues, such as hanging stockings or telling the number of children, are integrated into a whole view of the new world that is known and in which the problems can be managed.

In the interpsychic dimension, the parent transforms the inner representation of the deceased from the role it played in the bereaved's life before the death to the role it will play in the new intrapsychic equilibrium. The inner representation is not simply memory, but is a part of the ego, the characterization or thematic memories of the object, and the emotional states connected with the characterization (Fairbairn 1952; Kernburg 1976). Because there seems to be an exchange between aspects of the inner representation, we often see that activity in one affects the others. Thus, a transformation in the parental role to helping and nurturing others in the group is usually accompanied by the emergence of a more positive and less stressful memory of the lost child. We find that at the same time parents are bonding to the group, they are also reworking the bond with the deceased child.

CONCLUSION

Parental bereavement is a permanent condition. The parents have reached resolution by learning to live in a world that includes the fact that children die, and especially that their child died. They have found a place for the dead child in their ongoing life by introjection and identification. They have found new equilibria in the world and in themselves. They live, albeit somewhat more tentatively and sometimes more delicately, but often more fully and usually more caringly in a new and sadder world. TCF clearly shares common elements with other self-help groups. Especially in the experiential dimension that moves toward a renewed equilibrium between the self and the social environment, we are probably seeing dynamics that could be found in many self-help groups. But the quality or character of the interpsychic dimension is unique to TCF. The parents' bond with their dead child becomes part of the bond between the members in a way that facilitates a reworking of the bond with the dead child. As we have seen, the interpsychic dimension in TCF is part of the intrapsychic resolution for the members. Thus it is the particular character of the dynamics within TCF that helps the resolution of the particular character of parental grief.

REFERENCES

Anisfeld, E., and E. Lipper. Early contact, social support, and mother-infant bonding. *Pediatrics* 72(1):79-83, 1983.
Arling, G. The elderly widow and her family, neighbors and friends. *J. Marriage Family* 38(4):757-767, 1976.
Borkman, T. Experiential knowledge: a new concept for the analysis of self-help groups. *Social Service Rev.* 50(3):445-456, 1976.
Bourne, S. The psychological effects of stillbirth on women and their doctors. *J. Royal College Gen. Practice* 16:103-112, 1968.

Bowlby, J. Processes of mourning. *Int. J. Psychoanalysis* 42:317-340, 1961.

―――――. *Attachment and Loss* Vols. 1-3 (*Attachment,* Vol. 1, 1969; *Separation: Anxiety and Anger,* Vol. 2, 1973; *Loss: Sadness and Depression,* Vol. 3, 1980). New York: Basic Books.

Bowling, A., and A. Cartwright. *Life After Death: A Study of the Elderly Widowed.* London: Tavistock, 1982.

Carr, D., and S.F. Knupp. Grief and perinatal loss. *J. Obstet. Gynecol. Neonatal Nursing* 14(2):130-139, 1985.

Cary, R.G. Weathering widowhood: problems and adjustment of the widowed during the first year. *Omega J. Death Dying* 10(2):163-174, 1979-80.

Dickoff, H., and M. Lakin. Patients' views of group psychotherapy: retrospections and interpretations. *Int. J. Group Psychotherapy* 13:61-73, 1963.

Edelstein, L. *Maternal Bereavement: Coping with the Unexpected Death of a Child.* New York: Praeger, 1984.

Fairbairn, W.D. *An Object-Relations Theory of the Personality.* New Nork: Basic Books, 1952.

Forrest, G.C., E. Standish, and J.D. Baum. Support after perinatal death: a study of support and counseling after perinatal bereavement. *Br. Med. J.* 285:1475-1479, 1982.

Hoeppner M., and D. Klass. Factors in affiliation with a self-help group for bereaved parents. In R. Pacholski and C.A. Corr (eds.), *Priorities in Death Education and Counseling.* Arlington, VA: Forum for Death Education and Counseling, 1982.

Hofer, M.A. Relationships as regulators: a psychobiologic perspective on bereavement. *Psychosomatic Med.* 46:183-197, 1984.

Hood, R. Eliciting mystical states of consciousness in semistructured nature experiences. *J. Scientific Study Religion* 16(2):155-163, 1977.

Horton, P.C. *Solace: The Missing Dimension in Psychiatry.* Chicago: University of Chicago Press, 1981.

Kernberg, O.F. *Object-Relations Theory and Clinical Psychoanalysis.* New York: Jason Aronson, 1976.

Knapp, R. *Beyond Endurance: When a Child Dies.* New York: Schocken, 1986.

Kowalski, K.E.M. Perinatal Death: An Ethnomethodological Study of Factors Influencing Parental Bereavement. Unpublished doctoral dissertation, University of Colorado, 1984.

Lopata, H.Z. *Women as Widows: Support Systems.* New York: Elsevier, 1979.

―――――. *Widowhood in an American City.* Cambridge, MA: Schenkman, 1973.

Maddison, D., and W.L. Walker. Factors affecting the outcome of conjugal bereavement. *Br. J. Psychiatry* 113:1057-1067, 1967.

Miller, A.A., G.A. Pollock, and H.E. Bernstein. An approach to the concept of identification. *Bull. Menninger Clinic* 32(4):239-252, 1968.

Parkes, C.M. *Bereavement: Studies of Grief in Adult Life.* New York: International Universities Press, 1972.

Parkes, C.M., and R.J. Brown. Health after bereavement: a controlled study of young Boston widows and widowers. *Psychosomatic Med.* 34(5):449-461, 1972.

Parkes, C.M., and R. Weiss. *Recovery from Bereavement.* New York: Basic Books, 1983.

Rando, T.S. (ed.). *Parental Loss of a Child.* Champaign, IL: Research Press, 1986.

Raphael, B. *The Anatomy of Bereavement.* New York: Basic Books, 1983.

Sanders, C.M. Comparison of younger and older spouses in bereavement outcome. *Omega J. Death Dying* 11(3):271-273, 1980-81.

Silverman, P.R. *Widow-to-Widow.* New York: Springer, 1986.

Spinetta, J.J., J.A. Swarner, and J.P. Sheposh. Effective parent coping following the death of a child from cancer. *J. Pediatric Psychology* 6(3):251-263, 1981.

Vachon, M.L.S., et al. Predictors and correlates of high distress in adaptation to conjugal bereavement. *Am. J. Psychiatry* 139:998-1002. 1982.

van der Avort, A., and P. van Harberden. Helping self-help groups: a developing theory. *Psychotherapy* 22:269-272, 1985.

Videka-Sherman, L. Coping with the death of a child: a study over time. *Am. J. Orthopsychiatry* 52(4):688-698, 1982.

Volkan, V. *Linking Objects and Linking Phenomena: A Study of the Forms, Symptoms, Metapsychology, and Therapy of Complicated Mourning.* New York: International Universities Press, 1981.

Worden, J.W. *Grief Counseling and Grief Therapy: A Handbook for the Mental Health Practitioner.* New York: Springer, 1982.

Yalom, Y.D. *The Theory and Practice of Group Psychotherapy,* Ed.2. New York: Basic Books, 1975.

23

Pilots in Gliders: The Professional's Role in a Cancer Wellness Group

David S. Tulsky, PhD and David F. Cella, PhD

A commonality between the professional psychotherapy group and the self-help group is that both attempt to promote wellness in each of the individual members. Despite having the same purpose, their methods of achieving it are quite different. While the traditional psychotherapy group achieves its goal through formal training, rules and theoretical beliefs about "wellness," the self-help group promotes wellness in the individual members by enlisting them in a helping community composed of others who are in a similar situation. Given that both helping forces are attempting to achieve the same goal, the differences between these delivery agencies is striking. So strong are these differences that professionals tend to shy away from self-help agencies, and self-help communities tend to mistrust professionals. This discord may stem from three sources: from uncompromising attitudinal convictions, beliefs and prejudices (Jacobs and Goodman 1989); from misperceptions between laypeople and professionals (Lenrow and Burch 1981); or from competition between professionals and self-help organizations (Silverman 1978).

The first reason for this discord is well described by Jacobs and Goodman (1989), who write that the professionals' attitude "may stem from our attachment and habituation to the familiar therapy model as *the* professional intervention" (p.536). Along the same lines, Lenrow and Burch (1981) point out that while professionals may regard self-help groups as having the resources to help, the groups would be more effective if their organizers acquired more formal training and technical skills. In short, some professionals erroneously believe that the self-help centers are ill-equipped to help others.

On the other hand, some self-help providers are equally skeptical of the professionals' ability or intentions. For instance, Silverman (1967, 1970) has described how fellow sufferers or veterans are best equipped to help new members by "normalizing" their problems. Other self-help providers have written that self-help groups are an alternative to the dehumanizing and ineffective care provided by formal professional medical systems (Gartner and Riessman 1977). Still others have mentioned distrusting the professionals' motives and actions when the two forces work together (Back and Taylor 1976) because they fear that the professional will try to take over the group, forcing the self-help organization to surrender its autonomy (Kleiman, Mantell and Alexander 1976). This lack of faith, trust and confidence between the professionals and the self-help organizers has contributed to the friction between the two treatment styles.

The second reason for the the misperception between groups may be an offshoot of the first. Most professionals lack familiarity with the potential of self-help groups to serve as a primary treatment of choice for some individuals. Instead they view the organizations as "hand-holding, morale-boosting, do-no-harm meetings of fellow sufferers" (Jacobs and Goodman 1989, p. 536). Sometimes this viewpoint stems from prejudice or a rigid dogma. Sometimes professionals may see mutual aid groups as self-sufficient and unwelcoming to professionals. Both of these views appear erroneous, yet these tenets have undoubtedly contributed to the distance between the self-help movement and professional therapists. Equally distancing, self-help groups may perceive professional helpers as essentially uncaring, unknowing or primarily interested in personal gain or profit.

The final possibility of the discord stems from basic competition (Silverman 1978). In a small market, two agencies that are attempting to meet the same goal of helping individuals may see each other as rivals, fighting to work with the same people. The professional may feel threatened by an organization that will provide services for a minimal fee or without charge, and, on the other side, the self-help provider may feel intimidated by the power, knowledge and wealth that the formal professional system represents.

Given these problems, the question arises about how a collaboration between the professional and self-help organization can evolve, function and benefit the self-help community as well as professionals. Silverman (1978) has described ways in which the professional can "cooperate" with a self-help group without "corrupting" it, "competing" with it or "copping out" to it. For instance, she suggests that professionals can do four things: make referrals, act as a consultant to existing groups, serve on professional advisory boards and initiate or help develop a new group. Furthermore, when professionals facilitate group interactions, they should not vehemently promote their own views, but instead, the role should be played down. In short, professionals should at most provide support in the background, ensuring that the group does not fall apart. The key to a successful collaboration between professionals and self-help agencies is that the professional must adopt the self-help model. This model allows group members to work out issues themselves whenever possible with minimal intervention. This is not that unfamiliar to most group therapists who are trained in process group therapy where one of the goals of the leader is to facilitate the ability of people to help one another (Yalom 1975; Wasserman and Danforth 1988).

Just as it is necessary for the professional to respect the autonomy of the self-help organization, it is important for the self-help community to trust and adopt input from professionals. Similar to the professional who seeks additional supervision or consultation from another professional, the self-help center can often benefit from a professional opinion from someone who is not invested in the immediate dynamics that surround the situation. Objective input should be regarded as helpful and not threatening.

THE CANCER WELLNESS CENTER

Given this background about the historical differences between professionals and self-help organizations, we will now shift the discussion to a specific self-help center, The Cancer Wellness Center (CWC), and our experiences with its members. The CWC is a newly formed organization staffed and run mostly by people with cancer or by family members of people with cancer who are active in their fight for recovery. The center has built a strong alliance with mental health professionals. They have hired private contractors to facilitate their groups as well as establishing a ''Clinical Advisory Committee'' to help with clinical decisions. Additionally, professionals were consulted at each step of the planning so that professional input was an integral part of each leg of the center's development.

At the core of the CWC's programs is a closed, eight-week group consisting of six to ten members. Also in the group is a facilitator, a professionally trained person who has been hired to sit in on the group sessions and bring out their potential. The facilitator's objective is to help the group operate as independently as possible. Facilitators become active only when it is absolutely necessary. Obviously, the point at which something becomes ''absolutely necessary'' will be different for different people. The facilitator's goal is not to preach rigid rules, but instead to share decision guidelines in the hope that this may help others when they decide whether it is necessary to intervene. An important point is that there are occasions when it is necessary to intervene and, when these arise, the deviations from the strict self-help model should be as nondirective as possible for the situation.

There are at least three occasions when it is important for the facilitator to become more active: when a safe environment must be promoted by preventing the fears of members from becoming too great; when it is necessary to divert uncontrolled negative affect; and when the group must be prevented from making a major, irreversible mistake.

As a case example, one of the authors was once involved as a facilitator of a couples group consisting of five people with cancer and their spouses.

All of the couples arrived at the CWC "in crisis." The members of the group who had cancer had metastatic disease, meaning the the cancer had spread beyond its original site and therefore was more life-threatening and probably not curable. Upon presentation at the first group, it became clear that we were dealing with ten needy individuals rather than five couples. The severity of the pain, worry, concern and anger present in each of the group members immediately caused re-evaluation of the facilitator's role, with a tension between true (leaderless) facilitation and a more active "mediator" role.

Promoting a Safe Environment

The facilitator must ensure that the group remains safe. Seeing the severity of the pain, in each of the ten group members was by itself insufficient to prompt a more active facilitator stance. It did, however, serve as a warning bell indicating the need to pay close attention to future signs. The facilitator must be careful not to step into a leadership role too quickly. Careful assessment is required before any intervention is initiated.

In the first session, the facilitator decided to become more active when a direct threat to the safety of the setting emerged. As some of the members began expressing their needs, it became apparent that it was overwhelming for some of the other members to listen and hear these needs. The facilitator, as an observer, watched as people revealed their fears, emotions and goals for the group. He also watched these same members being ignored by the others. People were cutting one another off. When the group members themselves voiced concern over the process, it was time to seize the opportunity and shift the role from the more passive facilitator to the more active leader. The facilitator suggested that a rule be made that allowed everyone to be "heard" in some way by at least one person. In short, the facilitator changed to a more active role by directing the group toward a common goal because the direction was necessary to help make the group environment safer for everyone.

Diverting Uncontrolled Negative Affect

The threat of uncontrolled negative affect arose when the group began to exhibit displaced anger. Members began subtly, and then not so subtly, to put down one of the participants who had asserted herself. In this instance, everyone began referring to her as "she" rather than by her first name. Since direct attacks against other members threaten the security of the group, it was necessary for the facilitator to intervene. He promptly reintroduced this member and suggested that people address one another on a first-name basis. Because this seemed to reflect poorly controlled (displaced) anger, which is a direct threat calling for prompt and direct action, immediate intervention by the facilitator seemed indicated.

The expression of overwhelming negative affect occurred more frequently than the other two criteria for facilitator involvement. The members were repeatedly faced with overwhelming, intense emotions for which they were ill-prepared. Later on in the group it occurred dramatically when one of the members died and another became quite ill. The emotions were overwhelming, in part because the news of the death came so suddenly. The members were not ready to confront or process their feelings about death. Unfortunately, the members had nowhere to hide. Everyone was thinking about death. Despite the flood of thoughts, there was little discussion about it. Instead, everyone appeared struck with an overwhelming, paralyzing fear. In this case, with such a traumatic event confronting the group, the facilitator decided to become more active and help the group test reality, express their fears and process their emotions.

Preventing Irreversible Mistakes

A third criterion for involvement is when the group is about to make a irreversible, major "mistake." An example occurred when the group decided impulsively to invite new members to join for the last three sessions of an eight-week, time-limited group. Among the organizers of the CWC, as well as among the directors of the Clinical Advisory Board, it was unanimously agreed that the addition of the new members would be very risky. However, it was also agreed that it was important to allow the group to make its own decisions and, in the event it occurs, to make its own mistakes. What occurred in the actual group, however, was an impulsive, sporadic movement to invite the new members in without any processing or discussion. This decision seemed to cross the imaginary boundary between a risky decision and a potentially grave error. As a result, the facilitator needed to become more active and raise objections until further discussion within the group took place. In this case, a direct intervention was made: the group was given the power to make a decision on the matter, but only *after* putting some thought into the potential consequences of their behavior. By allowing the members the power to decide, merely delaying their decision, rather than deciding for them, the facilitator attempted to preserve the group's power and integrity. However, by delaying their action, the facilitator also prevented the group from making an impulsive decision that could jeopardize their future group experience. After some discussion, the group decided against bringing in new members.

CONCLUSION

In this eight-week group, we were able to clarify three criteria in which a more active, professional role was appropriate. These were (1) to preserve the safety and security of each individual member of the group, as well as the group structure as a whole; (2) to buffer the group from material that was too intense and overwhelming (as well as testing reality when necessary); and (3) to prevent the group from making an irreversible and hasty mistake. This set of criteria is probably far from comprehensive. It does, however, outline and support the notion that there are instances when professional interventions are necessary in self-help groups. It is important to caution the professional about becoming active without carefully evaluating the situation to ensure that an intervention is absolutely necessary. Given that everyone's definition of "absolutely necessary" will differ, it is important to use one's best judgment. The key here, however, is that when one does make an intervention, one is deviating from the typical standard model of self-help. An understanding of this model should remind the facilitator that whenever interventions are initiated, they should be as limited and as mild as possible. The power should remain within the group rather than in the hands of the leader.

It is as if self-help groups are operating like gliders. Occasionally, they need steering from a pilot or a push from a motor. However, these gliders generally operate best by themselves. There may be instances when this is not true. Professionals in self-help groups are like pilots in a glider who, once in a while, slip into the plane, turn on the motor and steer. They do this when they judge that the glider is about to crash or take a nose dive. However, pilots in gliders are in unnatural positions. It is automatic for them to navigate, but in this case they are forced, for the good of the ride, to "turn off" this automatic process, letting other factors control the ride. In general, they serve the glider better by sitting back, watching and experiencing, rather than actively controlling. Professionals must learn this patience when working with self-help groups. Their skills are needed and will most likely be appreciated if they are able to develop new skills of inhibition.

The road, however, goes both ways. It is important that self-help agencies learn to trust professionals and to be able to utilize their knowledge. It is important to select the right professional, one who knows—or will learn—the theoretical premise behind self-help. Once the professional adopts this framework, there exists only one method to achieve the primary goal: the promotion of wellness. If the professional adheres to the agency's model, the self-help community must trust the professional's opinion and decisions—especially when an action is taken that "breaks the rules." In this way, the self-help community and the professional can work conjointly toward promoting wellness.

REFERENCES

Back, K.W., and R.C. Taylor. Self-help groups: tool or symbol? *J. Appl. Behav. Sci.* 12:295-309, 1976.

Gartner, A., and F. Riessman. *Self-Help in the Human Services.* San Francisco: Jossey-Bass, 1977.

Jacobs, M.K., and G. Goodman. Psychology and self-help groups: predictions on a partnership. *Am. Psychologist* 44:536-545, 1989.

Kleiman, M.A., J.E. Mantell, and E.S. Alexander. Collaboration and its discontents: the perils of partnership. *J. Appl. Behav. Sci.* 12:403-409, 1976.

Lenrow, P.B., and R.W. Burch. "Mutual Aid and Professional Services: Opposing or Complementary?" In Brian Gottlieb, ed., *Social Networks and Social Support.* Beverly Hills: Sage, 1981.

Silverman, P.R. Services to the widowed: first steps in a program of preventive intervention. *Community Mental Health J.* 3:37-44, 1967.

———. The widow as a caregiver in a program of preventive intervention with other widows. *Mental Hygiene* 54:540-547, 1970.

———. *Mutual Help Groups: A Guide for Mental Health Workers.* DHEW Publication No. ADM 78-646. Washington, DC: U.S. Government Printing Office, 1978.

Wasserman, H. and H.E. Danforth. *The Human Bond: Support Groups and Mutual Aid.* New York: Springer, 1988.

Yalom, I.D. *The Theory and Practice of Group Psychotherapy,* Ed. 2. New York: Basic Books, 1975.

24

Widows and Widowers:
A Self-Help Bereavement Group

Kathleen A. Pistone, PhD

Self-help groups have become increasingly popular within the past two decades. The design of the Widows and Widowers Bereavement Group, conducted in Westchester County, New York, is based on the premise that self-help groups are educational and productive in nature. It is also felt that active participation in the group can help improve the quality of one's life. In addition to building skills, gaining knowledge and support, this group provides a forum for exchanging ideas, thoughts and feelings. Attitudes regarding the traumatic change members are facing are also exchanged.

The group is led by members who have successfully completed their own grief tasks and have the desire and skill to reach out and assist others. A resource person is available so that misinformation is not given to the members. Eight meetings are scheduled on a bi-monthly basis, beginning at 7:30 and ending at 9:00 P.M. The sessions are held from late September until early June and take place in the lounge of a local parochial school. Potential members are generally referred by other members, family friends, pastors, doctors, therapists or hospital personnel. Flyers and bulletins announce the sessions. The group is designed for people who have been widowed for 2 months to 2 years. However, members who have been widowed longer and who have not finished their grief tasks but are now ready for this type of group are also welcome and accepted.

First-time members are generally oriented half an hour before the session or by means of a phone conference before the meeting. The orientation consists of describing the basic format and concept of the group, stressing the goal and the confidentiality, and well as urging a commitment to be part of the group by attending and participating in the eight sessions. The physical setup is informal and members sit at random in a circle so that each person can be clearly seen and heard. The age range varies, but the majority of members are in their fifties and sixties. Nevertheless, we have serviced people ranging from the mid-twenties to the mid-seventies.

The group operates on a voluntary basis and consists of persons who come together for mutual assistance. Although the members have a common problem and concern that they want to discuss and alleviate, they also have the built-in role of helping each other. As a result, the members move from a rather confused state to a very helpful one. The warm, accepting environment is conducive to communication. Relationships are formed and members have the opportunity to grow by learning from and modeling each other. Each adult brings a wealth of knowledge and personal experiences to the group and is a rich resource. Members also have the opportunity to network, exchange information and meet socially in between sessions.

Potential members of a group act on the basis that (1) the group will help solve their problems better than they can alone and (2) the goals of a particular group—and its ideology, socialization, program and procedures—are compatible with their own needs and outlook.

The goal of the Widows and Widowers Bereavement Group is for its members to adjust socially, emotionally and psychologically to their new situation, the end result being personal growth and change. The discovery of hope seems to be a major factor in the healing and adjustment process. Hope and growth can be felt throughout the sessions as new members observe the success, attitudes and gains made by their peers. The most important aspect of the group is assuming that its members can make their disrupted lives meaningful by learning, growing and reorienting themselves to a new life.

By acquiring new skills, seeing others as role models and developing a sense of cohesion, members gain the opportunity to have movement in their lives. They learn strategies for building a bright future. They learn that there is no time frame for healing and adjusting; members progress at their own pace. As time goes on and they become ready to accept their situation, they make changes and improve the quality of their lives. As a result, they are able to feel once more a sense of control over their own lives and can take that first step in the journey of healing and adjusting.

As the new members hear others talk about the success as well as the setbacks they've had in overcoming the disruption in their lives, they realize that they too can adjust to their "mateless" present and feel a sense of hope and encouragement. They realize that life goes on and that it can never be the same again. It will certainly be different but it also can be good. Knowing that their feelings are not unique helps them face the situation with more confidence and assurance. Members start to get in touch with their own feelings, to put aside their fears and to develop a renewed sense of self-worth. They get to know themselves in a whole new way and find an inner strength that they were unaware of previously. Members find that they can handle things better than they thought they could and are quite proud of themselves at times. Life seems once more to have meaning, more meaning than they ever thought it could.

There are basic challenges and dilemmas that all people face periodically. Some situations are common and routine, but others are quite traumatic and can produce a crisis. The sudden loss or drawn-out death of a mate can create social, economic and personal problems for which there are no ready-made answers or approaches. Group members soon realize that they do have options for controlling their lives. As they start to accept their new roles, they begin to work with the constraints that they previously believed to be beyond their control. Because of their differing personal backgrounds and histories, members handle their new lives in their own special way.

While we are highlighting the success of group members, we must also mention that not everyone responds favorably in self-help groups. There are tremendous variations in individual personalities, backgrounds, beliefs and values that influence one's ability to contribute to, participate in, and become part of a group. Even after determining a need for action and movement, the desire and determination to pursue and then carry out specific plans is not always possible for some people. Members who feel uncomfortable in the group usually drop out after the first or second session. Some feel the group process does not meet their needs. They do have the opportunity to rejoin as new series of sessions start throughout the year. Sometimes individual support and assistance are needed. Members who exhibit behavior that requires more in-depth care are encouraged to seek professional services.

Although the group is designed for widows and widowers, the number of widows, both regionally and nationally, far surpasses that of widowers. It is estimated that for every widower there are at least 10 widows. Our figures do not deviate much from the national ones; however, we have noted that at times the group has consisted of several men and only six or eight women. Regardless of the ratio, the perception that widows have about the grief experience of widowers is usually clarified at these sessions. The widowers who join us express their feelings of disbelief, and sometimes of anger or guilt, coupled with emptiness and loneliness. They also convey a sense of deep loss and disorientation. They share the painful emotions that one feels after the death of a mate. Their spouses were their companions, caretakers, confidants, lovers and best friends. In most cases the spouse made life meaningful and worthwhile. There was a comfort in knowing that a special person was there who responded and cared. In addition to the loss of a valued human being, the role changes that widowers face often include cooking, shopping, cleaning and making child-care as well as household decisions.

If there are young children at home the widower has the role of keeping the family together and being the singular head of the house. Older working children are generally self-sufficient and have their own social life. Some children encourage the surviving parent to date or get involved socially, but others feel a loyalty to the deceased parent and oppose any type of contact with the opposite sex.

Retired widowers who live alone often find the days and nights long and lonely. They have little motivation to do the things they had enjoyed when their wives were with them. In the beginning stages of grief, they feel that little meaning is left to life. Some join senior citizens centers or volunteer at their churches. As they complete their grief tasks, widowers tend to get more social invitations from family members and friends. It is quite common for widowers to remarry within a few years. The same is not true for widows. Widowers are in demand and they generally become aware of their new advantages.

Widows and widowers must deal with painful role changes, especially being "partnerless" in a couple-oriented society. Many widows lead lives with minimal support systems and are dependent on their children, especially their daughters. Over half of all widows live alone and eight out of every ten are heads of their own households. Many widows are also able to obtain and take advantage of societal resources.

Clearly, individual life styles, personal histories and circumstances bring specific problems and concerns for both widows and widowers. A major problem is that many survivors, regardless of age, do not have adequate contact with people who will listen to and assist them. In the majority of cases, our members feel that people do not want to talk about their grief. People want to feel that the survivor is doing well and getting on with life. Friends and relatives do not give them permission to grieve openly. Since their lives have returned to normal, they feel that the survivor's life should also be back to normal within a few months. Being together only on holidays, birthdays and anniversaries does not provide the day-to-day contact and support most people need; hence the popularity of support groups. Some of the basic problems or concerns expressed most frequently by members when the first enter the group are the following:

1. Lack of confidence, motivation and continuity in everyday living.
2. Lack of emotional support and understanding from family and friends.
3. Lack of self-awareness regarding emotions they are experiencing and time to grieve because of overscheduling.
4. Lack of belonging to an actual group, such as couples do.
5. Lack of acceptance of new role and status and of a desire to reinvest energies.

Through discussion, feedback and grief work, members start to regain confidence and motivation. They receive emotional support, insight, understanding and suggestions from their newly found friends. These same people assist them in becoming aware of some of the emotions they are experiencing. The members feel as though they are part of a group that gives them a sense of cohesion. As they start to understand their feelings, they are better able to handle their new role. They then take time to grieve and eventually reinvest their energies. Obviously, all of this is not accomplished in eight sessions, but members do have the option to return to the groups as new sessions begin throughout the year.

Certain basic curative factors have been identified in self-help groups, including (1) installation of hope; (2) universality; (3) imparting of information; (4) altruism; (5) development of socializing techniques; (6) imitative behavior; (7) group cohesiveness; (8) interpersonal learning and (9) existential factors. An additional factor is the recapitulation of the primary family, which should actually remain under the auspices of a family therapist.

Because of the increasing popularity of self-help groups, a number of key questions have evolved around them. Do people learn from external sources or through internal, unfolding processes? Moreover, do people learn through orgainzed, logical, segmented methods or through more holistic body-mind-spirit approaches?

Having dealt with groups of adults and children for more than 25 years, it is my observation that external activities provide the learner with a rich, meaningful, necessary experience. But the real learning and growth take place when we acquire knowledge and hope and then process them, which is a part of internal development. Many members are motivated because of the hope they receive in the group setting.

The most effective learning and growing require not only self-reflection and self-direction, but also input from external sources and objective observers. As mentioned previously, there is no pain greater than the pain of isolation. The men and women in self-help groups make every attempt to lessen their personal pain and improve the quality of their own lives while they are also helping others. It is axiomatic that when we help others, we are ultimately helping ourselves.

25

AIDS and Bereavement: Support Groups for Survivors

William G. Pheifer, MS, RN

The Centers for Disease Control (CDC) report that more than 85,000 people have been diagnosed with acquired immunodeficiency syndrome (AIDS). It is estimated that 1 to 3 million people have been infected with the human immunodeficiency virus (HIV) (Quinn 1987). Many of these people may go on to develop AIDS.

Of people who have been diagnosed with AIDS, approximately 59 percent were known to have died by 1987 and 67 percent by 1991. By the year 2000, it is projected there will be more than 1 million Americans who will have developed AIDS (*New York Times,* March 4, 1987). If current trends continue, we can expect over half a million AIDS-related deaths to have occurred in the United States by that year.

When considering the parents, siblings, spouses, children, friends and significant others—the survivors of people with AIDS (SOPWAs)—we are talking about millions of people who will be experiencing AIDS-related bereavements. Many survivors may need special resources to assist them in coping with their loss. Support groups may be an effective way to address this problem. Health and social service professionals can be instrumental in meeting the needs of this growing population of survivors by helping to start these types of groups.

SURVIVORS OF PEOPLE WITH AIDS

People with AIDS (PWAs) are a diverse group: gay and bisexual men, intravenous drug users, people who have received transfusions of blood or blood

The author wishes to acknowledge Clare Houseman, PhD, RN, CS of the College of Health Sciences at Old Dominion University for her participation in developing the model of survivorship discussed in this chapter.

products, sexual partners of PWAs, children of PWAs. In other words the group embraces homosexuals, bisexuals and heterosexuals, men and women, young and old.

If PWAs are a diverse group, then it follows that SOPWAs are as well. Survivors can be divided into subgroups for discussion: (1) survivors of people who contracted AIDS through sexual transmission, (2) survivors of those who contracted AIDS from needles or blood, and (3) survivors of those who contracted AIDS as newborns.

Among survivors of people who contracted AIDS from sexual contact, the largest percentage are survivors of gay or bisexual men. Some of these survivors may be in high-risk groups or may have HIV or AIDS themselves. Some may have been unaware that their significant other was gay or bisexual until diagnosed with AIDS. Some may be ashamed of their relationship to a PWA. Many of these survivors experience anger—at the disease, at the lack of resources or at the deceased PWA.

In looking at survivors of people who contracted AIDS from needles or blood, we can categorize them further into survivors of people who were intravenous drug users and survivors of those who received transfusions of blood or blood products. Again, some of these survivors are at risk themselves. Some may have been unaware of the drug use of their significant other and may be ashamed of the activities that resulted in transmission. Some of the survivors may be enraged at the health care system that was responsible for transmission but unable to produce a cure.

Finally, there are the survivors of those who contracted AIDS as newborns. Some of these survivors may have been responsible for the transmission of HIV to the infant. Many are members of minority groups and may have few resources.

High-Risk Bereavement Factors

Several factors have been identified that place people at high risk for complicated grief reactions (Bowlby 1980; Kuprio, Koskenvuo and Rita 1987; Parkes and Weiss 1983; Shuchter 1986). In a study by Geis, Fuller and Rush (1986), SOPWAs are described as possessing many of these high-risk bereavement factors.

Stigma is a major factor associated with an AIDS-related death. In our society there is inherent discomfort with illness, death and grief (Trant 1987); AIDS involves all three. In addition, AIDS-related deaths often involve the controversial subjects of sexuality or drug use. And there is also the hysteria and confusion associated with HIV and AIDS. Subsequently, the survivor may feel the need to hide the cause of death from family or social contacts (Geis, Fuller and Rush 1986).

Many SOPWAs may have been involved in gay relationships. In these circumstances, society often fails to recognize the validity of what was essentially a spousal relationship (Trant 1987). As a result, we see some survivors who may perceive no support for mourning or no one with whom they can risk sharing their feelings. SOPWAs may feel pressured to behave outwardly as if no loss has occurred, even though their entire life may have been disrupted.

At times the relationships between the SOPWA and the deceased may have been strained due to conflicts related to lifestyle choices. When this has been the case, feelings of guilt may complicate the grief process.

The grief experienced by SOPWAs can also be complicated by the untimely nature of AIDS deaths. The largest percentage of PWAs are between 20 and 40 years of age. Many survivors are confronted with mortality (their own as well as their significant others') at an age when people do not usually have to confront these issues (Trant 1987).

Another risk factor is the fear and anxiety of having potentially been exposed to HIV, or the guilt that may occur if the survivors feel they may have been responsible for transmission of the virus. Finally, there is the anger and helplessness associated with being a SOPWA. These feelings can be associated with the lack of knowledge about HIV and AIDS, the lack of treatment alternatives, the absence of a cure, the limited health and social service resources, and other circumstances surrounding the AIDS-related death.

Some SOPWAs have personal and social support systems, but far too many may perceive themselves as having few, if any, resources or supports. It is essential to the mental health of our communities that we begin to identify accessible sources of support for this group of survivors.

BEREAVEMENT SUPPORT GROUPS

SOPWAs may need support in completing the tasks that are necessary to successful survivorship. The term survivor is used here to describe any person who has experienced a significant bereavement and who seeks to adapt to a loss. Survivorship implies that *grief* (the intrapersonal component of the experience after bereavement) and *mourning* (the interpersonal and behavioral manifestations or rituals related to the experience of grief) are experienced in a productive manner. The *tasks of survivorship* are those tasks that survivors undertake, related to grief and mourning, in attempting to process their loss. These include recognition, realization, acknowledgment and adaptation.

Recognition refers to appreciation of the loss. This implies identification of membership in a select group that has experienced bereavement. The very existence of support groups for SOPWAs validates the reality of a survivor's bereavement related to AIDS. Survivors are granted acceptance into the general category of the bereaved, and the fact that groups specific to SOPWAs exist substantiates the uniqueness of this group. The survivor can recognize that the loss has occurred by association with others in similar circumstances.

Realization relates to the survivor's perception of the impact of the loss (the effect on emotions and on one's life). This includes awareness of the need to express feelings related to the loss. Support groups assist survivors to actualize their loss; to accept the reality and finality of the loss they have experienced. This is begun by talking about the deceased, the death, and the grieving rituals that were carried out (Worden 1982). A full recognition and realization of loss may take weeks or months. In any death, but especially in AIDS-related deaths, there may be few people with whom the SOPWA feels able to discuss these events, which may prolong the grief process.

In AIDS-related deaths, actualization of the loss can also be complicated by the fact that survivors are sometimes separated from the deceased at death and not included in grieving rituals, which may be arranged by family members who do not accept the relationship between the survivor and the deceased. Participation in a support group may function as an alternate form of grieving ritual for these survivors.

Acknowledgment involves admitting the loss to others and receiving assent from others as to the relevance of their loss. This also includes accepting the right to experience grief and to mourn. Survivors have a human need for acknowledgment of the losses, their feelings, the normalcy of these feelings, and their right to experience and express these feelings. Survivors of any loss often have trouble with feelings such as anger, guilt, anxiety and helplessness (Worden 1982). SOPWAs often experience these feelings, as well as fear, denial, isolation, uncertainty, inadequacy, ambivalence, paranoia, confusion and despair. In order to promote resolution, it is essential that the survivor be facilitated in expressing these difficult feelings. An atmosphere of understanding, relatedness, acceptance and nurturance is necessary to accomplish this (Pheifer and Houseman 1988). Support groups can provide this environment.

Survivors need time to grieve in order to acknowledge their loss (Worden 1982). Experts suggest the grief process takes several weeks to a few years. The amount of time depends not only on the survivor and the relationship, but on a myriad of other factors. All too often the needs of the bereaved differ from the expectations of others. SOPWAs may see themselves as having few resources to grant them the "luxury" of time to grieve. Participation in support groups provides a place, time and structure to process grief at the survivor's own pace.

Participation in support groups can also serve to help the bereaved identify normal behaviors associated with grief (Worden 1982). Persons who have experienced a loss may question their own state of mind. Survivors may experience an inability to concentrate, memory loss, ruminations about the deceased, preoccupation with their own health, mood swings, and a variety of other symptoms. The SOPWA may need validation of these experiences as part of the grief process. Group members can help to fulfill this function by sharing their experiences.

Adaption suggests adjustment to the loss. This starts with mourning and may progress to helping others with their losses. Survivors may need ongoing support in the weeks, months or years following bereavement. Support groups can ensure the long-term availablilty that is necessary (Worden 1982). Survivors may especially need support during critical periods that arise throughout the survival process, such as anniversaries, birthdays and holidays. Bereavement groups represent an excellent way of providing this support.

Adaptation to loss also means continuing to live without the deceased. This can be promoted by identifying areas of the survivor's life that have been affected and assisting in problem-solving strategies to promote functioning independently of the deceased (Worden 1982). The extent of this task may differ depending on the relationship of the SOPWAs to the deceased and their respective roles. It may be related to loss of a primary support person, sexual partner or confidant. The bereavement group may be able to help since members will have experienced similar losses. Group members can discuss the ways in which they have moved forward with their lives and the adjustments they have made.

The survivor may also need to think about forming new relationships (Worden 1982). This may be a particular area of concern for survivors who have been in loving relationships with a PWA. Not only does the SOPWA have to deal with the usual emotions that accompany forming new relationships after the death of a partner, but HIV and AIDS add a new dimension to the problem. Survivors may have been exposed to or have AIDS themselves. They may be uncertain of how to approach relationships, fear rejection, or feel they have no right to new relationships. Since they have experienced similar feelings, group members may be more able to accept these feelings. Group members who have dealt with these issues may be able to share knowledge about HIV and AIDS, safe sex and other concerns that the SOPWA may need. Participation in support groups also allows the survivor to relate to others in a group, which may emphasize the benefits of relating to other people.

Each survivor brings his own defenses and coping strategies in attempting to adapt after a bereavement (Worden 1982). As group relationships develop, the usefulness and adaptability of coping mechanisms can be explored. If self-destructive strategies are employed, the group can point out the negativity of these and assist in exploring more adaptive coping strategies.

This model summarizes the tasks that can be facilitated through participation in bereavement groups for SOPWAs. As survivors accomplish these tasks, they are actively engaged in survival—an adaptive grieving process. Moving forward through the difficult process of grieving is what successful survivorship is all about.

EVOLUTION OF A SUPPORT GROUP

Bereavement support groups for SOPWAs are most readily available in larger metropolitan areas. During the early years of the AIDS crisis, the majority of cases were reported in these more densely populated areas. As AIDS spreads into middle America, the need for services increases. SOPWAs are found throughout the nation in every segment of society.

There are several problems that may be encountered when initiating support groups for SOPWAs. The first one is the lack of community support or funding for services to SOPWAs. In many areas of the country services for people living with HIV and AIDS are just starting to be developed. Often these services focus on education and some resources for individuals who have HIV or AIDS. The survivor of an AIDS-related death is often forgotten, possibly due to the emphasis of these agencies on helping people to live with AIDS. Perhaps it is time that all the people who are affected by HIV and AIDS are given consideration and not just the person who is infected with the virus.

The second problem involves accessing the SOPWAs. Since there is generally no one source that can be relied on to get the information out, some creativity may be necessary to let people know that the bereavement group exists. When beginning the support group in Norfolk, Virginia, we were fortunate to have the support of the local AIDS service organization. They sent letters to families and significant others of deceased clients. This agency also referred in cases of loved ones and friends of newly deceased PWAs. In addition, letters with information about the group were sent to hospitals, mental health professionals, clergy and other bereavement groups. Notices were also placed in the local newspapers.

Support services for SOPWAs are most often available under the auspices of gay-oriented groups or AIDS service organizations. This sometimes presents a conflict for survivors who may not be comfortable seeking help from gay or AIDS-related organizations. In order to address this issue, our group was held in a neutral location at a local university.

Despite the preparation, getting started still presented a challenge for us. Beginning a support group for a specialized population is a long process. We started by setting up liberal criteria for group membership, decided on an open-ended group format, and determined that meetings would be held weekly for 90 minutes. One of the most difficult parts was trying to avoid frustration in the early weeks of the group. For the first two weeks no one showed up except the two identified group leaders. Finally, in the third week one person came. Holding a group with two leaders and one member is an interesting experience. After several more weeks, a second person began to attend. By the time the group had been meeting for four months, a core group of six people were attending on a regular basis.

Roles for Professionals

There are several important roles that can be played by professionals in the initiation of bereavement support groups for SOPWAs. The first is to identify the need for the group. Because of the stigma related to AIDS deaths, survivors may have a tendency to isolate and may even feel that they are the only SOPWAs in their area. Health and social service professionals often have a broader perspective on the needs of the community and may be better able to identify the need for this type of group in a particular community.

Professionals may be able to identify a health, community, or special interest group that would be willing to sponsor the bereavement support group. Sponsorship generally involves providing a location for meetings and sometimes some clerical support for providing information about the group.

Professionals may also be able to provide a stabilizing influence during the initial group meetings. By having identified leaders, the group will be better able to weather the early months when attendance may be low. Professionals can be available to provide support to whomever attends until the group has built up a core membership. Professionals may also be able to help facilitate interaction during early groups. Communicating about death and feelings is often difficult. Group leaders may be able to encourage participation in discussions and promote problem solving. As the group develops, members may begin to take on these functions.

The role of the professional who starts a group of this type may change over time. In the Norfolk group, the professional leader continued with the group for the first year. By the completion of that year, group members were able to maintain the group on their own and assumed full responsibility for the group using a self-help format.

SUMMARY

The potential for dysfunctional grieving has been demonstrated through identification of multiple high-risk bereavement factors that are characteristic of SOPWAs (Houseman and Pheifer 1988). Bereavement support groups can help survivors to engage in the tasks of successful survivorship, which should result in positive progression through the grief process. Among the other ways in which professionals can address these bereavement issues are:

- to provide education about AIDS and bereavement related to AIDS;
- to provide direct support to SOPWAs;
- to be familiar with and refer to resources for SOPWAs.

The epidemic of HIV and AIDS has presented many challenges to this society, some of which are just now beginning to be recognized. Attending to the needs of SOPWAs is just one of those challenges. When future generations evaluate the effectiveness of our society's response to this epidemic, let us hope they will see that we were able to effectively address the whole broad array of issues arising from the AIDS crisis.

REFERENCES

Bowlby, J. *Attachment and Loss, Vol. 3.* London: Hogarth Press, 1980.

Frierson, R.L., and S.B. Lippmann. Psychological implication of AIDS. *Am. Family Physician* 35(3):109-116, 1987.

Geis, S.B., R.L. Fuller, and J. Rush. Lovers of AIDS victims: psychosocial stresses and counseling needs. *Death Studies* 10:43-53, 1986.

Grief Education Institute. *Bereavement Support Groups Leadership Manual.* Denver: Grief Education Institute, 1986.

Houseman, C., and W.G. Pheifer. Potential for unresolved grief in survivors of persons with AIDS. *Arch. Psychiatric Nursing* 2(5):296-301, 1988.

Kupprio, J., M. Koskenvuo, and H. Rita. Mortality after bereavement: a prospective study of 95,647 widowed persons. *Am. J. Public Health* 77(3):283-287, 1987.

Parkes, C.M., and R.S. Weiss. *Recovery from Bereavement.* New York: Basic Books, 1983.

Pheifer, W.G., and C. Houseman. Bereavement and AIDS: a framework for intervention. *J. Psychosocial Nursing* 26(10):21-26, 1988.

Quinn, T.C. The global epidemiology of the acquired immunodeficiency syndrome. In B.K. Silverman and A. Waddell, eds., *The Report of the Surgeon General's Workshop on Children with HIV Infection and Their Families.* Washington, DC: U.S. Department of Health and Human Services, 1987.

Shuchter, S.R. *Dimensions of Grief.* San Francisco: Jossey-Bass, 1986.

Trant, B. AIDS has created a new form of bereavement. *Canad. Med. Assoc. J.* 136(2):194, 1987.

Worden, J.W. *Grief Counseling and Grief Therapy.* New York: Springer, 1982.

26

Self-Help in Catastrophic Illness: Centers for Attitudinal Healing

Maureen A. Milligan, PhD

This chapter will discuss how Centers for Attitudinal Healing complement the traditional health care system's approach to health by supporting the many crucial human dimensions that the traditional medical model often neglects. It will describe Centers for Attitudinal Healing and contrast them with the traditional medical models of health in order to familiarize health care professionals and others with the benefits of this valuable resource in disease intervention and support.

BACKGROUND

The first Center for Attitudinal Healing was opened in California in 1975 by Dr. Jerry Jampolsky to offer self-help support for children with catastrophic illnesses (typically cancer) and their families. Today more than 50 centers throughout the United States and abroad provide support for both children and adults with catastrophic illness, their families, and others experiencing loss. The Centers offer, at no cost, what many traditional medical systems fail to provide: support for the spiritual, psychological and emotional needs of patients and their families, as well as a method for developing healthier attitudinal habits (Jampolsky 1983).

The Centers utilize specially trained volunteers to facilitate self-help for groups of ill adults, children, siblings, parents and others affected by illness and loss. They provide a safe, supportive and structured atmosphere within which individuals can share their fears, experiences, beliefs and struggles associated with loss and disease. The focus is on emotional and spiritual needs. Participants find that by reaching outside of themselves and support- ing others, they move out of their own isolation, pain and fear and thus help themselves. Feelings and fears about death and other losses are listened to, shared and accepted, thus providing individuals with a freedom of expression and exploration not often available in the traditional technological medical model.

The Centers, however, are more than just another place to facilitate self-help. They are based on a particular psychospiritual philosophy that utilizes basic spiritual principles to facilitate the development of healthful attitudes. The philosophical basis of the Centers contrasts with that held in the traditional view of health care. Before detailing this philosophy, we will briefly consider the traditional medical model's approach to health and the resultant problems, which are addressed by Centers for Attitudinal Healing.

THE TRADITIONAL MEDICAL MODEL OF HEALTH CARE

Traditionally, Western health care models have tended to treat patients primarily as physical bodies rather than as multifaceted persons who also have emotional, psychological, social and spiritual aspects and needs (Gadow 1980; Leder 1984). This model has its roots in seventeenth-century developments. The Church suppressed the work of scientists such as Copernicus and Galileo when spiritual and physical beliefs began to conflict. Enlightenment scientists felt it necessary to distinguish the physical from the spiritual realm in order for science to advance without the Church's interference.

René Descartes, one of the fathers of modern philosophy, established a dualistic metaphysics that distinguished the physical and spiritual realms, thus buying science freedom from the Church. His metaphysics held that physical matter, the subject of science, was separate from the spirit, the subject of the Church (Descartes 1979). The price of this freedom was the development in science of a dualistic way of thinking about body and spirit as radically different and separate. The body was thought to be a passive, separate mechanism commanded by the mind to carry out certain functions. It was thus amenable to technological mechanistic interventions such as those practiced today in acute health care. A person's mind or spirit was thought to have little to do with the healthy operation of the body mechanism.

In medicine these dualistic seeds have been nurtured by the Flexnerian model of medicine, which emphasizes the scientific aspect of health care and by the prodigious growth of medical technology. Scientific and technical skills have often taken precedence over personal and caring skills. Medical doctors in particular have traditionally been given minimal training concerning the importance of personal interaction with patients, the expression of their emotions, as well as the patient's psychological and spiritual well-being.

Given this dualistic philosophy of mind/body separation, the total cause-and-effect structure of illness and health are naturally thought to be confined to the mechanism of the physical body and its material environment. Health is often given a narrowly physical interpretation that concentrates only on physical performance and well-being. Thus medical science often focuses on the body alone, utilizing technology in attempts to control and cure the body. Some of the consequences of adopting this traditional model are as follows:

1. Patients' psychospiritual needs become a relatively minor detail, something relegated to the social workers if they have time. State of mind, attitude and the subjective reality of the person who has a disease have received minimal clinical attention under this premise of dualism. Curing the body takes precedence over caring for the person, who is often neglected.
2. The person may become a passive and largely absent recipient of care, rather than an actively involved participant. If mind and attitude are extraneous to the process of disease and health, the patient has little to offer in an interaction with a physician.
3. Patient dependency on the physician is another consequence of the dualistic model. Unless patients are schooled in medicine, they must simply trust that the physician knows best.
4. Responsibility for health or illness is ultimately thought to be the physician's. The patient must accurately report symptoms and follow the recommended regimen, but the ultimate success or failure of the treatment lies in the hands of the physician.
5. The person is often a secondary consideration, while the body remains the focus of attention.

Part of the difficulty inherent in the traditional medical model results from the mind-body dualism and the subsequent myopic concentration on the body mechanism (chemistry and biology) and mechanistic methods of treatment: technological testing, manipulation and intervention. By challenging some of the limiting premises of this model, Centers for Attitudinal Healing help to discover different attitudes and avenues toward health.

**THE CENTERS' PHILOSOPHY:
PEACE AS A DIFFERENT DEFINITION OF HEALTH**

Dr. Jampolsky, aware of the shortcomings of the traditional medical model, based the Centers' philosophy on spiritual principles derived from Nancy Schucman and William Thetford's 1975 book, *A Course in Miracles* (Jampolsky 1983). The "Course" is itself metaphysically dualistic, but its dualism differs from that of Descartes or the traditional medical model. It holds that there are only two ways of being and perceiving: one is based on and operates out of fear and hate, and the other is based on and operates out of peace and love (Jampolsky 1981). The most distinctive characteristic of attitudinal healing can be summed up in the first principle of attitudinal healing: Health is defined as *inner peace*. Health begins in the mind, in one's attitude and one's habitual ways of perceiving and interacting in the world. A peaceful person is a healthy person. Thus, in contrast to the traditional medical model, mind or spirit is of primary concern in the Centers' philosophy.

By anchoring the concept of health in the mind, attitudinal healing has shifted the traditional focus of health from the body. Attitudinal healing, however, does not interfere with regular traditional medical treatments or in any way advise against them. Rather, it complements what medical science and technology can achieve. It goes beyond the medical model to address the medical model's emotional and spiritual lacunae. The philosophy of attitudinal healing acknowledges the interaction of mind and body. It acknowledges the reality of the psychological, emotional, social and spiritual needs of the patient, and it stresses an individual's active role in health attainment and promotion.

ATTITUDE AND CHRONIC DISEASE

Health promotion and education are correct in recognizing that some diseases, in particular the stubborn frontier of some chronic diseases, are not discrete. They are indicative of a life style, a personal history or way of being in the world (Justice 1987; Kimball 1981; Matthews-Simonton 1980; Solomon and Temoshok 1987). Because some chronic disease develops within the scope of a personal history, discrete, acute answers to chronic disease fail. A different approach to certain kinds of healing is called for.

The healing of diseases cultivated within a personal context must be promoted within a personal context. Whereas most health promotion requires a rehabituation concerning diet or exercise, the Centers' philosophy goes further to require a radical restructuring of one's total way of being in the world: habitual ways of perceiving, thinking, interpreting and behaving. Healthful, peaceful attitudes, perceptions and behaviors need to be integrated into life styles to promote health, both psychospiritual and physical. Like the successful Alcoholics Anonymous program, the Centers' philosophy necessitates the development of a different way of being in the world, and like AA programs, the Centers direct a medical community confounded by chronic disease to new alternative methods in health.

The precepts of attitudinal healing, like those of health promotion, stress the active involvement and commitment of each individual in attaining health. In contrast to the older medical model, one cannot simply passively request intervention from a health care professional who, it is hoped, will magically absolve one of disease. Attitudinal healing emphasizes the individual's role and responsibility in *choosing* to adopt attitudes that promote inner peace and health.

Since the Centers define health as peace, the project of becoming healthy and staying healthy requires that one habituate oneself to peaceful attitudes. The dualism presupposed by the Centers is between love/peace and hate/fear. Thus attitudinal healing is a process of dropping fearful attitudes, perceptions and beliefs that interfere with peace, and adopting loving attitudes, perceptions and beliefs that promote peace.

THE PRINCIPLES OF ATTITUDINAL HEALING

The process of re-habituating oneself and one's way of being in the world is outlined in the principles of attitudinal healing. Attitudinal healing assumes that people are fundamentally loving and peaceful. Yet past fearful experiences and subsequent habitual ways of perceiving and reacting to the world, as well as fears of a future that we believe will resemble the past, cloak our fundamental nature in fear. This blocks our access to our fundamental nature: love and peace. If, for example, one had been constantly disappointed and had one's trust dashed as a child, one may habitually look for and perhaps "see" betrayal, even where it does not exist. One might decide to stop trusting others. The future may be perceived fearfully, as a realm full of possibilities of betrayal. Living in such a fearful way inhibits the ability to experience peace and love.

Peace is developed by practicing "principles" of attitudinal healing in order to re-habituate to a new way of perceiving and being in the world. This re-habituation process is supported by following the principles of attitudinal healing. As was mentioned previously, Jampolsky adopted many of the central principles of the Centers for Attitudinal Healing from *A Course in Miracles,* and discusses seven of these principles in *Teach Only Love* (1983). The seven principles are as follows:

1. *Health is inner peace.* Therefore, healing is letting go of fear. To make changing the body our goal is to fail to recognize that our single goal is peace of mind.
2. *The essence of our being is love.* Love cannot be hindered by what is merely physical. Therefore, we believe the mind has no limits; nothing is impossible; and all disease is potentially reversible. Because love is eternal, death need not be viewed fearfully.
3. *Giving is receiving.* When our attention is on giving and joining with others, fear is removed and we accept healing for ourselves.
4. *All minds are joined.* Therefore, all healing is self-healing. Our inner peace will of itself pass to others once we accept it for ourselves.
5. *Now is the only time there is.* Pain, grief, depression, guilt and other forms of fear disappear when the mind is focused in loving peace on this instant.
6. *Decisions are made by learning to listen to the preference for peace within us.* There is no right or wrong behavior. The only meaningful choice is between fear and love.

7. *Forgiveness is the way to true health and happiness.* By not judging, we release the past and let go of our fears of the future. In so doing, we come to see that everyone is our teacher and that every circumstance is an opportunity for growth in happiness, peace and love.

Participants and volunteers incorporate and integrate these principles through interaction with the Centers for Attitudinal Healing during weekly "Group Nights." On these nights, various groups are composed of ill children, their siblings, parents and significant others, or ill adults, and are facilitated by trained volunteers. Discussion in this supportive atmosphere facilitates expression and exploration of feelings, self-help, opportunities for helping others and integration of the principles of attitudinal healing for dealing with illness and other difficult aspects of life. Through these principles and the shared fellowship of a helping community that supports and promotes these principles, the Centers facilitate healing both for the families who come to the Centers for support in the face of loss and for the specially trained volunteers.

ATTITUDINAL HEALING AND EFFECTS ON PHYSICAL HEALTH

While the primary concern of attitudinal healing is inner peace rather than the body's condition, inner peace may incidentally improve the body's condition. Research in neurophysiology, immune studies and biopsychosocial approaches to medicine support the importance of the Center's emphasis on psychospiritual state and attitude. Such work finds evidence for the link between mind and body, and emotions and health.

Psychosomatic medicine believes that "human illness cannot be conceptualized or treated by a single factor–single disease approach, but that all illness depends on a multiplicity of factors involving the somatic and psychological processes of the individual in relationship to the environment" (Kimball 1981, p. 132). Similarly, the biopsychosocial model in medicine takes genetic, biological, emotional, behavioral, situational and cultural factors into consideration of the pathogenesis of disease (Solomon and Temoshok 1987; Rolland 1984).

Psychoneuroimmunology explores the effects of emotions, attitudes, personality, ways of perceiving and subsequent behaviors on physical health. Many studies have shown the deleterious effects of negative or pessimistic attitudes on health. Kobasa and Maddi, for instance, studied the effects of stress on Illinois Bell Telephone businesspersons after divestiture. The key factor in whether or not stress resulted in physical illness was an individual's way of looking at and dealing with stressful events. Those who stayed healthy had an optimistic way of looking at situations; they developed a sense of control and an ability to put difficulties in perspective (Justice 1987, p. 58). Martin Seligman of the University of Pennsylvania also considers the way in which one perceives events and the decisions one makes concerning causes and implications of those events as crucial to the way stressful events effect health (Justice 1987, p. 233). Solomon and Temoshok (1987), as well as other researchers, have found links between personality types and the course of AIDS (Moulton et al. 1987).

Furthermore, studies show that individuals who are actively involved in situations, and perceive themselves as active and able to exert some control in those situations, are healthier than individuals who view themselves as passive, dependent, or helpless victims of a situation (Justice 1987, pp. 141-151). Clearly, personality and attitude play a role in illness and health.

CONTRASTING THE TRADITIONAL MEDICAL MODEL

The principles of attitudinal healing are in contrast to those of the traditional medical model. Attention is paid to individuals' psychospiritual-emotional state. Facilitators are trained to listen and allow people to explore, express and share their feelings. People are treated as persons who happen to have a disease, rather than diseases that happen to have a host.

Furthermore, individuals are seen as responsible, as having choices for the way they perceive reality and for their subsequent actions. While they are not held responsible for contracting a disease, they are held responsible for the way they react to their condition. They learn that they have a choice either to root their perceptions in fear and see the world negatively, or to root their perceptions in peace.

Since the Centers' philosophy holds individuals responsible for choices, it also makes them less dependent. Instead of perceiving oneself as a victim, either of someone's abuse or bad temper, or of a disease, one begins to see and accept one's own power to extend love to others, to care for oneself and to make the best of things that cannot be changed. Individuals perceive themselves as active, powerful and responsible, and in the process, often improve their physical health, as well as their psychospiritual well-being.

COMPLEMENTING THE MEDICAL MODEL

Centers for Attitudinal Healing both challenge and complement the traditional medical model by emphasizing and facilitating the psychospiritual approach to health care. By requiring individual involvement in health and a willingness to change attitudes and perceptions, they ask much more of people than the traditional model does. But they also offer more than any pill or surgery can: spiritual growth and support, and a way to develop inner peace. Chronic diseases and "diseases of the spirit" such as alcoholism and other types of addiction may be particularly amenable to the Center's approach to health. As we face some of the seemingly impermeable frontiers in modern medicine, the lessons of attitudinal healing may assist us in our goals of promoting peace and health for others and in achieving them for ourselves.

REFERENCES

Descartes, R. *Meditations on First Philosophy* (1641). (Translated by D.A. Cress.) Indianapolis: Hackett, 1979.

Gadow, S. Body and self: a dialectic. *J. Med. Philosophy* 5: 172-185, 1980.

Jampolsky, J. *Love is Letting Go of Fear.* Toronto: Bantam, 1981.

_____. *Teach Only Love: The Seven Principles of Attitudinal Healing.* Toronto: Bantam, 1983.

Justice, B. *Who Gets Sick? Thinking and Health.* Houston: Peak Press, 1987.

Kimball, C.P. *The Biopsychosocial Approach to the Patient.* Baltimore: Williams & Wilkins, 1981.

Leder, D. Medicine and paradigms of embodiment. *J. Med. Philosophy* 9:29-43, 1984.

Matthews-Simonton, S., O.C. Simonton, and J.L. Creighton. *Getting Well Again.* Toronto: Bantam, 1980.

Moulton, J.M., D.M. Sweet, L. Temoshok, and J.S. Mandel. Attributions of blame and responsibility in relation to distress and health behavior change in people with AIDS and AIDS-related complex. *J. Appl. Social Psychol.* 17:493-506, 1987.

Rolland, J. Toward a psychosocial typology of chronic and life-threatening illness. *Family Systems Med.* 2:245-262, 1984.

Schucman, N., and W. Thetford. *A Course in Miracles.* Tiburon, CA: The Foundation for Inner Peace, 1975.

Solomon, G.F., and L. Temoshok. A psychoneuroimmunologic perspective on AIDS research: questions, preliminary findings, and suggestions. *J. Appl. Social Psychol.* 17:287, 1987.

27

Sudden Infant Death Syndrome: The Compassionate Friends and the Indiana State SIDS Project

Chris McDonald

An infant has died for no apparent reason. First responders (police and paramedics) are called. After investigation, the parents will be told the cause of death was sudden infant death syndrome. SIDS, the sudden and unexpected death of apparently healthy babies, is the major cause of death of infants between the ages of 1 month and 1 year in the United States. As many as 8000 American babies die as a result of sudden infant death syndrome every year (a ratio of 2 per 1000 live births).

The babies are not the victims of a "freakish disease." SIDS is at least as old as the Old Testament and seems to have been at least as frequent in the eighteenth and nineteenth centuries as it is today. SIDS is a definite medical entity. It is not contagious, and it seldom occurs after 1 year of age. SIDS cannot be predicted or prevented, even by a physician. There seems to be no relationship between SIDS and prenatal care or the baby's body weight. Victims appear healthy prior to death. There appears to be no suffering. Death occurs very rapidly, usually during sleep, and generally strikes males. There is a higher incidence during the winter months, when the disease may mimic the symptoms of a cold. Research to date indicates that the cause of SIDS is not suffocation, aspiration or regurgitation.

SIDS is not apnea. Apnea is an unexplained episode of cessation of breathing lasting for 20 seconds or longer, or a shorter respiratory pause associated with bradycardia, cyanosis or pallor.

The infant dying of SIDS during the night and found in the morning will sometimes resemble an abused child because the blood has pooled to the soft tissue areas, and there may be froth flecked with blood at the mouth and nose. Due to the suspicious appearance of the baby, many parents or caretakers have been arrested and charged with child abuse.

In Indiana, approximately 200 infants die of SIDS every year. Since the early 1980s, The Compassionate Friends (TCF) and the SIDS Project of the Indiana State Board of Health have worked as a team in Indiana communities to inform the public and first responders about the dynamics of a SIDS death.

Owing to several cases involving SIDS families in northwestern Indiana, The Compassionate Friends asked the state board of health to present an informational panel to the community. Invited to be part of the planning were representatives from the state board of health, a local board of health, three police departments and an area coroner's office, in addition to local clergy, funeral directors, hospital emergency room personnel and emergency medical technicians. During the planning we were informed that many of the first responders did not have even basic information about SIDS and felt that a seminar should be given to them first. As a result, a seminar just for first responders was presented twice in the same day at two different locations to accommodate the changing of shifts of the first responders. The police departments made attendance mandatory for their officers.

The program included a pathologist, who presented facts and showed slides to acquaint the audience with the appearance of a typical SIDS baby. Two bereaved parents illustrated how first responders might behave with the parents of a SIDS baby. One of the objectives of the program was to remind first responders that they can either help or hurt parents who are trying to deal with their grief. Will first responders be able to show knowledge, understanding and compassion, or will they appear unprepared? From the beginning, parents need to hear the facts about SIDS, because society has so many misconceptions about the subject. Parents are often besieged with questions, such as, Why didn't you breast-feed? Did you use too many covers? Didn't you check the baby during the night? Wouldn't a monitor have saved the baby? Was the baby sick? and Why didn't you take the baby to the doctor?

The positive responder will likely have a soft voice, a gentle touch, a willingness to transport a child while knowing that child is dead, and correct information on a suspected SIDS death. Telling the parents that the death was not their fault is a must. The negative responder may unconsciously find fault with the parents because of a first impression of their appearance or living conditions. Negative statements and body language can be very accusatory and destructive. (The program presenters used a "Bad Guy, Good Guy" format, with the "Bad Guy" acting first, in order to leave the audience with an uplifted feeling.) What is conveyed, verbally and nonverbally, to the parents at the first response will be reviewed and "replayed" by the family for a long time after the death. The panel encouraged the audience not to be afraid to use the word "dead" when talking about the child.

A year later, Indiana's first statewide SIDS seminar was held. One presentation to bereaved parents and personnel concerned how a SIDS case can be effectively and compassionately handled. During the first 24 hours after a child dies of SIDS, many people become involved:

1. *Police.* There are procedures police must follow after a death in the home. Asking about what happened, in a kind voice, is a good way to begin.
2. *Emergency medical technicians.* EMTs arrive to transport the child to the hospital.
3. *Medical examiner.* The ME or coroner may also be called to the home or hospital; he may offer supportive services to the family and may even make the call to The Compassionate Friends.
4. *Emergency room staff.* If the child is in the ER, the staff should ask the parents if they would like to hold their child.
5. *Clergy.* Members of the clergy are usually called by the family or hospital. They may give comfort by a simple touch or a hug. Parents should not be told, "The death is God's will."
6. *Funeral director.* The funeral director should offer many options as to arrangements and possible keepsakes for the parents.
7. *The Compassionate Friends.* After confirmation of SIDS by an autopsy, TCF may be called by any of the persons above to contact the parents within the first 24 hours.

All of these people have had contact with the family for only a short time, but all need to know and share with the parents the accurate facts about SIDS. When the family has been treated with kindness and compassion, a "good grief" has begun for the family, which will help immensely in the years to come. A few weeks following the death, a supportive in-home visit is usually made by a nurse from the local board of health, accompanied if possible by another SIDS parent.

Throughout the project, the Indiana State Board of Health has been a good source of information for TCF representatives, as well as for bereaved parents seeking answers to their questions. Networking with the state board of health has opened many doors to professionals for help with seminars and presentations. Through the board we have received mini-grants, useful films and much up-to-date information. The Indiana State Board of Health has given credibility to The Compassionate Friends as a viable community service organization. In turn we at TCF have let them know what is going on in our communities, including prevailing misconceptions and the need for greater community awareness.

A mutually beneficial relationship needs a firm commitment from the state board coordinator and from TCF leaders at the local and state levels. Such a relationship can work, and we have proved it.

28

Group Structure and Group Dynamics for Ex-Mental Patients

Robert E. Emerick, PhD

The claim that "self-help works" deserves objective evaluation by researchers from outside the mental health system and the self-help movement. My desire to study the self-help method with particular reference to ex-mental patient groups led me to the question, What different types of groups are there? My sociology background suggested that I begin with a descriptive study of the entire ex-mental patient self-help movement in order to develop an understanding of the range and diversity of types of groups within the movement.

This chapter presents a classification of ex-mental patient self-help groups based on an examination of the relationships between four variables: two structural variables called "group affiliation" and "group structure," and two aspects of group dynamics: "service provided," which reflects *intra*group dynamics, and "regular group contacts," an aspect of *inter*group dynamics.

The mental health self-help movement is composed of many different types of groups. At one end of the spectrum are groups that are politically conservative, pro-psychiatry and formally affiliated with a national self-help organization that promotes a particular self-help "method." These groups provide their members with some form of "alternative therapy" directed toward individual growth. At the other end of the spectrum are the radical groups that may affiliate loosely with local or developing national movement organizations, are anti-psychiatry and provide their members with opportunities for involvement in political activism, legal advocacy work and other "social change" types of activities. In the middle are the bulk of the self-help movement groups, the moderate groups engaged in a broad range of activities and organizational affiliations that reflect their political neutrality. These moderate groups constitute the heart of the mental patient self-help movement today, as well as indicating the future direction of the movement. Nonetheless, it is important to understand the historical and potential future impact on the movement of the groups at both ends of the spectrum. The radical and conservative groups provide both definition and beneficial diversity to the mental patient self-help movement.

RESEARCH DESIGN

The Sample: Primary Consumer Ex-Mental Patient Self-Help Groups

Although the literature indicates that there are thousands of self-help groups in this country, the parameters of the population of ex-mental patient self-help groups are largely unknown (see Gartner and Riesman 1977; Katz and Bender 1976; Borman et al. 1982; Lieberman and Borman 1979). Accordingly, a "snowball sample" of groups was developed by reviewing articles in mental patient movement newsletters and magazines and by attending a number of self-help conferences. A basic informational questionnaire was developed and mailed out to all groups in the snowball sample. One of the questions asked for the names and addresses of other comparable or competing mental health self-help groups. Following these leads, the sample of movement groups was further developed with eight separate "waves" of questionnaire mailings.

In analyzing the content of newsletter articles, and after talking with hundreds of members of mental health self-help groups, it became apparent that the most important distinction that people in the movement make is between "primary" consumer groups (groups of former mental patients) and "secondary" consumer groups (groups composed of parents and relatives of mental patients, and sometimes professionals). In general these two kinds of groups are considered to be antithetical to one another—philosophically, politically and pragmatically. It was determined that the present research would be directed exclusively to the study of primary, rather than secondary, consumer groups.

The focus of the research was thus determined to be groups that are both *primary mental health consumer groups* (those composed of ex-mental patients, rather than family members or relatives) and *self-help groups* (those claiming to promote mutual peer help, rather than traditional types of psychiatric or psychological therapy involving hierarchical therapist-client relationships).

The Questionnaire

The questionnaire was composed of 20 questions designed to elicit basic demographic information about the groups, as well as descriptive information about how the groups are structured, the kinds of activities they engage in and the political values they promote, particularly in regard to the "mental health system."

A total of 140 groups returned questionnaires. After eliminating the incomplete and nonrelevant questionnaires, the remaining 104 groups constitute the sample of primary consumer mental patient self-help groups for the present study. Obviously, since we have no basis for knowing the extent of the total population of such groups, our findings are offered as only suggestive of the nature of the mental patient self-help movement.

Data Processing and Analysis

Since this is an exploratory descriptive study of a group whose population parameters are still unknown, the data generated by the questionnaire items are treated as "nonparametric" measures of nominal and ordinal variables. The major statistic used in this study is percentage figures, although the nonparametric "contingency coefficient" measure of correlation (C) and chi-square tests of statistical significance are computed for all cross-tabulation tables (see Siegel 1956).

THE VARIABLES

The Structural Variables: Group Affiliation and Group Structure

In an earlier project we analyzed the demographic factors of group location, group age and group size in the mental patient movement (Emerick 1989). That analysis was organized in terms of two structural variables called "group affiliation" and "group structure."

GROUP AFFILIATION

Groups in the mental health self-help movement are popularly identified in terms of categories of formal or informal group affiliation. These categories are important because they identify groups in terms of the various political ideologies in the movement (Emerick 1990).

Movement activists speak and write primarily about two major, although still informal, national grassroots movement affiliations known as the National Alliance of Mental Patients (NAMP) and the National Mental Health Consumers Association (NMHCA). NAMP is widely considered to be the more "radical" organization, while NMHCA (pronounced "nim-ka") is thought of as the "moderate" or "conservative" group. In addition there is widespread awareness of a number of local grassroots groups organized into statewide networks, such as the California Network of Mental Health Clients (CNMHC). A number of movement groups remain in the category of "non-affiliated" groups. Finally, movement activists consider the several national satellite spin-off organizations, such as Recovery Inc., GROW, and Emotions Anonymous, to constitute a separate or marginal movement category of formal "national" group affiliations (see Lee 1976; Rappaport and Seidman 1985; Galanter 1988).

Each group in the sample was thus classified into one of five categories of group affiliation according to its response to the affiliation question and, when known, its public affiliational identity.

GROUP STRUCTURE

Group structure is a composite dimension based on a group's type of leadership and membership vis-à-vis psychiatry. This classification was developed by Judi Chamberlin, a major figure in the mental health patient movement, in her book *On Our Own: Patient-Controlled Alternatives to the Mental Health System* (1978). Chamberlin classifies groups based on how they deal with the problem of whether or not to include psychiatrists and other mental health professionals in their membership or leadership cohorts. Most mental patient self-help groups do not allow professionals to participate in leadership capacities. Those groups that do are referred to as "partnership groups" and are based on a structural model that theoretically promotes a kind of sharing of leadership responsibilities between professionals and patients-as-partners. Within the client-led groups there are two different models that reflect type of membership. The most radical groups reject professionals within their membership in any capacity and are known as "separatist groups." Groups that allow professionals in auxiliary roles are called "supportive groups." Thus, the three categories of group structure include (1) the most radical (anti-psychiatric) "separatist" groups, (2) the moderate (psychiatrically neutral) "supportive" groups and (3) the most conservative (pro-psychiatric) "partnership" groups.

The "group structure" classification of each group in the sample was determined on the basis of how the group answered a question on "the kinds of people who use your services" and another question on "the kinds of leaders in your organization." Any mention of professionals in leadership roles led to the classification of the groups as a "partnership" group, and any mention of professionals in the group membership was used to classify the group as a "supportive" group. Groups without professionals, either in leadership or membership roles, were classified as "separatist" groups.

The Dynamic Variables:
Service Provided and Regular Group Contacts

In recent years increasing awareness of the importance of the self-help movement in this country has led social scientists to study these groups in terms of the kinds of service provided to members. After reviewing these studies we developed the variable of "service provided," a measure of intra-group dynamics (Emerick 1989). A second dynamic variable—"regular group contacts"—is a measure of intergroup activities in the mental patient self-help movement.

SERVICE PROVIDED

Sample groups were asked to describe the types of service provided within their groups. Based on our data and a review of the literature on models of self-help groups (Sagarin 1969; Katz and Bender 1976; Gartner and Reissman 1977; Zinman 1987), we developed a service typology of groups. This includes the whole range of services provided, from revolutionary protest and radical advocacy activities on the left to conservative alternative therapy services on the right. Our typology of six categories of services includes three types of "social change" services (advocacy-legal, educational-technical assistance and information referral) and three types of "individual growth" services (drop-in centers, group support and alternative therapy).

REGULAR GROUP CONTACTS

Groups in the sample were asked to name other self-help organizations with which they have "regular contacts." The sample groups were classified into four regular-group-contact categories of "none," "low," "medium" and "high," based on whether they mentioned no other groups, one group, two or three groups, or four or more groups, respectively.

THE FINDINGS

The structural variables of group affiliation and group structure are examined below in terms of their relationships, first with each other and then with each of the two dynamic variables of service provided and regular group contacts. Finally we look at the relationship between the two dynamic variables.

Group Affiliation and Group Structure

Table 1 demonstrates the overwhelmingly moderate nature of the mental health self-help movement today. Nearly 80 percent of the groups (83 out of 104) are located in the three central affiliation categories—NMHCA, local and non-affiliated groups. Similarly, the central structure category—supportive groups—includes 62.5 percent (65 out of 104) of the sample groups. Mental patient self-help groups are "bunched up"—overrepresented—in the moderate ideological and structural categories. With relatively few groups in the extreme affiliation and structural categories, it is reasonable to argue that the moderate groups are the heart of the movement today. Indeed, the three central cells in Table 1—NMHCA, local and non-affiliated groups that are in the supportive structure row—account for more than half (52.9 percent) of the sample groups.

Table 1.
Group Affiliation by Group Structure: All 104 Sample Groups

Group Structure	NAMP N	%	NMHCA N	%	Local N	%	Non-Affil. N	%	National N	%	Total N	%
				Group Affiliation								
Separatist	5	(55.6)	3	(16.7)	4	(14.3)	5	(13.5)	0	(0.0)	17	(16.4)
Supportive	4	(44.4)	14	(77.8)	20	(71.4)	21	(56.8)	6	(50.0)	65	(62.5)
Partnership	0	(0.00)	1	(5.5)	4	(14.3)	11	(29.7)	6	(50.0)	22	(21.1)
TOTAL	9	(100.0)	18	(100.0)	28	(100.0)	37	(100.0)	12	(100.0)	104	(100.0)

Chi-square = 22.99; p < 0.01; C = 0.43.

Table 1 also shows that there is a statistically significant relationship between group affiliation and group structure (C = 0.43, p < 0.01). Notice in the left-hand column of Table 1 that the most radical (anti-psychiatry) NAMP groups are concentrated in the radical separatist (55.6 percent) and moderate supportive (44.4 percent) categories of group structure, with no groups at all in the conservative partnership category. Conversely, at the other end of Table 1, the most conservative (pro-psychiatry) national affiliation groups are found in the most conservative structural category of partnership groups (50.0 percent) and the moderate supportive category (50.0 percent), with no groups at all in the separatist category.

Following the same trend, the second most radical category of NMHCA groups tends to be concentrated in the supportive (77.8 percent) and separatist (16.7 percent) structural categories, with a few groups in the partnership category (5.5 percent). Balancing this off, the non-affiliated groups are found in the second most conservative position, with most groups in the supportive (56.8 percent) and partnership (29.7 percent) categories, and a few in the separatist category (13.5 percent).

Finally, the central affiliation category of local groups is symmetrically distributed throughout the structural categories with 14.3 percent of its groups in both the separatist and partnership categories and 71.4 percent in the central supportive category.

Next we analyze the first of the dynamic variables—service provided—by comparing the relationships between this intragroup activity and the two structural variables of group affiliation and group structure. The more ideological factor of group affiliation is shown to be more helpful than the factor of group structure in making sense of the distribution of types of service provided in ex-mental patient groups.

Tables 2 and 3 show that, despite the moderate nature of the mental patient movement, it is clearly more accurately labeled as a social movement than a collection of alternative therapy groups. Nearly two-thirds of the sample groups (62.5 percent) are classified as "social change" groups, based on the types of service provided, while the other one-third of the sample constitutes the "individual growth" contingent.

Table 2.

Group Affiliation by Service Provided: All 104 Sample Groups

Service Provided	Group Affiliation										
	NAMP		NMHCA		Local		Non-Affil.		National		Total
	N	%	N	%	N	%	N	%	N	%	N	%
Social Change	7	(77.8)	12	(66.7)	17	(60.7)	25	(67.6)	4	(33.3)	65 (62.5)
Individual Growth	2	(22.2)	6	(33.3)	11	(39.3)	12	(32.4)	8	(66.7)	39 (37.5)
TOTAL	9	(100.0)	18	(100.0)	28	(100.0)	37	(100.0)	12	(100.0)	104(100.0)

Chi-square = 5.82; $p < 0.30$; C = 0.23.

Table 3.

Group Structure by Service Provided: All 104 Sample Groups

Service Provided	Group Structure							
	Separatist		Supportive		Partnership		Total	
	N	%	N	%	N	%	N	%
Social Change	13	(76.5)	38	(58.5)	14	(63.6)	65	(62.5)
Individual Growth	4	(23.5)	27	(41.5)	8	(36.4)	39	(37.5)
TOTAL	17	(100.0)	65	(100.0)	22	(100.0)	104	(100.0)

Chi-square = 1.88; $p < 0.50$; C = 0.13.

Group Affiliation and Service Provided

In Table 2 we see the differential distribution of services provided throughout movement groups based on group affiliation. Four of the five categories of group affiliation—NAMP, NMHCA, local and non-affiliated groups—are seen to be similarly dominated by groups with a "social change" orientation. Sixty to nearly 78 percent of these groups offer outward-focused, social change services to their members.

In distinct contrast, the national affiliation category is dominated by groups offering "individual growth" services to their members (66.7 percent). It is in this sense that these formal national self-help organizations constitute the "alternative therapy" wing of the self-help movement and may be thought of as "marginal" to or outside of the general social reform orientation of the mental patient movement.

Group Structure and Service Provided

Table 3 shows that the factor of group structure has a less clear influence on service provided than does group affiliation. All three structural categories include a predominance of social change groups (58.5 to 76.5 percent). Even the most conservative partnership groups are decisively more social change–oriented in their services provided (63.6 percent) than they are individual growth–oriented (37.5 percent). Apparently, the way a group is structured vis-à-vis psychiatry has less to do with the type of service offered than does its affiliation with other self-help organizations (C = 0.13 versus C = 0.23).

Group Affiliation and Regular Group Contacts

Next we examine the relationship between the structural variable of group affiliation and the intergroup dynamic variable of "regular group contacts." This analysis includes assessing the relationship between these two variables by controlling for a third variable—service provided. The analysis shows that the strong relationship between group affiliation and regular group contacts is even more powerful when the type of service provided is controlled.

Table 4 shows that the groups are fairly evenly distributed between the four categories of "none," "low," "medium" and "high" regular group contacts (23.1, 25.9, 28.8 and 22.1 percent, respectively). Table 4 also shows that the distribution of regular group contacts varies dramatically with the type of group affiliation. In general, the more radical the group affiliation, the greater the frequency of contact with other groups. Conversely, the more conservative the group's affiliation, the greater the likelihood of infrequent or no contact with other groups.

Table 4.
Group Affiliation by Regular Group Contacts: All 104 Sample Groups

| Regular Group Contacts | Group Affiliation | | | | | | | | | | |
| | NAMP | | NMHCA | | Local | | Non-Affil. | | National | | Total | |
	N	%	N	%	N	%	N	%	N	%	N	%
None	0	(0.0)	1	(5.6)	3	(10.7)	15	(40.5)	5	(41.7)	24	(23.1)
Low	2	(22.2)	5	(27.8)	8	(28.6)	7	(18.9)	5	(41.7)	27	(25.9)
Medium	3	(33.3)	9	(50.0)	9	(32.1)	8	(21.6)	1	(8.3)	15	(28.8)
High	4	(44.4)	3	(16.7)	8	(28.6)	7	(18.9)	1	(8.3)	23	(22.1)
TOTAL	9	(100.0)	18	(100.0)	28	(100.0)	37	(100.0)	12	(100.0)	104	(100.0)

Chi-square = 26.17; p < 0.02; C = 0.45.

Looking at the extreme cases in Table 4, we see that the most radical NAMP groups are concentrated in the "medium" and "high" contact categories (77.7 percent), with no groups at all in the "none" category of group contacts. Conversely, the most conservative national groups are concentrated in the "low" and "none" categories of group contacts (83.4 percent), with only one group (8.3 percent) in each of the "medium" and "high" contact categories. The other three categories of group affiliation—NMHCA, local and non-affiliated—fall appropriately between these two extremes.

The indication is that, with the exception of the non-affiliated groups where greater isolation is to be expected, only the national affiliation groups are "marginal" or "out of the loop" of the mental health self-help movement. Among the NAMP, NMHCA and local affiliation categories, very few groups report total isolation from other self-help groups (0, 5.6 and 10.7 percent, respectively). These frequent contact groups *are* the mental patient movement and thus are actively involved in interaction with other groups in the movement.

Table 5.
Group Affiliation by Regular Group Contacts: 65 Social Change Groups

Regular Group Contacts	Group Affiliation										
	NAMP		NMHCA		Local		Non-Affil.		National		Total	
	N	%	N	%	N	%	N	%	N	%	N	%
None	0	(0.0)	1	(8.3)	1	(5.9)	8	(32.0)	0	(0.0)	10	(15.4)
Low	2	(28.6)	3	(25.0)	2	(11.8)	6	(24.0)	4	(100.0)	17	(26.2)
Medium	2	(28.6)	6	(50.0)	7	(41.2)	5	(20.0)	0	(0.0)	20	(30.8)
High	3	(42.8)	2	(16.7)	7	(41.2)	6	(24.0)	0	(0.0)	18	(27.7)
TOTAL	7	(100.0)	12	(100.0)	17	(100.0)	25	(100.0)	4	(100.0)	65	(100.0)

Chi-square = 24.65; $p < 0.02$; C = 0.52.

We suspect that the strong correlation between group affiliation and regular group contacts might be even more pronounced if we controlled for the type of service provided. Thus, Tables 5 and 6 examine the relationship by looking separately at the "social change" groups and the "individual growth" groups, respectively.

Table 5 shows that when we look only at the 65 social change groups in the sample, the original correlation between group affiliation and regular group contacts is even more pronounced (C = 0.52 versus C = 0.45). Among these social change or "movement" groups, only 15.4 percent claim no contacts with other groups, compared to 23.1 percent for the whole sample and 35.9 percent for individual growth groups (Tables 4 and 6, respectively). Table 5 also shows the highest concentration of groups in the low, medium and high contact categories. Thus, for example, among the 65 social change groups, 27.7 percent report "high" contact with other groups, compared to 22.1 percent for the sample (Table 4) and only 12.8 percent for the individual growth groups (Table 6).

Table 6.
Group Affiliation by Regular Group Contacts: 39 Individual Growth Groups

Regular Group Contacts	Group Affiliation										
	NAMP		NMHCA		Local		Non-Affil.		National		Total	
	N	%	N	%	N	%	N	%	N	%	N	%
None	0	(0.0)	0	(0.0)	2	(18.2)	7	(58.3)	5	(62.5)	14	(35.9)
Low	0	(0.0)	2	(33.3)	6	(54.5)	1	(8.3)	1	(12.5)	10	(25.6)
Medium	1	(50.0)	3	(50.0)	2	(18.2)	3	(25.0)	1	(12.5)	10	(25.6)
High	1	(50.0)	1	(16.7)	1	(9.1)	1	(8.3)	1	(12.5)	5	(12.8)
TOTAL	2	(100.0)	6	(100.0)	11	(100.0)	12	(100.0)	8	(100.0)	39	(100.0)

Chi-square = 15.81; $p < 0.20$; C = 0.54.

Table 6 shows the strongest correlation between group affiliation and regular group contacts (C = 0.54), although it is not statistically significant. Within the 39 individual growth groups the variation in the distribution of regular group contacts is very clear. None of the NAMP or NMHCA groups show up in the "none" category of contacts, while 62.5 percent of the national groups have no contacts.

Group Structure and Regular Group Contacts

Tables 7, 8 and 9 assess the relationship between group structure and regular group contacts, first for the entire sample, and then controlling for service provided. As these tables show, the variable of group structure is not as powerful a predictor of regular group contacts as the variable of group affiliation.

Table 7.
Group Structure by Regular Group Contacts: All 104 Sample Groups

Regular Group Contacts	Group Structure							
	Separatist		Supportive		Partnership		Total	
	N	%	N	%	N	%	N	%
None	4	(23.5)	15	(23.1)	5	(22.7)	24	(23.1)
Low	4	(23.5)	14	(21.5)	9	(40.9)	27	(25.9)
Medium	4	(23.5)	23	(35.4)	2	(13.6)	30	(28.8)
High	5	(29.4)	13	(20.0)	5	(22.7)	23	(22.1)
TOTAL	17	(100.0)	65	(100.0)	22	(100.0)	104	(100.0)

Chi-square = 5.86; $p < 0.50$; C = 0.23.

Table 7 shows that the correlation between group structure and regular group contacts is weak (C = 0.23). Tables 8 and 9 show that controlling for the variable of service provided strengthens the correlation for social change groups (C = 0.32) but weakens it for individual growth groups (C = 0.21). In all cases, the correlations are not statistically significant.

Table 8.

Group Structure by Regular Group Contacts: 65 Social Change Groups

Regular Group Contacts	Group Structure							
	Separatist		Supportive		Partnership		Total	
	N	%	N	%	N	%	N	%
None	3	(23.1)	6	(15.8)	1	(7.1)	10	(15.4)
Low	3	(23.1)	7	(18.4)	7	(50.0)	17	(26.2)
Medium	3	(23.1)	15	(39.5)	2	(14.3)	20	(30.8)
High	4	(30.7)	10	(26.3)	4	(28.6)	18	(27.7)
TOTAL	13	(100.0)	38	(100.0)	14	(100.0)	65	(100.0)

Chi-square = 7.58; $p < 0.30$; C = 0.32.

Table 9.

Group Structure by Regular Group Contacts: 39 Individual Growth Groups

Regular Group Contacts	Group Structure							
	Separatist		Supportive		Partnership		Total	
	N	%	N	%	N	%	N	%
None	1	(25.0)	9	(33.3)	4	(50.0)	14	(35.9)
Low	1	(25.0)	7	(25.9)	2	(25.0)	10	(25.6)
Medium	1	(25.0)	8	(29.6)	1	(12.5)	10	(25.6)
High	1	(25.0)	3	(11.1)	1	(12.5)	5	(12.8)
TOTAL	4	(100.0)	27	(100.0)	8	(100.0)	39	(100.0)

Chi-square = 1.86; $p < 0.95$; C = 0.21.

Table 7 shows that the fairly equal distribution of groups among categories of regular group contacts for the whole sample is largely maintained in each of the three structural categories. The only significant "movement" of these data is seen in the partnership category of groups, comparing the distributions in Tables 8 and 9.

Service Provided and Regular Group Contacts

We now proceed to a consideration of the final relationship between the two dynamic variables of service provided and regular group contacts. Table 10 shows that there is a correlation, albeit a weak one, between service provided and regular group contacts (C = 0.25). We see a definite relationship here between social change groups and a greater tendency for group contacts, on the one hand, and individual growth groups and a greater tendency to be isolated from other groups. Again, despite a fairly equal distribution of sample groups throughout the four group contact categories, the social change groups are underrepresented in the "none" category (15.4 percent), while the individual growth groups are overrepresented there (35.9 percent). Conversely, the social change groups are more frequent in the "high" contact category (27.7 percent), while the individual growth groups are less frequently there (12.8 percent).

Table 10.

Service Provided by Regular Group Contacts: All 104 Sample Groups

Regular Group Contacts	Service Provided					
	Social Change Groups		Individual Growth Groups		Total	
	N	%	N	%	N	%
None	10	(15.4)	14	(35.9)	24	(23.1)
Low	17	(26.2)	10	(25.6)	27	(25.9)
Medium	20	(30.8)	10	(25.6)	30	(28.8)
High	18	(27.7)	5	(12.8)	23	(22.1)
TOTAL	65	(100.0)	39	(100.0)	104	(100.0)

Chi-square = 7.11; $p < 0.10$; C = 0.25.

SUMMARY AND CONCLUSIONS

This chapter analyzes data collected from 104 mental patient self-help groups in terms of the relationships between two structural variables (group affiliation and group structure) and two dynamic variables (service provided and regular group contacts). In general, group affiliation explains more of the variance in two dynamic variables than does group structure. In addition, group affiliation appears to be an ideological variable that accounts for variations in group structure.

Our data suggest a strong trend toward moderation in the mental patient movement, with most groups affiliating themselves with politically neutral ideologies and adopting a moderate supportive structure. Nonetheless, our data also show that the mental health self-help movement is composed of a large variety of types of groups. The most radical anti-psychiatry affiliation groups (NAMP) are concentrated in the most radical separatist category of group structure. The most conservative pro-psychiatry "national" affiliation groups are concentrated in the most conservative "partnership" structural category. The politically moderate groups (NMHCA, local and non-affiliated) are clustered in the moderate supportive category of group structure.

Despite the strong trend toward moderation, nearly two-thirds of the groups in the mental patient movement promote progressive, social change activities typical of groups involved in a social movement, rather than the socially regressive and isolationist alternative therapy concerns of the individual growth groups. In general, the more radical the groups are, in terms of the categories of group affiliation, the more likely they are to offer one of the outer-focused, social reform types of service. Most of the groups in our sample—NAMP, NMHCA, local and non-affiliated groups—are shown to be primarily social change groups. The more conservative the groups are, as measured by the variable of group affiliation, the more likely they are to offer one of the inner-focused, individual reform types of service. Only the national affiliation category of groups in our sample is dominated by individual growth groups and thus is classified as "marginal" to the mental patient social movement.

It is apparent that the categories of group structure are less informative in helping us make sense of group dynamics than are the categories of group affiliation. Even the most conservative partnership groups are decisively more social reform–oriented than they are individual reform–oriented.

Our data show that the more radical the group affiliation, the greater the frequency of regular contacts with other groups. Conversely, the more conservative the group's affiliation, the greater the likelihood of infrequent or no contact with other groups. Only the most conservative national affiliation groups are found to be significantly isolated from other groups in the self-help movement. Group structure is not a significant predictor of degree of group contact.

Finally, we found that the two types of group dynamics discussed here—service provided and regular group contacts—are predictably related to each other in terms of degree of radicalism-conservatism. That is, the more radical the group's service, the more actively involved the group is in the networking process. Conversely, the more conservative the group's service provided, the less likely the group is to be involved in networking. Active involvement in the informal networking process is associated with the more radical, outer-focused, social reform types of group services, while lack of networking involvement is associated with more conservative, inner-focused, individual reform types of service among self-help groups.

The data presented in this chapter lend support to traditional sociological assumptions about the relationship between the way groups are structured and the kinds of dynamics that take place within and between them. Our data show that the more radical the group, the greater the probability that the group is actively involved in social change activities and high levels of networking with other groups in the mental patient movement. The more conservative the group, the more likely it is to be involved in providing individual growth activities and thus to remain uninvolved in the movement networking process. The strong anti-psychiatric history of this social movement is thus perpetuated by the fact that the most conservative and pro-psychiatric groups tend to be the least actively involved in networking with other groups in the movement. Clearly, the informational, political and economic benefits of active involvement in the networking processes are not as important to those groups involved with individual growth activities as they are to the social change groups.

The relatively small number of conservative groups tend to emphasize self-help as a form of "alternative therapy," thus promoting groups modeled on the inner-focused, individual reform orientation of the traditional mental health system. The major portion of movement groups are the more radical and moderate groups that emphasize the notion of self-help as a basis for various types of social reform that may reject or challenge the traditional assumptions of the mental health system. These social change groups tend to promote outer-focused activities that most people outside of the movement would characterize as "anti-establishment" or "radical." Mutual protection and support for the social reform values and goals of these groups appear to be sought and obtained through the elaboration of an extensive system of networking contacts between the groups.

REFERENCES

Borman, L.D., L.E. Borck, R. Hess, and F.L. Pasquale (eds.). *Helping People to Help Themselves: Self-Help and Prevention*. New York: Haworth, 1982.

Chamberlin, J. *On Our Own: Patient-Controlled Alternatives to the Mental Health System*. New York: McGraw-Hill, 1978.

Emerick, R.E. Group demographics in the mental patient movement: group location, age, and size as political factors. *Community Mental Health J.* 25(4):277-300, 1989.

————. Self-help groups for former patients: relations with mental health professionals. *Hosp. Community Psychiatry* 41(4):401-407, 1990.

Galanter, M. Zealous self-help groups as adjuncts to psychiatric treatment: a study of Recovery, Inc. *Am. J. Psychiatry* 145(10):1248-1253, 1988.

Gartner, A., and F. Riessman. *Self-Help in the Human Services*. San Francisco: Jossey-Bass, 1977.

Katz, A.H., and E.I. Bender. *The Strength in Us: Self-Help Groups in the Modern World*. New York: New Viewpoints, 1976.

Lee, D.T. Therapeutic Type: Recovery, Inc. In A.H. Katz and E.I. Bender (eds.), *The Strength in Us: Self-Help Groups in the Modern World*. New York: New Viewpoints, 1976.

Lieberman, M.A., and L.D. Borman. *Self-Help Groups for Coping with Crisis*. San Francisco: Jossey-Bass, 1979.

Rappaport, J., and E. Seidman. Collaborative research with a mutual help organization. *Social Policy* Winter 1985, pp. 12-24.

Sagarin, E. *Odd Man In: Societies of Deviants in America*. Chicago: Quadrangle, 1969.

Siegel, S. *Nonparametric Statistics for the Behavioral Sciences*. New York: McGraw-Hill, 1956.

Zinman, S. Definition of Self-Help Groups. In S. Budd and S. Zinman (eds.), *Reaching Across: Mental Health Clients Helping Each Other*. Riverside, CA: California Network of Mental Health Clients, 1987.

29

Self-Help Groups and Aging

David Haber, PhD

More than 10 million older persons are living in the community and coping with a chronic impairment that limits their daily activity. The number of such persons will more than double over the next 30 years and the community long-term care assistance they will need may overwhelm professional and institutional resources. Moreover, community long-term care assistance requires social and emotional support to care recipients—and caregivers as well—that professionals cannot be expected to provide. In addition, geographical mobility and the decline of the birth rate will limit the number of relatives who can provide timely assistance.

To meet the increased demand for chronic care assistance the self-help group has become the fastest growing self-help activity today. Over 15 million Americans, young and old, have joined these groups, most in the past five years.

Self-help groups are associations of people who come together to become better informed about their impairment, knowledgeable about more appropriate health care services and resources, and more capable of coping with the emotional, physical and financial burdens associated with chronic conditions.

By 1983 self-help groups were the number one source of assistance for health problems that impact on mental health. A national probability sample revealed that more individuals utilized self-help groups than sought help from mental health professionals or consulted with clergy. The likely explanation for this growth is the unique set of strengths associated with self-help groups. For instance, self-help participants are *empowered* through volunteering to join, willingness to share leadership, and capacity to take a positive attitude toward adversity.

A second unique aspect of self-help groups is *accessibility*, with members available in emergencies, over prolonged periods of time and in a preventive capacity—before emergencies arise. There are no barriers to access such as costs, bureaucratic forms, appointment times, transportation out of the neighborhood, impersonal officials or unresponsive regulations. The vicissitudes of public spending on human services do not limit self-help accessibility.

Given the number of chronic health conditions that disproportionately affect persons age 60 and over, the increased involvement of aging persons and their caregivers in self-help groups has great potential. Also, due to quicker hospital discharges and the aging of the aged, many of the seven million Americans who are providing assistance to an older relative on any given day are experiencing considerable stress. Moreover, one-third of these caregivers are age 65 and over themselves. Thus, it is not surprising that caregiver groups for the elderly are growing rapidly throughout the country.

Health challenges with a particular impact on older persons and their caregivers include those that focus on cancer, heart and stroke patients and their family members; persons with hearing and visual impairment; and patients with arthritis, Parkinson's disease, lung problems and Alzheimer's disease.

TARGET AREAS

To encourage greater participation in self-help groups among older persons and their caregivers, several new target areas need to be examined including (1) hospitals, (2) religious institutions, (3) Area Agencies on Aging and the service provider network, (4) professionals in general and (5) the work setting.

Hospitals

Over half the patients in hospitals are geriatric patients. In this era of cost containment geriatric patients are being discharged from the hospital more quickly than a decade ago. Family members are concerned about the ongoing health management problems they will be encountering after the older person leaves the hospital. Many are quite grateful to have the opportunity to share their concerns and gather information about health care and community resources at a hospital-based self-help group.

Religious Institutions

Researchers report that the religious institution is the most important resource for the older person outside of the family. Moreover, the elderly constitute the largest age group in organized religion. The church or synagogue is not only a vital resource for older persons, but the most common host site for a self-help group.

The Aging Network

The aging network consists of more than the 57 State and 672 Area Agencies on Aging. It consists of 20,000 service provider organizations that can refer clients, or give assistance, to self-help groups. To avoid transportation problems that may prevent older persons or caregivers from joining a self-help group, service providers or Area Agency on Aging personnel can encourage the formation of a group at a site where older persons already congregate, like a congregate living facility, senior center, nursing home, nutrition site, church or hospital.

Professionals

Many self-help groups are started by professionals such as social workers, nurses, counselors, clergy and physicians. Moreover, professionals can make referrals, provide expertise and resources and influence policymakers. Self-help groups in turn provide the social and emotional support to patients that professionals are not able to provide. They can also extend the professionals' influence in the community, bring new information to the attention of professionals and policymakers and take political action in favor of policies that benefit professionals and self-help group members alike.

The Work Setting

A large minority of employees look after an aging parent, and sometimes this responsibility conflicts with their work duties. As employers recognize the growing need to help locate care for older parents, elder care programs are emerging around the nation. Elder care programs at the work site often involve self-help groups as well as information and referral services. Among other uses of self-help groups in the workplace are for promoting programs that change employee behavior, such as smoking cessation and weight reduction programs.

Afterword

Alfred H. Katz, DSW

"Everywhere burning waters rise," wrote a poet of the civil rights movement, and the same words might be applied to the less spectacular and dramatic but still powerful and important rise of self-help groups. They are springing up everywhere. As revealed by this book's wide-ranging subject matter, self-help embodies simultaneously a philosophy, methods that have a common base but vary a good deal, and a vast array of organizations that comprise a major and enduring social force.

The Symposium on the Impact of Life-Threatening Conditions, some of whose papers have been adapted for this book, took place almost two years before the initiation of the Gulf War, in January 1991. It was in no way surprising that this recent "life-threatening" situation also evoked self-help responses from dependents, relatives and some armed services personnel who dissented from the war's purposes and did not wish to be associated with it.

All over the United States, spouses, parents and other relatives of persons in the armed services followed classic self-help principles in organizing to secure better resources for dependents, an equitable allocation of call-ups and risks for service personnel and reserves, and respectful consideration for the consciences of dissenters. Self-help clearinghouses noted that a large number of local, regional and national organizations on the self-help model were quickly and spontaneously created; many have continued to pursue these aims.

To those who have followed the dynamic growth of the self-help initiatives, especially over the past two decades, these most recent manifestations of the power and necessity of self-help organizations causes no surprise. So many of the social trends and forces of the late twentieth century have emphasized that *people acting on their own behalf* is an expression of democratic citizenship, even if the actions taken have no specific political context.

Thus, much of the material in this book has underlined that in the health field laypersons are spurred to self-organization because they have experienced, suffered from and were determined to overcome the perceived inadequacy or irrelevance of health services planned, dominated, adminis-

298

tered and rendered exclusively by conventionally trained professionals. Over 30 years ago, in conducting my study of self-help groups formed by parents of handicapped children,* I became aware of two factors: first, the parents' awareness of gaps in professional services so that their needs and those of their children were not being fully met, and second, the gains and benefits parents received both in knowledge and in a sense of community from participation in self-help groups. These two motifs have continued as major engines in the forward thrust of self-help, and are illustrated and made explicit in almost every chapter in this book.

Self-help is a dynamic and many-sided phenomenon, constantly evolving and taking new forms as social conditions change. No conference or book, even as comprehensive and detailed as this one, can hope to represent more than a partial reality, a temporary slice of the state of knowledge existing at a given time. Unpredictable developments in a few years time may make some of the formulations seem obsolete or primitive.

This perspective holds true throughout the current self-help literature, and applies as well to the present volume. Yet it constitutes one of the most complete "state of the art" works on self-help ever published. Its contributors have explored, reflected on, and acutely described and analyzed how and why self-help benefits patients, their families and significant others who confront and learn to deal with a wide spectrum of illnesses and conditions. The conditions discussed have ranged from the needs of patients on life-support services to those with AIDS, from lupus to Alzheimer's disease, from multiple sclerosis to hearing loss, and from cancer to sudden infant death syndrome.

These wide discussions of self-help applications in serious, long-term, sometimes terminal, situations put forward several effective self-help models for aiding patient and family adaptation to the psychosocial disruptions and crises of chronic illnesses, including those with a known genetic cause. Not only have patient and family situations and needs been dealt with, but some chapters have considered the dilemmas and conflicts that arise for health professionals whose clinical work involves such patients and families. A number of key policy and organizational issues have been discussed: public vs. private funding, the relationships of professional services and lay groups, the role of religious and spiritual factors, and leadership "burnout," among other important topics.

The chapters in the first section of the book have dealt with issues that are of major significance to all self-help groups, whether those of the "12-step" or of the "non-12-step" varieties. The fundamental question of how empowerment of individuals, families and groups is fostered by self-help participation has been cogently analyzed in the opening chapter. The chapters that follow have discussed provocatively and with differing personal emphases the existing and desirable patterns of professional caregiver/self-

---

*A.H. Katz. *Parents of the Handicapped,* Springfield, IL: Charles C Thomas, 1961.

help group relationships. Others have considered the aging population as an opportunity and natural locus for self-help programs. The roles of self-help clearinghouses and of local religious congregations have also been usefully analyzed.

As a systematic thrust into a dynamically evolving and complex field, this book will be an important resource both for self-help group activists and professional providers. Its content is both accurate and timely, and while no book can have all the answers, this one provides an excellent platform for further study and development.

Index of Groups
and Conditions

T

Tay-Sach Parents' Telephone Network, 121

TCF. *See* Compassionate Friends.

Telephone conferencing in mutual support, 121, 220-223

Test Positive Aware Network (TPA), 15, 27

TMJ (temporomandibular joint) syndrome, 118

Trefpunt Zelfhulp (Belgium), 18

Turner's syndrome. *See* International Turner's Syndrome Society.

U

Urban Self-Help Project (Illinois), 24

U.S. Bureau of Health Professions, 40-41

W

Washington Business Group on Health, 46

Wellness Community, The, 196-204

Widows and Widowers Bereavement Group, 257-261

World Health Organizations, xxvii, 5, 14, 21

World Institute on Disability, 229

Y

Y-Me, 91

Year 2000 National Health Objectives Consortium, 43